Popular Science

HOMEOWNER'S ENCYCLOPEDIA

FULLER & DEES

TIMES MIRROR

New York • Los Angeles • Montgomery

© Fuller & Dees MCMLXXIV
3734 Atlanta Highway, Montgomery, Alabama 36109

Library of Congress Cataloging in Publication Data
Main entry under title: Popular Science Homeowner's Encyclopedia

1. Dwellings — Maintenance and repair — Amateurs' manuals. 2. Repairing —
Amateurs' manuals. 3. Do-it-yourself work. I. Title: Homeowner's encyclopedia.
TH4817.3.P66   643'.7'03   74-19190
Complete Set ISBN 0-87197-070-8
Volume III ISBN 0-87197-073-2

Popular Science

Science

HOMEOWNER'S
ENCYCLOPEDIA

Home Air Conditioning

Air conditioning in the fullest sense of the term, means the artificial control of air temperature, air motion, air moisture content (humidity), and airborne pollutant level (dust, pollen and soot). An air conditioner is a mechanical device designed to perform these functions.

Specifically, an air conditioner is a mechanical device that will *reduce* air temperature and moisture content during periods of high ambient temperature and humidity. This is done by circulating the air past a chilled surface: the air temperature drops and, simultaneously, airborne water vapor condenses out of the air onto the cold surface. For this reason, the heart of any air conditioner is a self-contained refrigeration system.

Air coolers are often used to lower air temperature in hot, dry (low-humidity) climates. These are not air conditioners; they work on a totally different principle. Typically, air is blown through a water-soaked pad, causing rapid evaporation of the moisture. A substantial amount of heat is required to transform the water from liquid to vapor (approximately 1000 BTU per pound), and this heat is taken from the air moving through the wet pad, lowering its temperature in the process, but raising the relative humidity.

An evaporative air cooler can lower air temperature several degrees *if* the original moisture content is low enough. Practically speaking, the relative humidity must be less than 40 percent for an air cooler to work satisfactorily.

TYPES OF AIR CONDITIONERS

Broadly speaking, all home air conditioners fall into two categories: *Unitary* (or self-contained) air conditioners that include the complete mechanism in a single package. Window-mount, "through-the-wall" and attic-mount central units are unitary air conditioners. *Built-up* air conditioners composed of two or more interconnected sub-assemblies (that may be located apart from

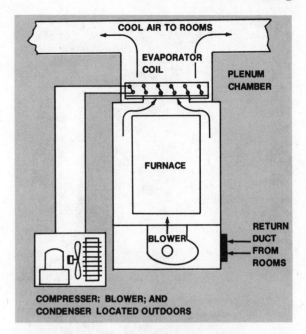

A Built-Up Central Air Conditioning System

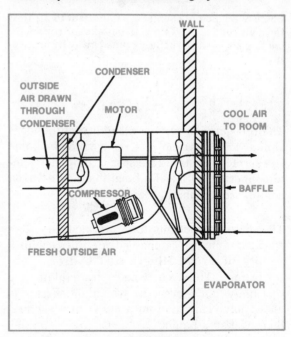

A Unitary Air Conditioning System

each other). Many central air conditioning systems designed to cool an entire house are built-up units. In general, built-up systems can be much larger than unitary air conditioners, and they have somewhat greater flexibility to adapt to different architectural requirements.

765

Louvers on side of cabinet are important to air flow through condenser. This is the intake for condenser cooling air. Keep shrubbery pruned away from openings.

PRINCIPLES OF REFRIGERATION

The refrigeration system in an air conditioner is similar to the system in a refrigerator or home freezer. It consists of three basic components interconnected by metal tubing: the motor-driven compressor, evaporator and the condenser.

The three components form a sealed, loop-like configuration that is charged (or filled) with a supply of Freon (fluorinated hydrocarbon) refrigerant. The system cools by exploiting a *thermodynamic cycle* in which the Freon is alternately changed from a liquid to a gas and then back to a liquid.

Liquid Freon enters the evaporator (via a small flow-limiting expansion valve) where it evaporates into a gas. When this happens, heat is removed from the aluminum evaporator structure, chilling its metal surfaces. The newly-formed Freon gas moves from the evaporator to the compressor. Here, the gas is compressed to several times its original pressure

and in the process, its temperature rises sharply. Finally, the warm, compressed Freon gas enters the condenser where it condenses back into liquid form, and releases the heat it contains to the condenser's aluminum surfaces.

You will note that the refrigeration system does not dispose of heat, it *moves* it from the evaporator to the condenser. Both the evaporator and condenser are *heat exchangers* built very much like an automobile radiator; Freon flows through tubes within the structure, while air flows over fins that surround the tubes. In an operating air conditioner, the evaporator serves as the chilled surface mentioned earlier; the condenser "rejects" the heat absorbed by the evaporator to the ambient air *outside* the air conditioned room or building.

A PRACTICAL AIR CONDITIONER

In addition to the refrigeration system, four other components are necessary to create a practical air conditioner: a pair of motor-driven blowers to force room air through the evaporator fin structure and ambient air through the condenser; a filter placed below the evaporator to remove airborne pollutants; a thermostat to control the air conditioner's operation in response to changing indoor air temperature and a water drain system to collect and dispose of moisture that has condensed on the evaporator surfaces.

A unitary air conditioner is likely to have a single motor to power both the evaporator and condenser air blowers. The condenser blower is often a simple multi-blade fan, while the evaporator blower is usually a squirrel cage type blower capable of pushing the cooled air a greater distance into the room. By contrast, built-up systems invariably use separate evaporator and condenser blowers.

A typical home central air conditioning system consists of two separate units. The compressor, condenser, and condenser blower are contained within a metal enclosure mounted outside the house; the evaporator is installed within the plenum chamber at the head of the cold-air duct work that serves the house, directly above the evaporator blower.

If the home has a forced hot air heating system, the evaporator is usually mounted in the heating system plenum chamber over the furnace, thus the heater blower serves double-duty during summer months, as does the existing duct work. (Note: When such an installation is contemplated, a heating system serviceman should examine the blower and motor to make certain that they have sufficient capacity for the more strenuous air conditioner service.)

VENTILATION

Most unitary room air conditioners have the capacity to draw uncooled outside air into the room at the same time they circulate cooled room air. Such ventilation supplements the *infiltration* (to be discussed shortly) to keep inside air fresh and free of stale odors.

Louvers on front panel of air conditioners should be turned upwards to allow proper circulation of room air.

COOLING CAPACITY

Air conditioner cooling capacity is frequently stated in two different units: British Thermal Units per hour (BTU/hr) or tons per day (or, simply, as "Tons"). A BTU is the amount of heat that will raise one pound of water one degree Fahrenheit in temperature. Conversely, removing one BTU from a pound of water will lower its temperature one degree F. An air conditioner

27,000 BTU/hr, for example, is capable of removing this much heat from the air passing through its evaporator during each hour of operation.

A ton is not a measure of heat in itself; its use is best illustrated by an example: A *one ton* air conditioner can remove the same amount of heat in a 24 hour period as would be absorbed by one ton of ice melting in 24 hours. This is equivalent to 287,200 BTU's per day, or 11966.7 BTU/hr. The equivalency between BTU/hr and "ton" is usually rounded off to 12,000 BTU/hr. Thus, one "ton" equals 12,000 BTU/hr.

An operating air conditioner consumes a substantial amount of electrical energy. Even portable 5000 BTU/hr window-mount units draw about 900 watts. Surprisingly, the electrical consumption of various units within a given cooling capacity range can be different. To evaluate the efficiency of an air conditioner, simply divide its BTU/hr rating by its wattage rating; the higher the number in the answer is, the better. Most large unitary and central air conditioners will produce answers greater than 7; small "portable" units will probably score between 6 and 7. (Note: If the wattage rating is not specified, it can quickly be calculated by multiplying current draw, measured in Amperes, by operating voltage.) Example: Two 120-volt AC air conditioners, A and B, have the following ratings. Compare efficiencies.

A: 6500-BTU/hr; 8.9-Amperes current draw
B: 7000-BTU/hr; 9.1-Amperes current draw

Step 1: Calculate wattage ratings of both units:

A: 120 x 8.9 = 1068 watts
B: 120 x 9.1 = watts

Step 2: Divide the BTU/hr ratings by the wattage ratings calculated in Step 1:

A: 6500 / 1068 = 6.1 (approximately)
B: 7000 / 1092 = 6.4 (approximately)

Air conditioner B is more efficient because it provides more cooling per watt than model A.

As a rough rule of thumb (the actual number obviously depends on climate and air conditioner efficiency) a typical air conditioner in a temperate climate will consume about 3000 kilowatt-hours through a cooling season for each 12,000 BTU/hr cooling capacity.

POWER REQUIREMENTS

Many portable window-mount unitary air conditioners are designed for 120-volt AC operation and can be plugged into any wall outlet. However, since the Electrical Code requires that plug-in appliances not draw more than 12 amperes of current, the cooling capacity of these small machines is limited to a maximum of perhaps 9000 or 10,000 BTU/hr. Higher capacity units (both large unitary and built-up central air conditioners) are designed to be powered by 240-volts AC (much like an electric range or dryer) and must be connected to the house's electrical service entrance panel via an appropriate circuit breaker or fuse (typically a dual 40-Ampere/40-Ampere unit). Number 8 or number 6 copper wire can be used in most installations.

Note: The wiring of large unitary or central air conditioning systems is not a chore for the amateur electrician. Not only can 240-volts AC be lethal, but doing a proper job requires specialized tools and equipment.

FILTERS

To provide cooling, an air conditioner must move large volumes of air through a room or house. Filtering is necessary to remove dust, lint, and larger particles of airborne pollutants that would otherwise be blown about the cooled room. Two types of filters are widely used: disposable, throw away filters made of spun glass, plastic foam, metallic mesh, or other fibrous material, and washable filters, most often made of plastic foam or metal mesh.

It is important that the filter be kept clean. A clogged filter dramatically slows down air flow through the evaporator coil, severely lowering cooling capacity. In a small unitary air conditioner, a clogged filter may also trap moisture

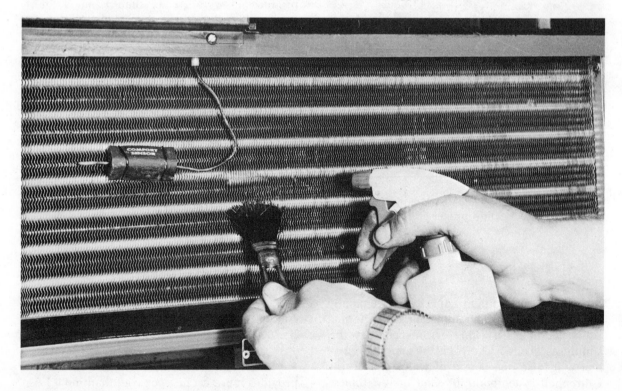

If coils become clogged with lint that bypasses filter, they should be cleaned with strong detergent and water or special cleaning solution available from refrigeration supply houses.

next to the evaporator coil; this, in conjunction with reduced air flow, can cause a layer of ice to form on the coil, completely blocking air movement.

COOLING CAPACITY REQUIREMENTS

An air conditioner must overcome a variety of different heat sources in order to cool and dehumidify the air within a room or house. In technical terms, there is a *heat gain* (measured in BTU/hr) that represents the *load* on the air conditioner. This heat gain is the total heat brought into the room or house each hour from the following major sources: Heat conduction through the walls, ceiling (or roof), solid doors, and floors. Because the interior temperature of an air-conditioned room or house is lower than the outdoor temperature, heat flows from outside to inside. The *rate* of heat flow depends on the temperature difference (the greater the difference, the greater the flow), and on the insulating qualities of the wall, floor, doors, and roof (the better the insulating properties, the slower the flow).

Heat conduction and solar radiation through glass windows and doors are also sources of heat gain. Heat flows through glass components for the reasons given above; in addition, sunlight streaming through glass windows and doors heats the interior space substantially (this is the major reason a closed car becomes so hot inside on a sunny summer day). Solar heating can be reduced significantly by closing draperies, blinds, or shades on a sunny day.

Heat is also produced by electric lights and appliances. Over 95 percent of the electrical energy flowing into a light bulb is converted directly to heat . . . a 100 watt bulb produces almost 350 BTU/hr. Similarly, appliances such as refrigerators, electric ranges, toasters, and irons, all release heat as they operate. The average hourly heat gain from lighting and appliances in a typical home is about 2000 BTU hr.

The human body is a source of heat, the quantity of heat produced depends on the level of physical activity, and can range past 2000 BTU/hr during strenuous exercise. An *average* heat produc-

tion is 400 BTU/hr per person (the amount produced by a seated adult doing light work).

Finally, there is *latent* heat moisture. The task of dehumidifying air requires that heat be absorbed. Specifically, about 8000 BTU/hr must be absorbed to eliminate one gallon of water from the air in one hour. A certain amount of infiltration of outside air is desirable to provide fresh air inside the air-conditioned interior. Infiltration takes place through minute cracks and pores, crevices in caulking and frequently opened doors.

Estimating heat gain accurately in order to determine the required cooling capacity of an air conditioner is complex. Careful consideration must be given to geography, climate, house size and shape, amount of insulation, number of occupants, size and location of windows, color of roof, degree of attic ventilation, and other related factors. The estimating procedures given are presented as general guides to cooling requirements. A prospective air conditioner purchaser should request that a complete analysis be done by a professional air conditioning contractor (or knowledgeable salesman.

To estimate the cooling requirements of a house, think of it as one large room and ignore interior walls or ceilings. Then multiply the total volume (in cubic feet) of the air within room or house by 3.5 to determine the BTU/hr estimate.

Note: this procedure usually produces an estimate that is somewhat too large although it is usually within 10 percent in warm climates.

EXCESSIVE CAPACITY

A common error, particularly by purchasers of unitary air conditioners, is to buy too powerful a machine. Excessive capacity can lead to an uncomfortable cool and damp interior environment. This is because the process of dehumidification requires that room air repeatedly circulate over the chilled evaporator coils. A too-large unitary unit — which will include a large blower — may cool room air so rapidly that the thermostat switches the unit off before enough moisture has been taken from the air to lower the humidity significantly.

Home Alarm Systems

While it is true that there is no such thing as an absolutely burglar-proof installation, a combination of deterrents will be effective. It is now possible to have a home security system that is tailored to your family's needs. As wholly new products, or in combination with older ones, electronic devices are to be found for sale in telephone supply companies, some hardware stores, leading department stores, and electronic supply houses. Either in kit form or easily installed by a local electrician, these systems are more reliable, smaller, and generally less expensive than their forerunners.

Look for and apply realistic, rather than maximum, protection. The more actual value a person needs to keep secure, the greater the protective measures that are justified. If you can afford it, consider a reputable professional alarm service. The Yellow Pages list companies who sell, install, service, and monitor their own fire and burglar detection equipment. They offer several protection options, which are paid for on a monthly basis.

Check the telephone book and local newspapers for the names of dealers who sell do-it-yourself systems. If you don't know a dealer, or would like to check the reputation of an individual dealer consult the Better Business Bureau.

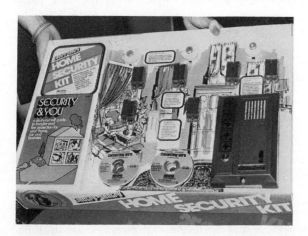

One manufacturer sells a security system in a do-it-yourself kit.

Unless you know the dealer or the alarm service personally, be sure that you check their reliability as there are fraudulent schemes based on the sale of a home security service. Equally important as the dealer's reputation is the dependability of the equipment. Underwriter's Laboratories, Inc. tests electrical products to make sure they meet national safety standards. Their booklet, "Accident, Automotive and Burglary Protection", contains a list of all burglar protection systems listed by UL. To obtain a copy, write to: Underwriter's Laboratories, Inc., Publications Dept., 207 East Ohio St., Chicago, Ill. 60611.

One basic decision should be made before selecting the components for any system. Do you prefer an alarm that employs sirens, horns, or bells to alert you or your neighbors that your house has an intrusion or fire? This kind usually will scare off the intruder, which may be best. Or does a system that can direct-dial the police, report the fire, or tie into a monitoring service suit you better? Most alarm systems can be adapted to your choice.

Decide which system or combination suits your home best. The kind of protection you need depends on whether you live in an apartment with only one vulnerable entrance (the door), or a private house or apartment with several doors and a number of windows near ground level.

Keep in mind that the security system is a supplement to solid locks on doors and windows. If these are insecure or easily circumvented (such as a lock that can be opened by merely breaking a nearby pane or glass and reaching around), a security system offers only a second line of defense. Also remember that the best alarm system will not deter a burglar if you forget to turn it on. One-third of all home burglaries occur when householders forget to lock the doors and, if the alarm is not on either, the burglar has free rein.

KINDS OF SYSTEMS

Alarm systems may be classified according to the limits they are designed to protect; hence, the names *spot*, *perimeter* and *volume* detection systems.

"Spot" alarm units like these protect only one point of entry. Battery-powered, each contains a horn that sounds if its sensor switch is tripped. Multiple units are needed to protect all doors and windows.

Spot or Point Protection

Spot or point protection devices are only useful where the entry or intrusion point can be anticipated (as from a window, door or sky light). They include such defenses as battery-powered door and window alarms that sound a built-in horn if entry is forced, and foil tapes along the edges of window glass, guarding against both broken glass as well as actual opening of the window. Other spot detectors include special floor mats, stress tensors mounted under the floor joists so that pressure on the floor above sets off the appropriate alarm. Care buttons and special medical assistance buttons may be wired to this basic system or may be interconnected with a more sophisticated central security system.

Perimeter Systems

Perimeter systems, though the most difficult to install, offer the greatest degree of protection and flexibility. In a complete system all doors and windows are fitted with magnetic or contact switches that trigger the alarm when one is broken. Since nearly every room is wired, adding fire protection to a perimeter system is easy. Heat or smoke sensors are simply wired into the same circuit the switches are on.

A basic perimeter system consists of a central control box or console (sometimes containing a key switch, batteries and horn), exterior bell or siren and window and door switches. An advantage of a perimeter system is that it may easily be expanded as desired or required.

More expensive and sophisticated perimeter alarms are both AC and battery operated. If there is a power failure or an intentionally cut power line, such units switch over to battery automatically and the system is still on. Such a system is valuable if you live in an apartment building where the fusebox is located outside your apartment.

An effective system of any kind should include both internal and external alarms or bells. An external signal will alert neighbors and police while you are away. The internal alarm tells the intruder that he has been detected. Incidentally, if you plan to go away, instruct a dependable neighbor on the operation of your system, in case it accidentally goes off. And, if you add fire protection to your system, use a different sounding alarm to easily distinguish between a fire and an intruder.

Volume or Area-Protection Systems

If the spot or perimeter protection fails to detect an intruder, the space within the perimeter can be made hostile to a burglar by a volume or area-protection system. Ultrasonic detectors fill a room with sound waves that cannot be heard, but any movement disturbs the orderly wave pattern of the empty room and sets off the alarm. Photoelectric systems use a tiny light source and series of mirrors to bounce an invisible light beam around a room in zig-zag fashion. If it is interrupted by a burglar, the alarm goes off.

For fire safety, heat detectors and smoke detectors provide invaluable area protection, giving early warning of serious temperature rise or presence of smoke in the air while a fire is still small enough to make your escape possible.

TYPICAL WIRED ALARM SYSTEM

A typical home security system includes protective features against burglars and fires. Most of its sensors are simple switches that respond to opening or closing of a door or window, or to heat rise. The smoke detector is a somewhat more elaborate electronic unit (described separately, later) that supplies a switch-like signal.

Central Panel

The components are connected by wire to the central panel, a wall-mounted unit containing the electronics that sorts out the sensor inputs and controls alarm devices. Door and window intruder detection switches form a continuous loop for a small current to flow from the panel, through the closed switches and wiring, back through a drop relay in the panel. When the alarm is set, the drop relay's contacts (which control power to the alarm) are normally held open, so the alarm remains silent. However, if an intruder opens a window, its sensor switch opens, breaking the current path. Instantly the drop relay's contacts close and the alarm sounds. Once the relay operates, the sensor switch loop loses control of it. Even if the window is closed and the switch returned to normal, the alarm continues to sound. The relay must be reset by actuating a switch at the central panel.

The fire/smoke detection circuit is somewhat different. Rather than a loop, heat and smoke detectors are wired across one another so that if enough current flows through any single path, it will trigger the alarm.

Inside the panel, an electronic latch circuit is tripped, activating a switching circuit that pulses on and off at regular intervals just like the turn signal flasher in your car. That switch, however, applies current pulses to alarm devices inside and outside your home to rouse the deepest sleeper while summoning help from the community.

SWITCH-TYPE SENSORS

All-Purpose Detector Switch

The most important part of the alarm system is the all-purpose detector switch. It can be recessed into any window or door because its spring-loaded beveled nose is easily pushed in by sliding or butting surfaces. Opening a door or window causes that nose to pop out, opening a pair of switch contacts which signal the central panel that security has been breeched. A tamper

Spring-loaded butt-end of this tamper switch is easily actuated by sash-type window. Switch can also be located under an object, so that its removal triggers alarm.

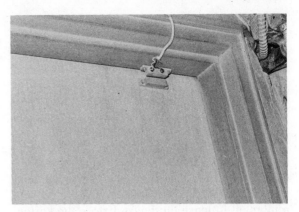

Magnetic proximity switch simplified door or window installation since both parts are surface-mounting.

switch is similar, but has a long nose with flat ends. This makes it suitable for protecting sash or casement windows or in other applications where a flat surface will close against the switch end.

Magnetic Proximity Switch

Another universal detector is the magnetic proximity switch. It consists of two parts: a bar magnet embedded in a plastic mount, and a switch capsule containing two slender, magnetically sensitive reeds. The magnet mounts on a closed door or window so that it lies opposite the reed switch. The field of the magnet normally holds the reeds pressed tightly against one another. The magnet is moved away by opening a door or window, and the reeds spring apart,

breaking an electrical circuit and signalling the central panel.

The magnet switch is mounted on either the edge of the door or frame; it must not be installed on the hinge side. For proper fucntioning, the switch and its magnet must be accurately aligned and separated by no more than 3/16 of an inch. If the door and frame do not line up perfectly or if there is a molding which interferes, the switch, magnet or both may require thin wooden or plastic shims for alignment.

Heat and Smoke Detectors

These components are placed high on ceilings and walls where natural convection currents bring warm air or smoke. Usually, one or two smoke detectors are adequate to cover a home by virtue of their great sensitivity. But, each room should have a heat detector, since the fire warning these give may be later than that provided by the smoke detector.

Alarm Horn and Beacon

Bells were once the principal alert devices in home security alarms, but horns are the big noise in security systems today. A combination flashing beacon and horn unit can be placed at the peak of a house or, on a TV antenna mast, perhaps. It features a 3 inch in diameter electric vibrator horn that sounds off with loudness equal to a car horn. It radiates a visual distress signal, as well. On top of the horn is an automotive-type lamp inside an amber lens.

Most basic package systems such as the wired type just described do not include the extras such as window foil, pressure switches and ultrasonic alarms. They do offer perimeter and fire protection and are adaptable to inclusion of almost any protective device or system. Optional exit/entry controls are also available. A key-operated switch in a tamper-proof housing, or a central panel time delay switch which gives you a moment to leave the house before the system arms itself, with a similar delay on entry can be added to a perimeter system.

Package protection is a worthwhile, economical investment for many homeowners, even those who plan to use it as the nucleus of a larger, more comprehensive system.

WIRELESS ALARM SYSTEMS

The ultimate in simplicity of installation is the wireless alarm system. It speeds up installation and eliminates all unsightly wires. Two radio-control approaches are used: via air and by power line. The system which sends alarm signals through the air from remotely located transmitters also allows the use of small, pocket-carried devices which by pressing a button can report personal distress situations to a central receiver. Any number of transmitters may be used with a single receiver. When a transmitter is activated, a sophisticated coded radio signal is sent over the air to activate the receiver which controls the alarm. These radio controls are recommended for use as panic or holdup buttons, since they are no bigger than a pack of cigarettes and can be carried in hand, pocket or purse. The receiver can be placed about 200 feet from the farthest transmitter, under normal conditions. Walls and metal surfaces will reduce its range.

Such a wireless remote control system can be used to activate an automatic dialer when it receives a signal from a portable transmitter. Transmitters can also be connected to sensors that send out a radio signal when they sense

A truly "wireless" alarm system. Ultrasonic motion detector responds to movement in room by applying power to transmitter module plugged into its side outlet. Transmitter signal is coupled to receiver by riding on power line. Receiver may actuate bell or dialing mechanism.

smoke, fire, illegal entry or any other sudden emergency.

Though emergency telephone dialers are most widely used as the device which automatically summons the police in the event of a burglary and the fire department at the occurrence of a fire, they can also function as a means of securing emergency medical aid. It is often impossible for an invalid, heart patient or elderly person to make an emergency call to a doctor or hospital for medical attention in a hurry. An automatic dialer, receiver and panic button transmitter makes it possible to place this vital call by simply pressing the wireless panic button from *anywhere* in the home. The rest is done automatically. The entire system requires fifteen minutes to half an hour to install, including connections to the telephone line.

The power line-coupled wireless scheme is called the *carrier current* system. Standard house wiring is used as the transmission medium. Here, a high-frequency control signal is superimposed on the 60-cycle power which comes through the power outlet. The control electronics, which receives its power from the same lines, also receives the signals through the lines.

The alarm receiver may be plugged in anywhere in the house as may any of the sensors. Each sensor has its own transmitter which is simply plugged into the nearest socket.

An ideal alarm system for the aged, shut-ins, or invalids who must summon local help immediately is a wireless system which consists of a simple *on-off* switch on a line-cord, which is plugged into any 120 volt AC outlet together with the alarm trigger. The alarm bell, which has its own built-in receiver, may be placed indoors or outdoors, in a spot protected from the weather. It may even be placed at a neighbor's house, provided his house is wired to the same power transformer. When the manual control cord is switched on, the alarm trigger sends its unique signal right through the power line to the alarm bell which turns on and continues to ring until the manual control cord is turned off.

Wireless alarms are very flexible. For example, an alarm trigger and an ultrasonic motion detector, provide instant space protection. Any sensor (fire, smoke, vibration, foil, photoelectric or other devices) can be connected to a wireless transmitter module.

HEAT DETECTORS

Heat detectors respond to excessive temperature rise caused by outbreak of a fire. The button-like detector contains a concave metal disc which is a tightly held-together combination of two metals

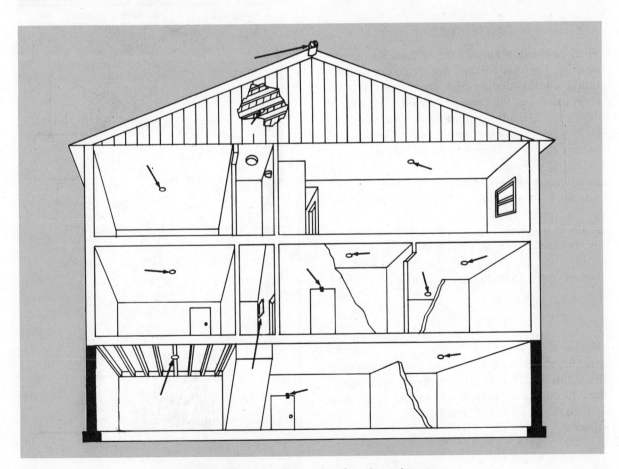

Arrows indicate position of various heat detectors.

that expand at different rates when heated. The material is called *bimetal* and, so long as air temperature is within reasonable limits, the disc is held away by its internal stress from closing a fixed contact. As the air is heated by flame, however, one side of the disc expands more rapidly than the other, unbalancing the normal mechanical stress, causing the disc to snap in the opposite direction and press against a pushrod which closes a set of contacts. This circuit closure signals the central alarm panel that a fire is in progress.

The degree of mechanical stress fixed in the disc at the factory sets the temperature at which the heat detector will operate. 135° F and 195° F are typical actuation levels. The 135° thermostats are optimized for normal room use, whereas the 195° thermostat should be used in attics, near heaters or in hot kitchens where temperatures can exceed 100° F.

Locating A Heat Detector

When heat-laden air hits the ceiling, it spreads laterally. For this reason, fire detectors are installed on the ceiling and are most effective when located at the center of a room. But that is often very difficult if not impossible. In practice, the location is determined by ease of access for making the wire connections. When detectors cannot be placed at the center of a room, they should never be ceiling-mounted closer to a wall than six inches, as that part of the room where the wall meets the ceiling is a "dead" air space which is bypassed by swirls of hot air from a fire. Where there is no other alternative, a detector may be placed on a wall, not less than six inches or more than 12 inches below the ceiling line.

SMOKE DETECTORS

"Where there's smoke, there's fire" is trite but true. Smoke precedes flame in most household fires, and its effects are often more devestating than flame, since poisonous carbon monoxide and noxious gases are smoke's principal constitutents.

The majority of household fires start as slow smoldering fires and generate a good deal of

poisonous smoke before breaking into open flames. Statistics show that 75 percent of the fatalities in home fires are caused by suffocation and not by heat of flames. Thus, a smoke detector can save time and lives by sensing smoke in early stages of fire before the smoke reaches a lethal concentration.

The smoke detector is a radical departure from other sensor elements in the home security system. It makes use of the simple principle of optics that light travels in a straight line through clear air. A small light source is so arranged that a beam of light shines into a chamber surrounded by non-reflective but very porous polyurethane foam. A light-sensitive photocell is mounted at a right angle to a light source, so that it is aimed at the normal clear air within the chamber. Ordinarily, there is no way that the light

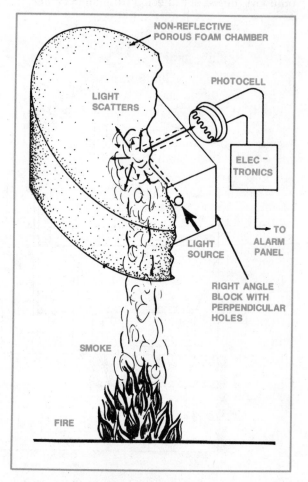

Smoke Detector

beam can strike the cell. Thus, the cell normally presents no path for current flow.

However, if smoke comes into the porous polyurethane foam chamber on rising thermal air currents, the smoke detector responds to visible light scattered by the smoke. The light from the source is scattered and some strikes the photocell. The cell then conducts, causing the electronic circuitry to trigger a horn or send a signal so the central panel can start to sound the alarm.

Although smoke detectors are rather expensive, just one may suffice for basic protection in the average home where the bedrooms are all on a single floor. Generally, the most acceptable location is the common hallway between bedrooms through which smoke must travel to reach the sleeping occupants. In a two story dwelling where the bedrooms are usually on the second floor, it is best to place a smoke detector at the head of the stairwell.

Additional secondary locations to be considered for smoke detector installation are the kitchen, where cooking is done, the laundry, where ironing and cleaning pose fire hazards, the basement near the heating plant, and the living room and other areas where smokers may congregate. To provide additional protection from a slow-burning fire in bedding or upholstery, consider installing a smoke detector in each bedroom of your home.

Foil tape on first floor windows sound the alarm should a window be opened or broken.

SPECIAL PROTECTION DEVICES

Window Foil

A narrow strip of a thin, conductive metal ribbon taped all around the edge of a glass door or window provides reliable perimeter protection, Breaking or cutting the glass will rip the foil, interrupting the continuous series-loop protective circuit and setting off the alarm. Self-adhesive metallic foil tape (about $^3/_8''$ wide) and terminal blocks make foil installation relatively easy. Just follow these step-by-step instructions and use reasonable care.

1. Use a straight edge and a grease pencil to mark off the foil location, but do so on the *outside* of the window to be protected. (Generally, foil is best run between three and six inches from the edges depending upon the size of the window.)

2. Using ammonia or an alcohol (not wax) based cleaner, clean the *inside* surface of the glass, where the foil will be applied.

3. Unroll a little of the foil, peel off some of the backing paper and start application from the edge of the frame. Leave a few extra inches of tape at the start to attach later to the foil connection blocks.

4. Apply the foil to the *inside* of the glass following the pattern drawn on the *outside*. Keep the foil tape smooth (without wrinkles) and straight.

5. At a corner, make a double fold.

6. If the foil must pass over metal separators such as those found in casement windows, make certain an insulator is used between the foil and the separator. A single strip of electrical tape over the metal part is suitable as an insulator. The tape should cover all the metal but only about $^1/_{16}$ of an inch of the glass. Run the metal foil over the tape.

7. To repair breaks or make splices, press the splice in place, cover with clear cellophane tape. Then puncture in five or more places with a sharp pin to insure a good electrical contact.

8. Use the back of a pack of book matches to smooth the foil as it is applied and press it lightly in place.

9. Where the foil installation is complete, attach the foil connection blocks by removing the protective tape on their backs to expose the pressure-sensitive adhesive and pressing them into place.
10. Run the window foil up on the block and attach by tightening the screws or soldering depending on the type of block used.
11. If the foil has been installed on a hinged door or window, use a door cord on the hinge side for system connections.
12. After the installation is completed, the foil can be protected from accidental scratching or abrasion (as well as from the chemicals used in window cleaning) by covering the entire length with suitable foil varnish, overlapping the foil by about ¼ of an inch on each edge.

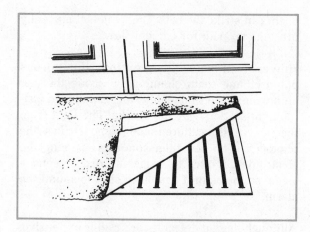

Entrance Mat Protection

doors, stairways and hallways. Of all the types of spot protection available, pressure sensitive mat switches are the most economical and least likely to give false alarms. Inside the mat slender pressure-sensitive ribbons run parallel to each other from one edge of the mat to the other. These ribbons are wired so they make (or break) contact when stepped upon. The mats are so thin that they are completely invisible when placed underneath regular carpeting or rugs at any locations that need to be protected. Mats may have single or double connecting wires for either open or closed circuit system installations and they are available in various sizes from stairtread width to continuous length of 30 inch runners.

Vibration Detectors

A vibration detector supplements other sensory devices used in burglary protection installations. They are often employed in closed-circuit alarm systems to protect against intrusion through windows, walls or ceilings, but can also protect specific objects such as safes or cabinets. The mechanism will initiate an alarm when a forcible blow strikes the protected surface. Thus, the impact of a jimmy or pry-bar can be sensed before the intruder has gained entry to the premises. Vibration contacts can be adjusted for greater or lesser sensitivity, by turning a screw under the cover to make possible use on any surface such as glass windows, plaster board construction, and even cement walls. When properly adjusted, normal building vibration will have little effect on the contacts. However, they will respond very

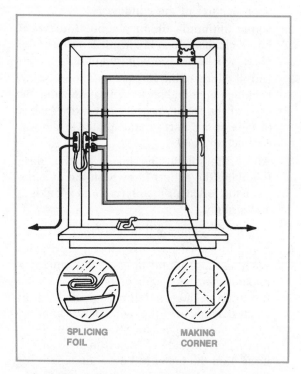

SPLICING FOIL MAKING CORNER

A window foil alarm system is easily installed.

Pressure Sensitive Mat Switches

Pressure sensitive mats are simple to install and provide inexpensive, highly reliable spot protection. They offer an excellent and very economical way to trap an intruder at hard-to-protect locations such as the threshold of sliding glass

effectively to sharp blows as normally occur when someone tries to break through a door, window or wall.

When protecting windows, the best installation method is to mount the vibration contacts on the surface frame rather than directly on the glass. This reduces the danger of false alarms from the vibrations caused by heavy vehicles passing by, or from the impact of rain, sleet or wind on a window.

For maximum economy (extended coverage) and minimum danger of false alarms the preferred method of installing vibration contacts on walls or ceiling is to mount the contacts on furring strips.

Panic Button

A very desirable, easy-to-include component of any alarm system is the so-called panic-button. One or more of these simple pushbuttons should be located in strategic places throughout the home, beside the front door, next to a bed, or in a clothes closet where one might hide during a burglary. When the button is pressed, *regardless whether the system is armed or not,* an immediate alarm condition will result. Such a button has very important usage during holdup at-

An emergency or panic button can signal distress of any type. These are especially helpful for elderly people.

tempts in the daytime, when the alarm system is not usually on, as is the case when doors and windows are open, or even at times when the system is on and an intruder has managed to enter in some way without triggering the protective detectors. (This is usually possible only in the most marginal systems.) Pressing the panic button will divert the intruder's attention away from you, and that can be vital!

Ultrasonic Alarm

Of all the *volume* intrusion protection devices, perhaps none is as tamperproof, easy to set up and foolproof in operation as the system based on high frequency sound waves called an ultrasonic alarm. It is a motion-activated solid-state device which emits a high frequency tone that literally saturates the protected area from walls to floor to ceiling, including doorways, windows and skylights, filling the air with waves transmitted at a pitch far above the range of human hearing. These waves, which are called ultrasonic waves, are bounced all around the protected area and then come back to the unit for sensing. As long as everything is motionless within the protected area, the pitch remains constant. The ultrasonic alarm is activated, however, when it senses the change in the wave pattern from a moving object.

Operation of all ultrasonic intrusion alarms is based on the *Doppler effect,* named after Christian Johann Doppler, the Austrian scientist who discovered it. This, simply, has to do with the fact that the sound of a moving object seems to change as it passes you.

The units typically house a transmitter of ultrasound energy and a receiver which listens for the transmitter's high-pitched signal. The volume of room air provides the coupling between the two, and so, ultrasound waves penetrate into every square inch of the protected area. This means that all reflected waves bouncing off walls, floor, ceiling, doors and furniture continuously reach the receiver. As long as the pattern does not change, the receiver does not register that anything is moving within the room. However, any moving object will produce a Doppler effect change-in-pitch of some of these

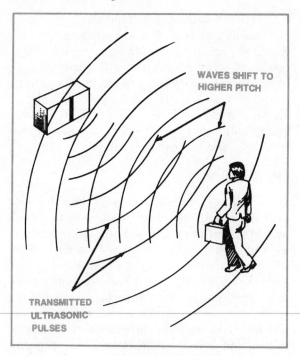

WAVES SHIFT TO
HIGHER PITCH

TRANSMITTED
ULTRASONIC
PULSES

The Doppler Effect

reflections. It is these waves of slightly different pitch that trigger the receiver's sensitive circuitry and cause the alarm to sound.

Remember that the ultrasonic alarm detects movement within the area of transmitted ultrasonic waves. For best transmission, the unit should be placed on a solid object such as a desk, built-in bookcase, or wall shelf. It should face the area to be protected, but should not face things which normally move or vibrate, such as large picture windows, curtains or air conditioners. It may be possible for air currents from heating and cooling ducts to trigger the unit. Since hot air is less dense than cold air, the boundary between the two can register as a moving object—especially if the air is blown directly toward the unit.

Photoelectric System

Most intrusion detectors require that the prowler make *direct physical contact* with a sensor, open a door, break a window, or step on a mat, or with something to which the sensor is attached. With the photoelectric system, he merely interrupts a light beam and instantly the alarm goes off.

Popularly called an *electric eye,* the photo-electric detection and alarm system basically consists of two major parts: a light source (projector) and a light sensitive detector (receiver). The projector, located on one side of the protected area, transmits a beam of light across the area to a receiver. Any interruption of this light beam will trigger an alarm.

Photoelectric detection systems are versatile. They may be used indoors or outdoors. They may, for example, be used to detect unauthorized entry to a private driveway by placing the projector on one side of the road and the receiver on the opposite side, so that the light beam will be interrupted by an approaching vehicle. A similar arrangement may be used to guard a gate, door, window, or even a whole line of doors or windows along one side of a hallway or building. With the use of mirrors, the light beam may be "bent" (up to 90°) to allow one beam to guard more than a single straight path. So, two or more systems, together with mirrors may be used to establish a "light fence" around an enclosure or a home, thus affording complete *perimeter* protection.

Photoelectric systems can also furnish *area* and *point* protection. Mirrors can criss-cross a single light beam across an entire area. If the light beam is broken at any point, the alarm will be actuated. Point protection can be achieved by directing a light beam at a mirror attached to the protected object such as on the door of a safe. The receiver picks up the reflected light so that anyone standing in front of the object, or opening its door, even from the side, will trip the alarm.

A shortcoming of this family of alarms is that any shifting of the light source or the receiver can trigger the alarm. To provide trouble-free performance, a photoelectric system *must be rigidly installed.*

A few manufacturers offer photoelectric security alarms that provide area protection, but do not require specific projector light sources. These systems monitor the average light level in the guarded area and detect *change* in the absorption or reflection of background light caused by an intruder's movement. A sudden change in average light intensity caused by an intruder using a flashlight, switching on a light or even by his shadow falling on a normally bright area, will actuate the alarm.

Photoelectric systems can be used independently or in combination with other systems such as those designed around foils, switches and traps.

Local Alarms

When an intrusion has taken place, smoke is sensed or a fire has been detected, an alarm must be sounded to call attention to the emergency condition. This can be achieved with a remote alarm like a dialer or with local alarms such as bells, buzzers, horns or sirens.

To alert occupants of a home, passersby and neighbors to a dangerous situation, these alarms should obviously be as loud as possible to have the highest probability of attracting attention so help can be summoned. The traditional large bell is relatively inexpensive, but one disadvantage is that the range of sound is limited to a few hundred feet.

Sirens have the power-handling capability required for long-distance transmission and their distinctive sound is clearly differentiated from background noise. Their characteristic rise and fall in pitch is attention-producing.

Powerful electronic sirens with no moving parts can be heard as far as one mile away. They are variously called an Electronic Whooper or Wailing Siren and produce a distinctive pulsating sound similar to that of a police or fire siren.

Vibrator-type horns are another useful sound source for home alarms. A useful adjacent to the bell, horn or siren is a weatherproof revolving or flashing emergency light that radiates a long range visual distress signal that is obviously most effective after dark. In some instances, combination audible and visual alarm units are available. These are usually placed high at the peak of the roof of a side wall or mast, so that the flashing beacon is clearly visible and the alarm sound dispersed.

Automatic Telephone Dialer

The local alarm which a bell, horn or siren provides depends exclusively on the cooperation of those within earshot. To be truly effective, an alarm must reach the ears of a reactive group such as the local police or fire department. Though it is a silent alarm, the telephone dialer has become one of the most effective developments in the security field.

A telephone dialer is an ingenious add-on to any alarm system. It detects and reports emergencies by *automatically* dialing telephone numbers which have been set and delivers previously recorded messages that fit the situation: one for fire, one for burglary. The dialer does not interfere with normal use of the telephone, yet when an emergency is detected, it is connected automatically to the telephone line and begins playing a prerecorded tape containing the telephone number or numbers to be called (in the form of a series of pulses). When the number has been dialed, the tape continues to play and delivers an audible emergency message to each party who is called.

Dialers are available with a wide spectrum of characteristics. Some use double channel tapes, where each channel can call up to four separate numbers and deliver a prerecorded message. Separate calls and messages can be made in the event of fire or burglary. Furthermore, such a dialer is designed to repeat the dialing sequence in the event that a number is busy when first dialed. In addition the dialers have the capability to prevent an extension phone from interferring with emergency dial out.

Some dialers come equipped with standby battery power so that the dialing sequence will always take place in the event of accidental or intentional interruption of AC power. Dialers can also be used for many other purposes such as monitoring refrigerator temperatures, water levels, or the medical status of the sick and elderly. With the proper attachments, a dialer can be remotely triggered by strategically located pushbutton or portable transmitter.

Home Appliance Selection

WHEN TO BUY

When to buy should be one of the first decisions you make. If you are building a new home or remodeling an old one, major appliances can be selected over a period of many months, and the item will be held for delivery (usually without a storage charge, but ask) until you need it. Midwinter, just after Christmas, and in late summer before the new models come in, are sale times for appliance bargains.

The worst time to buy, of course, is when the appliance you now own breaks down and you are under pressure to replace it immediately. If this is the case, do not let the salesman know. He may talk you into buying a more expensive model than you planned, or another choice that the store needs to sell. You should be able to strike a bargain and get a good discount on anything the store is eager to sell. Take time at least to go to the local library and check on anything you are considering. Arm yourself with a copy of the annual Consumer Report to use as a talking point, and then strike a deal.

Whenever you buy, cash is usually the cheapest. Some people hesitate to use cash for if the appliance is unsatisfactory or defective it may be difficult to get a replacement or service once the item is paid for. Try to buy an appliance then, on a 30-day, no interest charge account, or if possible, a 90-day no interest account. Many dealers will sell on this basis provided you have a good credit rating and make a substantial down payment. Paying for a major appliance by use of a revolving charge account or finance company means adding 18%, sometimes more, which can be an addition of a hundred dollars or more to the basic cost of the appliance.

A TRADE-IN

It is not likely that you can lower the price of the appliance by a trade-in. If a dealer does quote you a figure on your old appliance, he may be adding it on to the price of a new one by not giving you a discount or free installation. He cannot afford to repair and guarantee the old appliance. He may even charge to haul it away. The best bet is to sell the appliance privately. One mail-order company gives the price of a want-ad with every appliance sale, because it does not want to bother with trade-ins.

A local dealer who handles nationally known appliance brands is probably the safest way to buy, especially if you live in a non-metropolitan area and know the dealer personally. It is even better if he is someone who belongs to your club or church.

Next best is a large mail order company or local department store, especially if they offer prompt service on repairs. These places may try to sell you insurance on repair service after the first year. This is not a good purchase. The store will have your insurance money to use during the year your new appliance is fully guaranteed. After that, the most expensive parts such as transmission in the washer, motor in a refrigerator or freezer are still guaranteed. Major appliances often run for years without substantial repair costs.

Mail order appliances are made by national manufacturers to mail order specifications and are often the same models (with slight variation in color and options) sold at higher prices under the manufacturer's own name through other dealers. Mail order companies have frequent sales and bargains in appliances, but often provide no installation service.

Be suspicious if a well-known brand is suddenly offered at drastic price reductions. Find out from other dealers if a company is going to stop producing a certain appliance. That bargain might turn out to be a discontinued model and parts or service would be impossible to get in future years.

CHOOSING A RANGE AND OVEN

Consider these points: Gas vs. electric is probably a matter of personal preference. Gas is often the cheaper fuel. Supplying 240-volt service can add to the cost of an electric range and oven.

Both gas and electric ovens come with self-cleaning features. Continuous cleaning (catalytic) occurs in a gas oven lined with a material which breaks down oven soil each time the oven is used. Cleaning is not perfect, but the process adds nothing to the cost of operation. In an electric oven the cleaning process is a separate operation which uses high heat at a rather high cost in energy. Repair costs are high in a catalytic oven should it break down. Energy consumption can be reduced if oven spills are wiped up as soon as they occur and the self-cleaning process is limited to a few times a year.

A ceramic cook top on an electric range is easy to clean, and can be used as extra counter space when cooking is not being done. However, spills must be wiped up often and a special cleaner used. Be sure that the ceramic top is subdivided into two or four sections, rather than a single surface, to reduce replacement costs. Though durable, the ceramic surface can be cracked or broken if a heavy pan is dropped onto it.

Choose a range and oven with ease of cleaning as a factor. Such items as: accessories and burners that come off or apart easily for washing, a surface top that lifts or removes for cleaning, an easily removable oven door, an oven liner (if this is a feature) which is easy to wash in a sink or inexpensive to replace, knobs and handles that wipe off easily or are removable for washing are all important. Chrome, decoration, and even the manufacturer's nameplate can be dirt catchers. Dark colors and stainless steel show fingerprints and spills quickly.

Location of controls is important if there are children and elderly people about.

Be sure you will use extras such as built-in rotisserie, shish-kebob attachment, timer oven, or meat-minder before choosing such a model. Each can add $50 or more to the price of the appliance. Timed-programmed cooking may be worth its price where both man and woman are

Courtesy of Frigidaire Division, General Motors, Corp.

A touch of the finger activates the control panel and brings computer technology into kitchen appliances. This range has a glass ceramic smooth surface cooktop.

fulltime wage earners and want their dinner ready when they come home.

An extra microwave oven with a browning element is an energy saver. It operates on an ordinary appliance circuit, but should not share its use with other appliances. Special locks and seals protect the user from the radiant energy which heats or cooks food in a few minutes (a fraction of the time needed in an ordinary oven). Cooking utensils of paper, china, glass ceramic, and some

Courtesy of General Electric Major Appliances Division

Countertop microwave oven shown here is a good size for heating soup right in the bowl, or a sandwich on a paper napkin, or for thawing a prepared dinner.

plastics can be used. Heart pacemakers are affected by microwave energy. If someone in your family wears one, consult your physician before purchasing a microwave oven. Because a microwave oven requires no special wiring nor installation, it is a good consideration for a vacation cabin.

CHOOSING A DISHWASHER

This appliance, now found in forty percent of all homes, will save time, produce spotless dishes, destroy harmful bacteria, do away with a routine chore, and usually consumes less water than does manual dishwashing. It can be a tremendous help for a family which entertains frequently, where everyone is fully employed outside the home, or where the children eat many snacks around the clock.

Choose a portable model if you rent, or if a built-in would destroy kitchen efficiency. Though a portable is more expensive than a built-in

Courtesy of General Electric Major Appliances Division

Potscrubber dishwasher with a scrub cycle cleans baked-on or dried-on food from pots and pans and flushes particles away in the soft food disposer. This unit has space for large pots and pans and a random loading rack for odd-shaped dishes.

model, it hooks up instantly without special plumbing or wiring. Its disadvantage is that it must be used at the sink and may block passage in the kitchen as well as access to sink faucets while it is operating. Look for a model with a faucet bypass.

Unless you will make conversion within a year or so, a model convertible from portable to built-in is not a good buy. An inexpensive or used portable now, replaced by the exact built-in you want when you are ready for it, is the better choice.

A front loading dishwasher is more convenient than top loading. Portables usually load from the top, therefore, choose one which has a fold-back rack exposing the dishes below. A chopping block on a dishwasher is handy, and saves the cost of installing one elsewhere.

Be sure your water heater can deliver 140° to 160° water and that the spray arms beneath each rack distribute water thoroughly on every dish.

Check for a soft food disposer. If there is not one, food may collect and block drainage of water.

Manufacturer's figures on number of place settings the machine will hold is not important. Check it out to see whether large pans and platters will fit, whether the racks are adjustable for random loading, and if there is a small basket to hold bottle or lid tops.

Numerous cycles are no asset. Regular and rinse-and-hold are used the most.

Some machines come equipped with a special dispenser to hold a wetting agent to prevent hard water spotting. A cheaper solution is to buy a detergent that contains a wetting agent.

Dishwashers are noisy, especially when used in the evening when quiet is most desired. Listening to an empty machine in the store will not help. Check the consumer magazines for information. They test loaded machines through all their cycles and rate the noise levels. Alternatively, listen to dishwashers in homes of your friends before you buy.

GARBAGE DISPOSALS

These appliances are mandatory in some areas, illegal in others. Check with your buliding inspector before buying one. All ordinary garbage, except large bones, cornhusks, and tough fruit pits, can be ground by a sturdy disposal. A standard four inch sink opening will take almost any model.

This appliance can be used with a septic tank. The usual requirements are: a 750-gallon tank for a two-bedroom house, a 900-gallon tank for three bedrooms, and a 1000-gallon tank for four bedrooms. A disposal cannot be used if your home has a cesspool.

There are two types of disposals: a batch feed which operates only with the cover on (safer when there are children) and a continuous feed disposer, controlled by a separate switch, which continues to grind waste as long as the electricity is on. The batch feed type is slower to use, and may cost more initially. Buy a good one, which is rubber mounted for less noise, and with a half horsepower motor. Look for a model with pivoted cutters that resists jamming. Some models have an overload reset button on the bottom of the unit which can be pressed to restart the disposer if the motor has stopped because of an overload.

TRASH COMPACTORS

Trash compactors are comparative newcomers in the kitchen. A compactor does not do away with trash, but it will compress the week's debris for a family of four into a neat bundle a fourth its usual bulk.

If you pay for garbage service by volume, a compactor could earn back its cost. However, it will take up extra space in your kitchen. The usual model is 15″ wide and 24″ deep.

A freestanding model with hardwood cutting board top will save the price of a cabinet and counter.

In choosing a compactor, buy one which can neither operate nor can the door be opened without use of a key.

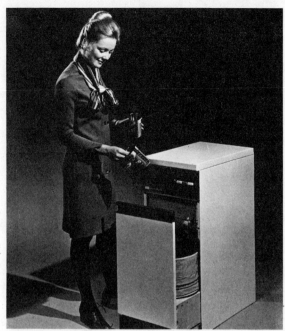

Courtesy of Frigidaire Division of General Motors Corp.

A free-standing compactor, such as this one, does not need to be housed in a cabinet or take up counter space. It is a good choice for the family that rents.

Most types use special plastic bags. Choose a type which can be used without a bag, or which uses ordinary kitchen bags.

Also consider whether the deodorizer is sprayed automatically, or must be done manually each time trash is compacted.

Owners of some compactors complain that there is still odor in spite of deodorizers. Care must be taken to place large cans and bottles near the center of the container to minimize danger from broken glass and sharp edges when putting in additional trash.

If you recycle metal and glass, the compactor will not have much to do. If you do not recycle, remember that a compactor smashes everything into one chunk, and there is no possibility of anyone retrieving the useful materials within at the dump.

Regardless of the compacted shape, the trash still weighs the same as if you had put it into several garbage cans. A child will not be able to cart out that 30 lb. sack.

CHOOSING A REFRIGERATOR-FREEZER

Unless you buy meat a side at a time, have a garden, and purchase food in bulk lots, you probably will need a refrigerator-freezer rather than a separate freezer.

Here are some tips to help you choose wisely: There is no economy in buying a small refrigerator. Crowding reduces effectiveness of cooling and speeds spoilage. Most refrigerator interiors look larger when they are empty.

When comparing models in a store ask the dealer to let you see a specification sheet. Look for the figure called net shelf area given in square feet. This is a better way to judge usable space than the cubic footage figure usually given. With the net shelf area figure you can compare models which look similar but may differ greatly when it comes to stowing food.

Operating cost of a frostfree model runs fifty percent higher than for a manual defrost type. But anyone who neglects defrosting will still be wasting electrical energy and operating costs will be high.

Consider the size of the new appliance. Make sure that a larger model fits the space now occupied by the old one and that it will go through the door.

Consider the noise factor. Check the consumer magazines for reports on the noise nuisance in models they test. Automatic defrost models run most of the time which could be annoying if your bedroom is near the kitchen.

Without built-in wheels the appliance may be difficult to move for cleaning. Some dealers call wheels an extra and charge $5 or more for them.

Check the kind of insulation the appliance has. In some types wires and coolant coils are buried in foam insulation. A repair job might involve the cost of replacing insulation.

Heavy chromed steel or aluminum are the best materials for shelves.

Courtesy of General Electric Major Appliances Division

This refrigerator dispenses crushed ice directly into a glass.

The shelves should be adjustable and shelf supports wide enough to keep shelves from giving way when heavily loaded. Metal is more reliable than plastic for supports.

Notice the materials used for vegetable and meat keepers and the liner of the refrigerator. Plastic is porous, can absorb odors, may become brittle in old age. Porcelained steel surfaces are more durable and are becoming harder to find.

The vegetable crisper should have a tight lid and meat keeper have its own cold-air duct to keep the temperature 5° below the recommended 37° for the rest of the refrigerator.

The controls should be easy to read and reach.

Consider the way the door opens. Some have reversible doors, but there may be an extra charge for this feature. Also, if the door needs to be opened more than 90° to permit removal of shelves or bins for cleaning, be sure that your kitchen can accommodate this, as you will not be able to place the refrigerator next to a wall.

If there is no ice maker, do you plan to add one? An add-on ice maker is often less efficient than a built-in. An add-on may also add another $50

Courtesy of Frigidaire Division, General Motors Corp.

In this kitchen the refrigerator would be convenient to use from the adjoining counter if the door were reversed. Fortunately this is a reversible model of a two door top freezer-refrigerator, a good choice for the family which moves often and has to cope with frequent changes of kitchen arrangement.

or more to the cost if you need a plumber to install it.

CHOOSING A FREEZER

First decide whether you really need one. It is not true that a freezer pays for itself because of what it saves on food. Unless a freezer is extensively used, it costs more than it saves. Do not be taken in by the free food for a year gimmick. That freezer will be ridiculously high in price, and the food he gives you may be neither the best quality nor of sufficient variety to be of use to your family.

In choosing a freezer, be aware of these factors: In deciding between a chest type or upright, the cost is higher for the upright, but it is easier to clean, use and house than the chest type. It is difficult to find or remove foods from a chest type unit.

The frostfree feature is a luxury. A freezer needs defrosting only once or twice a year. The best buy is a manual defrost chest type freezer with a push button flash-defrost and a bottom drain.

It is a good precaution to choose a freezer with a lock and an alarm system to tell you if the electricity has been off, or if the freezer is not operating properly. These items are important, especially if freezer is kept in a garage or basement where it may not be checked every day, or where intruders could easily help themselves.

Look for a bargain in a used freezer. People who move a long distance, or who are not getting much use out of a freezer, may sell at a loss. Be sure to check out a used freezer with a thermometer. The temperature should hold a steady zero or below.

AUTOMATIC WASHERS

These appliances are either top loaders, which are the dominant type or front loaders which have a simpler mechanism, consume less water and detergent, offer easier maintenance and leave space above for a dryer.

Courtesy of General Electric Major Appliances Division

A dispensall washer can handle a large family wash in the big tub or a small load in the mini-basket. Dispenser automatically dilutes and adds laundry agents needed. Variable water levels can be used according to wash load size.

Basically all machines are alike but there is a difference in price, depending on the features chosen.

Features which to choose from are these: *Permanent-press cycle.* This cycle is almost essential for today's fabrics with special finishes and made of materials such as polyester knit. Actually this cycle means that the unit washes at a slower speed, uses cool water and spins slowly for a short time to preserve the finish and keep material from wrinkling. Once a permanent-press fabric is wrinkled it may never recover.

Special soak cycle. Any machine can be adapted to soaking clothes, and the length of the soak period can be adjusted by the user therefore, a built-in soak cycle may not be necessary.

Rinse cycles. Most machines have at least two rinse cycles. Therefore, additional rinse cycles are not essential. Efficiency of rinse methods is determined more by whether the water level is high enough to cover the clothes completely and whether the user has been careful not to

Courtesy of Frigidaire Division, General Motors Corporation

This space saving top-loading washer with dryer above, is suitable for placing in a closet, hallway, small bathroom or kitchen.

overcrowd the machine or use too much detergent.

Programmed washers are convenient, but costly. A push button tells the washer the type load. The washer chooses correct water temperature, length of wash period and puts in the correct amount of detergent, bleach and fabric softener. The high cost of a programmed washer is also reflected in greater frequency of repair.

Choose a washer with adequate capacity for your family needs. If you buy too small a model you will find it is overcrowded and get a poor washing result.

Consider the amount of energy consumed by various machines. The manufacturer's specification sheet will tell you total, as well as hot water only, consumption. Choose a machine that will operate on a low water level, when only a few items need to be washed.

Automatic dryers are available in both gas and eletric models. Most electric units require a 220-240 volt connection but a few models are available which work on 115-volt.

In regions where natural gas is available fuel cost for a gas model is about half that of the cost of electricity. An electric dryer, though initially less expensive than a gas model, may not save much if a new circuit (220-volt) is needed.

When buying a dryer look for: A convenient lint filter with a choice of temperatures from cold air fluff to hot are needed to suit all types of garments. A model with a drying sensor will stop the machine when clothes are just right to prevent them from wrinkling. A model with a porcelain top (not enamel) is stain resistant and worth the extra cost if the top is used for a work surface.

Washer-dryer combinations are still available. They are expensive, need frequent repair, and when one half of the unit goes the other will need to be discarded also. Their big advantage is compactness. A better choice would be either a stacking unit or a combination with washer below and dryer offset above and at the back.

PROBLEMS WITH MAJOR APPLIANCES

At some time you may buy an appliance which is poorly made, or find that the dealer or service agent will neither exchange nor repair an unsatisfactory machine. Write directly to the manufacturer first, giving details. If you get no reply or are not satisfied with action taken, go to the Major Appliance Consumer Action Panel, an industry-sponsored but independent group that acts as mediator between consumer and manufacturer. Write MACAP, 20 North Wacker Dr., Chicago, Ill. 60606 or call collect this phone number 312-236-3165. Be prepared to supply this information: Your name, address, phone number; type of appliance, brand, model and serial numbers; the dealer's name and address; service agent's name and address if different from dealer; location of appliance and a clear description of the problem. Some leading appliance manufacturers now have their own hot-line complaint departments. Be sure to ask your appliance dealer about it.

WHICH AND HOW MANY SMALL APPLIANCES

This is a matter of how often the appliance will be used, and whether there is sufficient storage and counter space to warrant adding another item. Small kitchen appliances can be great electrical energy savers, because they require less energy than an electric range. A new fry pan which fries, bakes, broils and has a separate warming tray does all the jobs a large oven can do and would be adequate for two people. It has the further advantage that it can be used at the table, taken along to a vacation cabin, washed in a sink, and replaced for about $30 when it is no longer working properly.

Whatever the appliance you are considering, whether it be a toaster, or an electric comb to untangle your hair, review the following before you make a choice: Take into consideration what you now own before buying another appliance; check consumer information booklets and consumer magazines before making a decision and comparison shop. Prices vary greatly among discount houses, supermarkets, mail order houses and department stores, all of which handle the same items. Buy at the time of the year when there are sales or before new models arrive. Study labels, fact tags, booklets and guarantee slips attached to the sample models in the store display. Discuss your purchase with friends who own similar appliances to find out how satisfied they are with performance of the item, excellence of the guarantee, and whether service and parts are available. If you do not pay for the item within a month, add at least an 18 percent credit charge to the purchase cost.

Home Batteries

Alessandro Volta discovered that two dissimilar metals, immersed in a solution of acid and water, chemically generated electricity. Volta called his invention a *cell,* a term still used today although the term *battery* (which really means a group of cells), is used as a catch-all word.

The Voltaic cell is the predecessor of all present-day primary and secondary batteries. Chemical energy stored in a battery is converted into electric current when the battery is discharged. This electric current is produced directly by chemical reactions which occur entirely within the battery. Many combinations of chemicals have been tried, with varying degrees of success, as energy storage systems. Each type of battery

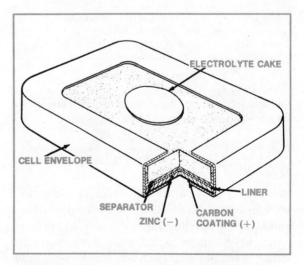

Miniature LeClanche Cell Used In (9V) Batteries

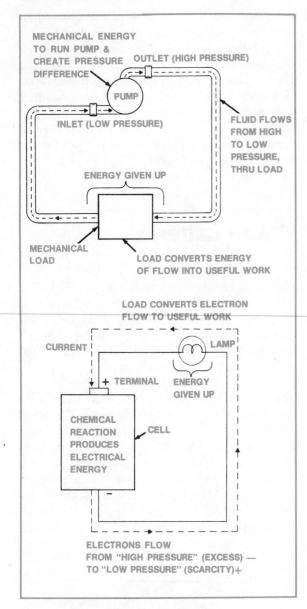

A battery is like a pump.

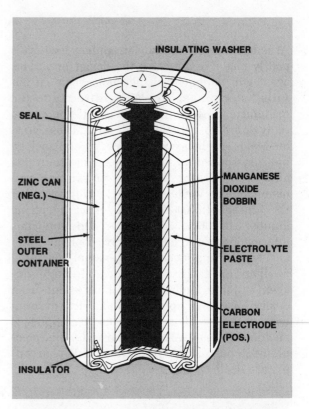

Construction of LeClanche's Zinc-Carbon Cell

has advantages and disadvantages with regard to its physical and electrical characteristics.

BATTERIES — A SOURCE OF READY-TO-GO ENERGY

With literally hundreds of physically interchangeable "look-alikes," which one is best suited for a specific application? With battery costs continuing to go up, and battery usage increasing ten per cent per year, it is important to get the right battery. Manufacturers make their products for specific applications, but very few battery purchasers really know if they buy the right one for their specific application. The "look-alike" character of different batteries in the store makes the odds against the uninformed user buying the *right* battery for a particular application slim.

For example, all size D batteries fit the same holder, and all have a nominal 1.5 volt rating. There, however, the resemblance *ends*. Usually the purchaser finds three different battery types: familiar carbon-zinc *flashlight* batteries, *transistor* batteries and *alkaline* batteries. Distinguished by their different internal chemistries, each of these battery types is designed for a specific job. Carbon-zinc batteries are custom tailored to moderate, steady current demands — just the kind of load presented by the filament of a flashlight lamp. Transistor batteries are also carbon-zinc batteries, but specially modified to deliver steady voltage under current demands that are mostly low, but occasionally and briefly, moderate. Just the thing to energize a transistor

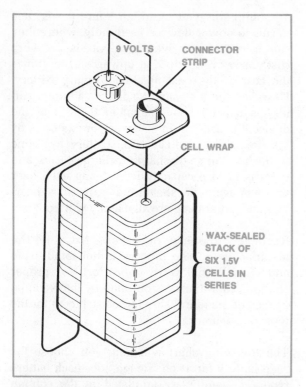

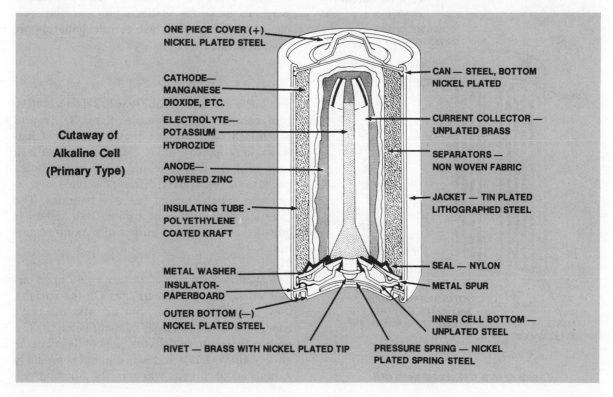

portable radio, but not a good choice to power a flashlight.

Neither of the two preceding types is a strong performer in any motor-powered device. Unlike lamps and transistors, DC motors have a voracious appetite for current at start-up and when slowed-down under load. Cassette recorders that stop mid-reel, motorized toys that stop after a few minutes and portable shavers that do not cut well are good examples of the problems caused using a carbon-zinc battery where you should not. That introduces the *alkaline battery*. Similar to the carbon-zinc battery, the alkaline type features a large reserve for peak current demands which makes it a good choice for motor-powered applications. But, there are three catches. First, the alkaline is likely to drive a motorpowered device more slowly, even though longer, than a carbon-zinc battery. Secondly, the alkaline types tend to "salt" over a period of time. That is, a whitish powder forms at the terminals which can corrode, or at very least, insulate the battery from the terminals of the holder. Equipment not used for long periods of time may not give satisfactory service when

Construction of a carbon-zinc "transistor" battery widely used in solid-state radios and entertainment devices.

needed. Alkalines used in place of carbon-zinc types in low current applications are more expensive, costing about three times as much as a carbon-zinc type. Use it as a highly reliable energy source for a device that draws large peak currents (recorders, electronic photoflash, etc.), but do not assume that the alkaline battery can last *longer* than a carbon-zinc battery just because it can withstand more punishment in use. In moderate drain applications, such as a flashlight, performance will be close to equivalent.

Compounding the problems of selecting the right battery for equipment is the availability of rechargeable *secondary* batteries in the same package as the single-use *primary* types just described. Nickel-cadmium batteries (also called *nicads*) are not meant to be thrown away after use. They can be recharged using a charging unit that plugs into the household AC power. Most cordless appliances come equipped with these batteries and have a built-in or plug-in charger. In a pinch, a carbon-zinc or alkaline battery can be used to run a device while its rechargeables

are being revived. And, in some cases, use nicads to power devices used daily, where they can be recharged overnight. Nicads are very costly, however, priced at upwards of ten times the cost of the best alkaline primary battery. However, the life span of a nickel-cadmium battery is usually about equal to the life of the device it is used in. In a shaver, for example, by the time the nickel-cadmium battery has gone through 500 or so discharge-recharge cycles, and it starts to lose capacity from being used over and over again, the shaver motor, brushes, bearings and cutter head are all usually worn out too.

Recharge primary batteries? No, say the manufacturers. The process is not totally safe and is really not worth the effort, for proper charging conditions (as outlined by the National Bureau of Standards) are far too stringent for the typical consumer.

The following chart will help you choose the right battery for a specific job. Jobs each battery type can handle are tabulated in the column under the other characteristics that spell out the great difference between. Costs of operation are included plus several other important considerations. To make the distinctions clear, the technical terms engineers use to rate batteries are used & defined.

BATTERY POINTERS

Similarity of size is a poor way to select a battery replacement. For example: Size "D" round photoflash batteries and regular flashlight batteries look exactly alike. Using the photoflash unit in a flashlight would be a poor choice because of the widely different service capacities and capabilities of the two batteries. The chemical composition of a photoflash battery is adjusted to favor brief surges of maximum current.

The alkaline battery has the same 1.5V open circuit voltage as the carbon-zinc. On the surface, they look quite similar, but the alkaline cell's energy content discharges at lower voltages. The carbon-zinc battery delivers most of its available energy above 1.25V and is just about completely exhausted at 1 volt, whereas the alkaline cell

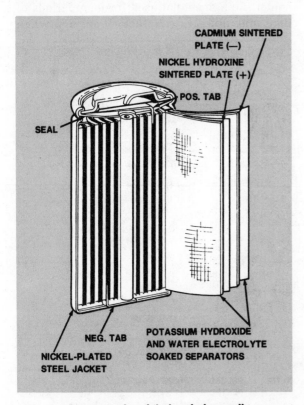

CADMIUM SINTERED PLATE (—)

NICKEL HYDROXINE SINTERED PLATE (+)

POS. TAB

SEAL

NEG. TAB

NICKEL-PLATED STEEL JACKET

POTASSIUM HYDROXIDE AND WATER ELECTROLYTE SOAKED SEPARATORS

Cutaway of a nickel cadmium cell.

yields most of its energy below 1.25 volts and still has quite a reserve left below 1 volt.

To preserve the energy in any unused battery, store it in an airtight bag at normal refrigerator temperature. When ready to use it, let it warm up to room temperature in its wrapper to avoid condensation of moisture on metal parts.

For ecological reasons, it is suggested that mercury and silver oxide batteries can be returned to the seller or a business specializing in reclaiming heavy metals. If not recycled, used batteries are best disposed of in well-designed landfill sites. Batteries may explode if disposed of in fires.

BATTERY FACTS		
CHARACTERISTICS	**TYPE**	
	Carbon-Zinc	Alkaline	Nickel-Cadmium
End-of-Life Voltage Voltage at the battery terminal (measured under load) which signals that a battery has reached exhaustion.	0.7 to 1.0V	0.7 to 1.1V	1.0V
Ampere-Hour Capacity (D cell) A relative measure of the amount of current a battery can deliver in a specified length of time. The higher the rating, the more energy the battery can make available.	2-8Ah	Up to 11Ah	4Ah
Cost of Use	30 cents — general purpose type (throw away) 35 cents — premium type (throw away)	$1.00 (throw away)	Purchase price approximately $10. Use cost: 3.5 cents per charge/discharge cycle.
Cost Per Ampere Hour	4 to 20 cents	About 9 cents	About $1/2$ cent (assuming 500 charge/discharge cycles)
Jobs Each Battery Type Can Handle	Flashlight, games, radios, clocks, toys (small), highway flasher, novelties, instruments. Intermittent, low current drains.	Shavers, movies, cameras, photoflash, large toys, TV sets, radios, bicycle lights and horns, tape recorders, model planes, calculators, slide viewers, heavy duty lighting, walkie-talkies, telephone answering machines, motor-driven devices. Heavy current drains.	Shavers, calculators, toothbrushes, knives, photoflash, drills, hedge clippers, grass trimmers, tape recorders, emergency lighting, TV sets, radios, instrument movie cameras, hearing aids, amplifiers, slide projectors, portable tools, alarms, gasoline engine starters, dictating machines, transmitters, low or high current drains — intermittent or continuous.
Attributes	Nonrechargeable, with efficiency best on low current, on/off electrical jobs.	Rechargeable and nonrechargeable. Most efficient on portable equipment with higher current demands: good shelf life 50% to 100% more energy than carbon-zinc batteries.	Rechargeable many times, more rugged than most types, with excellent shelf-life.
Nominal Voltage	1.5V	1.5V	1.25V
Energy Density Ratio of battery energy to weight expressed in watt-hours/pound.	5-40	20-40	12-17

BATTERY FACTS

CHARACTERISTICS	TYPE		
Rechargeable	No	No	Yes
Self-Discharge Rate a Month at 70° F A measure of how quickly a primary (or secondary) battery loses capacity when standing idle.	0.8% (Good)	0.6% (Better)	5-15% (Poor)
Low Temperature Limit Temperature at which a battery's ampere-hour capacity is halved, due to cold's making chemical reaction sluggish.	20° F	15° F	Store — 40° F Discharge — 20° F Charge — 32° F
High Temperature Limit Temperature at which a battery's internal reaction becomes excessive and self-discharge rises sharply.	120° F	140° F	Store — 140° F but shelf-discharge is rapid. Discharge — 113° F Charge — 90° F
Shelf Life For a primary battery, the time measured from the date of manufacture at a storage temperature of 70° F, after which the battery retains only a percentage (usually 90%) of its original ampere-hour capacity.	1-2 years (at 70° F)	Up to 3 years (at 70° F)	Charge retention poor. Must be recharged if idle more than 30 days.

OTHER BATTERY TERMS

Battery	A device which produces electrical current as a direct consequence of a chemical reaction between two dissimilar materials.
Primary Battery	A battery that is used once and discharged. Primary batteries are not intended to be recharged.
Secondary Battery	A battery that can be recharged and used over and over.
Charging (or Recharging)	The process of reversing a chemical reaction in the battery by applying an external source of current. Charging alters the chemical composition of battery materials, making it again possible for the battery to generate current as the material reacts.
Load	The circuit or component through which the battery forces current flow. Lamps and motors are typical examples of loads.

Home Buying
[SEE PURCHASING A HOME.]

Home Calculators

A calculator is an electronic device that performs addition, subtraction, multiplication and division. It consists of a housing, a keybord, a circuit board, a display on which the numbers are seen and an LSI (large-scale integrated circuit) chip.

This large-scale integrated circuit, smaller than your little finger nail, is the secret of the personal calculator which is rapidly becoming a well known household appliance. Continuing developments in chip production are making what started out as a several-hundred-dollar luxury, a home necessity at one-tenth the original price.

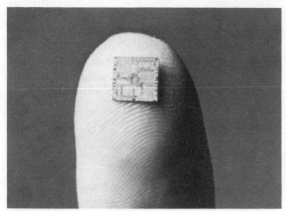

Courtesy of Texas Instruments, Inc.

Here are some of the things a calculator can do in your home. It can tell you how to save important money on your grocery purchases and where to deposit those savings for maximum return. It can calculate the length of a rafter and the angle at which to set your circular saw.

A home calculator is a great help in personal finances such as income taxes. It will quickly figure all individual entries and then enable you to test different methods of filing for the best results. It also helps prevent a special audit due to mathematical errors.

When does it pay to drive your car? What's your gas mileage? With the increase in gasoline prices it becomes a necessity to know and, your calculator makes it easy to find out. If you are driving abroad and want to know how many miles to the gallon the car is getting, you will appreciate electronic help even more. Getting from liters and kilometers to miles and gallons is a real chore with paper and pencil. Calculators will ease the shock for all of us as the metric system begins to penetrate American daily life.

Money exchange is one reason that travelers are beginning to slip calculators into shirt pockets. With dollar values fluctuating daily, the actual cost-to-you of a prospective purchase calls for a calculation based on the rate you actually paid for your peseta or franc. If you are contemplating a European trip, a home calculator may be a very helpful item to take along.

Painstaking surveys have shown that an average shopper can take 20 percent off the family groc-

ery bill without loss of either food enjoyment or nutrition by adopting better budgeting methods. A major saving is in price comparisons, since one equivalent product may sell for half to three-fourth the price of its competitor. But how is the shopper to choose among the 4$^1/_2$ oz. package at 2 for 73c, the family (12 oz.) size on special today at 69c and the jumbo pack, or 3 months supply, of 5$^1/_2$ lbs. for $5.39? The portable calculator will take only seconds to figure that the prices per ounce are about 8c, 5$^3/_4$c and just over 6c.

You have learned that as usual, the little package is expensive. For once, (although this happens surprisingly often) the rule of the-bigger-the-cheaper does not hold. Therefore, buy the middle size which saves, as the calculator will further inform you, 29 percent compared to the little packages, 6 percent compared to the big, an awkward choice.

Is it worth while to keep a running total as you go through a supermarket? For some people it surely is, especially if the shopper is limited to a budget. It is also protection against inadvertent, but very common, overcharges at the cash register. (Some come from the checker's ringing up an item twice, some from misreading, but most are failure to credit the day's special price when it is not marked on the package.)

To calculate markups, including sales taxes, and discounts, touch the percent key found on a few

Courtesy of Victor Comptometer Corp.

One unusual feature of the low-medium priced Victor "Vic" is its snap-on cover that protects it and also forms a cradle for comfortable angle of use. K key on the board is pushed only when constant is wanted.

calculators and you can add or subtract these instantly. Without the special key it is still an easy calculation. Do this: think of the price of something with 5 percent sales tax added as 1.05 times the price. Think of $19.98 less 20 percent as .80 times $19.98.

In deciding where to invest your money for the largest return, consider the following: it is no secret that banks can make mistakes, therefore, balancing your monthly statement is just normal prudence. If there is an elusive discrepancy, try adding up all the cashed checks separately and subtracting from the beginning balance to see if the error may have been in your day-to-day arithmetic on the stubs.

This and other personal-finance calculations, including social security and annuities and insurance, are natural fields for your calculator. It will tell you how much more seven percent interest is worth to you when compounded daily or quarterly instead of annually as well as a somewhat more striking fact: let the usual 1$\frac{1}{2}$ percent-per-month charge account run for a year and it will cost you not the annual rate of 18 percent that you are told but actually 19.56 percent.

Games become more fun when you have an easy way to calculate probabilities. Many computations of odds in bridge, horse racing, lotteries, and roulette involve tiresomely large numbers, but a personal calculator will handle the big numbers just as easily and just as quickly as if they were little ones.

How well a personal calculator will do these jobs for you will depend somewhat on what model you choose, and a good deal more on the tricks you learn in using it. Even the calculator manufacturers don't know many of these as they are being discovered or invented by ingenious users and passed around informally.

BUYING INFORMATION

Like a car, the calculator you choose may come as the basic model, or with almost any conceivable mix of optional extras at the usual extra price. These extras are important and not too hard to understand. You can be sure that any

machine you buy will add, subtract, multiply and divide. It will handle at least six digits. Almost all models display self-illuminated answers which can be read in darkness or subdued light, and all the small ones can be used on batteries. Beyond those characteristics, there are many refinements and extras to consider in choosing a home calculator.

Power Source

Power source may be your first major consideration. A unit that works on dry cells only can be a nuisance if it uses the obscure and expensive Type N and needs them every three hours of operation, as one widely sold calculator does. An otherwise quite similar machine, widely sold at about the same price, uses an under $1 type of dry cell and goes perhaps 15 hours on it. If your expected use is limited, this kind of disposable-battery model may be fine for you. Be sure to check first on battery cost, availability and running time, and consider the advantage of a model that uses the same kind of battery as other devices you own. Some models can be kept going in an emergency by taking a battery from either a transistor radio or a garage-door opener. For greater use, get either a machine that saves on batteries by having an adaptor for plugging into house current or one using rechargeable batteries.

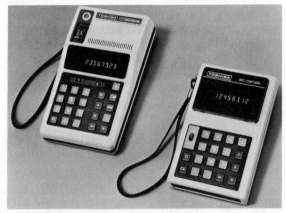

Courtesy of Toshiba America, Inc.

Slightly greater size with its liberal keyboard space makes the Toshiba pocket-sized calculators easier to use than the vest-pocket minis. Both models seen have automatic constant, one at left percent, sign-change and memory keys as well.

Mechanics

Compare machines for ease of operation for you. Some have keys too crowded for stubby fingers. Others have off-on switches that operate so easily they may turn on in your pocket and ruin their battery while others are extremely hard to activate.

If you may use your machine in the field, take a look at the display under bright light to be sure it can still be read easily. If you will use it mostly at a desk, check the viewing angle. Some have legs for tilting. If you are color blind note that some calculators have green instead of the usual red light-emitting-diode numbers.

Size, especially thickness, and weight vary considerably. You should favor one of the bigger machines which is still pocket-sized for mostly home use, and the tiny type for frequent carrying.

Logic

Essentially this means: Does the machine think your way or must you adapt to it? Mini-calculators generally started with what is called arithmetic logic, but many now offer somewhat simpler circuitry — known, oddly enough, as algebraic logic.

How to tell? Try an elementary subtraction problem, such as 6 minus 4 just that way. . . . If you get 2 that's the simpler logic. To do this problem on many models will require you to hit the 6, plus, 4, and minus keys in that order. (That minus key you hit last may have both minus and equals marked on it.) There are a few problems where this kind of logic may help, but it can confuse the new or occasional user. Even if it does not bother you, you may still have to consider this aspect, if it is to be used by other members of the household.

Number of Digits

Much more versatile than the ordinary 6-digit calculator is the one displaying 8 digits. (Ten and 12 digit displays are generally confined to larger, desk-top machines.) If the calculator is to be used for anything more than check-balancing and household accounts, you will probably need more than six digits. There are units that display only six digits while having a bank of six more which can be brought up by pressing a flip switch. The system is a little awkward and this extra capacity is not available for some operations, but if you foresee multiplying numbers that will produce really big products, this could be the one you should choose.

Reciprocals

You may not think you will ever want to figure reciprocals, but they have a lot of uses. Reciprocals are used to figure electric resistance, since the joint conductance of several conductors is found by adding together the reciprocals of the resistances.

Work problems such as; if Jim could do the job alone in 8 days; John could do it alone in 5, how long will it take them working together? can be worked on the calculator. Since the reciprocal of a number is the fraction or decimal you get when you divide 1 by that number, there is a special trick for getting it. You could, of course, just ring up 1 and then divide by the number. But often the number of which you want the reciprocal is the one already on your machine and you don't want to have to copy it off on a piece of paper and then put it back into the machine after punching the 1. The special trick is this: just divide the number by itself twice. The first step automatically produces the 1 you need, and the second step gives you the reciprocal.

Very Large Numbers

Beyond 8 (on some models, 6) digits, work stops and a warning sign pops on. With some calculators, there is no warning and digits begin falling off at the right.

Expensive machines solve this problem with scientific notation. What the scientific machine does is show the first 8 digits, all it has room for, and tell you how many zeros you must tack on to make your answer the right size. To get the same result, you can reduce the problem to manageable size and keep track of the decimal places.

Home Calculators

For a problem involving the number of days in a year, you might want to raise 365 to the 6th power, a number with far too many digits for ordinary calculators. Move the decimal point two places to the left and operate with 3.65 instead. The answer you get will be 2364.5972. But you know you have taken two places off the original number and then used the number six times. Add those 12 places you owe and you have the result you needed: 2,364,597,200,000,000. (In scientific notation, which is often the easiest way to record and to use such a number, you could call it $2,364.5972 \times 10^{12}$ or $23,645,972 \times 10^{8}$.)

Sometimes you can bypass the problem altogether. The formula for figuring out how many different poker hands can be dealt calls for dividing the product of all the numbers from 52 to 48 by the product of all the numbers from 5 to 1. If you write that down you will discover you can reduce the size of the numerator, and get rid entirely of the denominator, by some simple canceling. This process brings the chore down to the capacity of the calculator and tells you there are 2,598,960 things that could happen to you on the first deal.

Would you like to try both canceling and mental scientific notation on a single problem? Calculate the number of possible hands at bridge — all the possible groups of 13 cards that can be dealt from a deck of 52. Following the rule of combinations, the denominator will consist of the digits from 1 through 13 multiplied. The number you get will tell you that the chance of your getting 13 spades in you next bridge hand is 1 in 635,013,550,000.

Rearrange

Unless your home calculator has somewhere to store a partial result while doing the rest of the work, you will have trouble with sum-of-products problems. You can solve this kind of problem by rearranging it into a straightline task. Suppose you have these three products to add up: 5,888 x 4; 6.981 x 166; 59.4487 x 5. How do you go about it?

With any calculator, but especially one having a constant that works on addition, there is a timesaver when at least one number is small in all but one of the pairs.

In the example given, begin by multiplying together the pair in the middle because they are both big. Then just add 5,888 four times and 59,4487 five times.

Decimal

The lowest-priced machines sometimes come with fixed decimal, preset for 2 places. This is convenient for dollars-and-cents chores, but can badly restrict precision in many other calculations. No decimals means no fractions either; if you try to divide 3 by 9 on such a machine the only answer it can give is zero. The great majority of calculators have what is called full floating decimal. That means the decimal point can be placed anywhere in any number entered and it will take care of itself. Combining advantages of both systems is the floating decimal that can also be preset where you want it; or the kind that gives you a choice between full float and two place setting, or between full, two place and four places.

Overflow

Any but the least expensive calculators will have some way to warn you that it finds your problem too big for its abilities. It will either read-out all 9s or some special symbol will show up at the left. Given a number too small, that is, too large in a negative way, some other odd symbol should pop up. This, naturally, is called underflow. Such a warning is necessary to prevent errors.

Rounding

Any time a number gets too many decimal places for your machine, the excess will be dropped. And when a number gets into too many decimals for the operator's needs, he can drop them. Rounding is more accurate than dropping decimals. It means that 33.339 becomes 33.34 instead of 33.33. At least two of the medium-priced machines know how to do this for you to two decimal places. What these particular machines do is let you choose. If you punch out 3.33333 times 2, for instance, and then hit the times key

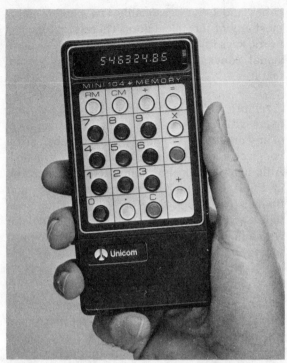

Courtesy of Unicom Systems

Shown here on a medium-priced calculator are features a buyer should know about. Special features, all discussed in the text, include memory and rounding off.

again, you will read the answer in full: 6.66666. But if you use the equals key instead for the final punch, what you will read is the rounded-off product: 6.67.

Constant

Just about all the personal calculators outside the lowest price bracket now have some form of constant.

Suppose you want to know the circumferences of a number of different circles. That naturally calls for multiplying their various diameters by pi. If you want to be very accurate, tap out pi to 7 decimal places: 3.1415927. Then all that is necessary is to multiply this constant by the different circle diameters without entering the value of pi again. The constant is very convenient for money conversions, prices and discounts, inches to centimeters, and so on.

Most mini machines have automatic constants that keep working unless you cancel them. Some

have constant keys, often marked K, which allow you to choose ahead of time whether you want this feature to be in operation. This convenience can lead to one special problem: you must remember to switch it off one step in advance of when it is needed or it will make your whole calculation wrong.

A constant will also work on division. Check the instruction booklet to find out if it functions for addition and subtraction too.

Memory

Ordinarily characteristic of more elaborate machines, this is a feature now offered on a few in the medium price range. When you see one or more keys with M on them, often MC or CM or RM or MR, they are probably for this useful function. A memory makes it simple to do a series of multiplication problems, for example, storing the product of each and finally adding them all together.

Courtesy of Bowmar

The Bowmar range of handheld calculators includes everything from simple personal machines to this upper-middle priced scientific model. With recourse to special techniques and tables, most of its functions can be duplicated on the less-expensive personal models — as explained in the accompanying text — but more slowly, of course.

Home Calculators

You might use a calculator to compare pre-ounce costs of competing products in family grocery shopping in addition to adding up the costs of all the things you are buying. The only trouble is, you will need two calculators, one for each operation, unless yours has a memory in which you can store the running total while making your new calculation.

More Functions.

As you get into somewhat higher price ranges you will find calculators offering a few special capabilities. The most common is the *percent key*. If you do a lot of work with discounts and markups you will find this a convenience. Also available is a *square-root key*. Most users can get along without this nicely, though, since it is not at all hard to calculate a square root on the machine. And if you need square roots frequently you could keep a table of them at hand.

A key for producing *powers,* squares, cubes, and so on, can be essential in working with some problems that call for very high powers, but a squaring key alone is not especially valuable. There is usually a method for getting squares,

Courtesy of Hewlett-Packard

Handheld calculators were seized upon initially by scientists, engineers, business people. This ultra-sophisticated scientific model sells for about 40 times the price of the simplest miniature calculator that is quite adequate for most household needs.

cubes and other reasonably low powers using most any of the calculators. Therefore, for most users, keys for roots and powers classify as occasional conveniences rather than as important features.

A *reciprocal* key is another specialized key most users will not find to be essential. The reciprocal of any number is 1 divided by that number, so on your calculator it comes out a decimal fraction. Although reciprocals are important and come up in fields as varied as electric resistance and financial planning, they are simple enough to figure with the regular keys on any calculator with a floating decimal. You merely have to push several buttons instead of one.

Pre-set Numbers

If you are going to make frequent use of certain numbers, especially ones containing more than two or three digits, it is handy to have special keys that produce them automatically. Most often found on medium-priced calculators is a key for pi. This feature saves you the effort of striking several keys instead of one. A set of keys for the most-used metric equivalents is offered on some machines; one turns the regular digit keys into these when you want them. More elaborate calculators have whole sets of keys that give you logarithms and a variety of trigonometric functions. Again, if you use these things only occasionally you will find it feasible to enter them from tables, using an ordinary calculator.

TRICKS IN USING CALCULATORS

Since the complex scientific calculators and the specialized commercial models are still not produced for true mass consumption, their prices remain relatively high. The ordinary household user may prefer the economy of buying a simpler model and using it to perform calculations that the manufacturer did not plan for it. Here are a couple of quick examples, followed by many more, of how you can do specialized things and take shortcuts with an ordinary calculator.

1. You have added up a series of long numbers and now you want to divide into (not by) some

number, such as 999. With an ordinary calculator, one that has no memory, how can you do this without stopping to memorize the total or write it on a piece of paper and then entering it again after entering the 999?

The answer—divide the total by itself twice and then multiply by the 999. What you have done is convert the number to a decimal equal to 1 over the number (its reciprocal, as mentioned earlier) and multiplying by the reciprocal of a number is equal to dividing by the number.

2. Again you have added up a series of numbers. But this time you want to subtract your total from, say, 999. To do this, just use the change-sign key and then add; on some calculators the minus key will do to make this change of sign. If not, the simplest procedure is to go ahead backwards: subtract the 999 from your total and ignore, or change, the sign of the answer.

Counting

You will not learn counting from your instruction booklet which is unfortunate since this is a task each machine does in its own way. It is a useful trick, too, for counting items at the supermarket, the box office or in traffic. With some calculators, generally those with an automatic constant that works with all functions, you can count by just hitting the 1 and then the plus repeatedly. If the calculator has a constant (K) switch, turn that on first. If it has a K key, the procedure will probably be to hit successively the 1, equals, K buttons, then the plus repeatedly. To count by 2's, just use the 2 key instead. To count backwards or correct a mistake, touch the minus.

If these methods fail, it may be that the constant on your machine works only with multiplication and division. In this case, load the entry with zeros and ones in such a way that each time you multiply, the product increases by slightly more than 1, but so slightly more that the difference is at the tail end of so many decimals that the machine will drop it as excess. You do this by multiplying 1.0000001 by 10000000. (You need not count the zeros; just put in enough to fill the machine.) Now each time you touch the equals key, the digit at far right will increase by 1.

That is how you do it for a model that is designed so the first number you enter becomes the constant. For machines with which it is the second number, do the same multiplication, but in reverse order. With some of the simplest calculators, counting can be done only by pressing both 1 and plus keys each time.

Square and More

Most calculators can be taught to square and cube without your having to enter the number more than once. That's important if it is a number like 3.1415927, as it frequently is. When you have taught your calculator the procedure you will find it is almost as handy as having a special squaring button.

If your machine has a K key, hit the number, equals, K, in that order. Then hit the times button once for square, twice for cube and so on for any power you fancy.

With an automatic constant all you need do is hit the number, the times, and then the equals (repeatedly for higher powers). If the constant is governed by a switch, turn it on first.

You can square almost as quickly as on a machine with a special button for the job. But what if you want something like this, the 23rd power of a 3-digit number? Use a shortcut that you may remember from high school algebra. After reaching the 11th power, square that to immediately get the 22nd power. Multiply once more by the original number, and there you are.

Adapt this method to find any power too tedious to pursue step-by-step. Just remember that you multiply by adding exponents: cube a number, square that cube, and you have the 9th power.

Square Roots and Diagonals

You are laying out a cabin and want its corners to be square. By squaring the lengths of the sides, adding these squares together and finding the square root you can find the length of the diagonal of a rectangle. You begin by making a careful guess what the square root might be. Then, on your calculator, you divide the original number by the guessed root, add the amount of the guess, then divide by 2.

In other words, to obtain the square root of 150, recall that 12 times 12 is 144. Take 12 for your guess and divide 150 by 12, then add 12, and divide by 2. Result: 12.25. Check by squaring 12.25 on your machine to get 150.0625, which is close enough for most purposes.

To get an even more exact answer, repeat, using the new root instead of your guess. Divide 150 by 12.25, add 12.25, divide by 2, and you will get a square root that squares to 150.03123.

Beyond Square Roots

There are similar approximate-and-refine formulas for deriving cube roots and worse, but experience has taught me and the calculator that we can get results faster in these instances by pure guess and try. And no formula to remember.

The way to find cube roots involves some trial and error. To find the cube root of 1,234, for instance, begin by guessing 10.5 since 10 is the cube root of 1,000 and therefore, somewhat small.

In cubing 10.5, you find that is too small also, so you try 10.7, which cubes to 1225 plus. You are close, so you try 10.72. That proves too small, but 10.73 proves too big, so the answer is in between. Within a couple of more tries you will find that the cube of 10.726 is 1233.9948, so that is as close as the answer can be without using an inordinate number of decimal places.

FIGURING PERCENTAGES

Many medium priced calculators boast percentage keys. For regular business use the key is well worth its extra cost. But, for occasional use a basic model can work percentage without recourse to a special key. The basic rule to remember is instead of hitting the number and then the percent key, just hit the decimal point and then the number, so that you have moved the point two places to the left. Thus 25% becomes .25; 12$\frac{1}{2}$% becomes .125; and 4% becomes .04.

Equally useful, keep in mind that a discounted price can be found directly by first subtracting the discount percentage from 1. For example:

you are thinking of ordering a $127.50 bicycle on which you have been offered a 22$\frac{1}{2}$ percent discount. Set 1 on your machine, subtract .225, multiply by 127.50 — and the answer is $98.81. (If the price is subject to 6 percent sales tax, multiply by 1.06 to find the grand total the easiest way.)

Interest

Here is something most people with savings or mortgages or installment payments want to figure sooner or later. With a few formulas you can turn your little calculator into a commercial machine.

Simple interest: this tells you what you will owe a month or a year from now if you borrow money today. To find it, multiply the interest rate by the time, add 1, then multiply by the principal amount. For $250 borrowed for 6 months at 12$\frac{1}{2}$% simple interest, multiply .125 by $\frac{1}{2}$, add 1 and then multiply by $250 to find that you will have $265.63 to pay.

Compound interest gets more interesting and more complicated. The formula tells you to add 1 to the interest rate, then raise this total to a power equal to the number of periods involved, then multiply this factor by the amount of money. Just remember that *number of periods* means number of times compounding occurs and the interest rate desired is the one for the period used for compounding, not necessarily for a year.

How much will $1,200 be worth if you leave it in a savings account where it will be compounded semi-annually for 5 years at 6$\frac{1}{2}$% ? Thinking of 6$\frac{1}{2}$ as the decimal 6.5, divide it by 100 (because it is a percentage) and then by 2 because compounding is to be twice a year. Add 1, and the display will read 1.0325. Multiply that by itself 9 times to raise it to the 10th power, because there are 10 half-yearly interest periods in 5 years. The resulting factor multiplied by the amount of money should tell you that your $1,200 will swell to $1,652.27.

Cutting A Rafter

Begin this with the Pythagorean theorem and square root, both of which have already been touched on. You are building a cabin, with a shed roof. The structure is 10 feet, 8 inches high on one side and 7 feet high on the other, and the walls are 12 feet apart. How long must you cut the rafters, not including any overhang?

In effect, each rafter is the hypotenuse of a right triangle of which the sides are 12 feet and 3 feet, 8 inches. The only difficult part of such a problem are the feet and inches. Probably the easiest method, until the metric system is in full force, is turning everything into inches. This means using larger numbers, but with an electronic calculator that makes little difference. Therefore, 12 feet becomes 144 inches, which squared is 20,736. That added to the squares of 44 inches makes 22,672. We have already discussed the method for finding the square root of a number which is what you do next.

As it happens, if you make your initial guess the rather logical 150 (smallest round number greater than 144) that first trial will produce an answer so close to perfect there will be no need to go further. You are to cut your rafter to 12 feet, 6.57333 inches. Which, is a little more than 12 feet, 6½ inches. (If you want to be a more precise carpenter, feed that decimal fraction of an inch, .57333 into your calculator, multiply by 16, and find that it really comes to 12 feet, 6⁹/₁₆ inches plus.)

If you want to figure out how to set your saw to make that cut so that it will be parallel to floor or wall, you will need a trigonometry table. The tangent of either of those little angles in a right triangle is what you get when you divide the length of the far side by the length of the near side, in this case 44 divided by 144. Look up the resulting .3055555 in the tan column of a table of trigonometry functions and you will find it comes as near to 17 degrees as makes no difference. So that's where to set your radial saw there or at 90 minus 17, depending upon which rafter cut is being made.

With these ideas as a start you can go on to turn your relatively simple personal calculator into the functional equivalent of a scientific model with its elaborate keyboard and formidable price tag. All you need is a few math tables: trig func-

tions, logarithms, metric conversions. These might be photocopied to convenient size and encased in plastic to become a permanent part of your calculator's equipment.

Even the simplest of personal or household electronic calculators is a marvel that multiplies not only numbers but your power to cope with an increasing complex and mathematical world. With it you take a quantum jump that may remind you of the day you switched from a handsaw to power equipment.

Home Construction
[SEE FLOOR CONSTRUCTION; FOOTINGS & FOUNDATIONS; FRAMING; ROOF CONSTRUCTION; STAIR CONSTRUCTION; WALL & CEILING CONSTRUCTION.]

Home Heating Systems

Heating systems can be classified into two kinds: the *space heaters* and the *central heaters*. Fireplaces and electric resistance heaters fall into the first category. Each heats the air directly and thus, usually serves only individual areas. Central heat systems manufacture heat in one of several kinds of furnaces, then distribute it to all parts of the house by a heat-conveying network of pipes or ducts. These are often described by naming both fuel and the heat-carrying medium used in the system (e.g., gas/warm air, oil/hot water, coal/steam, or any other interchangeable combination of these fuel and media). In some instances, a system may have acquired a special name, such as *radiant heat,* although it could also be technically described by the fuel/medium generic name, as well. For simplicity, the sections which follow describe systems by heat-carrying medium. In later sections, furnaces will be described by the type of fuel used.

WARM-AIR HEATING SYSTEMS

Basically two types of systems are found in this category: *gravity* and *forced.*

Gravity Warm-Air Systems

Gravity warm-air systems originated in the era of Queen Victoria and represent an improvement on the fireplace.

Gravity warm-air systems are of two kinds, the wall furnace and the central furnace variety. In the central system a single furnace is used to heat a number of rooms. The furnace usually is located in the basement, although some are designed for use on the main floor. The heat is ducted to the various areas of the house where it is needed. The air is warmed in a chamber surrounding the enclosed firebox of the furnace. It then rises and flows through ducts and risers to the rooms above, entering through registers located in the floor or at the baseboards. (In installations with the furnace on the main floor, the registers are usually located high on the walls or in the ceiling of the rooms since the furnace must be *below* the registers.) Return air ducts at the floor allow the cool air from the rooms to return to the furnace for recirculation.

In wall furnace space heater systems, one or a number of smaller furnaces are used. These furnaces are located either under the floor or on the wall of the rooms to be heated. Each furnace serves the room or rooms in its immediate vicinity. Heated air from the furnace rises and circulates into the room space. The cool air at the floor is continuously drawn back into the furnace for reheating. Automatic controls are used with gravity warm-air systems to regulate the heating.

There are no moving parts in the gravity warm-air circulating system, therefore it works in silence. The disadvantage of this system is that the ducted air does not move with much force. It cannot push its way through a conventional dust filter without slowing down too much for efficient heating, hence gravity hot-air systems are usually unfiltered.

The gentle flow also makes it necessary to keep the hot-air ducts short to avoid too great a heat loss along the way. So the hot-air registers are usually at the inside walls of the rooms which are closest to the furnace situated in the center of the basement. The return air registers are at the outside walls. (They have to be on the opposite side of the room in order to draw the hot-air flow across.) Thus, the hot air floats past the warmer inner walls first.

Then, as it cools, it descends past the colder outside walls and windows and enters the return registers for its downward glide to the furnace again. As a result, the outside areas of some rooms may be chilly on very cold nights. Also, natural air flow may make the unit slow to respond to the thermostat.

Forced Warm-Air Systems

With an electric motor-powered blower to increase the air flow, the warm-air system has become the heating choice of modern home builders. An advantage of this sytem is that the ducting and blower of a forced warm-air system can also be used to circulate cold air from a central air conditioning unit during summer weather. Thus, the cost of one system helps to defray the cost of the other.

As a heating plant, the forced warm-air system works this way: the blower sucks in cool air

Gravity hot-air system relies on fraction of an ounce difference in weight of heated air and cold air for circulatory effect.

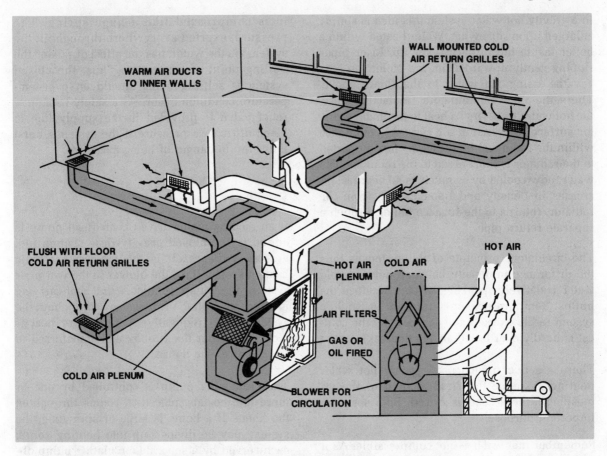

WARM AIR DUCTS TO INNER WALLS

WALL MOUNTED COLD AIR RETURN GRILLES

FLUSH WITH FLOOR COLD AIR RETURN GRILLES

HOT AIR PLENUM

COLD AIR

HOT AIR

AIR FILTERS

GAS OR OIL FIRED

COLD AIR PLENUM

BLOWER FOR CIRCULATION

Forced warm-air system distributes heat evenly throughout home, overcoming several drawbacks of gravity system.

from the return ducts, all of which are now joined to a common, large duct containing a filter. Dust particles and lint are trapped by the filter material and the air passes through the whirling blades of the blower which forces it into the air chamber surrounding the firebox. Heat transfers to the air and the high-velocity air stream carries the heat away from the hot furnace surfaces and into the rooms above much more rapidly than in the gravity system. Therefore, more heat is available from the same size furnace with forced-air instead of a gravity system. As the forced-air stream can travel in any direction, the furnace can be taken out of the cellar and installed anywhere in the house, including the attic.

HOT-WATER HEATING SYSTEMS

Water is a better conductor of heat than air and it takes more time to absorb and release its heat than air. These advantages give it a slight advantage over warm-air heating systems where even-temperature whole-house heating is desired.

Both air and water are *fluids* and so it is not unusual that there should be great similarity between the systems which deliver the heat. There are gravity hot-water systems and there are forced hot-water systems (which are usually called *hydronic systems*).

Gravity Hot-Water Heating System

Water, like air, expands when heated. Thus, hot water occupies more space for a given weight than does denser cold water. Thus, when water is being heated in a boiler, the hottest water rises, "floating" on the cooler, denser water, below.

In a gravity hot water system this idea is simply enlarged upon somewhat. Water heated within a boiler inside the furnace floats up. Riser pipes sloping gently upward from the boiler top convey the rising hot water to the floors above. There, the pipes join radiators. Contacting these, the hot water transfers its heat to the metal radiator surface. Convection air currents commence within the room and by these, the heat imparted to the radiator is transferred to the room air. The water, now cooled by as much as 40 degrees, increases in density and upon exiting from the radiator, returns to the furnace boiler through a separate return pipe.

The circulatory principle of the system is thus the difference in density between hot and cold water (relatively speaking, of course, since the hottest temperature encountered in such a system rarely exceeds 180 degrees and the coldest is hardly ever less than 130 degrees).

There are two branches of gravity hot water heating systems: the first is open to the atmosphere, the second is closed. Both serve an important purpose.

Remember that water is not compressible. As it increases in volume while being heated, some part of the system has to physically "give" or the boiler or piping would burst. This contingency is covered in the open system by an expansion tank located above the highest point in the system, usually in the attic. The tank is open and has an overflow tube near the top, leading to a drainpipe. As the water level in the system rises with temperature change, the system is kept at a constant atmospheric pressure by relieving expanded water volume into the tank. Where heat increases and hence, expansion, are excessive, the system relieves itself into the drain system.

A disadvantage of the open system is that it does not prevent steam formation within the system should heat accidentally rise beyond controlled limits. In a closed system the expansion tank is sealed and airtight, although there is air space within. At normal room temperature, air pressure inside the tank is equal to that outside. But, when the water in the system is being heated and it expands into the tank, the air within

is compressed like a huge spring. The pressure, exerted everywhere throughout the system via the water, has the effect of raising the boiling point of the water. Thus, the closed system is self-regulating should an over-temperature condition occur. As a safety backup, a relief valve is provided in the supply line to bleed off excess pressure if the system's burst limits are in danger of being exceeded.

Hydronic (Forced Hot-Water) Heating Systems

If an electric motor-driven centrifugal pump is added to the closed gravity-flow system just described the result is the modern *hydronic* heating system. Like the blower in the warm-air system, the pump circulates the heat-carrying medium through the furnace and throughout the system more frequently, so that more heat is picked up from the firebox and transferred to the rooms of the house.

The circulating pump is controlled by one or more thermostats, placed in rooms throughout the home. If a home is large or sprawling, the system may be divided up into *heating zones,* each served by a separate circulating pump obtaining its hot water supply from a common furnace.

Water heated in the furnace of the hydronic system is distributed through pipe to special radiators called *convectors*. Usually, these are low-profile, baseboard mounted units consisting of a pipe length fitted with metal radiating fins, enclosed behind a decorative exterior piece that admits cool, floor-level air at the bottom and exudes warmed air from the top front. Heated water flowing through the pipe simply transfers its heat to the pipes and fins. The large surface area of the fins is in contact with a considerable volume of air. As heat transfers from the fins to the air, the warmed air rises and is replaced by cooler air from floor level. Thus begins the convection flow which results in warming of the air throughout the room.

How Convectors Are Arranged

The two-pipe convection of the gravity hot-water system is still considered the best choice in

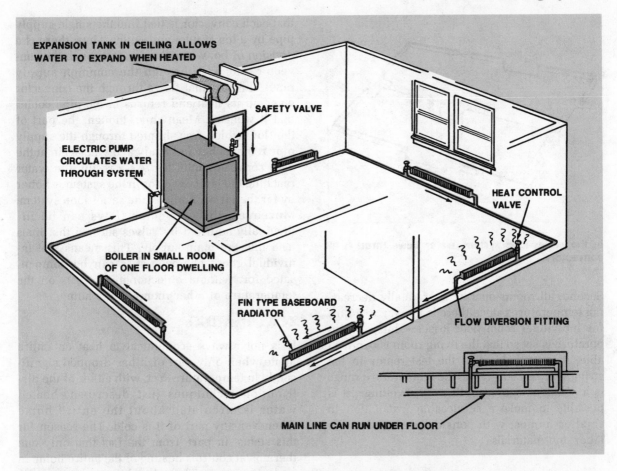

EXPANSION TANK IN CEILING ALLOWS
WATER TO EXPAND WHEN HEATED

SAFETY VALVE

ELECTRIC PUMP
CIRCULATES WATER
THROUGH SYSTEM

HEAT CONTROL
VALVE

BOILER IN SMALL ROOM
OF ONE FLOOR DWELLING

FIN TYPE BASEBOARD
RADIATOR

FLOW DIVERSION FITTING

MAIN LINE CAN RUN UNDER FLOOR

In the forced hot-water heating system, a circulator pump routes heated water throughout the system dozens of times more often than in a gravity hot-water system. Water stays hotter, conveys more heat to convectors.

forced systems where a large home is to be heated with forced hot water heat. But, there are other, less costly alternatives: the *series-loop* system and the *one-pipe system.*

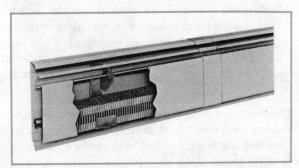

The inside story of a convector: pipe arrayed with fins runs entire lineal length of convector.

Series-Loop System

In the series-loop system, heated water expelled from the furnace by pressure of the circulating pump is carried by a pipe to the inlet of a convector.

The convector outlet joins another pipe, leading to a second convector, which in turn, links up to a third, a fourth, and so on. The outlet of the last convector in the "loop" returns the water, now minus its heat, to the furnace.

Though least costly to install, the system has some disadvantages: first, no convector in the loop can be turned down or shut off since that would affect the flow through all convectors.

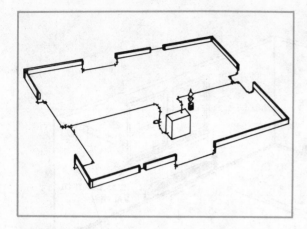

In the series-loop system, water flows through all convectors.

Second, all rooms operate at gradually decreasing temperatures since there is no way to adjust for individual room heat losses. Thus, if temperature is set so that the living room is comfortable, it is probable that the last rooms in the string will be cool. While the temperature range is a disadvantage in multi-story dwellings, it is possible to make a serviceable installation in smaller homes, with considerable savings in labor and materials.

One-Pipe System

The gradual cooling of the water is overcome in the *one-pipe system*. In this, a common pipe carries heated water from the furnace to each of several convectors. The important difference is

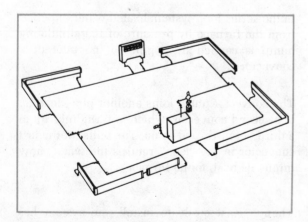

One-pipe system affords means of "balancing" heat delivery through separate valving at convectors.

that each convector is tied into the single supply pipe by a tee at inlet and outlet. Thus, there is a *division* of hot water flow: part through the convector and part through the common supply pipe. The part that flows through the convector gives up its heat and returns to the pipe cooler that it went in. Meanwhile, though, the part of the flow which was shunted through the supply pipe remains hot and ready to divide again at the next convector inlet tee. As a result, the water reaching the last convector in the system is hotter by far than it would be in the series loop system. Moreover, the convector flows can be individually adjusted by valves set into the pipes teed into the main supply. This means that individual room characteristics can be compensated for, without objectionable effects on the temperature of other rooms in the home.

ZONE HEATING

It is not always economical to heat an entire home when only part of it has dropped significantly in temperature. Yet, with either of the distribution techniques just described, heated water is circulated about the entire home whenever any part of it is cold. The reason for this stems, in part, from the fact that only one thermostat controls heating of the entire home in such a system. Thus, the home represents a *single heating zone*. The steam rises in insulated pipes to radiators, pushing air within the pipes and radiators ahead of it. The air is vented out of the radiators through valves which shut when the steam enters under pressure. The hot steam contacts and gives up its heat to the cool radiator inner surfaces, condensing back into water. The radiator and pipes are pitched at an angle so that condensing water flows back down the steam pipes. As steam condenses, a partial vacuum is created that draws more steam up and into the radiator. Very quickly, the radiator heats up and transfers its warmth to the air and objects about it by radiation and convection.

One solution is to provide more than one thermostat and individual piping arrangements, so that the home is divided up into two or more heating zones. Such an arrangement, common in split-level and sprawling ranch homes, recognizes the fact that heat should be delivered only where it is needed.

In practice, two or more series-loop or one-pipe systems are installed in the home, each connects back to the furnace and circulator through individual electrically operated solenoid valves, and each is controlled by a thermostat within a heating zone. When no zone thermostat calls for heat, the gas in the furnace is off, the circulator pump is off and the solenoid valves of the system are closed (blocking water flow). Let us now assume that one heating zone thermostat's contacts close. Immediately, the fuel supply to the furnace is turned on, the circulator pump is turned on and the solenoid valve of the zone demanding heat is opened. As a result, water circulates only through the convectors of the zone demanding heat; the closed solenoid valves of the other zones prevent flow through their convectors. As the circulating water conveys heat from the furnace boiler to the convectors, the rooms in the affected zone warm to the point where the thermostat opens.

This turns off both the fuel supply to the boiler and the circulating pump and closes the zone valve. Of course, water can circulate in more than one zone, but flow through the convectors depends upon a controlling on-off signal from each zone's thermostat.

In heating systems for large homes and in homes where a playroom or extra living space has been added, there may be no zone valves. Instead, separate circulating pumps may be installed, controlling the flow through individual heating zones. A thermostat simply switches on the fuel and a zone circulating pump when heat is needed. Water does not circulate in those zones in which the circulating pumps are immobile.

RADIANT SYSTEMS

Some homes that lack basements are built on concrete foundations with slab-type floors. This can be an advantage since it allows easy installation of a special hot-water heating system called *radiant heat*. Actually, a network of small diameter pipes is laid in the slab and convected to the circulating pump of the system. The network forms what is called a *radiant* panel when covered with a thin layer of poured concrete. This panel replaces the usual convectors and

acts like one big low-temperature radiator. In effect, heated water circulating through the pipes transfers its heat to the concrete panel. A large volume of air is in contact with the panel, in contrast to the tiny fraction of room air that is in contact with the small surface area of a convector. Thus, the radiant panel nowhere approaches the temperature reached by a radiator, yet the room grows warm.

Because the concrete panel gains and loses heat slowly, there is quite a lag between the time the room thermostat signals for heat and the time that the panel is warm enough to impart heat to the room air. For this reason, many homes with radiant heat use an indoor/outdoor thermostat. In such systems, a bimetal switch located in a glass case outside the house senses outdoor air temperature. A change in outdoor air temperature will ultimately change indoor temperature. So, these systems start the heating system in advance of a drop in indoor temperature. This compensates for radiant heat's natural lag and keeps room temperature steady in the comfort zone.

Radiant Wall and Ceiling Systems

Not as common as the floor systems, radiant wall and ceiling systems are space-saving answers to the problem of supplying heat to rooms where convectors would be unsightly or would consume too much wall space.

Courtesy of Hunter Division, Robbins , Myers, Inc.

Baseboard heaters are usually controlled by a wall-mounted line voltage thermostat, though some come equipped with built-in temperature controls.

Radiant Wall Panel: Almost always placed on an interior wall, the radiant panel comprises a plumbing circuit of small diameter tubing through which water heated in the furnace is pumped by a circulator. A zone valve and thermostat may be used in the water circuit, just as in a convector hot water system. The principle is as described earlier: the hot water transfers its heat to the plaster and metal lath of the panel. These, in turn, radiate warmth into the air of the room. To prevent heat loss into rooms or closets which share the wall in which the panel is installed, at least three inches of insulation are placed behind the panel.

Radiant Ceiling Panel: Heat from the ceiling solves the heating problem where there are rugs on the floor or heavy drapes on the wall. Since a radiant panel needs a clear path to the area it is going to heat, the ceiling may be the best place for the heat. The ceiling panel tubes are usually embedded five to nine inches apart in a plaster bed containing metal lath.

Because there is no concrete slab, the ceiling panel's heat-up lag is far less than that of the floor type. Also, with proper planning, some heat from a downstairs ceiling panel can warm the floor of the second story. (Though you cannot rely upon this for complete heating of a second level, it may reduce the total heating needs of the upstairs system.)

STEAM HEATING SYSTEM

Water which is heated to 212° F (100° C) at sea level becomes *steam.* Steam carries heat just as effectively as hot water and it is faster to get from source to radiator. Generally, too, steam delivers more heat energy to a radiator because its temperature is greater than the cooler 180° F (68° C) that is the usual maximum in hydronic systems. Steam also circulates under its own pressure in a system, not by forced draft of a circulating pump or blower fan.

In the steam system, water is heated in a boiler within the furnace until it boils, becoming steam.

HOW FUELS AND FURNACES WORK

Wood and coal were the predominant fuels of home heating systems during the first half of this century. These bulky fuels did not readily lend themselves to use in convenient automatic furnaces, however, and today natural gas and number two oil are the chief fuels used in home heating systems.

Gas and the Gas Furnace

The modern gas furnace is designed to burn hydrocarbon gases such as methane, ethane, propane and butane. The first two are prominent constituents of *natural petroleum gas,* the fossil fuel obtained from deep wells. The second two are called *condensables,* which are extracted from natural gas then liquified and bottled under pressure. These fuels are widely used in mobile homes, recreational vehicles and vacation homes and usually are referred to as LPG (Liquified Petroleum Gas) rather than by their more exact chemical names. All of these gases will burn; all are generally rated nontoxic and nonpoisonous. However, in their natural state, none has any odor which could make leak detection hazardous. And so, gas producers add *odorant materials* containing sulfur compounds which give the peculiar garlic-like odor to heating gas. Very little odorant is needed to produce a strong,

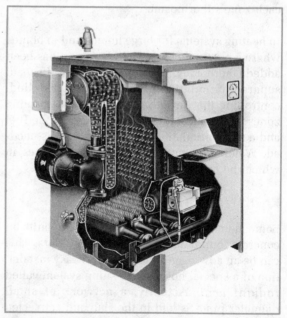

Courtesy of American Standard

A gas-fired forced hot water (hydronic) system furnace where circulator pump is shown at left, moving water through hollow core of heat exchanger.

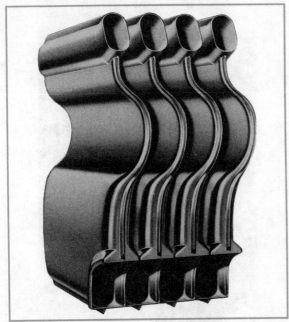

Courtesy of Lennox Industries

Heat exchanger of modern warm-air furnace present considerable surface area to air draft flowing over and about outer surface.

easily detected odor. The sulfur burns in the ignited gas and produces no color or harmful products.

The heat energy produced when burning a fuel gas is commonly expressed in British thermal units (BTU). One BTU of heat will raise the temperature of one pound of water, one degree fahrenheit.

Here is how a gas furnace works: The gas supply line enters the furnace through a main manual shut-off valve and an automatic safety valve that blocks gas flow if the pilot flame is out. Next in line is a pressure regulator. This element contains a spring-loaded diaphragm that reduces line pressure and holds it to a steady lower valve, even if line pressure changes markedly because of peaks in gas use by others. The gas then enters a tee and a small amount flows down a narrow-diameter tube to supply the pilot flame. The flame runs continuously and is positioned near the burner head jets. Next to the pilot flame is a metal capsule called a *thermocouple.* The pilot flame's heat causes this sensing device to generate a tiny electrical current which is just enough to hold open the automatic valve in the

gas supply line. If the pilot flame goes out for any reason, the cool thermocouple ceases to generate holding current for the automatic valve and it snaps shut, blocking gas flow into the furnace.

Beyond the pilot flame supply line is the main gas valve, which controls gas flow to the burner jets. Ordinarily, this electrically-operated valve is controlled by a room or zone thermostat. However, it is not unusual for other devices, such as a water temperature high limit switch in a hydronic system to be wired into the control circuit. In this way, gas supply can be shut off when the thermostat is satisfied, or if a failure occurs in the thermostat line, gas will shut off before the water turns to steam and dangerously raises system pressures.

When the main gas valve is actuated, gas flows through the pipe, mixes with air at one or more shutter-like openings in the burner jet casting and the fuel-air combination is ignited by the pilot flame. Burner jets are arranged so that the heat of combustion is spread evenly over the surface to be heated.

In a warm-air system furnace, the gas flames supply energy to a *heat exchanger.* The heat exchanger is a series of ducts, arranged so that air can be blown through them, while their outside surfaces are heated. The purpose is to transfer the heat from the gas flame to the air moving within the exchanger, but to prevent any combustion products from mingling with the warmed air. The circulating air supply is provided by a motorized blower in a sealed chamber below the heat exchanger and burner. The air supply is drawn in from the return duct system through a filter, to further minimize circulation of combustion by-products. Most gas furnaces are designed to provide a 100-degree temperature rise across the heat exchanger. Thus, if air enters at 60° F, it will leave the furnace at about 160° F.

In a hot-water system furnace, the gas burner jets heat the surface of a boiler, thereby transmitting heat to the water within. Heated water is pumped from the boiler to the room or zone demanding heat. Cooled water returning from the zone convectors is reheated and recir-

Courtesy of Lennox Industries

Nozzle (center) atomizes oil fed through tube under pressure for pump at right. Squirrel-cage blower forces air draft through ports in plate surrounding nozzle, driving volatile fuel vapor past spark electrodes.

culated in a continuous flowing cycle. Generally, the heat rise calculated for water circulating in the system is also about 100°, measured from boiler input to output. Thus, water entering at 60° F will leave at about 160° F. To prevent damage to the system from steam hammering and pressure buildup, a high-limit switch is ordinarily included and set to turn off the gas when the water temperature reaches a maximum of 180° F.

Oil and the Oil-Burning Furnace

Residential No. 2 heating oil is a fraction of crude petroleum. It is one of the left-over materials which remain after more volatile and flammable constituents (gasoline, kerosene, etc.) have been distilled from the crude oil. As a result, heating oil must be coaxed into burning by atomizing it, then mixing it with large amounts of air (to bring sluggish oil molecules into contact with oxygen molecules), then igniting the mixture with a continuous, hot electric arc. Once ignited, heating oil yields a high-energy flame which can be used to heat water in a boiler (for hydronic or steam systems) or air passing through a heat exchanger in warm-air systems.

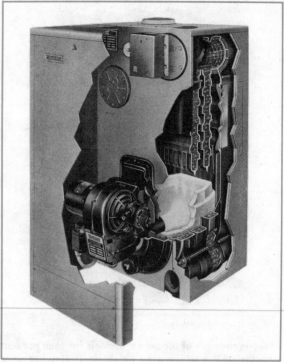

Courtesy of American Standard

Gun-type oil-fired hot water heating system furnace uses heat exchanger similar to gas-fired furnace.

Kinds of Oil-Burning Furnaces

Two principal types of oil burner mechanisms are used today: the *high-pressure gun type* and the *forced-air vaporizing type*. The gun-type burner consists of a pressurizing pump which forces oil through a nozzle to convert it into a fine mist. A fan forces the mist to mix with air and the fuel-air mixture is ignited by a continuous electric spark, produced by a special transformer that steps normal household AC power up to thousands of spark-gap leaping volts. The flame front issuing from the pressure gun is directed into a chamber lined with special firebrick. The heat within the chamber is then directed to the boiler or heat exchanger. Combustion gases and products exit through a smoke pipe connecting to the flue pipe of the chimney.

The forced-air vaporizing oil burner is not as common as the gun-type, its principal use being in small space-heater furnaces. Fuel enters through a control valve and runs to a pool below the fire pot. The walls of the pot are drilled through to allow passage of air and oil fumes.

Air is supplied by a small blower fan. An electric discharge ignites oil fumes in the upper fire pot and the heat causes more oil to evaporate and mix with the inrushing air from the blower fan. A pilot flame keeps the fire going and the oil pool is replenished as fuel is consumed.

Quieter than the gun-type burner, the vaporizing burner also has fewer moving parts. But, it does require competent maintenance since its functioning depends so heavily on the air draft. Sooty accumulations can reduce burner efficiency and produce a yellow flame, rich in poisonous carbon monoxide. Regular, seasonal maintenance is the best protection against hazards from any fuel-burning heating system.

Fuel Oil Storage

Most municipalities regulate the amount of fuel oil you can store in tanks in your basement. According to the National Board of Fire Underwriters, a basement oil storage tank should not exceed 275-gallon capacity and you should not have more than two tanks indoors. (If greater capacity is needed, tanks should be installed underground, outside the home.) Minimum separation between an indoor tank and the oil-burning furnace is seven feet. All tanks should be vented to outside air and the filling lines should also be outside the home for flammable fume safety.

Controlling the Oil-Burning Furnace

The control system is determined by the distribution method and number of zones. Generally, however, the thermostat in the room or zone calling for heat will energize *both* the gun-type burner (or blower fan in the vaporizing burner) and will begin circulation of air (in warm-air systems) or start the circulator pump (in hydronic systems). The steam system, being self-distributing, requires only the startup of the burner.

Whichever type system is in use, however, a safety stack-switch is provided in *all* systems. This switch is heat-sensing and is designed to operate as hot combustion gases exit from the oil burner through the smoke pipe. Thus, when the thermostat switches on the burner and fuel supply, the stack switch confirms that the fuel has

ignited. If it does not, power is shut off to the burner to prevent unignited fuel from being sprayed into the combustion chamber. Generally, when a stack switch shuts off the burner it is an indication of trouble requiring competent, professional service. Most stack switches have a reset button. If the burner shuts off, press the button and try again. If there is still no ignition, get knowledgeable help.

Chimneys

No combustion furnace, whether wood, coal, oil or gas-burning, will burn very long or well without an adequate supply of oxygen. That is one reason for the chimney in the heating system. Not only does it pipe away noxious gases and any smoke produced in combustion, but it also provides the draft that sucks air into the furnace to bring the combustion process to peak heat. To permit any furnace to develop maximum output and efficiency, a chimney must be clean and free of obstructions. Anything that reduces draft wastes energy.

Chimneys can be masonry types or asbestos-jacketed sheet metal tubes, depending upon local codes. Esthetics favor the traditional brick, but economy dictates metal. Either type works well and may be installed to rise on the exterior or within the interior of the home. Exterior designs are wasteful of energy since any heat entering the flue pipe at the bottom is essentially out-of-doors. In an interior-rising design, the walls of the chimney radiate heat within the insulation limits of the home and so there is some recapture of energy which enters the chimney.

Heat causes a chimney to expand somewhat and so its planning should include careful attention to a solid foundation. If a brick chimney is to be outside the home, its walls should be at least eight inches thick. Inside chimneys are not subjected to the ravages of weather and are supported somewhat by the house structure. Thus, the wall of an inside brick chimney need not exceed four inches. If you are planning a masonry chimney, however, add about five inches to the wall thickness to assure an adequate margin of safety.

Underwriters Laboratories and the National Fire Protection Association both offer safety guidelines for the installation of a chimney. It is important that the chimney extend at least four feet above any object, structure or surface within a horizontal span of ten feet in all directions. If the chimney is to rise through a flat roof, its top should be at least four feet above the roof surface. Of course, if your roof is gabled and the chimney is to rise through the peak, the minimum recommended height is two feet, measured from the arch of the roof to the chimney top. Local building and zoning codes may enter into a chimney installation and your safest course is to consult the building department or town engineer for up-to-date requirements.

From an operational standpoint, it is best to allow a flue area of about 100 square inches (figured by multiplying the widthwise dimensions). The exact shape of the flue pipe is unimportant, but sufficient area must be allowed to assure a good, free draft. Remember that combustion products must be freely expelled to make room in the furnace for a fresh charge of oxygen-rich air. A badly designed chimney that expels gases slowly can halve the efficiency of your furnace and send heating costs soaring.

Even if your chimney is well designed, it is bound to accumulate soot and dirt over a period of time. Cleanup is not difficult and the results can be well worth the time invested. Because cleaning is done from the top of the chimney, gravity will pull any loosened debris into the base of the chimney. Depending upon the layout of your heating system, this may mean that loosened soot will fall into the basement or enter the furnace.

It is wise to disconnect the smoke pipe from the furnace, blocking the pipe's free end with heavy paper or tying a heavy-duty plastic rubbish bag around the pipe end to catch the fallout of your clean-up activities.

Next, prepare a chimney sweep by filling a coarse burlap or heavy canvas bag with bricks or stone (for weight) until it fits snugly into the chimney flue pipe. Attach the sweep to a sturdy rope. Thoroughly wet down the sweep with water, then insert it into the flue and lower it to the bottom. Raise and lower the sweep to loosen the soot on the walls of the flue.

Afterwards, you may wish to vacuum clean the case end of the chimney, to be sure that you have cleared away any rubble that might affect your furnace's performance. Any particular matter that has worked its way to the smoke pipe can be shaken into a rubbish bag.

ELECTRICAL HEATING SYSTEMS

Central Electric Heating

Central electric heating systems can be divided into three principal categories: *electric warm-air furnace, electric boiler and central system with duct heaters.* These systems use a duct or piping system to distribute heat to the living area. They require a central fan or pump to move the heating medium through the system. The control systems for electric heat furnaces, boilers and duct heaters are all very similar.

How Electricity is Converted into Heat

Wires are like pipes for electrical current flow. And, just as small diameter pipes oppose the flow of water in a plumbing system, so special wire conductors (called heating elements) resist the flow of electrical current. In the process, the heating elements grow hot, often to the point where they emit a cherry red glow. It is in the electrical resistance of the conductor, that energy in the form of electricity is transformed into heat energy.

Courtesy of Lennox Industries

Electrical resistance heater uses coils of special alloy wire to convert current flow into heat.

With the elimination of combustion, the need for a chimney is also eliminated. Also, apart from a blower or circulator pump, there are no moving parts in the electric furnace, making it lowest in cost to install and maintain. There are, however, economic penalities in electric heating in some regions of the country where electricity is very expensive. These tend to offset somewhat the otherwise very practical advantages of central electrical heating. There are other ways to use electrical heat economically, and that is in *space heating* of single rooms, additions, workshops and garages, with baseboard or radiant systems and in *supplementary* heating, with the installation of compact wall or ceiling units designed to add to the heating provided by another system.

Electric Warm-Air Furnaces

An electric warm-air furnace consists of a cabinet housing a blower, heating elements and control system. It is similar to a fossil fuel (gas, oil) furnace, except that the heating elements replace the burner and there is no heat ex-

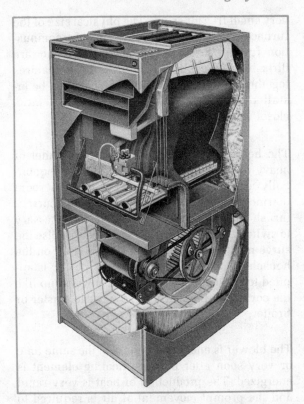

This is an "upflow" warm-air furnace. Cool air is drawn in at floor level by the blower, passed over the heat exchanger, and warm air exits from the top, ready for distribution to rooms via ducting.

changer or flue (since there are no products of combustion that must be removed). Generally the electric furnace contains a number of heating elements which are arranged in banks for ease of control. The furnace cabinet also encloses the air filter and the blower which moves the air through the heating section and the air distribution system (duct work) to the living spaces.

Modern warm-air electric furnaces are extremely flexible in their application possibilities. They may be readily combined with a central cooling system, an electronic air cleaner and a humidifier to provide year round comfort conditioning. Most are adaptable to upflow (basement), downflow (attic) or horizontal (same floor) applications without major modification. This is because there is no need for the heating elements to be in any one position. The heating unit itself is well insulated, and there is no combustion air required, so it can be installed in a

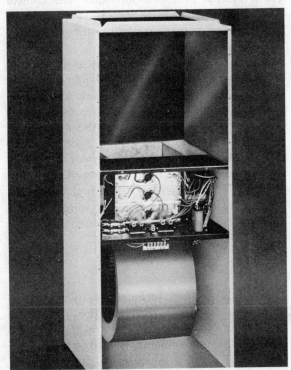

Courtesy of Fasco

Simplicity of this warm-air electric furnace is revealed in this inside view.

very small free air space. The physical size of the furnace is usually smaller than that of a combustion furnace because the heating elements are directly in the air stream. All these features together mean that the electric furnace can be installed almost anywhere — basement, attic, closet or right in the living space.

The heart of the electric furnace is a panel of heavy-duty heating elements. Power is sequentially applied to these elements when a room thermostat calls for heat. (So great is the current inrush to the heating elements that it is necessary to switch them on in a 1-2-3 sequence, or else the surge might cause annoying voltage drop on the household power supply line.) As power is applied to the heating elements, they warm up like the corresponding parts of an electric toaster or broiler.

The blower is energized before, at the same time or very soon after the first heating element is energized. The production of heat is very rapid and the prompt movement of air is required to prevent overheating in the furnace. At the end of the call for heat, the blower remains on until the last element is de-energized. It is not necessary that it remain on for an extended period to remove residual heat from the system, since the production of heat stops about as quickly as it started and there is no heavy heat exchanger to retain heat.

Over-temperature protection is provided in the furnace, in case the thermostat fails. Generally, each heating element is energized through a snap-action switch which responds to excessive temperature by snapping open, disconnecting power to the element and allowing it to cool.

Electric Boiler Heating System

The electric boiler system is functionally analogous to a central warm-air furnace: a centrally heated medium is distributed to the living area where its heat is released to warm the space. The differences are that water is the centrally heated medium instead of air, a piping system replaces the warm air ductwork and a circulator pump replaces the central blower.

The electric boiler is compact, generally having a water capacity of only two or three gallons and small enough to be hung on a wall in the home. Its small size is possible because water has a much higher heat carrying capacity than air, and the electric elements are immersed directly in the water. This not only saves space but provides very rapid heating of the water, since nearly all the heat produced by the elements is transferred directly to the water. The heated water is piped directly to the room convectors where its stored heat is delivered to the air. Distribution of the water can be easily controlled by zone valves under control of separate zone thermostats.

The electric boiler has the same control requirements as the electric warm-air furnace: room air temperature sensing, limit protection, load switching and distribution (circulator) control. The most common control system consists of a low voltage thermostat, transformer, solenoid type switching relay and an aquastat immersion type hot water limit. The boiler also includes a mechanical pressure-temperature relief valve to guard against pressure build-ups. The control system may also include zone valves if areas of the home are to be separately heat controlled.

A solenoid type switching relay is commonly used to switch the heating load in the electric boiler. The switching relay has up to five separate snap switches. One of these is designated for circulator control, and this switch will make first and break last on a call for heat. The relay uses a mechanical lever system to provide a slight delay between the operation of the switches. This delay allows the circulator to start before the heating elements are energized, and also reduces excessive instantaneous power demand.

Electric Duct Heaters

A complete electric duct heating system does not employ a central furnace as the main heat source, but, instead, uses a central fan to move air to the heating elements located in the duct at the room location (or in the diffusing room register). There may be a tempering heater at the fan location to prevent the circulation of cold air to rooms in which the heaters are off.

The central fan system offers advantages of individual room or zone control and is adaptable to central air conditioning, air cleaning, outdoor ventilation and humidification if desired. A duct heater may supply one room or several rooms and be controlled by a zone thermostat. Operation of a duct heater is similar to that of the heating element section of an electric furnace. It contains the elements and terminal connectors, and includes (as does the electric furnace) limits (usually a snap disc for each element), fuses and transformer. The housing is designed so the heater will fit into common sized ductwork.

Electric Baseboard Heaters

Baseboard heaters are among the most popular units for heating condominiums, apartments and additions to established homes. They are used for general comfort heating in both residential and commercial buildings, and may be used as either the total heating plant or for supplementary heat.

Baseboard heaters are available in a wide range of sizes and heat-output ratings. They can be conveniently placed under windows and along outside walls to offset heat losses and "cold-wall" effects. Most models are *convective,* requiring only free air circulation across the heating element; some are radiant, requiring a good placement in the room.

For fire and smoldering protection, in case drapes, pillows or clothing block the airflow through the baseboard heater, nearly all units have built-in limits (power cutoffs) that detect too high a temperature within the unit and break the circuit until the element cools to a safe temperature.

MAINTAINING THE HOME HEATING SYSTEM

In these days of rising costs, it is very likely that you will be able to perform the routine maintenance your heating plant needs. Since just about every part in any home heating system has been given the most careful attention in engineering design, the probability that you will be confronted by a major failure is minimal. But, failures *do* happen and if one should occur, a decision has to be made: can you tackle the job, or should you call in a professional?

Generally speaking, if you cannot find and fix the problem in ten minutes, call a repairman. Chances are that any fault beyond a blown-out pilot, tripped circuit breaker or furnace control switch cannot be fixed without special knowledge, tools or equipment. Delving into a heating system without any of these may result in your unknowingly inducing *other* failures which can sharply increase your repair costs.

What to Do if the Heat Doesn't Come

If your system becomes inoperative or will not deliver adequate heat, check the key areas spelled out in the following checklist first.

Be sure that the main power switch of the furnace is in the *on* position.

Check the thermostat setting. (If the thermostat also controls the air conditioning system, be sure that the switch on the thermostat's side is in the HEAT position.) Also, if the thermostat is an older model with open contacts, dust may be choking its operation, or pitting at the contacts may be preventing current flow needed to energize the heating system. Remove the cover, gently blow out dust or dislodge delicately with a new, *clean,* soft, long-bristle brush. Clean contacts by inserting a business card (or piece of paper) between them, close the contacts and rub the card back and forth. *Never file contacts or use an abrasive medium.* If the fine plating of the contacts is breached, you have to replace the thermostat.

In a forced-air system make sure that the switch controlling electrical power to the blower fan is in the correct position.

Look for tripped or blown circuit breakers or fuses supplying electrical power to the furnace, circulator pump or fan. (These are usually located at the main wiring box of your home.) Replace a blown fuse or reset the circuit breaker, as necessary.

With an electric furnace, each heating element is protected by a fuse within the furnace, itself.

After checking main supply breakers or fuses, turn off the power to the furnace, open the access door and check the element fuses. If one or more of these are defective, replace with fuses of the correct type and restore power.

In an electrical heating system with baseboard element heaters, make sure curtains or furniture are not jammed against the baseboard. These can cause element overheating, opening a safety heat-sensing switch which cuts off power to prevent fire. Clearing the blockage and allowing the element to cool down will reset the switch automatically.

In a forced-air system check to see if the main air filter is dirt-clogged and plugged. This can cause the furnace safety controls to shut off the fuel supply. Replace the air filter, if necessary, and follow the reset procedure prescribed by the furnace manufacturer.

If yours is an oil heating system, is there fuel in the tank? (Check the level indicator to be sure.) Is the primary safety control locked out? Wait five minutes, then move the level button to the reset position. Is the pump motor reset button locked out? Wait five minutes and push to reset. If neither procedure works, or if the furnace starts, then stops, call your serviceman.

Improving Heating System Performance

If your monthly fuel bill seems to be higher, if the furnace seems to be on all the time even on mild days, or if one area seems much warmer or cooler than another, chances are your heating system has acquired a few problems, not the kinds of problems that cause catastrophic failures, but the more insidious variety that waste money and cause early wearout of heating system components.

Dust, soot, airborne grease and neglect are the chief factors in lack of heating system efficiency. Dirt and soot are thermal insulators. They act as a blanketing layer that blocks contact between surfaces of a radiator or convector and the surrounding air. Thus, the transfer of heat is retarded, and the small amount of heat that does reach the room air may not be adequate to overcome

heat losses. The result is a room that feels cool and does not warm sufficiently to satisfy the thermostat, or requires a longer-than-normal running time of the furnace.

Once or twice each season, thoroughly vacuum the interiors of baseboard units, convectors and radiators to clear away dust, assure free air passage and promote efficient heat transfer. Inside a thermostat, a dust layer settling on the bimetal can also prolong a furnace cycle, making the thermostat slow to respond to room air temperature changes. A thermostat that lags in turn-on and turn-off is a serious waster of heat. A clean soft brush will remove dust from the thermostat bimetal with worthwhile results. (Don't

ever try to clean with solvents or water. Likewise, don't attempt to lubricate a thermostat; it is meant to run *dry*.)

Wherever air moves, dust and dirt move with it. And, if you have a warm-air heating system, the amount of these undesirables increases in direct proportion to the amount of air it uses. Older, gravity warm-air systems have no filters since they rely on the fraction-of-an-ounce difference in weight between hot and cool air for circulatory effect. The absence of a filter makes these systems vulnerable to dust build-ups in ductwork, which retards airflow and chokes off warmth. Regular vacuuming of ducts and the use of room electronic air cleaners can alleviate this problem with the bonus of reduced house cleaning, dusting and repainting, since tiny dust particles will be removed before they can be distributed throughout your home. Of course, the need to clean up circulating air is greater in the forced-warm-air system, but the built-in duct filter can be cleaned or replaced whenever dirt, grease and dust plug the filter's pores. You can also install an electronic air cleaner right in the duct, for continuous filtration of the air circulated about your home. Most in-duct cleaners pass the air through a panel of activated charcoal to trap odors in the air, then, through two grid-like screens, charged with high-voltage DC electricity. As airborne particles pass through the first grid, they are charged positively. As they next approach the negative grid, these charged particles are pulled right out of the airstream and held tightly. Periodically, the air cleaner should be counterflushed (with electricity off) with fresh water that washes the trapped particles down the drain.

In some forced warm-air furnaces, the filter is located in the air entry chamber of the furnace, below the heat exchanger. Two common types of filter are the *slab* and the *hammock*. The slab is the typical, flat, disposable filter also found in air conditioning ducts. It is a "sandwich" of fiber glass and horsehair, held between two thin metal plates punched through with large diameter holes. When trapped contaminants reduce airflow through a slab filter do not try to clean it, replace it. The hammock filter differs, in that the frame is not throw-away but the fiber glass filter medium is. These are usually slide-out assemblies and must be removed from the furnace for replacement. It is wise to line the floor with paper or a drop cloth beforehand and have a large rubbish bag handy to receive the old dust-laden filter. Holding plates snap open to release the old medium and receive a new one. Once it is in place, simply slide the filter assembly back into the furnace and you are ready for another season or more.

Efficient air circulation also demands proper attention to the blower fan and motor. Do not overlook the drive belt linking the motor to the

Courtesy of Lennox Industries

The filter should be changed annually. To install, simply slide it back into place.

Courtesy of Lennox Industries

Be sure that the fan belt is taut to insure the efficiency of the blower.

fan shaft. A slipping belt reduces air delivery, adversely affecting household temperature. Inspect the belt for signs of obvious wear as belts wear, fray and stretch in normal use. If it looks good, check its tension. The belt should be as loose as possible without slippage. If necessary, loosen the motor mounting nut and move the motor to take up excessive belt slackness. The belt tension is just right if it can be deflected about ³/₄ of an inch at the center of its longest run to the fan pulley.

While you are checking the blower fan, oil the motor bearings, if necessary. Belt-drive motors usually have oiling ports. Seasonally, add a few drops of SAE No. 10, nondetergent oil to each port. If a motor has no oiling ports, it has been sealed with lubricant at the factory. No relubrication will be necessary in normal operation throughout its life. Direct-drive fan motors often have oiling ports, but are meant to operate for extended periods without relubrication. These motors are rarely as accessible as belt-drive motors and may need to be removed for lubrication after a number of heating seasons' service. Finish up by wiping fan blades and air chamber clean.

If you are satisfied that the heat-delivery part of your system is free of dust and dirt, check the heat-producing portion. In oil and gas-fired furnaces, a free and unobstructed draft to supply abundant oxygen for the burning of the fuel is essential. Since the air that is drawn into the furnace loses its oxygen, but picks up combustion products and carries them through the smoke pipe and up the chimney, there must be a continuous airflow. An obstruction anywhere in the chain will reduce combustion efficiency and cost extra heating dollars.

In a gas-fired furnace, the air supply to the flame results from convection. To allow free air flow, seasonally vacuum the furnace interior, paying particular attention to the cleaning of air entry ports and the space below the main burners. Be sure that dust is not blocking the burner throats and shutter openings, choking off air supply to the burner flames.

In an oil-fired furnace, air supply to the flame is forced. If the flame burns faintly or with a great deal of smoke thorough vacuuming of the air inlet (at least seasonally) is essential. Cleaning of the firebox and heat exchanger are also helpful in getting best performance.

An oil burner should be checked over by a qualified heating man each year before the system goes into operation. Usually your fuel supplier will provide this service, and all you must do is keep the unit clean and oiled. Oil burner nozzles should be replaced once a year. The continuous passage of oil at high pressure widens the passages in the nozzle resulting in the use of more fuel than is needed. This can also cause smoking. Experts say savings from this precaution can amount to $70 or more per year. If your serviceman is not replacing this inexpensive item, ask that he do so.

If the flame looks weak, check the oil-flow adjustment screw on the pump housing, located opposite the oil intake, and turn it until the flame burns brightly. If this has no effect, the trouble may be that the pump's oil filter is clogged. This can be inspected by first shutting off the burner power switch, then removing the pump cap to get at the filter. Remove and wash the filter outdoors in clean oil or kerosene.

In all cases, the smoke pipe and chimney must be cleaned periodically to preserve the flame-enriching draft that makes your heating system efficient.

Electric furnaces and baseboard systems do not require the same maintenance as combustion systems, but they do share a need for being kept clean. The draft in a warm-air electric furnace passes from the room into the heat chamber, thence to the remainder of the house, as does the airflow in a baseboard electric heater. In either case, occasional thorough vacuum cleaning will remove the dust layer that is inevitably deposited on heating surfaces by convection or fan-forced airflow.

Forced hot water systems usually employ automatic feed valves in the water inlet line to maintain the correct water level in the heating system. However, air dissolved in the water admitted to the system must inevitably come out of solution. This causes air-pockets to form at various points in the system. Unlike water, air is compressible. It can be compressed, like a spring, by a column of water under the force of a circulating pump. The problem is, the air starts to push back, preventing the heated water from flowing freely through one or more convectors. That is why it is essential to *bleed* each convector, by opening its air valve until airflow gives way to water. By releasing the trapped air, first from the upstairs units, then from the lower convectors, hot water circulates freely throughout the system, efficiently transferring warmth through unimpeded direct contact with the metallic convectors of the system.

In a steam system, the radiator vent valves are set to release air automatically. If plugged, they will prevent the steam from entering the radiator. You can sometimes unplug a valve by boiling it in water for twenty minutes or so. Check also that radiators are level on the floor. If not, condensed water will not drain properly, reducing heat output and often resulting in noises in the system. Wood leveling blocks can be slipped under the legs of the radiator to remedy this. A partially open shutoff valve can also produce hammering and knocking noises.

If a leak exists at a radiator shutoff valve, first try tightening the packing nut. If this fails, shut the valve, allow it to cool, then loosen and slide the packing nut up on the shaft. Wind valve packing, available at any hardware store, around the shaft under the nut, then retighten. On hot-water radiators the system must first be drained to a level below the defective radiator before this repair can be attempted.

CHECKING ELECTRICAL PARTS OF YOUR HEATING SYSTEM WITH A MULTIMETER

About the handiest electrical test instrument you can have around the home shop is a combination voltmeter, ammeter and resistance/continuity checker, called a *multimeter*. It is ideal for locating problems in heating control systems. With it, you can find such problems as an open winding in a low-voltage control transformer, check wiring and fuses for continuity, check operation of

control relays and switches, measure the output of a pilot flame limit relay sensor, check over-temperature limit switches for operation and check fan and circulator motors. The marvelously convenient part about the multimeter is that it measures voltages as low as a quarter of a volt (about one-sixth the output of a flashlight battery) and as high as 500 volts (about four and a half times higher than the power your household outlets supply). If your home heating system uses 220 volts (as do all electric furnaces and most large blower fan motors in forced-air systems) the multimeter provides the quickest and possibly the safest way to check line voltage and whether it is getting to where it should.

All multimeters come equipped with two carefully insulated test leads, each fitted with an insulated probe handle terminating in a metal, sharp-pointed tip. This allows you to hold the probes safely without danger of shock through accidental contact with hazardously high voltages. If you are to check power line voltage, set the switch of the multimeter to the range setting embracing the highest voltage expected (i.e. if you are expecting 120 volts, set the meter RANGE switch to the 250V scale. This will put a 120V reading at about the meter scale center. If you are working on the low-voltage side, where a heating system control transformer steps the current down to only 24 volts, you will want to set the meter to the 50-volt range).

In making a voltage measurement, locate both the *hot* and *neutral* wires. Test lead polarity

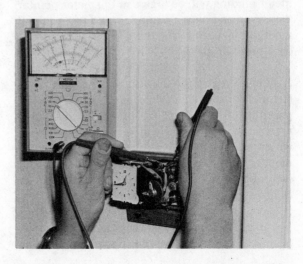

does not matter on AC, so place either the red or black test probe on either point. It is wise to hang or stand the meter so you do not have to hold it. You will need both hands to manipulate the two probes.

A good troubleshooting practice is to work backwards, from the thermostat or furnace control to the main fusebox if you are looking for the point at which a control voltage is lost. Check each junction and both sides of switches. If you suspect a switch is bad, shut off the power at the fusebox, then switch the multimeter to the *resistance* or *ohms* range. In this mode, a small battery within the meter attempts to push current through any conductor connecting the meter probes. The meter reports the results. If the conductor's resistance is low, the meter reads close to zero; if opposition to current flow is high, the meter reading will be high and the meter pointer may even indicate infinity (∞), which is about what you can expect if the probes were placed on a piece of glass.

A switch's resistance (as also a thermostat's contact resistance) should be as close to zero as possible for good operation. If you spot high resistance across a closed switch (that is, one which should be conducting current), replacement is probably in order. Open thermostat and control relay contacts, however, can probably be cleaned and restored to service.

The pilot flame sensor is a thermocouple which generates a low voltage when the flame heats the sensor housing. You can check the sensor's output with the low-voltage range of a multimeter right at the shut-off valve. Low or missing voltage means a short, or open circuit, bad connection or defective sensor. A quick continuity check will reveal which.

Some parts cannot be fixed easily. This includes control transformers that continuously step down the power line voltage to the 24-volt level where the thermostat and heating control relays operate. If you find no voltage across the secondary terminals (where there should be 24 volts), but there is power line voltage (about 117 volts) on the transformer primary, you will have to replace the transformer.

HOW A THERMOSTAT WORKS

A thermostat is an electrical switch which is activated by change in temperature, as well as by the human hand. Although you are involved in setting the temperature you desire the heating system to maintain in a particular area or throughout your home, thereafter, the thermostat operates free of human judgment, solely by measuring the difference between the temperature you set and the actual temperature of the air.

The temperature sensing mechanism of the thermostat is a *bimetal:* essentially, an alloy combination of two metals which respond very differently to even slight temperature changes. One metal expands more than the other when temperature increases. This causes the bimetal strip to bend in the direction of the metal which expands the least.

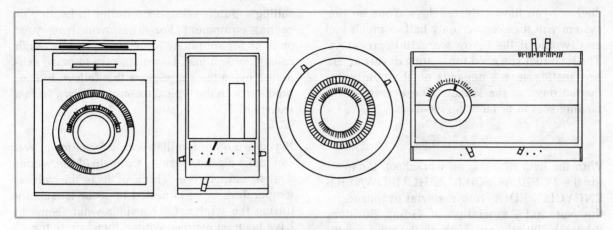

Varying Shapes of Thermostats.

In a modern thermostat, the bimetal is coiled, to save space, around a central shaft linked to the temperature setting knob. This linkage means that the free end moves in an arc in response to either temperature change or a manual adjustment. A glass bulb filled with mercury is fitted to the coil end and tilts one way or the other depending upon either rotation of the temperature knob or the effect of room air heat on the coiled bimetal strip.

Two electrical contacts in the glass bulb are bridged by the mercury when the angle of tilt and force of gravity cause the liquid metal to flow backward. This closes an electrical circuit to the furnace controls, beginning a heating cycle.

As heated air moves past the bimetal coil, it gradually loses tension. Slowly, the glass bulb is tilted in the opposite direction, until the mercury rolls away from the two contacts, breaking the circuit to the furnace controls and commencing the shutdown phase of the heating cycle.

As room air cools due to heat losses, the bimetal coil regains tension and in coiling more tightly, slowly swings the glass bulb over to the tilt angle at which the mercury switches on the furnace for another heating cycle.

Because the bimetal coil is extremely sensitive to relatively small temperature changes, a thermostat will easily hold a room within three degrees of any temperature set.

The location of the thermostat and the way it is used can have an influence not only on comfort, but also on the cost of heating. The thermostat should be on an inside wall — never on an outside wall. It should be in a room where it will not be exposed to drafts from the outside or to heat from such sources as a nearby radiator, register, fireplace, or even a candle or an electric light. All of these can cause the thermostat to function improperly, so that the house becomes too hot or too cool.

Do not change the thermostat setting any more than is necessary. It is best if you keep it at one setting throughout the day.

UNDERSTANDING "DEGREE-DAYS"

The degree-day and fuel consumption: The degree-day was developed by the American Gas Association in the 1920's as a simple means of estimating home heating fuel requirements accurately. Heat is not actually required in the average home when the outside mean temperature is 65 degrees Fahrenheit or higher. But, when the temperature is *below* 65 degrees, heat is required in proportion to the *difference* between 65 degrees and the *mean* outside temperature. (The mean temperature is half the sum of the highest and lowest temperatures that occur during the 24-hour period beginning and ending at midnight.) Each degree that the mean temperature is *below* 65 degrees is called a *degree-day.* Thus, if the mean temperature for a 24-hour midnight-to-midnight period is 60 degrees, you have 5 degree-days. Your heating system will thus require only half as much fuel as it would if the figure were 10 degree-days. The total fuel you need for heating during an entire heating season depends on the number of degree days in the season. The average for a heating season is 4,871 degree-days.

HEAT LOSS AND HEATING COSTS

With the help of a simple worksheet, (adapted for the POPULAR SCIENCE HOMEOWNER'S ENCYCLOPEDIA from material prepared by the National Association of Home Builders Research Foundation) such as the one accompanying this article, it is not difficult to calculate heat loss for any home and to translate this figure into fuel costs.

These figures have many uses. One is in choosing a furnace or other heating device of the proper capacity for a given house in your climate. Other decisions that can be made more intelligently with the help of these calculations are: how much insulation to use, whether to change furnace types and which of two otherwise similar houses will be more economical to own and live in. Influence of such factors as type of construction (frame compared to masonry, slab on grade, one or two story design), number of windows and kind of duct arrangement, on energy consumption and fuel budgets can be studied when these figures are in hand. Since some of them show how cost varies between one climate and another, they may be useful when choosing a region in which to live.

Making the worksheet calculations is simple enough for paper and pencil arithmetic, but it can be speeded up greatly if a small electronic calculator is available. Other basic information is required. To figure heat loss — as in choosing a size of furnace, for example — it is first necessary to know the winter design temperature of the area in which the house is located. To convert this figure into dollar costs, it is necessary to know fuel prices (obtained from oil dealer or public utility) and also winter degree days.

Design temperatures and degree days can be estimated or can usually be learned quickly by calling a public utility or a dealer in heating or cooling equipment. For areas away from your own, or for simplicity in making quick or rough calculations, it may be satisfactory to make estimates, using the suggestions that follow, in conjunction with the typical examples drawn from a variety of U. S. climates.

If you are quite familiar with your climate, you can make a good working estimate of the winter design temperature. Think of it as the coldest temperature to be expected to occur frequently during the winter. Or consider what seems to have been an average winter, then ignore the 72 coldest hours, and take as design temperature the coldest reading that remains. Another way to look at this is to choose the coldest temperature at which you might expect to have to heat your house to about 70 degrees Fahrenheit. You do not have to consider the temperature at sleeping hours when you will not have to heat to more than 50 to 60 degrees.

Typical Design Temperatures And Winter Degree Days

You may find your own locality, or one of similar climate, in the list that follows. These winter design temperatures and degree-days are those used by the American Society of Heating, Refrigerating and Air-Conditioning Engineers. Winter degree-days are found by noting how much each day of the winter averaged under 65 degrees and then adding up all these deficits. For each city listed, the first figure given is the winter design temperature in degrees Fahrenheit and the second is the number of winter degree days.

ALABAMA: Birmingham 19, 2600; Mobile 26, 1600; Montgomery 22, 2200.
ALASKA: Anchorage -25, 10800.
ARIZONA: Flagstaff), 7200; Phoenix 31, 1800; Yuma 37, 1000.
ARKANSAS: Fayetteville 9, 3400; Little Rock 19, 3200.
CALIFORNIA: Los Angeles 41, 2000; San Francisco 35, 3000; Yreka 13, 5400.
COLORADO: Denver -2, 6200- Leadville -9, 10,600.

CONNECTICUT: Hartford 1, 6200; New Haven 5, 5800.

DELAWARE: Dover 13, 4600; Wilmington 12, 5000.

DISTRICT OF COLUMBIA: Washington 12, 4200.

FLORIDA: Miami 42, 200; Tallahassee 25, 1400.

GEORGIA: Gainesville 16, 3200; Savannah 24, 1800.

HAWAII: Honolulu 60, no heating required.

IDAHO: Boise 4, 5800; Idaho Falls-12, 7200.

ILLINOIS: Carbondale 7, 4200; Chicago 3, 6600.

INDIANA: Bloomington 3, 4800; Indianapolis 0, 5600.

IOWA: Des Moines -7, 6600; Mason City -13, 7600.

KANSAS: Garden City -1, 5200; Wichita 5, 4600.

KENTUCKY: Covington 3, 5200; Paducah 10, 4200.

LOUISIANA: New Orleans 32, 1400; Shreveport 22, 2200.

MAINE: Bangor -8, 8000; Portland -5, 7600.

MARYLAND: Baltimore 12, 4600; Hagerstown 6, 5200.

MASSACHUSETTS: Boston 6, 5600; Pittsfield -5, 7600.

MICHIGAN: Detroit 4, 6200; Sault Ste. Marie -12, 9400.

MINNESOTA: Duluth -19, 10000; Minneapolis -14, 8400.

MISSISSIPPI: Biloxi 30, 1600; Jackson 21, 2200.

MISSOURI: Kansas City 4, 4800; St. Joseph -1, 5400.

MONTANA: Butte -24, 9800; Missoula -7, 8200.

NEBRASKA: Norfolk -11, 7000; Omaha 5, 6600.

NEVADA: Elko -13, 7400; Las Vegas 23, 2800; Reno 2, 6400.

NEW HAMPSHIRE: Keene -12, 7400; Portsmouth -2, 7200.

NEW JERSEY: Atlantic City 14, 4800; Paterson 8, 5400.

NEW MEXICO: Albuquerque 14, 4400; Santa Fe 7, 6200.

NEW YORK: New York 12, 5000; Watertown -14, 7200.

NORTH CAROLINA: Wilmington 23, 2400; Winston-Salem 14, 3600.

NORTH DAKOTA: Fargo -22, 9200; Grand Forks -26, 9800.

OHIO: Cincinnati 8, 4400; Dayton 0, 5600.

OKLAHOMA: Bartlesville 5, 4000; Oklahoma City 11, 3200.

OREGON: Baker -3, 7000; Eugene 22, 4800.

PENNSYLVANIA: Johnstown 1, 5600; Philadelphia 11, 4400.

RHODE ISLAND: Providence 6, 6000.

SOUTH CAROLINA: Charleston 23, 2000; Spartanburg 18, 3000.

SOUTH DAKOTA: Rapid City -9, 7400; Watertown -20, 8400.

TENNESSEE: Chattanooga 15, 3200; Memphis 17, 3200.

TEXAS: Brownsville 36, 600; Dallas 19, 2400; Lubbock 11, 3600.

UTAH: Ogden 7, 5600; Salt Lake City 5, 6000.

VERMONT: Burlington -12, 8200; Rutland -12, 8000.

VIRGINIA: Charlottesville 11, 4200; Norfolk 20, 3400.

WASHINGTON: Seattle 28, 5200; Spokane -2, 6600.

WEST VIRGINIA: Huntington 10, 4400; Wheeling 5, 5200.

WISCONSIN: Milwaukee -6, 7600; Wausau -18, 8400.

WYOMING: Cheyenne -6, 7400; Lander -16, 7800.

Having found, or estimated the design temperature for your locality, you can begin to fill out a heating worksheet

You will use the design temperature to calculate the temperature difference that your heating equipment must be chosen to cope with. For this purpose, you assume an inside design temperature of 70 degrees and subtract the winter design temperature from that. So if you live in the first city on the list above, Birmingham, you subtract 19 from 70 and enter 51 under Temperature Difference. For the last in the list, Lander, Wyoming, your Temperature Difference would be 86.

1. Enter, in the space provided at upper left of the worksheet, the total square feet of doors and windows. Depending upon whether you are figuring on storm windows and doors or other double glazing or just single glazing, multiply

this by the correct factor and also by the Temperature Difference. Enter this under Heat Loss.

2. Do the same for ceiling heat loss. Which of the multipliers you will use here will depend upon how much insulation you have or plan to use. (R-7 usually describes insulation about 2 to 2-1/2 inches thick; R-11, 3 to 4 inches thick; R-19, 5 to 7 inches.)

3. Enter the total square feet of frame-construction wall area and of masonry wall area in the two places provided. This is *gross* wall area; do not deduct for doors and windows. If a wall is 8 feet high and 20 feet long, enter it as 160 square feet even if it is mostly windows.

4. To calculate floor heat losses, note first that if the heating unit is in the basement no floor-loss calculation is necessary. Otherwise, enter the floor area unless construction is slab on ground. In that case, use linear feet of slab edge.

Now enter temperature difference on each line you are using, under that heading. After that, proceed to make the calculations, multiplying the footage figure by the multiplier and by the temperature difference. Enter these products under Heat Loss.

5. Figure duct heat loss, if any. If the ducts run through heated spaces you can assume no heat loss and skip this step. If they run through attics or crawl spaces, first multiply the floor area by the temperature difference. Then if you are using 1 inch flexible insulation on the ducts, multiply by 0.1. If 2 inch flexible or 1 inch rigid insulation, multiply by 0.07. Enter the result in the Heat Loss column. Since the principal value of these calculations is for making comparisons between alternatives, you may want to fill out the sheet at the same time for other possibilities.

In the filled out example, for a region having a winter design temperature of 5 degrees and, therefore, a temperature difference of 65, it has been assumed the glazing will be single. But three possible different amounts of insulation are being considered both for ceilings and for the frame walls.

6. For the first trial, the combination selected is R-19 insulation in the ceiling and R-11 in the walls (the maximum in both cases). Combined with the duct heat loss, this gives a calculated total of 59,520. The other two combinations considered, and entered in the two columns at the right, show the larger heat loss to be expected when thinner insulation is used.

7. To find the size furnace required, add approximately 50 per cent to the calculated heat loss. (This takes into account the efficiency factor, estimated at two-thirds.)

8. The final calculation will give an estimated cost of heating for a year. It requires one new figure, the Heating Index, which, in turn, is based on some other figures you'll have to obtain. These are: *degree days,* to be estimated from the typical examples given earlier or obtained from your public utility or fuel dealer; *cost of fuel,* from same source; and also, in the case of fuel oil, propane and butane, a figure called *seasonal efficiency.* For each of these fuels the Heating Index will be: Natural gas — multiply degree days by cost per therm and divide by seasonal efficiency (obtained from utility company or assumed to be .67). No. 2 fuel oil — multiply degree days by cost per gallon and divide by 1.41 times the seasonal efficiency. Electricity — except heat pumps, for which your power supplier should be consulted for calculations, which vary with climate conditions — multiply cost per kilowatt hour by 20.75.

Propane — multiply degree days by cost per gallon and divide by 1.02 times seasonal efficiency.

Butane — multiply degree days by cost per gallon and divide by 0.92 times seasonal efficiency.

Then, as the Worksheet shows, multiply your heat loss, calculated earlier, by this heating index and by 24, then divide by the temperature difference times 100,000. (If you are using an electronic calculator for this arithmetic, you will exceed the capacity of a six- or eight-digit machine while doing this. To avoid that problem, do the multiplying and the dividing alternately.)

HEATING WORKSHEET

BUILDING SECTION		WINDOW DOOR TYPE / INSUL. R	HEAT LOSS MULTIPLIER	TEMP. DIFF.	HEAT LOSS	TRIAL NO. 1	TRIAL NO. 2	TRIAL NO. 3
1. Windows, Doors		Double	1.10					
.... sq. ft.		Single	1.90					
2. Ceilings		R-19	0.05					
.... sq. ft.		R-11	0.08					
		R-7	0.12					
3. Walls (gross area)	Frame	R-11	0.07					
	.... sq. ft.	R-7	0.10					
		R-0	0.26					
	Masonry	R-7	0.11					
	.... sq. ft.	R-0	0.30					
4. Floors	Floors Other Than Concrete	R-19	0.05					
		R-11	0.08					
	.... sq. ft.	R-7	0.11					
		R-0	0.28					
	Concrete Slabs — Exposed Length Of Slab Edge	1″ x 24″ insulation	0.21					
		1″ x 12″ insulation	0.46					
	.... Lin. ft.	No insulation	0.81					
5. Duct Heat Loss (if applicable)								
6. TOTAL CALCULATED HEAT LOSS								

7. EQUIPMENT SIZE

8. ESTIMATED ANNUAL HEATING COST

$$\frac{\text{............................} \times \text{............................} \times 24}{\text{Total heat loss} \quad \text{Heating Index}} = \$ \text{................. / yr.}$$

$$\frac{\text{............................} \times 100{,}000}{\text{Temp. diff.}}$$

BUILDING SECTION		WINDOW DOOR TYPE / INSUL. R	HEAT LOSS MULTIPLIER	TEMP. DIFF.	HEAT LOSS	TRIAL NO. 1	TRIAL NO. 2	TRIAL NO. 3
1. Windows, Doors		Double	1.10					
2.60 sq. ft.		Single	1.90	65	32,110	32,110	32,110	32,110
2. Ceilings		R-19	0.05	65	4,450	4,450		
1,370 sq. ft.		R-11	0.08	65	7,120		7,120	
		R-7	0.12	65	10,690			10,690
3. Walls (gross area)	Frame	R-11	0.07	65	6,730	6,730		
	1,480 sq. ft.	R-7	0.10	65	9,620		9,620	
		R-0	0.26	65	25,010			25,010
5. Duct Heat Loss (if applicable)					6,230	6,230	6,230	6,230
6. TOTAL CALCULATED HEAT LOSS						49,520	55,080	74,040

7. EQUIPMENT SIZE — 80,000 | 80,000 | 105,000

8. ESTIMATED ANNUAL HEATING COST

$$\frac{49{,}520 \times 691 \times 24}{\text{Total heat loss} \quad \text{Heating Index}} = \$ \ 126 \text{ / yr.}$$

$$\frac{65 \times 100{,}000}{\text{Temp. diff.}}$$

If you are making alternative calculations to test the expected cost of different houses or different amounts of insulation in the same climate, proceed in somewhat different order for the purpose of reducing the amount of arithmetic. First multiply together just the heating index and 24, dividing by the temperature difference and by 100,000. This will give you a constant factor by which you can multiply different heat-loss totals to compare costs.

Home Improvement
[SEE REMODELING; ROOM ADDITIONS.]

Homeowner's Square

The homeowner's square combines the functions of a regular square with several other helpful devices. On this square are tables for converting inches to meters and fractions to decimals, a depth scale and a scale indicating board feet equivalents, volume and area formulas, a table showing quantity per pound for common and finishing nails of different sizes and a table that denotes the drill size for pilot holes for nine different screw gauge numbers. The homeowner's square is lightweight, has a tongue 16 inches long and $1^1/_2$ inches wide and a body 24 inches in length with a width of 2 inches. *SEE ALSO HAND TOOLS.*

Home Projects
[SEE PROJECTS.]

Home Safety

Most accidents in the home are caused by haste and carelessness. The battle against home accidents is fought in two stages: first identify hazards, and second change hazardous situations and behavior.

Falls

Falls in the home are responsible each year for about 75 percent of deaths. Some of the common causes of falls are scattered objects on lawns, walks, floors, and stairs; loose or broken handrails and porch railings; wet surfaces; lack of light in stairwells; frayed carpets and rugs; and highly waxed bare floors and stairs. Take the following precautions to eliminate these and other hazards.

1. Install safety bars and use safety strips to provide steady footing in bathtubs. Apply safety strips on the apron of a swimming pool.

2. Keep a kitchen step stool and a sturdy stepladder handy. Never stand on chairs or climb on cabinets or furniture to reach a high place. The stepladder should be tall enough for a person to reach the ceiling while standing two steps from the top. Never stand on the top step of a ladder.

3. Install safety locks on windows above the first floor, to prevent small children opening them far enough to fall out.

4. Establish rules prohibiting running on stairs and through the house.

5. Do not run electrical extension cords for long distances in the house. Install more outlets if needed.

6. Whether inside or outside, close off project work sites. Have safety or marker lights on out-

side work sites at night if possible. Clear all work areas of equipment and rubble when either finished or quitting temporarily.

7. Wipe up all spills immediately.

8. Mark the edges of steep or narrow basement steps with white or luminous paint or tape. If using tape, be sure it adheres to the steps.

9. Use rubber strips to anchor small rugs on slippery floors. Never use throw rugs at the top or bottom of a flight of stairs.

10. Install light switches at the top and bottom of stairways and at room entrances.

Burns and Fires

To avoid burns, which rank second as the cause of home deaths, take the following precautions:

1. Keep matches away from children. Do not carry loose matches in pockets.

2. Keep flammable materials away from open flame or any source of high heat. If the clearance between the stove top and wall cabinets is not at least 36 inches, fireproof the cabinets with a hood or shield.

3. Keep pot handles turned away from the front of the stove, so they will be out of the reach of children and out of the way as the cook moves around.

4. Use a pan lid to smother flames caused by burning grease or throw baking soda on the flames. Keep a supply of baking soda close to the stove. Never throw water on a grease fire. It will spread the flames. Never throw flour on a fire because it can literally explode in the flame.

5. Never use gasoline to start fires; the fumes are potentially explosive. Use only charcoal starters or kerosene, but never pour or squirt these fluids onto flames or live embers. Saturate the charcoal or kindling substance and light that instead.

6. Never smoke in bed. Be sure that smoking materials are always completely extinguished.

7. Never smoke around fuels, flammable liquids or easily ignited substances, such as sawdust and paint-soaked rags. Don't smoke around a filling station pump island.

8. Teach children to avoid hot objects and flames. Safely provide several explanatory lessons, such as guiding a small child's hand close to a candle flame, a hot pan, a radiator, or a cigarette ash. Hold the child's hand to be sure that he or she does not touch the sources of heat. Explain to the child that burns hurt.

9. Turn off or unplug an iron when leaving the room. Always set the iron down on its safety heel or a stand made of metal or asbestos.

10. Do not leave candles or lanterns aflame in an unoccupied room.

11. Never work around a gas stove or flames wearing clothing that burns readily.

Fire Emergency

Many small fires in the home can be extinguished with a carbon dioxide extinguisher. Electrical fires and burning grease and petroleum products can be controlled in small areas with such an extinguisher. Water works well in extinguishing wood, paper and fabric fires. A fine spray of water can be used on burning grease and petroleum products, but never throw water or direct a heavy hose stream on such a fire. Solid amounts of water will only spread the fire and possibly splash the burning substance onto other combustible materials. Remember that home methods are only effective against small fires. When you spot a fire, it is best to get everyone out of the house, then call the fire department.

Poisons

The victims of accidental poisonings are most often children under four years of age. The leading sources of poisoning are aspirin, insecticides and cleaning products. All medicines and other potentially toxic or injurious substances should be locked away from small children, not merely hidden or placed out of reach.

Hopper Windows

A hopper window swings inward on a hinged bottom sash. The window is opened and closed by a simple handle located in the top sash of the window, which turns and locks. Hopper windows are easily cleaned and maintained but may obstruct draperies or occupy valuable space near the window.

Horn
[SEE SYSTEMS, AUTOMOTIVE.]

Horse Rasp

The horse rasp is designed to file horses' hooves in preparation for its shoes. Although this is its main purpose, the horse rasp is also considered useful in filing wood. SEE ALSO HAND TOOLS.

Hose Adapter

A hose adapter is a galvanized steel pipe fitting. It has external threading on both ends with a hex nut-like divider. This divider holds the two halves of the fitting by screwing them together securely after the other pipe attachments have been made. SEE ALSO PIPE FITTINGS.

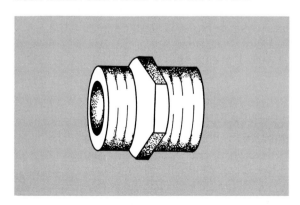

Hose Adapter

Hose Bib

A hose bib is another name for a sill cock. It is a threaded water faucet to which a hose can be connected. SEE ALSO FAUCET.

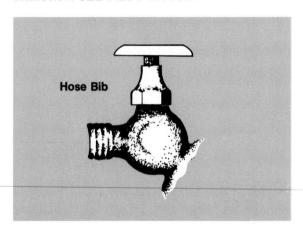

Hose Bib

Hot Air Heating System
[SEE HEATING SYSTEMS.]

Hotbeds
[SEE COLDFRAMES & HOTBEDS.]

Hot Glues

Hot glue, generally known as hide glue, is an extremely strong adhesive used in cabinetmaking. It can be bought in liquid form at most hardware stores and in flake or strip form at cabinetmaker's supply houses. Liquid hide glue comes ready to use and dries overnight. If bought in flake or strip form, hide glue must first be softened by soaking, then heated with a certain amount of water, as indicated in the manufacturer's instructions. It should be used immediately after heating, to prevent cooling and stiffening before the work is completed. Hide glue is not waterproof. SEE ALSO ADHESIVES.

Hot Plate Repair

Hot plates are very much like the heating element of an electric range that has been removed from the range top and put into its own small housing. Switches and the elements are very much the same except for the fact that most hot plates operate on 115 volts rather than 230 volts.

Two methods of controlling the heat range are used. One is a simple switch that controls a dual-element burner. Using the switch, either the inner or outer burner may be selected. Most newer hot plates use a cycling type switch similar to that found on ranges. A bimetal arm within the switch opens and closes a set of contacts at regular intervals depending on the switch setting. Toward the lower end of the heat scale the "on" periods are shorter and the "off" periods longer. This timing device serves to control the heat output of the burner.

If anything is spilled on the burner of a hot plate, unplug it and wipe up the spill immediately. If liquid reaches any electrical component it should be unplugged, wiped off and allowed to dry thoroughly before putting back into use. Don't try to use a hot plate to heat a room. The unit operating without a pan on it to absorb heat will cause its life to be reduced significantly.

This design by Corning illustrates how up-to-date hot plates have become. This one utilizes latest-design ceramic cooktop, thermostatic control of heat levels.

Unplug the hotplate before examining it. To service a hot plate, you can gain access to the burner in many newer models by simply unplugging it from the receptacle. Most older ones are held in place with a single screw. Wires may be connected with quick disconnect terminals or they may be fastened to the burners with screws. This heating element coil is not visible on most newer models — you'll need a VOM to check it.

The switch itself is also a sealed unit. It can be tested for continuity from the line terminal to the terminals leading to the heating element. When the switch is turned to the "on" position, it should indicate continuity.

Grease spilled around the switch knob is perhaps the biggest enemy of this type of switch. Once it gets on the contacts, it acts as an insulator and the resulting poor contact soon burns the switch out. If you exercise care in usage, these switches should last for many years.

If the hot plate won't work at all, check the receptacle with a table lamp. Check the cord at the plug and at the strain relief where it enters the appliance. If it's necessary to replace the wire at the terminal use the special heat-resistant type.

Don't use the hot plate if there is any indication of a shock hazard. Check the wiring and the element for a ground. Don't restore it to service until the condition is remedied. You'll have to use the VOM on the highest resistance scale to do this properly. *SEE ALSO APPLIANCE REPAIR, SMALL.*

Hot Water Faucet

A hot water faucet is connected to one of two water-heating devices usually found in the home, the hydronic or forced hot water system and the regular water heater system.

In the hydronic system, the faucet is connected to pipes, which receive heat from coiled tubing leading directly from the boiler. Regular faucet water and boiler water do not mix. The hydronic system also supplies winter heat for the home. If the house is to be left unheated, the water heater should be emptied through a hand-operated drain valve found at its lowest point. During this process, hot water faucets must be left open to clear the supply pipes. To re-activate the water-heating system, it should be completely filled with water. The hot water faucets should again be left open during this process, since water will run from them when the system is full. The heat source may then be turned on.

Regular water heaters provide hot water in large amounts. Since they are dependent on the fuel supply — oil, gas, or electricity, it takes a certain amount of time for them to provide a new supply of hot water after all has been used. *SEE ALSO FAUCET.*

Hot Water Heating Pipes

Hot water heating pipes usually run along outside walls of rooms, but occasionally they lead through inner walls so that all pipes in the system will be linked together properly. Because these pipes must be watertight, they require very adept pipe-joint work but basically, their arrangement is kept simple, much like water-supply pipes. Hot water heater pipes are arranged in four basic layouts in common hydronic systems: the series loop, one-pipe heating system, two-pipe system and zone system.

The simplest layout for hot water heating pipes, called the series loop, is especially good for small homes. Each radiator in this system is part of the main supply because all pipes are connected directly to the main supply boiler in one loop circling the house. There are very few fittings required. All radiators in the home must be turned on and kept on as vital to the entire working system which is controlled by one thermostat. Therefore, this arrangement would not be suitable for a big rambling house.

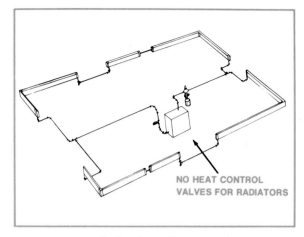

Series Loop System

The one-pipe system for individual room heat control consists of a circuit pipe leading from the top of the boiler and returning to the bottom part. Each radiator is not a vital part of this circuit, however, because each has a branch pipe carrying hot water to it from the main line. A separate branch pipe carries water back to the main circulator. There is a shut-off valve at each inlet for individual regulation.

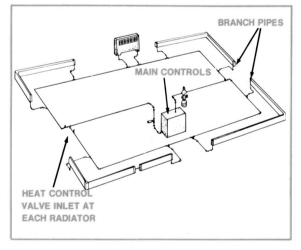

One-Pipe System

A T-shaped pipe fitting is used where the return pipe connects back into the circulating main in the one-pipe system. A dip in this T-fitting takes in water when the inlet valve is open and does not block the flow when the valve is closed. Though good for separate room control, the one-pipe system requires more pipe, more fittings and more installation.

The two-pipe system, good for large houses, is a gravity hot water system with a pump to force water through the pipes. It is different from the old gravity hot water system because of the pump. Hot water travels through a main and a branch pipe to each radiator. Cooled water going from the radiator flows through another branch pipe and return main pipe to the boiler. There is a bigger difference in temperatures from radiators along the line in this system than in the one-pipe system.

Zone heating is beneficial when a house has a T, L or U shape, is very long or is split level. It can be used in either forced-air or hydronic systems. This system has two or more separate circuits of pipe feeding the radiators either in the series loop or one-pipe arrangement. There are zone divisions, each with a separate thermostat. Electrically-operated valves in the supply pipes of a hydronic system make this possible. Hot water in the burner of a multiple-zone system is kept constant at a warm temperature and ready when needed. *SEE ALSO PLUMBING SYSTEMS.*

Hot Water Heating System
[SEE HEATING SYSTEMS.]

Hot Water Storage Tank

Water is reserved in a hot water storage tank until it is released to the system.

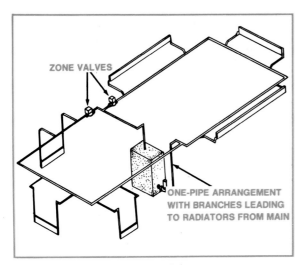

Zone System

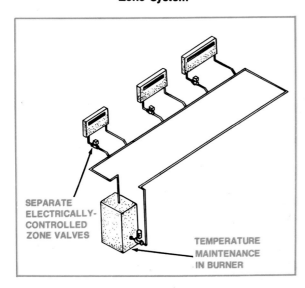

Multizone System

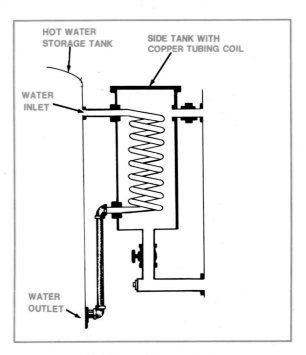

Hot Water Storage Tank

A hot water storage tank has a cold-water inlet which leads into it near the bottom and a hot-water outlet pipe which leads out at the top. In earlier models, cold water would enter the tank, become heated and rise to the top where it was piped to hot-water faucets. To keep the tank filled, cold water continually entered the tank, replacing the hot water which had been drained. Later this model was improved by the addition of a side tank with a copper tubing coil. The inlet and outlet remained the same. Water enters the side tank through the coil, becomes heated and returns to the storage tank.

When the water temperature is near boiling or the pressure is above normal, a relief valve which is attached to the storage tank lets water empty into a drain. This valve will close when the temperature and pressure return to normal. Burst tanks and other damage in the system can be prevented by the use of this valve.

Hot Wires

Hot wires are power-carrying wires through which current is actually passing. They are usually denoted by a red or black plastic coating over the wire itself. *SEE ALSO ELECTRICAL WIRING.*

House Decoration
[SEE DECORATING.]

House Designs

For most people, the purchase or construction of a house is the largest financial investment they will make. And, for the majority, a house becomes the most valuable financial asset and the major influence on their way of life. A well-designed house matches lifestyle and the interests of the family. It influences activities, but does not dominate them. The key to good house design begins with the family's understanding of its own needs and interest.

A well-designed house takes into account the total setting. If the view stretches across a wide expanse of land or water, the design should make it available by means of exterior glass and open, interior spaces. If the location is a city lot the design should turn inward, for privacy while creating a feeling of spaciousness within.

Good design considers the climate, landscape, terrain and sun. The design should provide ample access to the main living areas from the outside, space for entertaining and privacy for individual family members.

SINGLE-LEVEL HOUSES

A house with all of the living space on one level is most convenient for families that include small children or infirm persons. The single-level house allows access to the outdoors for rooms whose height above ground would isolate them in a multi-level house. The low roofline of the single-level house blends with the landscape of most lots. Furthermore, if lot space is available, a single-level house is easier to expand if a family needs more space.

In a single-level house, the design of the traffic pattern is especially important. Floor space must be divided into zones to create distinct areas for different activities. The space should be arranged so that access to one area does not require passage through another. Hall, courts, recesses and projections help provide a combination of privacy and access.

A design feature that can be included almost anywhere in a single-level house is the skylight. Each room can be opened to the sky through an opening in the roof covered with transparent or transluscent material. The skylight gives a feeling of spaciousness and reduces the need for artificial light.

Types of Single-Level Design

Single-Unit construction is the most common single-level house design. In this design, all the living areas adjoin in a single, continuous space.

Courtesy Red Cedar Shingle & Handsplit Shake Bureau

The shape of the house may be a simple square or rectangle, or it may have a more complex form that provides interesting projections and recesses. These features provide for privacy, interest, and more scenic views. For example, a house built around an interior court offers views of the court from many places in the house while screening the court and the interior of the house for privacy.

Pavilion design is another single-level design. A Pavilion-design house is made from two or more separate units, each with its own roof and walls, connected by a passageway or common area. The units, or pavilions, create individual zones for different activities. One pavilion serves as the zone for entertaining or family activities, containing the living room, dining room, and kitchen. A second pavilion is the parents' living area, with bedroom, bath, and sitting room. A third pavilion provides bedrooms, baths and play area for the children. Finally, another pavilion is the service area, with auto parking, laundry, utilities and storage. In such a house, parents can remain undisturbed while children entertain their friends.

MULTI-LEVEL HOUSES

A house with floor space on two or more levels has certain advantages over the single-level house. One important advantage is that it provides a large amount of living space while occupying a relatively small area on the lot. This factor is especially important in city locations, where lots are often small and outdoor space is at a premium.

835

Courtesy Red Cedar Shingle & Handsplit Shake Bureau

In the country, a multi-level house permits building on a wooded lot with a minimum loss of trees. The proportions of the house usually blend well with the height of the trees, and the upper living spaces often gain privacy from the screening effect of the trees. In some locations, the height of a multi-level house provides a better view. Multi-level houses can also use sloping lots that would be impossible for a single-level design. Finally, the multi-level house permits an economy of heating and cooling as their total area is arranged more compactly than a single-level house with the same floor space.

Natural lighting in the lower levels of a multi-level house requires more planning than in most single-level designs. The most common way to provide natural lighting is to build windows near the ceiling (called clerestories) and window-walls. Another way is to bring light into the upper levels through skylights and clerestories and allow that light to enter lower levels through open stairwells and internal balconies.

The naturally high roof line of a multi-level house permits certain rooms to have a two-story ceiling. Such rooms create a spacious feeling in the house, and may provide a dramatic focal point when used with imagination. For example, a living room with a two-story ceiling creates a feeling of spaciousness even when filled with people. A high, vertical space containing a stairway provides both a dramatic visual effect and an area of vertical continuity within the house. From the upper level, a balcony overlooking the lower level will share the feeling of openness felt below.

Another multi-level design is a house that occupies several levels, each overlapping the others, called a *split-level* house. Split-level houses are ideal for sloping lots, because the foundation does not require extensive excavation, and the "step-down" design provides more usable living space in a compact package. Another advantage is that the vertical separation between levels can be limited to a few steps rather than an entire

Courtesy Red Cedar Shingle & Handsplit Shake Bureau

flight of stairs, as in a two-story house, thus requiring less physical exertion.

Finally, the split-level house can be divided into the equivalent of three or four pavilions, each offering privacy from the others. (However, a house built in three or four overlapping levels takes up more of the lot than a two-story house of the same size, but not as much as a single-level house.)

COUNTRY HOUSES

Probably the greatest difference in design between a country house and a city house is the availability of space, both for building and for outdoor activities. The country house is usually designed to provide a relaxed and informal atmosphere.

Country houses are frequently designed as single-level houses. Since they are usually built where there is plenty of land, they can contain a larger area than houses built in the city. Usually,

a single-level house looks better in a country setting than a multi-level house. The low, broad profile matches the broad, open expanse of the land.

Inside a country house, the design is rustic and informal. The fireplace may be built of coarse field stones rather than brick, with a wider hearth. The mantel may be rough-hewn timber rather than finely-sculptured wood with delicate moldings. Floors may be built of wide boards stained and left bare or with area rugs, rather than carpeted. In a multi-level country house, stairways may be wider than in the multi-level city house. Window frames may be larger and look heavier.

Country exterior walls may be rough-sawn timber stained and allowed to weather, rather than smooth, painted wood or brick. Many typical characteristics of country houses are born of practical necessity, reflecting either the more

837

Courtesy Red Cedar Shingle & Handsplit Shake Bureau

Plants and decorative accents combine to create a unified decorating scheme.

casual life in country surroundings or the use of simpler building materials.

A country house needs to provide for outdoor living. Both children and adults tend to spend more time outdoors in the country. The design of the house should make cleaning easier and less frequent. Dirt-catching design features should be omitted wherever possible. The design should provide for the required housework to be done with the greatest ease. For example, a laundry-sewing room may be located in the bedroom area of the house rather than in the traditional service area, so that washing and mending can be done with a minimum of carrying.

The kitchen of a country house is traditionally large. It is often the place where the family congregates for meals and for family activities. Country kitchens need ample storage space. Shopping trips are less frequent than in the city, and may even be impossible in bad weather. Cupboards, refrigerators, freezers and other storage places need to hold larger quantities of

food and other supplies for longer periods of time in the country.

The semi-isolation of a country house must be reflected in the design by providing for times of emergency as well as normal times. The country house should be self-sufficient if bad weather cuts off electricity or bad roads isolate the family. An emergency generator will provide electricity, and stores of fuel, water and other supplies should be adequate to last for several days if necessary. The design of the house should provide for these special measures.

MOUNTAIN HOUSES

A house in the mountains should be designed to take advantage of spectacular mountain views. Windows should extend upward to offer an unobstructed view of high mountain peaks. Roof beams should be massive, sturdy, solid, large and rugged, and walls sturdy to blend with the surrounding terrain. The mountain house should also be functional and compatible with the activities of the people who live there.

The A-Frame house is one of the most efficient designs for use in the mountains. It can offer a high, unobstructed view of each end. During a mountain snowstorm, the steeply-pitched roof prevents snow from building up to a depth that can create excessive weight on the structure. Inside, the upper part of the *A* offers space for a second floor. If the second floor occupies only part of the house, the remaining one-level space has a feeling of great spaciousness. Two or more A-frame units can be combined to create a pavilion design with several zones. One zone can serve as the main living area, with an adjoining zone containing sleeping and bathing quarters. By careful planning, this design can provide the active family with sufficient space and privacy, while blending with the natural surroundings.

A well-designed mountain house combines rugged looks with sound engineering. The interior should reflect the surroundings. The surroundings in a mountain setting consist mainly of evergreen trees and large, angular rocks. This ruggedness can become part of the mountain house with a fireplace facing of large pieces of local rock. Interior walls and beams can be faced with unpainted pine, redwood or cedar. The wood surfaces may even be left in a rough-sawn finish. The vertical feel of the mountains can be reflected in vertical paneling with a minimum of horizontal railings, shelves and sills.

Heating and insulation are important in the design of a mountain house. Outdoor temperatures are cool even in summer because of the high altitude. In winter, weather conditions become severe with heavy snow and strong winds. Therefore, windows should be double panes of sturdy glass, strongly built and tightly sealed. The walls and roof should be well insulated to prevent heat loss. The heating system should circulate heat evenly. Warm air should not collect in the high reaches of an A-frame ceiling. The fireplace should be adequate to heat the house in case a power failure stops electric fans and pumps. All sources of heat should do double duty. For example, if a heater is provided for drying wet ski clothing or hiking jackets, that heat should be circulated throughout the house rather than being exhausted to the outside. The

same heat conservation should be practiced in the kitchen. Cooking odors can be removed by filters so that heated air can be kept within the house. Sleeping areas should be designed so that they can be closed off and kept cooler than living areas, thereby avoiding an additional demand for heat in relatively unoccupied areas.

SEASHORE HOUSE

There are a variety of ways to design a house to be compatible with the sea and the shore. The interior should have an open design that creates large, continuous living areas. The entrance can be designed so that it is visually shielded from the main living area, yet opens into it smoothly and easily. Wide, overhanging eaves contribute further to the feeling of expanse, and shield the interior from the mid-day glare of the sun. Paneling, shelving and railings should also contribute to the horizontal design of the house.

A house by the seashore needs to be designed to provide great flexibility. On pleasant, balmy days, the house should open wide to the outdoors, and be little more than a roof to protect against the mid-day sun. But on cold and damp days, the house should offer a safe and secure shelter from the elements, shutting out the weather and providing a feeling of protection.

Activities at the seashore dictate the design of the seashore house. Living is to be casual, and housekeeping needs should be minimized. Areas of the house that are used during the day will be in continual contact with sand and water, and should be designed to require a minimum of care and cleanup. Dining areas, bathrooms, and dressing areas should be accessible from the outside. Such areas may serve as a barrier between the casual and any formal living areas of the house.

With careful attention to detail, the seashore house can make use of elements of the shore environment in its decorating. For example, shifting patterns of light during the day can create a constant variety of shadow and light within the house through the use of clerestories, canopies, and overhangs. Light reflecting off the water can be used to provide constant changing patterns of light on walls and ceilings. Color schemes in the house can match or contrast with the colors of the sea. Both interior and exterior surfaces can reflect the weathered surfaces created on natural materials by the action of sea, wind, and sun.

Conditions on the seashore present special problems that should be considered in the design of a house. Winds are often strong and persistent. The roof and windows, therefore, need to be sturdy and well sealed to prevent entrance of air and water. If the house is located near the level of water, rather than on a cliff or behind a protecting landscape, spray may build up a salt crust on windows and exterior walls. Blowing sand can scour exterior surfaces and filter into the house through open doors, windows, and vents. The foundation of the house must allow for possible shifting ground caused by wind, waves, currents and the changing water table.

DESERT HOUSES

The desert climate is harsh and requires special features in a house. From the outside, the desert house may appear as solid and impenetrable as the desert itself. From the inside, it should offer a combination of visual continuity with the environment and physical isolation from the outside conditions.

Protection against hot weather requires thick, heavy construction materials. The traditional materials are brick, adobe and concrete. The roof must be thickly insulated and the eaves should provide a wide overhang for the windows. As an additional protection from the sun, windows should be fitted with working shutters, and the house may need to be air conditioned. In some desert houses, walls are built double with an air space between.

With proper design, the desert house can provide a visual continuity between the inside and the outside. For example, patios can be shielded from the direct rays of the sun by positioning them carefully to take advantage of shadows created by the house. An outdoor deck can be shielded from most of the sun's rays by a roof made of spaced lath (*a ramada*) that allows air to flow through easily. Windows can be positioned on the north and east sides of the house so that they do not receive the hot afternoon sun. And, of course, a pool or fountain offers both physical and psychological relief from the heat.

A traditional Southwestern or Pueblo style has evolved that makes use of natural materials and also provides the necessary protection against the environment. Basic colors are either the natural browns of desert soil or light-reflecting white. In a climate too harsh for most trees, the basic construction material is masonry, rather than lumber. Flooring is made of tile, stone or brick, rather than oak. Where lumber is used, it is widely spaced and made to contrast visually with the masonry. Arched doorways, windows and fireplace openings were first used because the original construction materials were not strong enough to support the weight of the house above squared openings. Today, this distinctive style is carried on in modern designs, lending a historical continuity to desert houses.

In desert houses there is less need for physical access than in houses built for more hospitable environments. Most family activity usually takes place inside the house rather than outside. Thus, the design requires fewer ways for the family to enter and leave the house. There also is less need for buffer areas between the inside and outside where outdoor clothing can be shed.

House Extension
[SEE ROOM ADDITIONS.]

House Painting
[SEE PAINTS & PAINTING.]

House Parts
[SEE BASIC PARTS OF A HOUSE.]

Courtesy of Florists Transworld Delivery.

Container grown plants can be massed for shape and color.

House Plants

House plants are used in decorating to provide color and warmth in a home or office. Because they are less costly than most furniture or accessories, house plants provide an inexpensive way to decorate. For the most part, house plants are free from insects and easy to care for. A local florist or publications about the many different types of house plants will give detailed instructions on choosing and caring for house plants. Some commonly used house plants include philodendron, fern, geranium, palm, bromeliad, pickaback, ivy and begonia.

ENVIRONMENT

Most house plants are able to survive in artificial as well as natural light. The amount of sun a plant can take depends on the type of plant and

Courtesy of Florists Transworld Delivery

The plants to be used in a terrarium are often limited only by the imagination of the gardener.

the intensity of the sun. As a general rule, leafy plants do well with little direct sun while flowering plants require more sun. House plants are often placed in windows. In winter, south or west windows provide strongest light, while in summer east windows are sunny. Turn plants often to keep growth even.

Because homes are usually warm with low humidity and house plants survive best in an environment similar to their natural habitat, most house plants are warm-country plants. Whatever the plant, a period of adjustment is normal when a plant is first moved to a new location.

CONTAINERS & LOCATIONS

House plants may be put in anything from clay pots to old household items, such as bean pots, dishes or baskets. Be sure the container has a drain hole in the bottom and rests on a saucer so that water will not collect in the bottom of the

pot. Hanging baskets and pots have become increasingly popular. Ease and convenience of watering, along with proper fastening, should be considered when placing a hanging plant.

All rooms are appropriate settings for plants. Bathrooms are particularly good because of the high humidity. Contrary to what many people think, plants in a bedroom use a very small amount of oxygen from the air at night and are, therefore, not detrimental.

CARE

Most house plants require minimum care. General rules may be offered, but it is best to observe how an individual plant reacts and develop your own method of care.

Courtesy of Florists Transworld Delivery

Green plants provide color accents in a monochromatic decorating scheme.

Ferns, ivy, and massed chrysanthemums create a lush spot of color.

House plants usually need extra humidity because their inside surroundings are often dry. Grouping plants helps raise the humidity. Spraying the leaves with water, either using a mister or placing larger plants in a shower, helps control humidity besides cleaning the leaves.

Watering is one of the major problems in the care of plants. How much to water depends on many factors: the kind of plant, the size of the pot and the condition of the roots. A general rule is to wait to water until the soil is dry ¹/₂ inch below the surface. Water should be able to run through a drain hole in the bottom of the pot. Another method involves placing the pot in water up to the rim until water seeps up to the surface. Self-watering pots contain a wick which soaks up water placed in the bottom portion of the pot.

Plant foods should be used according to the instructions on the package. Most plant foods are mixed with water and put on the plant once a month during spring, summer and fall months.

House plants add a touch of natural color to most rooms. Foliage plants are hardy in most situations.

If the roots of a plant become cramped, it is wise to repot it in a larger container. The new pot should be clean and have gravel in the bottom to keep the roots from standing in water. Potting mixtures may be used to fill in.

Household pesticides should be used occasionally to prevent insects from damaging plants. If a plant acquires insects, move it away from other plants and spray often until rid of pests.

TERRARIUMS

Terrariums are an ideal way to grow plants as they require little care. Any clear glass container, such as a brandy snifter, apothecary jar or fish tank, can be used. Plants that do well in terrariums include the African violet, maranta, philodendron, palm, coleus, croton and ivy.

Container-grown plants may be moved from inside the house to an outdoor living area during moderate weather.

The natural figure of the crewel is echoed in the lush foliage of the arrangements of foliage plants.

To make a terrarium, place a layer of charcoal on the bottom of the container. Add about an inch of gravel and then top with moss and a mixture of sand, peat moss and garden soil. Place plants carefully in the container using tweezers if the opening is small. Small plants should be placed in the front with taller ones in back. Add some water to the terrarium and then place a top over the container. The terrarium will need only occasional watering. If moisture is noticed on the side, remove the cover until it evaporates. Terrariums require some light, but do not expose to direct sunlight. *SEE ALSO LAWNS & GARDENS.*

Various shaped glass containers may be used for terrariums.

House Sewer
[SEE SEWER.]

How To Buy A New or Used Car
[SEE SYSTEMS, AUTOMOTIVE.]

Hub-Vent Fittings

A hub-vent fitting is a cast-iron soil pipe fitting. It joins cast-iron pipe of different sizes to change the diameter of the pipe at roof level. *SEE ALSO PIPE FITTINGS.*

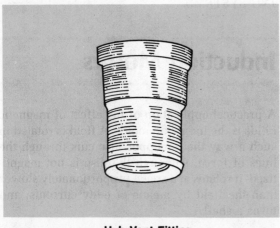

Hub-Vent Fitting

Humidifiers

A humidifier is a device, either attached to or a part of a heating system, which puts moisture back into the air. There are three basic types of humidifiers. The evaporative-plate type is mounted in the furnace and consists of plates that absorb water from a pan and return the moisture to the air as it moves through the furnace. The vaporizer type forms steam which is circulated throughout the home with the heated air. An atomizing humidifier sprays water into the cold-air return where it is picked up for circulation by the moving air. *SEE ALSO HEATING SYSTEMS.*

Hydraulic Cement

Hydraulic cement is a modified portland cement

mix, treated with small amounts of chemical agents to make the concrete resistant to water. Hydraulic cement sets in a matter of minutes and is excellent to use for filling a crack or hole in a basement floor or foundation. It is especially useful during wet seasons or under flooding conditions as the concrete sets under water. *SEE ALSO CEMENT PATCHING MATERIALS.*

Hydronic Heating System

A hydronic heating system includes a centrifugal pump that forces water through the system radiators, much like the pump in an automobile sends water through the car radiator. This forced flow eliminates the need for a large boiler, large pipes or having the boiler in the basement. The supply main and return main of the system are located in the top and bottom of the boiler, as in a regular heating system.

The water is fed through the radiators by a one or two pipe system or by a series loop system. The *one pipe system* allows individual room heat control but calls for more piping and installation procedures. The system includes branch piping and a shut-off valve which allows for the regulation of the quantity of water going into the radiator, or allows the system to be shut off completely.

The *two pipe system* is useful in large, rambling houses, because the hot water entering the radiator and the cooled water leaving flow through branch pipes, and do not mix. Consequently, the temperature difference in the radiators on each end of the supply line is considerably less.

The radiators in the *series loop system* are directly connected to the supply main, so that shutting off a single radiator would shut off the entire system. This system, therefore, is suitable for small, compact houses only. *SEE ALSO HEATING SYSTEMS.*

I Beam

The steel I beam has a cross section resembling the letter I and is used as a support for flooring. *SEE ALSO FLOOR CONSTRUCTION.*

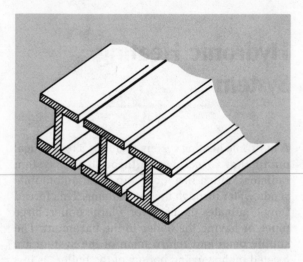

I Beam

Ignition Systems
[SEE SYSTEMS, AUTOMOTIVE.]

Indirect Lighting

Indirect lighting is used in homes mainly for decorative effects or for lighting displays and collections, such as pictures. This type of lighting includes cornice and valance lighting which reflects light on the wall and ceiling. Indirect lighting can be connected independently. *SEE ALSO LIGHTS & LIGHTING.*

Indoor/Outdoor Carpet
[SEE CARPET, INDOOR/OUTDOOR.]

Induced Draft

An induced draft is produced when air is pulled through the heating unit mechanically and forced up the chimney. This system reduces variations in performance caused from wind and outside temperature changes. *SEE ALSO HEATING SYSTEMS.*

Induction Motors

A practical application of the effect of magnetic fields is the induction motor. A field is rotated in such a way that a copper disc cuts through the lines of force. Although the disc is not magnetized, it rotates at a speed proportionately slower than the field by means of eddy currents, and turns a shaft.

This principle may be applied to all induction motors found in household appliances. A pair of

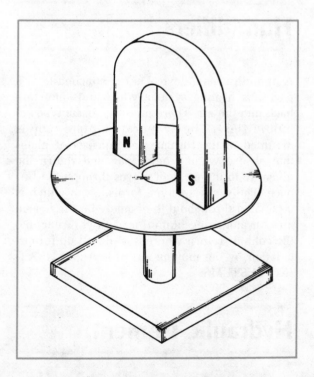

Basis of an induction motor.

windings are set in opposition of each other. When current is induced through the windings, the resulting field sets the rotor, or shaft, in motion. Induction motors in the form of split-phase motors are found in washing machines, fans and heater blowers. Devices that are not easily started require a capacitor, another variation of the induction motor. *SEE ALSO ELECTRIC MOTORS.*

Insect & Pest Control

Good house construction and tidy conditions inside and outside the house are the best protections against infestation by insects and pests. House sills built at least eight inches from the ground, with a metal flashing shield separating the entire foundation from the sill, will discourage both termites and carpenter ants from attacking the wood structure. When building, specify that all wood forms, lumber scraps and sawdust will be removed from the ground before the foundation is covered. Clean fill should be used to grade the property, as rubble from old construction sites is certain to contain insects and probably termites. Specify that earth under and around the foundation will be treated with chlordane. For the small extra cost involved, you can buy the best prevention available against insects and tunneling pests.

Termites feed on moist wood, so the places to look for termite attack are where moisture can enter the house. Scrutinize crawl spaces, under outside steps and porches and around the foundation to be sure that earth is not close to wood construction. Faulty roof flashing, clogged eaves and leaking downspouts can let enough moisture into the house to encourage termites at the foundation line, as can poor paint condition and unfilled cracks.

The three termite signals are: swarms of flying insects emerging from cracks and the ground in warm days of early spring; spent wings after a swarm, lying in drifts; and semicircular tunnels rising irregularly up basement walls, footings and foundations toward the wood of the house. The termite workers supply the rest of the population with food and cannot live in the air, so build tight tunnels to their target and chew on the inside of wood posts and beams, leaving hollowed ribs or perhaps a mere shell of important supports. Use an icepick or small drill, or tap with a hammer to test wood for termite damage. Door sills, stairs and basement windows are common points of attack as well as foundation sills, studs and beams. Outside, keep leaves and fallen limbs cleaned away from the house. Remove dead woody plants promptly.

Two methods are in wide use to control the termite problem. One is to dig a trench 30 inches deep along the entire foundation, pour in chlordane mixed with water as specified on the label and mix more of it with the earth when refilling the trench. This is hard work and will disrupt some foundation plantings, but it is probably the most effective method. Another is to use a long injection rod sold in hardware and garden-supply stores with poison pellets; connected to a hose, the poisoned water is forced into the ground through perforations in the rod. Insert the rod at close intervals to do a thorough job, for termites need only one clean space to make their approach.

Houses without basements and built on concrete aprons are most susceptible. If your house has been invaded, drill through the concrete and force large amounts of the chemical mixture into the earth under the apron or basement floor in a number of locations.

Ants, cockroaches, carpet beetles, flies, mosquitoes, moths, rodents and other pests come into the house in search of food or warmth and safe nesting. Others are brought in with food from stores, on clothing and pets. The best prevention is to inspect produce, grocery bags and your pets, keep food particles and spills wiped up and keep corners and shelves free of neglected papers. Tight-closing doors and screens are important. Where drain pipes and water pipes go through house or basement walls, spray well and close cracks tightly with treated stuffing. When pests are found in the house, spray entrances and window frames, taking care not to use pesticides dangerous to humans or pets. Try to find the pests' route and source.

A number of insects are helpful and should not be obliterated, including ladybugs, praying mantis, spiders (except red spider mites and black widow), bees, hornets and wasps. All help control destructive insects, and bees and their cousins fertilize plants by carrying pollen. Do not use spray or dust to control these insects.

An enlightened approach to using chemical pest and insect controls is to use as little as necessary, and only where there is a real problem. Applications can be increased, but it is hard to remove what has been used. Take every precaution to keep pesticides and insecticides away from food. Store containers under lock and key, and carefully dispose of empty containers.

HOUSEHOLD PESTS AND HOW TO CONTROL THEM

Ants form single files enroute from ant colony to food. Several files indicate more than one colony at work. Break files at entry points with insecticide. Use disinfectant regularly on surfaces where ants are seen. Keep sweets, ripe fruit and sugared drinks covered and stored safely. Wipe, spray or dust baseboards, doorways and window sills with insecticide when an invasion occurs. Follow maker's directions; read label carefully. Small metal ant traps containing kepone, available at supermarkets, are very effective against small food ants. Leave the traps at strategic locations for continuous control. Diazinon, lindane and malathion are very effective.

Bedbugs like dark, warm places, bite flesh, suck blood and lay eggs in hiding places. Have infested bedding cleaned and treated. Spray with lindane, malathion or pyrethrum in mattress seams and holes, under rugs and baseboards, wallpaper seams and cracks. If the problem is severe, have exterminators do a professional job.

Bees, hornets and wasps are normally helpful, but will attack humans and pets to protect nest or working territory. Search for nests in attic, eaves, wood piles and old trees. Do not destroy unless they are too near house and entrances or play areas. If necessary, destroy nests at night when creatures are dormant. Diazinon, malathion and naled may be used. If a person with allergies or history of dangerous bee-sting reaction is stung, call a physician at once.

Beetles, crickets and moths live indoors and out. Moths and beetles lay eggs where they eat. Early spring and fall are times to watch for them. Use powder or spray designed for use on cloth. Use in corners that collect dust, in clothes closets and under edges of carpets and upholstery. Have clothes and carpets cleaned with a preventive agent. Use moth crystals when storing woolens and furs in sealed cartons.

Roaches are active in the dark. Their main sources of food are old wallpaper paste, glue on old food labels, undisturbed pasta containers and starches. Spray where roaches are found and in nearby cracks, and remove attractions. Baygon, diazinon, lindane, malathion and ronnel are effective pesticides.

Ticks infest wildlife and pets outdoors. However, they may also be found in human hair and clothing, tall grass and brush. Brown ticks are usually nonpoisonous, others can leave infected sores and often are disease-carrying. Wash pets and human hair in disinfectant to kill eggs after removing ticks with tweezers. Diazinon, malathion and naled are effective sprays on wool carpets and clothing. Ticks that may carry Rocky Mountain fever should be removed by heat or pried off to avoid dangerous secretion.

Weevils and food beetles are usually brought into the house with grain and starch foods. Eggs in food may hatch and multiply while the food is stored. These are largely harmless, but unappetizing. Use disinfectant on food-storage shelves and flour tins, inspect old packages of food and watch flour as it is poured. Malathion and lindane sprayed on storage surfaces will control infestation.

Earwigs live on sugars in fruits, vegetables and flowers. They live outdoors by habit and bite when caught. To eradicate earwigs inspect garden produce and spray thresholds with household insecticides.

Fleas breed on plants as well as on animals, indoors and out, multiplying alarmingly fast. They infest carpets and clothing, attack humans when numbers increase and are disease-bearing. Put flea collars on dogs and cats. Inspect garden plants before bringing them into the house when fleas are around. Use flea powder on pets and wash them with treated soap when infested; use flea powder on pets' beds. Most pest controls except chlordane and lindane are used against fleas.

Houseflies breed in decaying matter. White maggot larvae, instantly recognizable, are found under stones in manured gardens as well as in garbage and carrion. They are disease-bearing. Keep animal matter such as manure and garbage well-sealed. Wash or spray garbage containers with disinfectant. Use insecticides designed for winged insects; malathion, pyrethrum and ronnel are effective. Close holes and cracks in screens. Double screen doors can be used where flies and mosquitoes are a serious problem. Set flypaper outside and inside doors.

Mosquitoes breed in standing water, wet eaves, bushes and bog. Preferring dark places, they may be found in a house under furniture. Basic protection is fine-mesh screening and mosquito repellent on skin. Use sprays designed for winged insects; malathion, methoxychlor and pyrethrum are conducive. To inhibit breeding, drain standing water, spray with oil or break up surface with small pebbles. A few types of mosquitoes carry malaria in known malarial areas.

Scorpions normally live outdoors under wood or rocks. In the house they will hide in dark, cozy places such as bedding, clothing and newspapers. Scorpions can be kept out of the house with water traps outside doors and porches. Put chlordane or lindane in the water traps. Wipe these pesticides on steps and thresholds, closet floors and shelves. Scorpions

sting when handled. Since this sting can be fatal to small children, medical attention should be called for at once.

Silverfish like dark, damp places where they will be undisturbed. They may eat wallpaper paste and box glue, as well as some textiles. Use malathion or pyrethrum on surfaces and in cracks, bottoms of trunks and other storage places.

FUNGICIDES	
Problems & Suggested Controls	
Anthracnose	Fermate
Brown Patch, Dollar Spot, Copper Spot	Captan, Dyrene, Daconil
Botyris Blight	Fermate
Chlorosis	Chelated Iron
Leaf Rust	Sulphur, Captan, Fermate
Potato Blight	Captan, Manzate
Powdery Mildew	Folpet, Dinocap, Karathane
Rust	Zineb
Snowmold	Dyrene
Tomato Blight	Maneb, Zineb

CONTROL OF HARMFUL RODENTS

Most rodents are serious disease-carriers and extremely destructive in the garden, in the house structure and where food is stored. They infect family pets and children by biting and with fleas and lice.

Mice, rats, chipmunks and squirrels which nest in ground holes or building walls, often tunnel or chew through wood to reach food and warmth. Generally, these disease-carrying rodents are active at night when they feel safe from predators. Since they multiply rapidly, an active cat is the best protection against mice, indoors and outdoors. Bait traps with fatty foods such as bacon or cheese. Place poisoned grain in crawl spaces, basements, behind cupboards and in attics—*only* if children cannot discover it or reach there. Poisoned grain is quite effective. Close holes in the foundation, lay carpenter's cloth over earth in crawl spaces and screen the

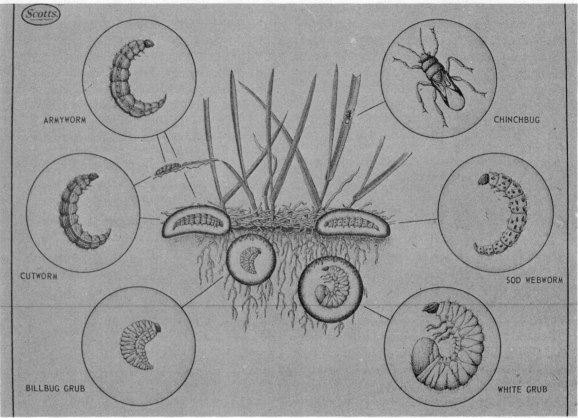

ARMYWORM

CHINCHBUG

CUTWORM

SOD WEBWORM

BILLBUG GRUB

WHITE GRUB

Courtesy of J. Converse, O.M. Scott & Sons Company.

chimney at its top with stout galvanized wire. Napthalene flakes repel rodents.

Rabbits eat vegetables, flowers, bark on woody bushes and tree trunks. They can destroy young trees. Animal repellent may drive rabbits out of a garden. Traps can be baited with the food they are destroying.

Bats usually sleep during the day and hunt for food at night. They enter houses through an attic or chimney. Since bats destroy insects, they should not be killed. Open doors and windows, turn off lights and a bat will probably leave willingly. Some carry rabies, so avoid being bitten. Napthalene flakes will repel bats from parts of the house and garden.

GARDEN PESTS

Prevention is the key to fighting off pests in the garden. Turning, loosening and aerating the soil

as soon as it can be worked in the spring helps desirable plants to grow strong and defeats weeds in the contest for space. Feeding plants and grass on schedule aids your plants and kills the weeds because they thrive in dry, starved soil. Dig out weeds that thrive and spread mulch around plants to prevent weed seed and roots from growing. Weeds play host to garden insects, and insects not only chew and suck nourished plants but carry diseases to the plants.

In early spring spray with an oil-based dormant spray and apply weed-killer to grass. This will kill weed seed and emergent insects before they can do damage.

Make friends with the birds, *regularly* feeding them at a well-protected bird feeder. When they make trees their home or spend time every day in a yard, they will eat huge numbers of insects. Buy live ladybugs and praying mantis from mail-order houses. If released in a garden, they will control many times their weight in harmful insects daily. Plant mint to drive away ants from hilling near doorways. Plant marigolds anywhere that nematodes are a problem; marigolds produce a chemical that the tiny worms can not take (nematodes cause root knot and weak growth in roses and other important plants).

Chrysanthemums repel aphids and thrips. Zinnias, nasturtiums, dill and garlic, planted in key spots, attract some insects away from vegetable crops and flower bushes. Hard spraying with the hose will wash off large collections of aphids and red spiders if the undersides of leaves and stems of plants are hit. Rose growers often use the hose to wash off heavy infestations before using chemicals. Water and oil traps can be set for slugs and Japanese beetles. A toad in cool, damp places of a garden will fill itself with insects.

WEED CONTROL	
Problems & Suggested Controls	
Bindweed	Benzac; Amino Triazole, 2, 4-D
Broad-Leaf Weeds (Dandelion, Plantain, etc.)	MCPA, 2, 4-D, Iron Sulphate
Bermuda Grass	Dalapon
Buckthorn	2, 4-D
Canada Thistle	Amino Triazole, 2, 4-D
Crabgrass	2, 4-D, PMAS; mow long and cultivate soil
Foxtail	Mow long and cultivate
Henbit	Silvex, 2, 4-D
Knotweed	2, 4-D, Silvex
Nutsedge	2, 4-D
Poison Ivy, Poison Oak	MCPA, 2, 4-D, Amino, Triazole, Ammonium Sulphate
Ragweed	2, 4-D
Red Sorrel	Silvex
Speedwell	2, 4-D

Courtesy of J. Converse, O.M. Scott & Sons Company.

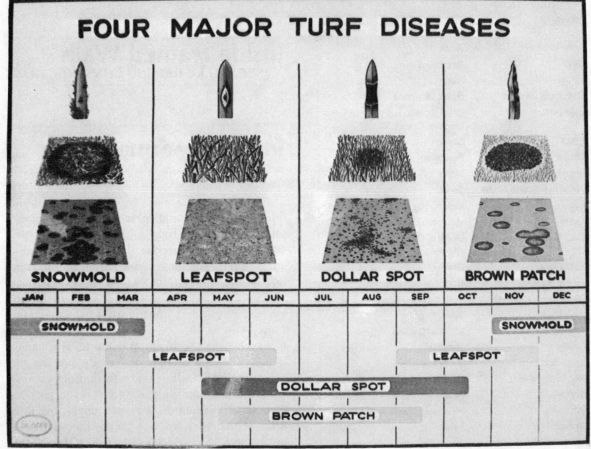

These methods and many others are natural approaches to maintaining a healthy garden. Good soil condition, plant nutrition and natural controls are the mainstays. When insecticides are really necessary, or experience tells you it is time to use one periodically, use it as an aid.

As specific garden problems arise during the season, find a specific control instead of heavily dousing everything in the garden with a number of insecticides and fungicides. Your garden will be a healthier place if low-toxicity insecticides such as rotenone, carbaryl, malathion, methoxychlor and pyrethrum are used. Using them for specific problems will make it harder for garden enemies to adjust to the control.

INSECTICIDES	
Problems & Suggested Controls	
Aphids	Malathion, Pyrethrum, Rotenone, Diazinon
Army Worm	Sevin
Cinch	Diazinon, Sevin
Corn Borer	Sevin
Cucumber Beetles	Sevin, Rotenone
Cutworm	Sevin, Rotenone, Pyrethrum Lindane, Diazinon
Fleas	Sevin, Malthion
Grubs	Rotenone
Gypsy Moth Larvae	Sevin
Japanese Beetle Grubs	Sevin
Lace Bug	Malathion, Lindane
Leafhopper	Malathion, Sevin, Diazinon
Leaf Miner	Lindane, Diazinon, Cygon (a systemic)
Leaf Roller	Lindane
Mealy Bugs	Rotenone, Malathion
Mexican Bean Beetle	Methoxychlor, Sevin
Pine Moth	Sevin, Cygon
Red Spider, Mites	Aramite, Diazinon, Malathion
Sawfly	Malathion plus Methoxychlor
Slugs and Snails	Metaldehyde Bait
Sod Webworm	Diazinon, Sevin
Thrips	Pyrethrum, Lindane, Malathion
White Fly	Malathion, Diazinon
Tomato Hornworm	Sevin

Inside Corner Molding

Inside corner molding covers the joint formed by the inside corner of a room, concealing uneven panel cuts and out-of-level corners. *SEE ALSO MOLDING & TRIM.*

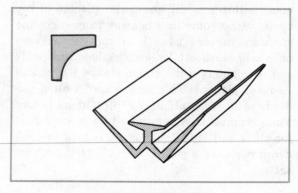

Inside Corner Molding

Inside Framed Walls
[SEE WALL & CEILING CONSTRUCTION.]

Inside Try Square

The inside try square is a try square or combination square used for checking inside corners and joints for perfect right angles. To use the try square for this purpose, lay the body of the square on the top edge of one corner of the structure. If the tongue falls flush with the side edge of the object from end to end, it is a true 90° angle. The combination square is used much the same way as the try square, except that you measure with the blade and the handle rather than with a body and tongue. By placing the right-angled handle inside the object on one wood surface and extending the blade perpendicular to the handle, you can check for light leaks which will indicate where the surface is not square. *SEE ALSO HAND TOOLS.*

Installing Electrical Switches

[SEE SWITCHES & OUTLETS.]

Instant-On

A cord set with a remote on-off switch and a simple semiconductor device called a *diode* is all it takes to build a useful device that eliminates the warm up time of the older tube-type AC/DC radio and gives you the instant-on function of today's transistor radios. The instant-on can also be used as a light dimmer for a night table lamp or the living room lamp.

Instant-on keeps your radio half-turned-on all the time. The filaments in the tubes stay warm, so when the set is turned on all the way, you do not have to wait while they heat up. An incidental advantage is that there is no current surge to blow a tube filament as could happen when full line voltage hits it cold. A minor disadvantage is that there is a slight current drain (about as much as an electric clock) to keep the filaments warm on stand-by.

The result is a five-second or less warm-up period, instead of half-a-minute. When turned off, instant-on's diode blocks the positive half-cycles of the power line AC voltage wave from the receiver so it cannot work.

Construction is simple since the instant-on is built into the switch of a remote control cord set (available at any hardware or electrical shop). Remove the two screws that hold the switch cover in place. Apply a little solder to one of the leads from the diode and solder it to the terminal to which one of the switch wires goes. Do the same for the other lead from the diode. That is all there is to the wiring. Before the cover can be replaced, it may be necessary to snip out a little of the plastic ribbing to make room for the diode.

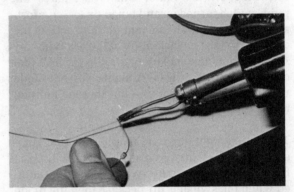

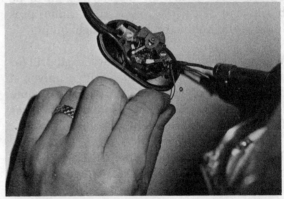

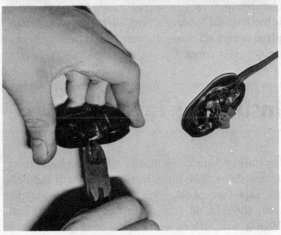

To use the instant-on, plug its cord into an AC outlet and plug the AC/DC radio into the instant-on's outlet. Turn the radio switch and the instant-on switch on. If the radio does not play, reverse *its* plug in the cord's socket. Now it will play. Set a comfortable volume and turn the switch on the instant-on to off. The radio will stop, but everytime you flip the switch of the instant-on, it wil start to play right away.

Of course, you can turn off the whole system by switching off the radio. Otherwise, leave the radio switch turned on and tuned up to a comfortable sound level. The instant-on then acts as the on-off switch. The instant-on can work with any AC/DC appliance including a radio (or TV) that draws 100 watts or less. A higher current diode would allow more watts — but there is not that much room inside the switch.

To use as a light dimmer, simply plug in a lamp cord instead of the radio's. The light will be at full brightness when the switch is on and dimmed when the switch is off because then the diode *blocks* half of each AC cycle so it cannot pass through the bulb to provide *full* light output.

You can also slow down an electric hand drill (or any low-drain appliance fitted with a universal or series-wound motor). Just plug its cord into the instant-on socket. One switch position gives full speed; the other, about half-speed.

The instant-on works with AC/DC appliances only. Any equipment labeled *AC only* may contain power transformers or induction-type electric motors (universal motors are all right) which could overheat or burn-out when supplied with half-wave current. Read the appliance name plate carefully.

Insulating Tape

Insulating tape is primarily used for insulating wire splices. The three basic varieties of insulating tape are plastic, rubber and friction tape, with the plastic type being the most popular. Plastic tape offers more insulating power than the other varieties regardless of thickness. This permits thorough taping with less bulk when the job is completed. Rubber tape is used in moist areas since it becomes more durable and water tight with age. Wrap rubber tape spirally with the tape edges overlapping for best results. Friction tape is generally used for insulating outdoor wiring. Occasionally, friction tape is wrapped over rubber tape to protect it from abrasion. When taping in cold, unheated areas, use special, low-temperature vinyl tape to prevent cracking.

Insulating tape should be started one tape width back from the area to be taped and wrapped in a spiral pattern. Cover slightly beyond the area to be insulated and begin wrapping in the opposite direction so that the spirals cross over each other. Allow a sufficient overlap on the tape edges for final wrapping so the finished job will be smooth with no loose ends.

Insulation

Insulation keeps a home warmer in the winter and cooler in the summer, making the house a more comfortable place to live all year long. It retards the rate of heat flow out of or into a house and eliminates drafts providing a more even distribution of heat throughout the house. The net effect of this is a reduction in the homeowner's electricity and fuel costs. If the house is located in the North, the insulation pays for itself within two or three years, but the amount of insulation needed depends upon the area of the country.

Insulation is applied most effectively during initial construction, but the handyman can accomplish excellent results with many kinds of insulating materials if he carefully follows manufacturer's instructions. Insulation can roughly be divided into several categories: poured or loose fill, blankets or batts, rigid boards and reflective foil. Most of these types of insulation operate on the same principle: they trap air in thousands of tiny pockets in their fibers preventing the passage of heat. Reflective foil insulation, on the other hand, reflects heat back to its source.

For best protection all walls as well as the roof should be insulated. If only the roof is accessible, it is still worthwhile to insulate the roof. Insulation can cause more trouble than benefit if a vapor barrier is not provided. A vapor barrier is a material (usually plastic, metal foil or asphalt paper) that does not absorb moisture or let water vapor pass through it. Water vapor will collect in the air pockets of insulation causing it to become wet and useless unless a vapor barrier prevents the flow of moisture. The vapor barrier may enclose the insulation on all sides or may be applied to only one side. To be effective, the vapor barrier must be facing the warm part of the house rather than the outside.

Loose fill insulation comes in bags and consists of particles of mineral wool, vermiculite or wood fiber. It is suitable for use between the rafters in unfinished attics and is also blown into the exterior walls of older homes with professional help. Loose fill insulation is relatively low cost, easy to use and fire resistant, but it tends to settle over the years and has no vapor barrier.

Blanket or batt insulation is used more often by the home handyman where framing is exposed. It is available in one to six inch thicknesses and in 15 to 16 inch widths to fit between studs and joists. Special butts up to 24 inches wide are available for widely spaced studs. Blanket and batt insulation is made of mineral wool, fiber glass, cellulose fiber or flame-proof cotton and covered with a paper or foil wrapper. There is a flange on both sides to permit nailing or stapling to framing. Blanket or batt insulation may be covered with foil or asphalt-permeated paper on one side acting as a vapor barrier. To make sure the vapor barrier is continuous and untorn, the paper flanges should overlap on the face of each stud. Blanket insulation is available in long rolls while batts come in shorter four to eight feet lengths.

Rigid board insulation is made of polystyrene plastic or compressed mineral wool and used on concrete, on walls and ceilings and inside the foundation before the concrete slabs are poured. It prevents heat loss from the edge of concrete slabs to the foundation. For use in a basement or attic, some of these panels come with decorative finishes so they serve as finish paneling as well as a form of insulation. However, rigid board insulation does not work as well as the bulkier insulation that is installed inside the wall.

Reflective foil insulation is a metal foil of several air-filled layers which depends on the number of layers rather than thickness for its effectiveness. Reflective foil comes folded in a single strip and pulls apart like an accordian to be installed. This insulation does a better job of keeping summer heat out than retaining house heat in the winter, but it can be as effective as bulk insulation if enough layers are used and sufficient air space is left on both sides of it. SEE ALSO WALL & CEILING INSULATION.

Insulators

Insulators are materials used to control the flow of electricity, heat, sound and the possibility of fire. They are numerous in types and variety but some of the more common are these: asbestos, rubber, plastic, fiberglass, mica and jute. Asbestos controls the hazard of fire and is usually found on the exterior walls of the house as a covering, e.g. asbestos siding. Rubber and plastic protect electrical cords from wear and shorts. Mica and jute are found in electronic equipment as a deterrent against shorts and burn-outs. Fiberglass is usually placed inside the interior walls to help in heating and sound control. SEE ALSO ACOUSTICS & SOUND CONTROL; ELECTRICAL WIRING; HEATING SYSTEMS; INSULATION; STEREO SYSTEMS; WALL & CEILING INSULATION.

Insurance Protection

Homeowners will invest a large part of their lifetime income in a residence. Loss of that home, either directly as a result of fire or tornado, or indirectly as a result of its sale to pay high hospital costs or personal liability judgments awarded in the courts, could mean financial disaster for a homeowner. This danger of loss is why it is so important for everyone to insure not only his house and its contents, but also his life, health, automobile and other property.

While it is possible that a person is spending more than he needs on insurance, it is more likely that he is underinsured or unprotected in some important areas. Check your present coverage against the guidelines in this article.

Insurance is sold by insurance companies that sell stock on the open market, by mutual insurance companies that are owned by the policyholders, by some savings and loan associations and by various lending organizations. To verify a company's good standing, check among family and friends and with the local Better Business Bureau or state insurance commission. Buy only from companies licensed to do business in the state. In the case of automobile insurance, make sure the company has representatives in possible future travel areas, particularly outside the United States.

LIFE INSURANCE

If a person is the sole support of a family, it is almost imperative that he carry some insurance on his life. While one might not be able to provide lifetime support after his death for all of his dependents, it is certainly possible to protect them for a time until they become self-supporting.

Three major types of life insurance plus endowment coverage are listed in the accompanying table.

Term life insurance requires the least current cash outlay for equal protection of the various kinds of insurance. Generally, it has no cash value (cannot be cashed in or borrowed against). For best protection, buy term life insurance that is both renewable and convertible. These features allow one to renew coverage (at a higher premium, of course) at the end of the stated term without a medical examination until a person is 65 or 70 and to convert the term policy to a whole-life policy without examination for continued coverage before age 65 or 70.

Whole-life or ordinary life insurance requires a greater cash outlay annually than term because it combines insurance with a savings plan. Its cash value increases from year to year as a result of the additional premium paid over and above the cost of protection, and it returns money to the policyholder should the policy be cashed in before death. Money may also be borrowed against a whole-life policy.

In addition to protecting dependents, life insurance often is used to pay off loans and mortgages, protect business partners and associates and pay inheritance taxes.

When a person takes out a life insurance policy, or sometime thereafter, the insured person may be offered the option of converting the policy to an annuity, payable to either the policyholder or the beneficiaries in a guaranteed amount over a period of years after a specified date.

Other insurance options are also available. All of these options add to the cost of basic insurance:

Double indemnity, which assures the beneficiaries twice the benefits under the policy if the insured dies because of an accident.

Waiver of premium, which suspends payment of premiums after someone has been disabled and unable to work for a stated number of months.

Guaranteed insurability, which allows an insured to pay extra premiums now for a guaranteed option to buy more insurance without medical examination at a specified later date.

Automatic premium loan, which is issued as a loan against the policy, to pay a premium on time should someone forget to pay the insured interest on this "loan".

AUTOMOBILE INSURANCE

Apart from the fact that a state may require someone to carry auto insurance, a car owner should at least protect himself against large per-

		TABLE					
		Types of Life Insurance					

Type	Period of payment	Period of coverage	Premiums**	Benefits Type	Benefits Amount	Form of payment	Cash value
Term	term indicated (1,5,10,20,30, years)	term	fixed for term; increased upon renewal for new term	death	face value	lump sum (or annuity option)	none
Whole or ordinary life	lifetime	lifetime	fixed	death	face value*	lump sum (or annuity option)	increases from year to year
Limited payment	period specified	lifetime	fixed for period	death	face value*	lump sum (or annuity option)	increases from year to year***
Endowment	to maturity of policy	to maturity of policy	fixed to maturity of policy	death or on maturity of policy	face value* as death benefit, or amount specified on maturity of policy	lump sum or annuity	increases from year to year***

*Benefits will be face value *minus* any outstanding loan against the policy at time of death.

**Some companies return a part of the premium annually in the form of a "dividend." Participating life insurance pays dividends in unguaranteed amounts for higher premiums; nonparticipating pays no dividends for lower premiums. The amount of the dividend depends upon the company's experience with that type of policy.

***Cash value may exceed premiums paid.

sonal liability judgments for bodily injury to others in an accident. If a person has borrowed money to buy a car, the lending agency more than likely requires the person to carry sufficient collision and comprehensive insurance to cover the car totally. Here are the basic coverages offered with auto insurance.

Personal Liability

A car owner should carry an absolute minimum of $25,000/$50,000 personal liability insurance. That is, $25,000 for injury to one person, up to $50,000 for injury to two or more persons in one accident. It is safer to have even greater coverage, particularly since the initial coverage

is of greatest cost to the car owner, and additional coverage is available for proportionately little extra expense.

A driver who is heavily insured will be backed all the way through the courts by his insurance company. Those drivers with minimum coverage may find the company willing to settle for the amount of the policy, leaving the driver the problem of defending himself against additional judgment.

Property Damage

The minimum property damage coverage recommended today is $10,000. Considering the possibility of multiple-car involvement in modern highway accidents, a car owner would be wise to insure for a greater amount.

Medical Payments

Most drivers carry insurance to pay medical expenses up to a stated amount per person for injury to him and others in the driver's car. This coverage is available for about $10 a year for $1,000 per person, which makes it an economical investment.

Collision

Even if collision insurance is not required by a lending agency, this coverage is a must if the car is new. It insures the new owner against damage to or total loss of the car in case of collision.

Comprehensive

Loan companies also frequently require a new car buyer to carry comprehensive insurance to cover the cost of damages to the car *not* caused by collision. Examples of such damages are those caused by flood, fire, storm, theft, and vandalism. This coverage is not expensive and is well worth the cost. Further protection is available to cover bodily injury to the insured in an accident involving a car operated by an uninsured driver.

A new approach to automobile insurance is no-fault insurance. Under no-fault, all insured drivers involved in an accident receive some compensation from their own insurance company for property damage and injury regardless of who is at fault. This type of insurance has been shown to cut the number of court cases drastically and thereby reduce the cost of insurance for all drivers.

An insurance company may offer a person a discount of 10 to 25 per cent of the cost of the policy if he is a good risk: if a person is a nondrinker; if a person has not had an accident costing more than $50 in the past 3 to 5 years: if the vehicle is a pickup truck; if a person drives less than 7500 miles a year; if a person has another car insured by the same company; if the insured's teenager has passed an accredited driver-training course or is a student ranking in the upper 20% of his class. Some companies offer discounts to groups of people who work or go to school together.

If a person is a member of a car pool, he may need to increase his liability coverage. Check with an insurance agent about insurance precautions for carpoolers.

HOMEOWNER'S INSURANCE

A homeowner's policy covers a variety of natural, accidental and personal risks involved in the ownership of residence and other property. Apartment dwellers often purchase homeowner's policies to protect furnishings and clothing against fire and theft.

The basic fire and extended coverage policy insures the homeowner against damage to or loss of property due to fire, smoke and water, lightning, windstorm, hail, explosives, riots, motor vehicles and aircraft, burglary, theft and vandalism. Almost all homeowner's policies also include personal liability insurance and some provision for expenses of living away from home for a time after a residence has been damaged or destroyed.

Fire

Insurance against damage to a home or garage by fire, lightning, or explosion pays up to the *face value* of the policy (not necessarily the value of your home) if, and only if, the insured amount equals at least 80 per cent of its replacement value at the time of the disaster. (See illustration.) Since the cost of fire insurance is divided equally among all policyholders, insurance companies understandably withhold full payment to anyone who has not carried a full share of the cost of coverage. The homeowner may also insure a residence for its full replacement value and receive full face value in the event of fire.

The replacement value of a home for purposes of fire insurance, either separate from or included in a homeowner's policy, should be updated annually. It is the insured's responsibility to do this. In figuring the replacement value, do not include the cost or value of the foundation or the land; (for insurance purposes, these are unaffected by fire). Do not forget the cost of im-

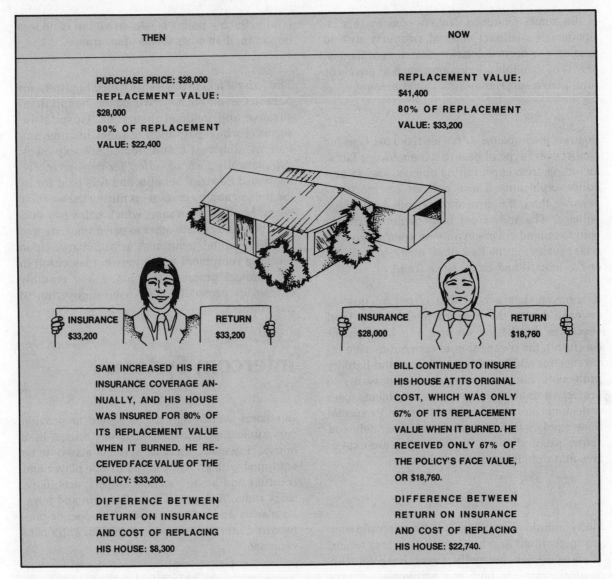

THEN	NOW
PURCHASE PRICE: $28,000	REPLACEMENT VALUE: $41,400
REPLACEMENT VALUE: $28,000	80% OF REPLACEMENT VALUE: $33,200
80% OF REPLACEMENT VALUE: $22,400	

INSURANCE $33,200   RETURN $33,200

INSURANCE $28,000   RETURN $18,760

SAM INCREASED HIS FIRE INSURANCE COVERAGE ANNUALLY, AND HIS HOUSE WAS INSURED FOR 80% OF ITS REPLACEMENT VALUE WHEN IT BURNED. HE RECEIVED FACE VALUE OF THE POLICY: $33,200.

DIFFERENCE BETWEEN RETURN ON INSURANCE AND COST OF REPLACING HIS HOUSE: $8,300

BILL CONTINUED TO INSURE HIS HOUSE AT ITS ORIGINAL COST, WHICH WAS ONLY 67% OF ITS REPLACEMENT VALUE WHEN IT BURNED. HE RECEIVED ONLY 67% OF THE POLICY'S FACE VALUE, OR $18,760.

DIFFERENCE BETWEEN RETURN ON INSURANCE AND COST OF REPLACING HIS HOUSE: $22,740.

Sam and Bill bought the same kind of house for the same price years ago.

provements made or the cost of rebuilding even those parts that might not be totally destroyed by fire, such as brick walls.

Personal Injury Liability

Liability insurance, which is usually included in a homeowner's policy and applies to all members of the family, protects the homeowner against claims for injury to others or damage to their property in the insured's home or outside the home, except for automobile accidents. If a guest should fall and injure himself, liability insurance would cover his medical expenses up to the amount specified in the policy, the cost of legal defense if he sues for damages and awards made by the court up to the limits of the policy. Swimming pool accidents and dog bites inflicted by the family pet are included in liability insurance unless they are specifically excluded.

Furnishings and Clothing

Homeowner's insurance usually covers furniture, clothing and other possessions against loss or damage by fire, theft at home or away from home, vandalism and so forth. The rate of coverage is usually 40-50 per cent of the amount

861

of the home insurance. Not covered by this insurance is ordinary loss of property due to breakage or normal deterioration, loss of money, or loss of valuable possessions, such as jewels or furs, above some minimum stated amount.

Special Protection

Insurance companies offer all-risk coverage for almost every type of hazard a homeowner faces, including freezeups, falling objects, and steam-boiler explosions. These policies are more expensive than the fire and extended coverage policies. The individual homeowner might do well to extend coverage only on special types of risks, such as tornadoes, theft away from home or credit card and bank check fraud.

If someone has a boat that is not adequately covered under the homeowner's policy (and check the limitations on size and horsepower carefully), the owner should take out marine insurance for additional loss, damage and liability protection. Someone who owns and wants to protect valuable furs, jewelry, art objects, coin collections and the like should take out a special floater policy that lists each item separately and shows proof of value. These floaters are expensive and not always easy to obtain.

HEALTH AND ACCIDENT INSURANCE

Many employers offer full-time employees group accident and hospitalization insurance. These policies normally cover hospital and medical costs for both the employee and the employee's dependents. Such expenses are hospital room and board, diagnostic services, surgical fees, doctors' visits, radiation therapy and outpatient care are usually covered up to stated amounts. Also included may be benefits for major medical expenses in cases of prolonged illness or accidental injury to pay additional costs not covered by the basic policy. A typical major medical provision might be 80% of all expenses not covered by the basic policy up to $25,000 maximum in a given benefit period.

If a group plan is not available, a person can buy an individual policy covering hospitalization and medical expenses incurred by a person and his family. Such a policy is expensive but is no less important than other forms of insurance.

The federal health insurance called Medicare for persons over 65 has two parts: hospital insurance and medical insurance. Hospital insurance, which pays most hospital, nursing, outpatient, diagnostic and home-care expenses, automatically goes into effect for persons receiving Social Security benefits and was paid for by the person and by employers during the working years. Medical insurance, which helps pay doctors' bills and certain other expenses not covered by the hospital insurance, is voluntary. Upon reaching retirement age, a person may enroll in the medical program and pay a low monthly charge for protection. The federal government pays the rest.

Intercom Systems

Intercoms were originally designed to provide communication between separate rooms in a house. However, intercom systems may now be equipped with an AM/FM radio, tape player and recorder and an automatic timer that acts like a clock radio. A doorbell amplifier, fire and burglar alarms and a front gate or door opener may be wired into the intercom system for extra convenience.

Speakers should be installed in the major rooms such as the bedroom, den, basement or recreational room, workshop and living room. In determining the placement for intercoms, remember that they are for saving steps and voices and keep in mind that up to 20 speakers may be installed in one home. Avoid placing speakers on exterior walls since moisture can damage the components.

When running the wire, use short routes and do not run the wires next to house power lines or through conduit. The wire chosen depends on the model, on the number of features wired into it and on how many speakers will be installed. Consult the manufacturer's specifications for

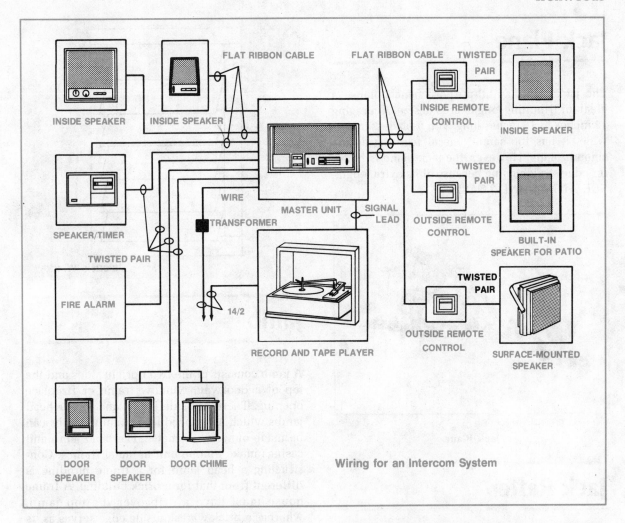

FLAT RIBBON CABLE

FLAT RIBBON CABLE

TWISTED PAIR

INSIDE SPEAKER

INSIDE SPEAKER

INSIDE REMOTE CONTROL

INSIDE SPEAKER

SPEAKER/TIMER

WIRE

MASTER UNIT

SIGNAL LEAD

TWISTED PAIR

OUTSIDE REMOTE CONTROL

BUILT-IN SPEAKER FOR PATIO

TRANSFORMER

TWISTED PAIR

TWISTED PAIR

FIRE ALARM

14/2

RECORD AND TAPE PLAYER

OUTSIDE REMOTE CONTROL

SURFACE-MOUNTED SPEAKER

DOOR SPEAKER

DOOR SPEAKER

DOOR CHIME

Wiring for an Intercom System

wire size and styles for the unit purchased. The illustration below shows a typical wiring system for the intercom master unit, speakers and other features. *SEE ALSO AUTOMATION; WIRELESS INTERCOMS.*

Internal Threads

Internal threads are the circular or spiraling grooves located inside screws, bolts and other types of fasteners that join with external threads without the use of fittings or adhesives. Internal threads are manufactured with gradations so that the grooves exactly fit an external thread of the same size.

Iron, Electric
[SEE ELECTRIC IRON REPAIR.]

Iron Pipe
[SEE CAST IRON PIPE.]

Ironwoods

Ironwoods is a term referring to those woods that are exceptionally hard. Classified as ironwoods are hickory, ebony and teak. *SEE ALSO WOOD IDENTIFICATION.*

Jack Plane

The jack plane, an all-purpose bench plane, is ideal for trimming long boards to size. Averaging 12 inches to 15 inches long with a blade 2 inches wide, it has the same general features as the smooth plane. However, the jack plane is better for edge straightening because of its extra length. *SEE ALSO HAND TOOLS.*

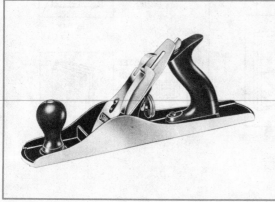

Courtesy of The Stanley Works

Jack Plane

Jack Rafter

A jack rafter is a short rafter framing located between the wall plate and a hip rafter, or between a hip or valley rafter and the roof ridge. *SEE ALSO ROOF CONSTRUCTION.*

Jalousie Window

A jalousie window is a window with small horizontal slats made of glass. Each end of these slats slip into metal frames which are attached to the entire window frame. A crank or lever moves the slats simultaneously. Jalousie windows provide good ventilation, but they are not air-tight and therefore used more often in the warmer climates.

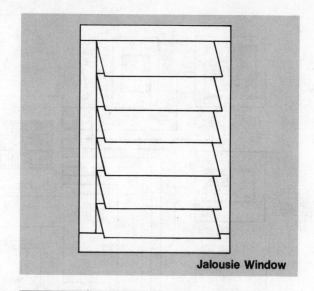

Jalousie Window

Jamb

A jamb consists of the two upright sides and the top of a doorway, window frame or fireplace opening. There are side jambs and top or head jambs which are placed horizontally. Jambs can be made of wood or metal. The head jamb and casings make up one unit in metal frames. Constructing a head jamb for a frame building is different from that for a brick building. A frame house must have a drip over the top jamb, whereas a brick wall's outside edge serves as its own drip. For adjusting the thickness of the window frame to different wall structures, a jamb extension of the required size may be applied. *SEE ALSO MOLDING & TRIM.*

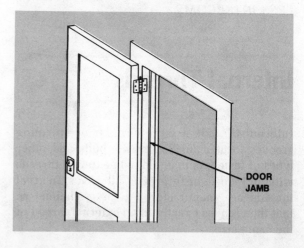

DOOR JAMB

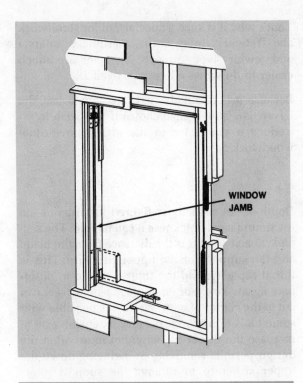

WINDOW JAMB

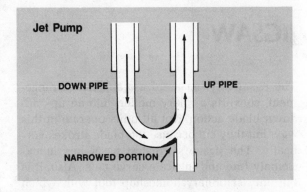

Jet Pump

DOWN PIPE — UP PIPE

NARROWED PORTION

Jig

A jig is a device which holds a piece of work and guides it in the correct position during assembly. Often this device is homemade.

There are different kinds of jigs used for various tasks, such as holding glasses for gluing, guiding tools for parallel cuts and drilling, honing plane irons, holding pipes and doweling. A jig can be made from scrap wood to act as a stand for holding a glass against its base while glue dries. Another type of jig can be made with scrap wood and a c-clamp to use as a guide in making a succession of parallel cuts. For emergency situations, a pipe-holding jig can be made by bolting two short lengths of 3/4 inch pipe together. A drill-sharpening jig sets the drill at the correct angle for grinding. Usually this type of jig is available at hardware stores. Jigs used for honing plane irons also set the irons at certain angles, usually 30°. Drill-guiding jigs are clamped to fit the hole size with the drill bit size. This helps in aligning the hole for precision. Doweling jigs are also used for aligning the holes.

Jet Pump

A jet pump is one of the types of well pumps that can be used in a deep well. This pump was designed according to Bernoulli's law that states the outward pressure of a fast moving fluid or gas decreases as its velocity increases. This new pressure is lower than the pressure of the stationary gas or fluid around it. The fluid with a higher pressure tends to be sucked toward and into the fast moving material. This is the principle used in pump-type bug sprayers.

The jet pump shoots a stream of water down the pipe and around a hairpin curve that is below water surface level. Because the bend in the curve becomes narrow at one point forming a Venturi tube, liquid must flow faster to pass through it. As the high speed stream that is lower than atmospheric pressure passes through this restricted area, the well water, having the higher atmospheric pressure, rushes up the pipe into the pump. Since more water is delivered than is sent, the surplus is transmitted to a water-storage tank. *SEE ALSO WELL PUMP SYSTEMS.*

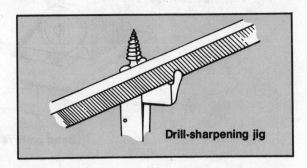

Drill-sharpening jig

JIGSAW

The jigsaw, by means of a crankshaft arrangement, converts a rotary motion into an up-and-down blade action. Not all units operate in this way, but they cut because the blade strokes vertically. The jigsaw's greatest asset lies in extremely fine and intricate curve cuts. Also, it is the only stationary homeshop tool with which you can do piercing, the technique that permits making internal cuts without a lead-in kerf from an edge of the stock.

The jigsaw should not be viewed as a toy machine. Since you can mount heavy blades and common depth-of-cut capacities run to about 2″, you can handle some quite heavy stock. The truth is, within its capacities, the jigsaw can do band-saw jobs, but there is no comparison in cut speed; the band saw will win everytime when compared solely on that basis. On the other hand, the jigsaw is king when it comes to very short-radius curves and extremely fine kerfs.

That's why it is such a special tool for scrollwork and fretwork. Inlay crafts, marquetry, intarsia and jewelry-type projects in metal are much easier to do when a jigsaw is available.

Because it is relatively easy and safe to use, the jigsaw is also a logical choice if you wish to introduce a youngster to the art of power-tool woodworking.

Gauging Capacity

Depth-of-cut capacity is figured in terms of the maximum stock thickness it can handle. The second capacity factor is the distance from the blade and the support for the upper structure. This is throat capacity, and the figure is used to designate jigsaw size. For example, an 18″ jigsaw can cut to the center of a 36″ circle. It's possible with some tools to use an accessory extension arm to increase the throat capacity, but more often the design permits removing or swinging down the upper structure to remove the support interference. Then, capacity is unlimited and the setup is called "sabre sawing." More will be said about this topic later, but generally this feature is

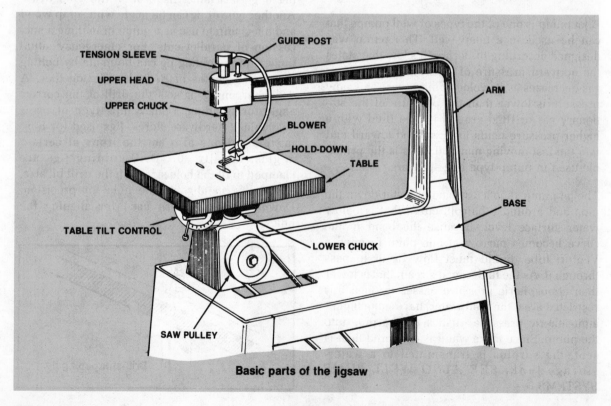

TENSION SLEEVE

GUIDE POST

UPPER HEAD

UPPER CHUCK

BLOWER

HOLD-DOWN

TABLE

ARM

BASE

TABLE TILT CONTROL

LOWER CHUCK

SAW PULLEY

Basic parts of the jigsaw

made possible by gripping a heavy-gauge blade in the lower chuck only.

Blade Mounting

Two chucks are provided. One is in the upper arm, the other below the table. Although designs may differ, the purpose of the chucks is to hold the blade taut between them. The amount of adjustment in the chuck and the method for achieving blade alignment can vary from tool to tool. Usually, a set of chuck blocks is provided. A setscrew on one side of the chuck lets you position one of the blocks in a more-or-less permanent position for most normal cutting; a setscrew on the opposite side moves the second chuck block so that the blade can be gripped securely. Some designs provide a permanent position for one of the blocks.

The important thing is to install the blade so it will *"jig"* in a true vertical line throughout the stroke travel. It must be vertical when viewed from the front and the side. One way to do this with assurance is to make yourself a guide. This guide is no more than a squared wood block

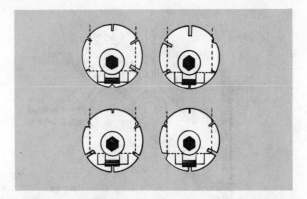

A universal guide is a disc with a slotted perimeter. Turn the disc to choose a slot that is right for the blade. The backup roller is set to lightly touch the back edge of the blade.

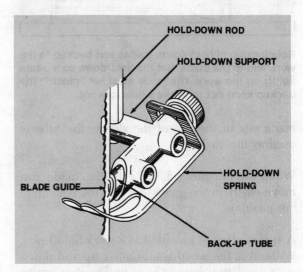

Another type (found on the Shopsmith jigsaw) has a split tube as a blade guide. This is encased in an adjustable sleeve that serves as the backup.

(about $3/4'' \times 4'' \times 4''$) with a straight kerf cut down the center of one edge. Holding the blade in the kerf as you tighten the chucks will assure alignment.

The blade backup is at the bottom of the guide post. Some of these are *universal*, being a slim, steel disc with various blade-size slots cut in the perimeter. You choose the slot that is suitable for the blade you are going to cut with and then adjust the device so the steel sleeve bears against the back edge of the blade. The degree of bearing should be a light-touch contact. Another design provides a split sleeve encased in a tube. The

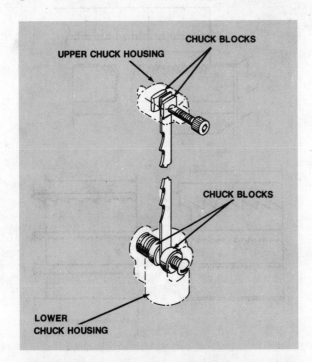

Jigsaw blades are gripped in both the upper and the lower chuck. When installing the blade, be sure that the teeth point downward.

867

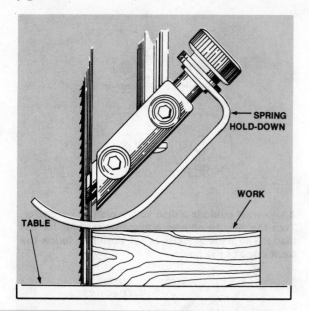

Relationship of hold-down, guides and backup to the work and to the blade. Set the hold-down so it bears lightly on the work. The guide must not "pinch"; the backup must not push the blade forward.

blade sits in the slot of the sleeve; the tube is used as the backup.

Whatever the method, be sure the blade can move easily in the guide and that the backup is not pushing.

A spring affair is provided as a work holddown. Without it, the wood would move up and down with the blade. Adjust the spring mechanism so it just touches the top surface of the work. Too much pressure can cause the spring to mar the work and interfere with a free feed. Too little pressure will be apparent because the work will chatter excessively.

Check the table for correct alignment. At 0, the angle between it and a side of the blade should be 90°. If your machine has a tilt scale and a table-stop screw, adjust them, if necessary, after you have checked the angle between the blade and the table.

Blades

Many types and sizes of blades are available, but they all fall into one of two general categories. Those that must be gripped in both the upper and lower chuck are called "jeweler's blades." Others, heavy enough and wide enough so they can function while gripped in the lower chuck only, are called "sabre blades."

There is a little bit of overlap here because some of the jeweler's blades are heavy enough to work as sabre blades. The general rule is to use the heavier blades as the stock thickness increases. Choose the widest and the fastest cutting blade as long as it does the job for you. Think about sabre blades and the heavier jeweler's blades when the stock reaches maximum depth-of-cut thickness and, when you are working on large material that makes it necessary for you to remove the upper arm of the machine.

Quite often, it's possible to use discarded band-saw blades and still-sharp sections of used hacksaw blades. These must be cut off or "snapped" to a suitable length. When the width of such items doesn't permit mounting in the jigsaw as is, you can always grind down the ends to the chuck size of your jigsaw.

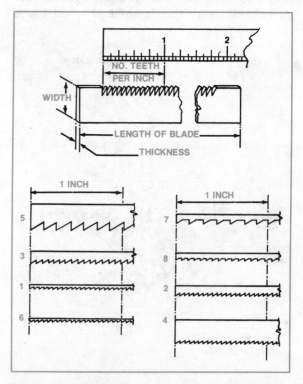

The eight examples of jigsaw blades represent a good assortment to have on hand. The numbers are defined in the chart — opposite page.

Blade	Blade Dimension			Operation				R.P.M.
	Thickness Inches	Width Inches	Teeth Per Inch	Stock Thickness (Inches)	Cut Radius	Kerf	Best For	
5	.028	.250	7	1/4 & up	large	coarse	soft & hard wood — pressed wood	745
3	.020	.110	15	1/8- 1/2 in metal, 1/8 & up in other material	medium	medium	metal — wood — bone — felt — paper	1175
1	.010	.040	18	1/16- 1/8	small	very fine	wood — bone — plastics	1600
6	.012	.023	20	up to 1/8	very small	fine	plastics — bone — fiber — comp. board	1050
7	.020	.070	7	up to 1/4	medium	medium	plastics — bone — hard rubber	1400
8	.010	.070	14	1/8- 1/2	medium	very fine	wood — plastics — bone — hard rubber	1525
2	.020	.110	20	1/16- 1/8	medium	medium	aluminum — copper — mild steel	940
4	.028	.250	20	3/32- 1/2 (1/4 max. in steel)	large	coarse	aluminum — copper — mild steel	830

Most jigsaws provide a device that permits you to "tension" the blade after it has been secured in the chucks. In most cases, it's merely a matter of pulling or pushing up on a cylinder that is part of the upper chuck assembly arm. It's even possible that the cylinder may be scaled for different blades. More tension is needed on fine blades than on heavy ones; however, producing too much tension will result in premature blade breakage. Probably the least tension that will do the job is the best to use. The operator's judgment is critical when deciding the degree of tension. You can easily be guided by well-defined indicators of poor tension adjustment. Cuts that are not square, blades breaking quickly, difficulty in following the cut line and obvious off-vertical movement of the blade when you are cutting clearly indicate the need for tension readjustment.

Basic Work Handling

Be relaxed and comfortable. Many jigsaw jobs take a long time to do, so as a strained position will tire you quickly and will affect the quality of your work. At most times, use the left hand as a guide to keep turning the work so the blade stays on the line; use the right hand to feed. However, there is so much twisting and turning involved with jigsawing that it is difficult to abide by one set rule.

Never crowd the blade, but on the other hand, do not be overly cautious. The teeth on the blade are there to cut, not to burnish. A steady, even feed that constantly produces sawdust is ideal. Don't force a wide blade to turn a corner that is too small for it. You'll end up burning the wood, breaking the blade and probably running off the line. Keep feed in a from-you-to-the-back-of-the-machine direction. It's the work you must keep turning, not the blade. Most jigsaw blades can be twisted when forced; and they will make cuts you never planned for, especially the finer, more flexible blades.

A good rule is to keep the side of the blade tangent to all curved lines. Worry about the teeth of the blade and the business of staying on the cut line.

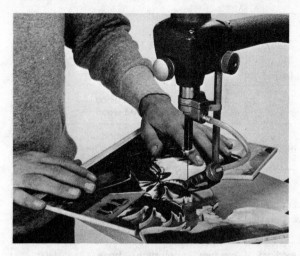

Good "normal" hand position is shown here. But, when cuts are as complicated as this, the operator's position as well as the hand position may be changed frequently.

If you feel that you are doing everything correctly and are still having difficulty making true cuts, check the relationship of the blade to the guides and the backup, as well as the degree of tension. If problems do occur, it will be mostly when you are doing intricate cutting with small jeweler's blades. The heavier blades will function in pretty good order even with some maladjustment. This is not the case with the others. However, because the jigsaw can negotiate extremely tight radii, the degree of backtracking and in-cutting possible is not nearly the same.

Patterns and Layout

A "pattern" can be simply an attractive picture that you snip from a magazine and cement to plywood. You can cut it out in profile to produce a silhouette-type project or you can cut in intricate, interlocking pieces to make a jigsaw puzzle.

When you work with an original design, you can draw it full-size on the wood or on a piece of paper that you then cement to the stock. The latter method destroys the pattern so if you need duplicates or wish to save the pattern for possible future use, transfer it to the wood by means of carbon paper. In the case of duplicate pieces, the first part you cut can be the template you use for marking other stock.

The transferring-by-squares method is still a fairly effective method when you have a ready-made pattern that you wish to transfer to wood, whether you wish to keep the same size of the original pattern, enlarge it or reduce it. What you do is mark off the pattern in squares of one size and mark off the work with same, larger or smaller squares. Then you just transfer the design square by square. This makes it easy to duplicate any design or pattern. If you make 1″ squares on the original and 2″ squares on the stock, you double the pattern size.

Sometimes, through planning and good layout, it's possible to cut small pieces from scrap so

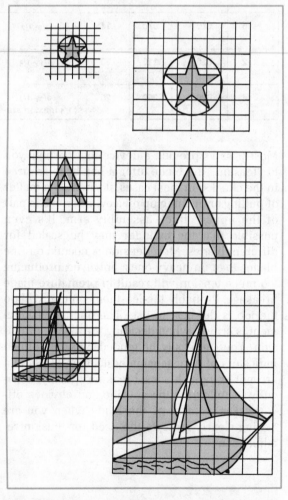

The enlarging-by-squares method is demonstrated here. Squares on the work are drawn 2x, 3x, etc., the size of the squares of the original. It can work the other way as well.

they may then be joined to form a large part. When you are cutting many parts from a single panel, it's wise to first make all the patterns you need and then lay them out on the panel. Thus, you can minimize waste and, more importantly, plan for a compatible grain direction on each of the pieces.

Piercing

It's possible to do piercing on a jigsaw because the blade is straight and secured at each end. Therefore, the blade may be passed through a hole in the work before it is secured in the chucks. This is intriguing because you can produce an internal design without a lead-in cut from an edge of stock. The common procedure is to loosen the blade from the upper chuck, pass it through the blade-insertion hole and then secure it in the upper chuck. Usual cutting procedures follow, but you do have to repeat the blade-insertion process for each cutout in the design.

When the cut is circular, the insertion hole may be drilled anywhere in the waste, but it does make sense to locate the insertion hole near the line simply because it reduces cutting time. Quite often, the insertion hole can be planned as part of the design; one example would be when you need a round corner. Choose a bit that will produce the radius you require and be accurate when you form the hole.

To cut a square corner, start from the insertion hole and approach the corner from one direction. Then backtrack to the hole and approach the corner from the second direction. Often, when you are using a fine blade, it's possible just to turn the corner. It will not be square; but when a tiny radius is not critical, this does not really matter.

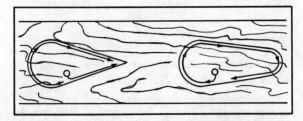

Typical feed direction on an example jigsaw job. Note that when the corner is acute, it is cleaned out by approaching from two directions. Follow the arrows.

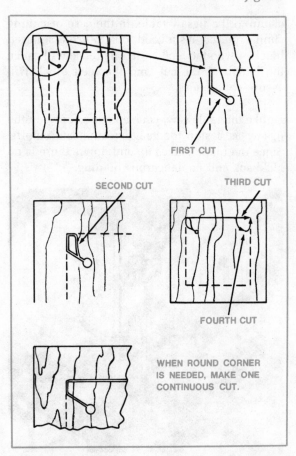

FIRST CUT

SECOND CUT

THIRD CUT

FOURTH CUT

WHEN ROUND CORNER IS NEEDED, MAKE ONE CONTINUOUS CUT.

A couple of ways to turn corners. The technique varies depending on whether the corner is square or round.

Wise jigsaw use calls for visualizing the shape and the cut before you start, if only to minimize the amount of cutting you must do to achieve a particular shape.

Choose blade sizes as you would for normal cutting: heavy blades for thick stock, smaller blades for thin material.

Straight Cuts

For most straight cuts, you will be working freehand, but there are occasions when setting up a guide can be useful. For example, when cutting squares for a checkerboard, doing slots or even cutting dowels to length, using a guide is most helpful.

The guide you use can be an improvised rip fence, simply a straight piece of wood that you clamp to the jigsaw table. In the case of cutting similar pieces, it's a good idea to use a squared block of wood to feed with. The fence will gauge the length of the cut, and the feed block will assure squareness.

Unlike the table saw, you can use a fence on the jigsaw as a stop for gauging duplicate cutoffs. Since the blade moves up and down, there is no kickback and no dangerous binding.

An improvised fence and a backup block is a good setup for doing work like this. Unlike the table saw, a fence can be used as a stop to gauge work length.

A fence is good to use when cutting slots, especially if you must do them in many pieces. When the slot has round ends, drill holes at each end of a common center line with the hole diameter matching the width of the slot. Insert the blade through one of the holes (as in piercing) and clamp the fence in place to guide the cut. After you have cut the first side, adjust the fence so you can cut the second side. If you require the same slot in many pieces, do the first-side cut in all of them before you adjust the fence.

If the slot has square ends, then you must do some freehand guiding after the slot sides are cut. Many craftsmen, when they require a lot of square-end slots, work as has been described for round-end slots; but they use a mortising chisel instead of a bit.

Remember that the jigsaw is not a speed tool. Feed slowly when using a fence and choose the heaviest blade that will produce the job you want. Guided cuts are tougher to do with the finer blades because they can twist so easily. When that happens, the blade simply moves off the line. Also, the work can move away from the guide. The answer is to use a good blade and a feed that permits the blade to cut without choking.

Pivot Cutting

You can cut accurate circles by using an auxiliary table that you clamp to the regular table. A nail that you drive through the auxiliary table acts as the pivot. It is very important for the pivot to be in line with the blade. The blades, because they are somewhat flexible, will tend to drift if you don't do a good job of locating the pivot point.

The extra table doesn't have to be more than a sheet of ¹/₄'' plywood or hardboard. Drill a hole through it so you can insert the jigsaw blade and, if you wish to use the same one for various size circles, drill a series of holes about ¹/₄'' apart on a common center line. Then you can insert the pivot through the hole that will give you the correct radius distance from the pivot to the blade.

A long nail as a pivot means you must drill a center hole through the work. If you wish to avoid this, just use a very short nail instead. Then you can simply press the work on it.

Thin blades, when used for pivot cutting, have more tendency to drift than heavy ones. If you must work with a thin blade, apply a bit more tension than you might normally do. In all cases, rotate the work slowly.

Bevel Cutting

Bevel cutting with a jigsaw enables you to form a deep bowl from a flat board.

If you jigsaw a disc in the center of a board, the disc will fall through. If you do the same thing but with the table tilted about 5°, the beveled disc will fall only part way through the beveled opening. The disc will jam like a stopper in a barrel.

If, instead of a single disc, you cut a series of concentric beveled rings, each would sink part way through the opening it was cut from; and you would end up with a cone shape. The more rings you cut, the deeper the cone will be.

When can this technique be used? Some of the things you can make include planters, raised

A blade insertion hole is required for each ring, drilled at the bevel angle used for the sawing.

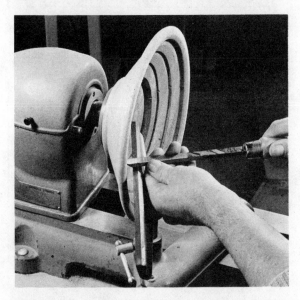

After the concentric rings are glued together in their projected position, the work can be face-plate mounted and turned. Thus a deep bowl can be made from a flat board.

bases, hollow hulls for boat models, trays with raised lips, signs with raised letters, panels with raised sections, drawer pulls cut directly from the drawer front and blanks for lathe-turning bowls, plates and trays. There are many possibilities to discover after you have tried the technique.

The shape you get depends on the contour of the sections, the wall thickness of the rings, the number you cut and the projection of each. For example, if you cut six concentric rings in a $3/4''$ board that is 6″ square, and each ring projects $1/2''$, you get a bowl shape that's 6″ across and $3^1/4''$ high. There is little point in trying to figure out beforehand just how much projection you'll get; it depends on the stock thickness, the table tilt and the kerf width. It's easier to make a trial cut in some scrap and then measure it.

The less table tilt you use, the greater the projection of each individual piece; the more pieces you cut, the greater the total projection. Using too little table tilt can add up to a difficult glue job when you assemble the rings. Try a table tilt of 2° to 5° in materials from $1/4''$ to $3/4''$ thick but don't use a blade that makes a heavy kerf. A blade that is .020″ thick by .110″ wide by 15 teeth to the inch works fairly well on the jigsaw. You can do this kind of thing on the band saw too. When working on that tool, choose a $1/8''$ or a $1/4''$ blade with a slight set.

These recommendations are just to get you started since there is no law that says you can't use heavier blades or lighter blades should they be compatible with the stock thickness.

When you cut, be sure to *always* keep the inside piece (the part that will project) on the same side of the blade. If you don't, you will change the bevel direction, and the parts will not fit.

Sabre Sawing

To do sabre sawing, grip a special sabre-saw blade or a very heavy jeweler's blade in the lower chuck only. You might wish to do this in the following two examples: when the work is heavy and tough and you feel a sabre blade will do the job best and when work size requires that

Sabre blades are held in the lower chuck only.

you remove the upper arm of the machine. In the latter situation, you have no choice since there is but one chuck to work with.

How you set up for sabre sawing depends on the machine you have. The chuck grip should be normal, but some tools have a special backup device for sabre-blade use. Check your owner's manual.

When doing pierced work in heavy stock where the use of a fine blade would be out of line, using a sabre blade can speed up the job because you don't have to go through the business of releasing from the upper chuck, inserting through the hole, resecuring in the upper chuck, etc. With the sabre blade you merely jump from one opening to another. The insertion holes are still required.

Don't force the work. Although the blades you use for this application are stiffer and heavier, they can still bend or twist. Feed so that the blade is doing the cutting at a speed it was designed for.

Inlay Work

The most common type of inlay work on the jigsaw is a kind of pad sawing. It calls for a selec-

tion of wood veneers that are fastened together between top and bottom boards with nails driven through the waste areas. The design you wish to inlay is drawn on the top board. Since all the veneers are cut at the same time by pad sawing, any piece cut out of one layer will fit the corresponding piece in another layer. The veneers must be selected for contrast both in color and in grain.

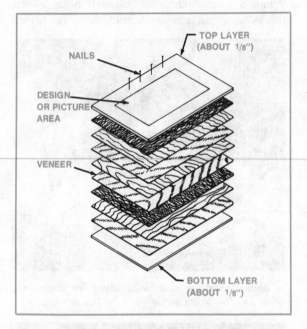

Pad sawing veneers provides the parts needed to do intricate and fascinating inlaid pictures. Any piece cut from one veneer will fit the corresponding hole in another.

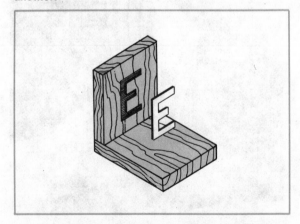

Intarsia is another type of inlay work. The design can be made on the jigsaw, rout or carve out of recess to fit it. Best to use the jigsawed design as a pattern for the recessing.

874

As the cutting proceeds, situate each separated piece on a flat board in the same position it occupied in the pad. This will eliminate having to search for and fit the pieces.

When the cutting is finished, the pieces are joined together by placing them on a sheet of gummed paper or something similar. The fully assembled picture is glued, paper side up, to a backup board. After the glue has dried, the paper is dampened with water and rubbed off. Then the exposed, inlaid picture is sanded and finished as desired. In most cases, a smooth, clear coating is used so the beauty of the veneers will not be hidden.

You can see that if the pad is made up of ten different sheets of veneer, you can actually get ten pictures. This is fine for wide-scale production, but a single-version selection of cut pieces should be made for the most promising results. This produces waste, but it is done for art's sake.

Another possibility is to work without making a pad. Then you cut each part of the picture from separate sheets of veneer. It can be done, but it calls for a lot more accuracy than you need when pad sawing. For all inlay work of this type, use a very fine blade. The kerf width must be minimal.

Cutting Sheet Metal

Metal cutting on the jigsaw is similar to cutting wood except you select a blade that is best for the material. Metal cutting blades are available in both jeweler's and sabre-blade types. It doesn't hurt to lubricate them with something like beeswax since this will help to make tight turns and reduce the possibility of breakage.

If you work directly on the regular table, you will find that burrs will accumulate as the blade cuts. This means a jagged edge and possible feed interference. Very thin material may actually bend because of the up-and-down blade action.

A simple way to get around all of this is to sandwich the sheet metal between pieces of scrap plywood. Another way is to use the auxiliary table shown for pivot cutting or to make a special table insert.

An easy way to get smooth edges on sheet metal cuts is to sandwich the work between pieces of scrap plywood. Tape will hold the pieces together.

Plastics

Certain plastics (phenolics) can be sawed easily with results about what you might expect from a hardwood.

When working with materials like plastics, use a coarser blade than you would normally and work at a slower speed. Speed and narrow kerfs combine to create enough heat to melt the plastic.

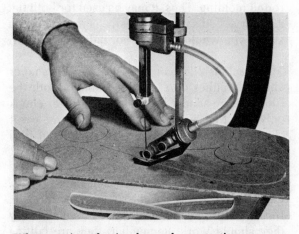

When cutting plastics, leave the protective paper on until after the cutting is done. Ordinary wood-cutting blades will work, however, a skip-tooth design is better.

Jigsaw

Although woodworking blades may be used, it's wiser to use a skip-tooth design. The spaces between the teeth help clear away the chips, and this helps to avoid overheating the work. Some plastics are soft enough so they actually weld directly behind the blade and cause it to bind.

Since most plastic you will use comes with a protective layer of paper, you have a ready-made surface for marking lines and designs. It's wise not to remove the paper until all the cutting has been done.

Pad Sawing Paper

You can saw paper cutouts easily if you sandwich the sheets of paper tightly between pieces of 1/8" or 1/4" plywood. The idea is to end up for cutting with what is the equivalent of a single, solid block. The tighter the pad, the better the results will be.

Use a blade that will take the turns you must do but try to work with one that is not too coarse. The other extreme is a blade so fine that the paper particles clog it quickly. This can result in burning the work. Properly done, paper cut in this fashion will have remarkably smooth edges.

Filing and Sanding

Special accessories are available for both filing and sanding. The standard sanding attachment has a semicircular shape like a piece of half-round molding. Thus, it may be used for both flat and curved edges. The abrasive is the same as a sleeve you would use on a normal drum sander.

The machine files come in a variety of shapes and with either a 1/8" or a 1/4" shank. Both the files and the sander are held in the lower chuck only. Most jigsaws provide a block in the lower chuck that has a V-cut in it. The shanks of files and sanders should be gripped in the "V."

Do these abrasive operations at slow speeds. Fast speeds will glaze the paper very quickly; files will simply scrape, which is not the way they should work. Remember, they are cutting tools. In general, you can use a higher speed as the abrasive gets coarser. In most cases, it's wise to make a special insert for the tool you are using

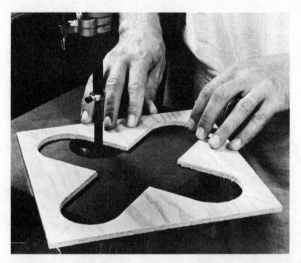

This sanding stick was made by mounting an emery board on a stiff metal backing. Shape at each end for gripping in the chucks. Files also can be used, held in the chuck V-block.

to minimize the opening around the cutter. This is especially important when you are filing or sanding very small pieces. With large work, it's often possible to work without any insert at all.

Don't jam the work against the abrasive. Since you work without a holddown, it's easy for the tool to lift the work from the table. Besides, trying to speed up the operation by forcing will gain you nothing. A gentle feed with fingers holding

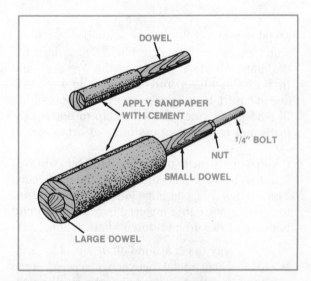

Make an assortment of "sanding drums", each with a center hole. Then, any one of them can be mounted on an arbor made by using a 1/4" bolt and nut.

the work down on the table is best. The feed should be just strong enough to keep the abrasive cutting.

There are various ways you can improvise filing and sanding attachments. Some craftsmen make use of broken files by grinding a shank on one end. It's even possible to use "needle" files. But do be careful since these can snap easily, and most of them have sharp points. A sanding attachment can be just a length of dowel with abrasive paper glued on it. One handy gadget is made from an emery stick. This item and a back-up piece of stiff sheet metal are cut to jigsaw-blade length and shaped at each end to fit the chucks. The unit is then gripped like a jigsaw blade.

If you check the standard, small drum sanders, you will find that many of them can be used in the jigsaw even though they are intended for use in a drill press or portable drill. Remember, however — and this is true of filing and sanding generally — production speed on the jigsaw will be slower.   *SEE ALSO BAND SAW; BENCH GRINDER; DRILL PRESS; JOINTER; LATHE; RADIAL ARM SAW; SHAPER; STATIONARY BELT & DISC SANDER; TABLE SAW.*

Jimmy Bar

A jimmy bar (sometimes referred to as a lining-up bar) is designed for close-quarter prying, nail pulling and aligning jobs. The average length of this bar is 16 inches. A jimmy bar is very useful in metal work because one end has a long slim taper for lining up bolt and rivet holes. *SEE ALSO HAND TOOLS.*

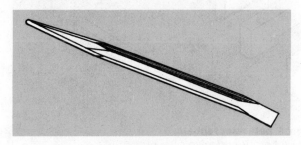

Jimmy Bar

Joining Sleeve

As a fiber pipe fitting, a joining sleeve connects lengths of fiber pipe. Since it is longer than a slip

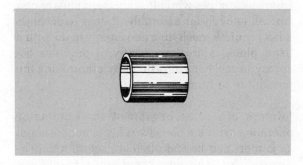

Joining Sleeve

coupling, this fitting is used to accommodate the tapered ends of fiber pipe. Since the principle of friction unites the elements of coal tar in the pipe to the fitting, the pipe is driven into the ends of the joining sleeve. *SEE ALSO PIPE FITTINGS.*

Joint Clamps

Joint clamps, which include the elbow, T's, reducer and adapter, are plastic pipe fittings. Usually made of metal, they slip on the ends of plastic pipe. While all but the adapter fit plastic to plastic, it fits plastic to metal. *SEE ALSO PIPE FITTINGS.*

Joint Clamp

Jointer

The jointer is a powered planer designed to remove a predetermined amount of material from stock edges while leaving them square and smooth enough for assembly. It does in seconds what requires much time and energy to do with a hand plane. More importantly, it provides accuracy in mechanical fashion by minimizing the possibility of human error.

Jointers are often organized for one-motor operation with a table saw. This is not essential as jointers can be and often are set up independently, but the combination affair does demonstrate the basic jointer function of smoothing edges after sizing cuts on the saw. The work pieces are overcut an amount to match the depth-of-cut setting on the jointer.

A jointer can be used for light surfacing operations, but this function does not put it in the "thickness planer" category. A jointer which removes thick amounts of material is a much heavier machine with features that include

A 4″ jointer is a more typical home workshop tool simply because it is cheaper. Depth-of-cut is ³/₈″, still pretty good for rabbeting work. Outfeed table is fixed; fence has a full tilt-range. Overall capacities are not impractical for general work that would be done by the home woodworker.

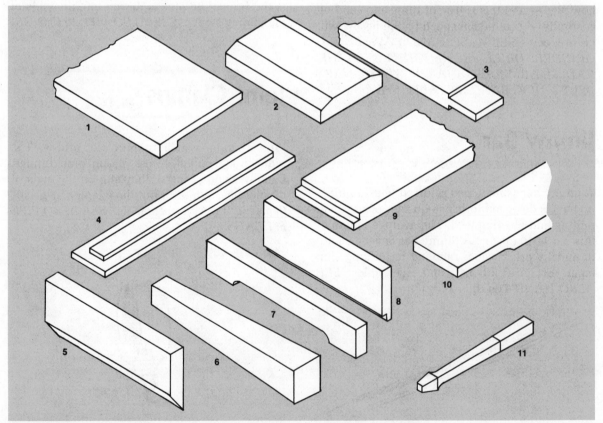

Typical jointer cuts: 1. wide rabbet; 2. chamfer; 3. stud tenon; 4. perimeter rabbets (raising); 5. bevel; 6. taper; 7. recess; 8. edge rabbet; 9. end rabbet; 10. surfacing (planing); 11. leg shapes

automatic feed, greater capacity, and a pretty good guarantee that, depending on your craftsmanship, the opposite surfaces of the work will be parallel after the cut.

A jointer will also do a variety of other operations well. It's more than a planer and, if used correctly, will do a fine job of forming rabbets and tenons, tapers, bevels and many other practical chores.

Parts of a Jointer

A three-knife cutterhead rotates between infeed and outfeed tables. The infeed table is adjustable to determine the amount of material you wish to remove. The outfeed table may or may not be fixed, which is a design feature that doesn't have too much effect on the range of the work you can do with this tool.

It's best for the infeed table to have a healthy rabbeting ledge, a positive depth-of-cut adjustment and a lock to hold the setting. The fence is usually a heavy affair that is adjustable angularly and laterally to the horizontal plane of the tables.

All jointers have spring-loaded guards designed to move aside during the pass and to come back quickly to cover the cutterhead after the cut. The guards are designed to be used. Doing without them is a poor excuse for taking big chances. Use all guards available.

Adjustment Factors

The horizontal plane of the outfeed table must be tangent to the cutting circle of the knives. All jointers provide for accomplishing and maintaining this critical relationship. To check, set a straightedge on the outfeed table so it juts out over the cutterhead and then rotate the cutterhead by hand. Each knife should just barely scrape the straightedge. If the straightedge is lifted or it the knife doesn't touch at all, adjustment is required.

When this chore is accomplished, set the infeed table to match the plane of the outfeed table and adjust the depth gauge to read "0."

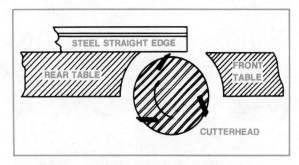

A straightedge, placed on the outfeed table, must be tangent to the cutting circle of the knives. This is essential for good jointer operation. Depending on the design of the machine, you adjust the table to the knives or the knives to the table.

Normal fence position (with quadrant reading "0") forms a 90° angle with the tables. If the fence is not in this exact position, you cannot consistently joint edges that are square to adjacent surfaces. Most jointers provide stops for common fence-tilt settings. Set these carefully so that correct angles are provided.

Edge Jointing

The general rule is to make all jointing cuts so the knives are cutting with the grain of the wood. It isn't always possible to follow this rule, but it does produce the most satisfactory results and also reduces the danger of kickback and splintering. When you work against the grain or across it, reduce feed speed to a minimum and keep cuts very light.

On normal work, depth-of-cut settings should not exceed $1/8''$. A $1/16''$, even a $1/32''$, setting is better if it gets the job done since it requires less power and wastes less wood. Often, on hardwoods or on large pieces, the job is done best by making a couple of light passes as opposed to a single heavy one. This is especially true with against-the-grain cuts and surfacing operations.

The jointing pass should be a smooth action from start to finish. Place the work edge firmly down on the infeed table with the adjacent surface snug against the fence. Use your left hand to maintain this work position and your right hand to feed. Move the work at reasonable speed and don't stop until you are well clear of the cutterhead. Such advice is sound only because it

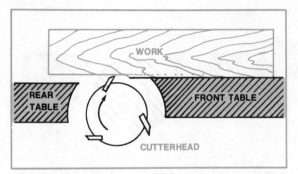

When the rear table is too low, the work will drop and be gouged.

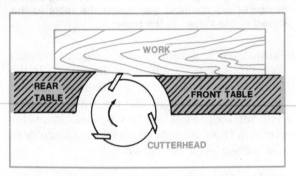

When it is too high, passing smoothly over the knives will be difficult.

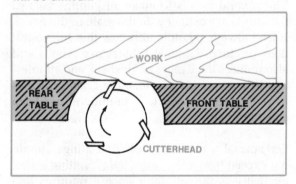

When rear table and knives are in correct alignment, work passes smoothly over the cutterhead and rests securely on the tables before and after the cut.

establishes a jump-off point. Work size, hardness of the wood, and the operation itself will also bear on how you hold the work and how fast you should feed.

Some operators feel the hands should never pass over the cutterhead. But if the guard is there and you are as alert as you should always be, this point isn't always valid unless the work size brings your hands too close to the cutters.

During jointer cuts, hand position should be such that the work is held firmly down on the tables and snug against the fence through the pass. Good idea to keep hands on top and back edges of the wood.

Jointing End Grain

If you do such jobs in one continuous pass, it's inevitable that the knives will split off a portion of wood at the very end of the pass. To avoid this problem, use a double-pass technique. Advance the work over the cutterhead only enough to joint an inch or two. Then lift the work, reverse its position and complete the job with a second pass. With plywood, judge the grain direction of the surface veneer as if you were working with solid stock.

When jointing four edges on a piece of work, do the end-grain cuts first in single passes. The

By trying to do the job in one pass, tearing will result at the end of the cut. This applies to cross-grain cuts on solid stock and to plywood.

third and fourth passes, made with the grain, will remove the imperfections left by the first two cuts. This method does not apply to plywood. On such material always use the double-pass method.

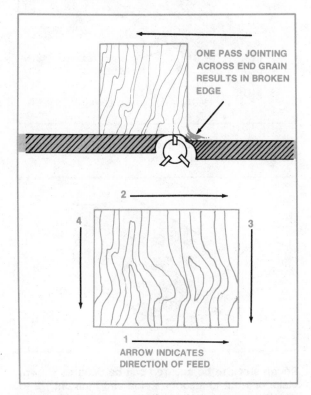

When jointing four edges, use a pass sequence as shown by the numbers. Cuts 3 and 4 will remove the imperfections at the ends of cuts 1 and 2.

Surfacing

Surfacing is almost the same as making a jointing pass except that the work is placed flat rather than on edge. Keep depth of cut to a minimum and use a very slow feed. It's very important to maintain uniform contact with the tables throughout the pass to avoid tapered cuts, gouges, and generally unsatisfactory results. In most cases, it's a good idea to work with a pusher-holddown tool.

Such an accessory, which you can make yourself, does more than help to do a good job. It provides a good degree of safety, especially when working with stock that could bring your hands too close to the knives.

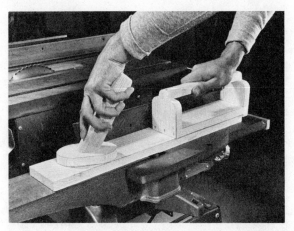

A fine way to organize for good pusher-holddown action on long stock is to make both the tools shown here.

Often, it's possible to do a surfacing cut with just one hand on a pusher-holddown tool. At other times it may be necessary to use your left hand to hold down the front edge of the stock while your right hand guides the holddown device at the rear. The whole matter is mostly a question of adjusting your position in relation to the length of the stock to make sure that the workpiece's contact with the table is continuous throughout the pass.

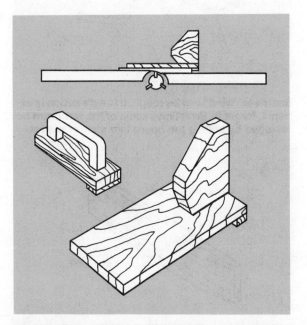

Construction details of a few basic pusher-holddowns. They should be a minimum of 12″ long by 4″ wide. The back ledge should be 1/4″ thick.

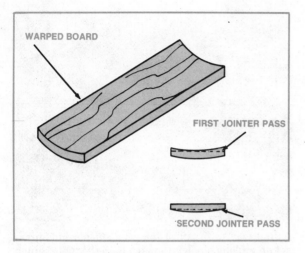

It is possible to do both sides on the jointer but guard against rocking when working on the convex surface.

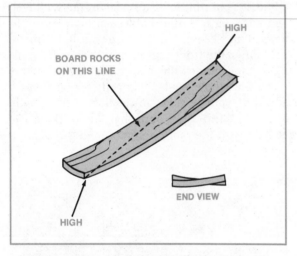

Boards in "wind" can be rough. If the distortion is extreme, forget it! Sometimes some of the wood can be salvaged by cutting the board into shorter pieces.

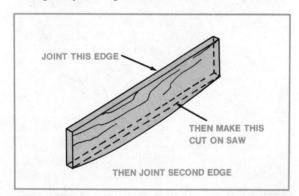

Work sequence when the stock is distorted on one edge only.

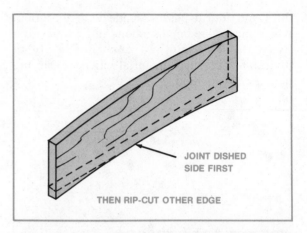

Stock that is distorted like this should be jointed on the dished side first.

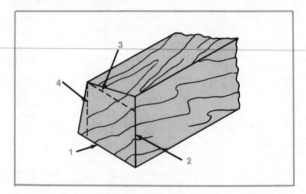

Rough stock to be squared can be done as shown. Make one cut to smooth a side and then cut #2 to smooth and square the adjacent edge. Make cuts 3 and 4 on the saw a bit oversize and then return to the jointer to smooth them.

Distorted Stock

"Dished" (hollowed or rounded inward) stock, even in some extreme cases, can be jointed if you work on the dished side first, making as many passes as you need to create a straight edge. If the opposite edge is also distorted, you can then do a rip cut to straighten that edge and end up with a second jointer pass.

Extra care is required if you are going to joint a curved edge since you'll have little bearing surface on the first pass or two. After these are accomplished, the job gets easier.

This kind of situation should be avoided, for example, on stock that has one straight edge. It would be better to use the one straight edge to ride the rip fence on a table saw to remove the distortion. Then you can do the jointer cuts.

Warped boards are dished across the width. With most jobs, the high points provide a pretty good bearing surface for the initial passes if you work with the concave side down. If the warp is uneven, set the board so it bears on the three highest points and keep it so placed through all the passes needed to remove the flaw.

The convex side is more difficult to do since you must be concerned with keeping surfaced side parallel to the tables if the board is to end up with parallel surfaces. In fact, it's usually wiser to use a table saw to remove the convex side after you have jointed away the concave side.

Boards in "wind," which is a full-length twist, are a different case. A very small amount of such material can be handled successfully if you work as you do with a simple warp. In extreme cases, don't even attempt it. Or, if you want to salvage as much as you can, cut the board into shorter lengths and see what you can then accomplish.

Rabbets and Tenons

The jointer is an excellent rabbeting machine as long as its maximum depth of cut is sufficient for your needs. Since most home workshop jointers will cut 1/2'' deep and the thickness of the wood you will be working with most often is 1'' or under, there really isn't much of a restriction here.

To organize for a rabbet, lock the fence from the front edge of the knives a distance equal to the rabbet-cut width. Set the infeed table to the rabbet depth. Place the work on the infeed table, snug against the fence, and advance over the knives as you would for any other job. When you need a deep cut on tough wood, it's wiser to make a couple of passes, adjusting for more depth of cut after each pass.

To create a tenon or a tongue, flip the stock and repeat the procedure. Such cuts on the end of stock are a little more difficult because you are working across the grain. It may be necessary to make the cuts more shallow and to reduce the

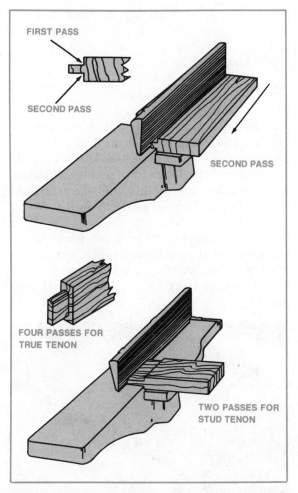

Fashion tongues or tenons simply by making matching cuts on opposite edges. The tenon passes are harder to do because there isn't much stock bearing against the fence. It's a good idea on such jobs to use a pusher-hold-down.

rate of feed, not only to make the cut smoother but to reduce the feathering and splintering that can occur at the end of the cut.

It's good practice to work with stock that has an overwidth of about 1/16''. Then, after the cross-grain rabbet or tenon cut, you can do a jointer pass to remove any imperfection.

In most situations where rabbets and tenons are cut across stock ends, it's a good idea to use a pusher-holddown device to do the feeding. Remember, too, on such jobs it's not possible to use the guard so you have an exposed cutterhead until the work itself covers the gap. Keep your hands well away from that area and be extra alert.

Cylinder Work

Rabbeting

Cutting a rabbet in a cylinder is entirely possible, but the initial problem that will be encountered shouldn't be minimized. You must hold the work firmly enough to guide it past the knives until the flat surface that is formed by the cut rests solidly on the outfeed table. At this point, the procedure is no different than the same job on flat stock.

Don't do this kind of cut on small dowels or on any piece too short to be held safely. Should you need to shape a short piece in such a manner, do it on the end of a long piece and then cut off what you require.

It is okay to rabbet a cylinder so long as you realize that the operator is the only control until there is enough flat to ride the outfeed table. Don't do this on pieces too small to handle safely.

Tenoning

The jointer can form tenons on cylinders and will guarantee similarity when the same shape is required on multiple pieces. The basic idea is to be able to rotate the stock against the direction of rotation of the cutterhead. The jointer fence may be used as a stop to gauge the length of the tenon, or you can use an L-shaped guide.

If the jointer knives are shaped at the ends to cut, as they are along the normal cutting edge, rest the work on the rabbeting ledge and go directly

forward to start the cut. If the knives are not so shaped, brace the work against the guide above the cutting circle and lower it slowly to make contact. Then, rotate the work to form the tenon.

An L-shaped guide block clamped to the infeed table positions the work for forming tenons on round stock. Guide position and depth-of-cut setting determine tenon diameter. Fence position determines its length. Turn work very slowly, keep hands clear of the knives.

Chamfers and Bevels

A chamfer and a bevel are similar and are made in much the same way. The chamfer does not remove the entire edge of the stock.

Bevels or chamfers are accomplished by tilting the fence to the angle desired. A closed angle is best since it creates a nook for the work. Even so, a clamped guide block keeps the work in correct position.

The best way to work is to tilt the fence so it forms a closed angle with the tables. This provides a tight nook to snug the work and keep it steady during the pass. If you work with the fence tilted in the opposite direction, be very careful to keep the work from sliding out from under you. Chamfers can often be accomplished in a single pass. Bevels usually require repeat passes.

V-Block Work

For a large percentage of routine shop work, the V-block jig provides greater convenience and more accuracy when you have to do the same job on many pieces.

The jig is a V-block with an offset that matches the tool's maximum depth of cut. It has its own fence, but this is just a means of attachment to the regular jointer fence. Attaching this and similar items to the jointer should not be a problem since all jointers usually have holes through the fence for just such purposes.

On maximum cuts, the forward end of the jig rests solidly on the outfeed table, but this changes as you reduce the cut. Therefore, don't bear down too heavily as you pass the knives. It's also possible to use a wooden shim between the jig and the table.

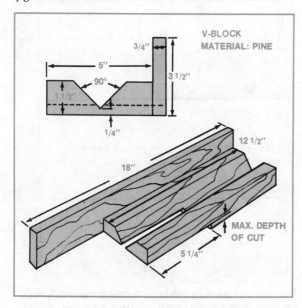

Construction details of the V-jig.

This jig can be used to create a flat on a cylinder, but don't use it for the same purpose on small dowels or on any piece that is too small to be held safely.

Octagonal Shapes

Making octagonal shapes with a jointer is a question of making similar bevel cuts on all four edges of a piece of stock that has been accurately squared. Set the fence at 45° and make the pass on each edge. Repeat passes are often required before the job can be considered finished.

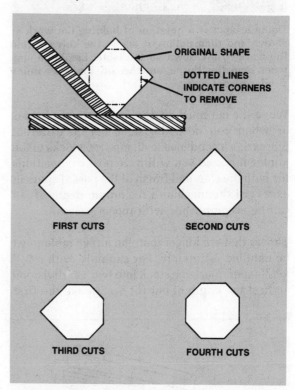

Working without the V-jig you can accomplish octagons on any piece regardless of size because now you can do repeat passes.

Tapering

You can do a simple taper by setting the infeed table to the depth of cut you want and then positioning the work so the starting point of the taper rests on the forward edge of the outfeed table. For a 12 inch x 3/8 inch taper, mark the work 12 inches in from one end and set the infeed table for the 3/8 inch cut. Rest the work as described, pull it toward you and you will achieve the taper.

Jointer

Doing a taper is a 'question of holding the work as shown and then pulling it across the knives. Hold the work firmly down on the table. Employ a stop when repeating the cut on other sides or when doing similar pieces.

When the cut must be duplicated on other sides or when you need the same cut on different pieces, it's a good idea to clamp stop blocks to the jointer fence so you will have positive positions for both the start and finish of the pass. Tapers in excess of the machine's maximum depth of cut can be accomplished with repeat passes.

Tapers that are longer than the infeed table must be handled differently. For example, with a 24″ x ³/₈″ taper, mark the stock into two 12″ divisions and set the depth of cut for ³/₆₄″. Make the first

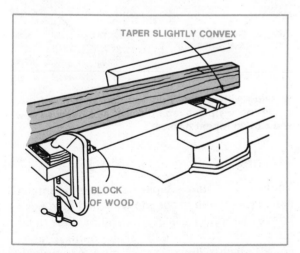

A block of wood can be used as shown when doing short end-tapers. The cut will be slightly convex. To eliminate the convex factor, tack-nail the height block to the work instead of clamping it to the table.

pass from the first 12″ mark and a second 12″ mark, and you will have the required taper.

Approximately the same procedures apply when you wish to limit the length of the taper while confining it to some midpoint. The idea is simply to clamp stop blocks to the fence on both infeed and outfeed sides of the cutterhead. These control the start and finish of the cut.

Variations of these techniques can be utilized extensively to produce legs, rails and similar parts for chairs, tables and such projects, or merely to add a design element to a component for any project.

Recessing

The recessing cut is often referred to as a "stopped chamfer." It's often seen on base mem-

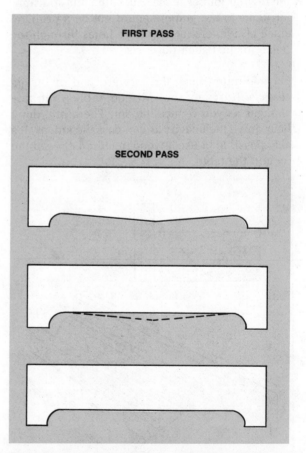

The second pass is made by turning the stock end-for-end. The center point (dotted line) can be removed or left as a decorative detail.

bers and bottoms of table and stand legs. When you have a jointer with a fixed outfeed table, the cut is made in two passes with stop blocks on the fence to gauge pass length. This still leaves a raised area in the center of the cut since all you've done is form opposite tapers. You can leave it, since it's quite decorative in itself, or remove it by cutting on another tool.

When the outfeed table is adjustable, you can do the cut in one pass merely by lowering both tables an equal amount. Whether you make the cut in one pass or two, you can't cut any deeper than the maximum setting of the jointer.

Coving

If you accept depth-of-cut limitations, you can do some respectable coving work on a jointer. The process involves passing work diagonally across the knives so the knife end produces the cove arc. When the knife ends are not shaped to cut, the work must be moved toward the end of the knife rather than into the end of the knives. When the knife ends are shaped to cut, then you can move work directly across them, parallel to the cutterhead, and get a cove cut.

Remember that the cove arc is limited by the tool's maximum setting. Because of this, you should not plan to produce an item such as a wooden rain gutter. However, the jointer as a coving tool can be utilized for moldings or molding details, for panel-edge shapes or for stock reduction that ends in a curve rather than a square corner.

The Pivot Jig

With the pivot jig, you can rotate stock as the knives cut and produce a perfect disc with a fine, ready-to-use edge. This jig provides a means of positioning work so it can be turned on a vertical plane. The center line of the pivot should be just forward of the center line of the cutterhead. There is a small arc of the cutting circle that can be used here, but it doesn't impose any critical limitation on depth of cut. Actually, if you wish to be a bit more flexible in the setup of the jig, you can slot the holes through which you bolt the jig to the jointer fence.

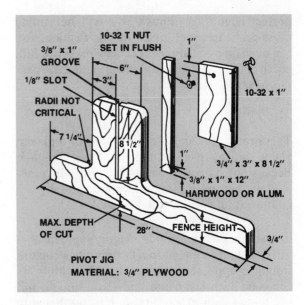

The pivot jig is a means of holding and turning work on a vertical plane. You can reduce the length of the jig if necessary but don't reduce its height. The pivot point is a heavy roofing nail.

To work with the pivot jig, mount the rough cut work on the pivot but clear of the knives. Hold the work firmly and lower it slowly to make contact. Then, turn the screw that locks the slide and rotate the work very slowly against the direction of rotation of the cutterhead. A slow, firm feed with a reasonable depth of cut will give you a

Rough-cut work is mounted on the pivot and then slowly turned against the direction-of-rotation of the cutterhead. For precise duplicates, make a mark on the slide after forming the first piece. Use the guard even though it isn't shown here.

perfect edge even though you will be cutting cross-grain in some areas. In this fashion, you can even do circular recess cuts by making a full-circle cut the first time and then limiting the pass the second time.

The Uniplane

This brand new tool is not a jointer or a planer, yet it can do many of the functions of either. Because of its cost (over $400.00), it will probably not become a common workshop tool, yet it is interesting enough to take a look at.

In essence, the uniplane is a highly sophisticated rotary planer mounted in a heavy-duty structure similar in appearance to a jointer. The cutting action is on a vertical plane, and it's so smooth and fast (better than 30,000 cuts per minute) that very little pressure is required to feed the work or keep the work in contact with the fence. There is no tendency for the work to be lifted or kicked back.

To use the machine correctly, you must make a pass that takes the work completely across the cutterhead area. Of the eight cutters in the head, four project .002 inches farther than the others. They are the "finishers" and do their job on the "up" side of the disc. The uniplane really makes a double cut, one when you enter the cut zone and a shave touch when you leave it.

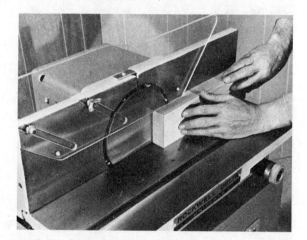

Uniplane's eight cutters revolve around outer rim of the visible disc. Machine cuts smoothly across end grain, produces perfectly smooth miters, chamfers and bevels.

Maximum depth of cut is only $1/8$ inch, but you will be more impressed by how little you can remove. Shavings off $1/64$ inch is a routine chore. Grain direction, in relation to the pass, has no effect on the finish you get as the finish will always be smooth. *SEE ALSO BAND SAW; BENCH GRINDER; DRILL PRESS; JIGSAW; LATHE; RADIAL ARM SAW; SHAPER; STATIONARY BELT & DISC SANDER; TABLE SAW.*

Joint Knife

A joint or broad knife is a short tool with a blunt edge which is used for plastering areas in walls and ceilings, scraping lumps off and spackling. This tool is similar to a putty knife, but normally is larger since it is used for bigger jobs. When purchasing a joint knife, select one made of a fine grade of steel.

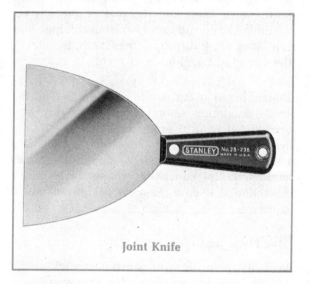

Joint Knife

Joints
[SEE FURNITURE MAKING; WOOD JOINTS.]

Joints, Cast Iron Pipe
[SEE PIPE JOINTS.]

Joints, Copper Pipe
[SEE COPPER PIPE & TUBING.]

Joints, Plumbing
[SEE PIPE JOINTS.]

Joist

A joist is a large timber used in frame construction to support floor and ceiling loads. The joists are laid horizontally in a parallel series, and are supported by girders, bearing walls or larger beams. Joists range from two to four inches in thickness, and width measurement for joists start at six inches. SEE ALSO FLOOR CONSTRUCTION.

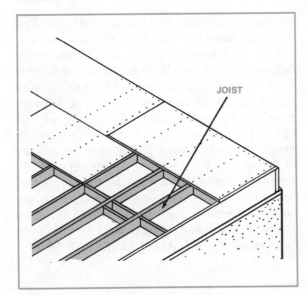

Joist Hanger

A joist hanger is a metal bracket used to fit on a beam and give support to the joist. SEE ALSO FLOOR CONSTRUCTION.

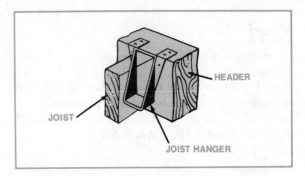

Joist Hanger

Junction Box

A junction box is a type of outlet box used to enclose splices or T connections in cable and as a mounting for some light fixtures. Junction boxes are octagonal (or square with flat corners) with an assortment of cover plates so that they can also be used as receptacle or fixture boxes. Most boxes are made of steel with "knockouts" in their sides and back to admit wires, conduit and nonmetallic or armored cable. Many junction boxes have built-in clamps for cable; if not, connectors fasten cable or conduit to the box.

Available in 4" and 3¼" sizes, the larger junction box is used most because it holds more wires without crowding. Junction boxes should always be placed in permanently accessible locations to permit easy entry to wire connections. SEE ALSO SWITCHES & OUTLETS.

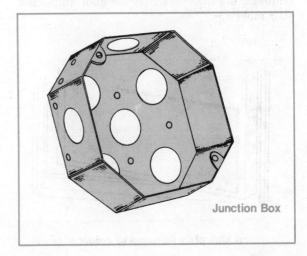

Junction Box

Kerf

A kerf is the cut made by a saw. Kerf also refers to cutting slits or notches on the underside of a piece of wood to permit bending. *SEE ALSO RADIAL ARM SAW; TABLE SAW.*

Keyhole Saw

[SEE COMPASS & KEYHOLE SAW.]

Key Wrench

Key wrench is another name for an Allen or setscrew wrench, which is used for adjusting headless setscrews. It is usually available in a set containing a size for every size setscrew. *SEE ALSO HAND TOOLS.*

Kick Plate

A kick plate is a metal or plastic shield fastened to the lower area on a door or stairs to protect against scuffing. The plate should be beveled on three sides and two inches narrower than the width of the door to allow for door stops and stair moldings.

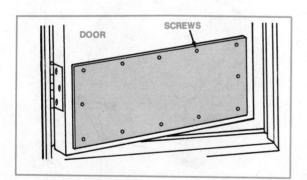

A kick plate fastened to a door.

Kiln Dried

Wood that has been exposed to artificial heat and controlled humidity to reduce its moisture content is said to be kiln dried.

Wood contains microscopic cells with hollow centers containing moisture. As a tree is growing, it retains water in and around these cells. When a tree is cut for lumber, this water is found in the cavities of all the wood fibers. Referred to as "free water" and "bound water," the moisture content can make up as much as a 100 to 200 percent ratio of kiln dried wood to green wood. In fact, a piece of lumber such as a 1 x 12 x 20 inch piece of redwood might contain 70 pounds, or 8.4 gallons, of water. *SEE ALSO LUMBER.*

Kilowatt Hours

Kilowatt hours indicate the amount of power that has been used by electrical fixtures and appliances in a house during a specific time, such as from month to month. Because a kilowatt hour is a larger and more convenient form of measuring electricity than a watt hour (one kilowatt hour equals 1,000 watt hours), the use of electricity is calculated and paid for in kilowatt hours. To figure kilowatt hours, take the wattage of the appliance being used, for instance a 1,000 watt iron, multiply the watts by the number of hours the item is used and that will equal the kilowatt hours. If the iron was used for four hours, it consumed 4,000 watt hours or four kilowatt hours. *SEE ALSO ELECTRICITY.*

Kitchen Design & Planning

Planning the kitchen, its relation to the outdoors as well as to other rooms of the house, and equipping it satisfactorily are a matter of each family's needs, habits and budget. Wall cabinets, sink and heavy mechanical appliances are permanent, expensive and difficult to change. Therefore, each kitchen should be arranged by arriving at the essentials.

To determine the type kitchen best suited for an individual family the following considerations should be kept in mind.

Does the family need a large kitchen with space for dining or is a small efficiency kitchen with dining elsewhere preferred?

Consider the plan. An open kitchen without a partition or door permits the kitchen workers to be a part of guest conversation, but it also transmits odors and steam and gives a view of cooking clutter.

If there will be a need for outdoor dining, the kitchen should have access to an outdoor deck or porch, or a pass-through for serving food. The view should also be considered as well as the climate. A kitchen on the east is cheerful in the morning, cool in the afternoon. A kitchen on the west is cheerful in winter, but can be uncomfortably warm in summer.

Family job schedules must be considered. Night workers and teenage activities call for meals at odd hours around the clock. Will it be necessary to include a large freezer to store ready-to-heat meals or a microwave oven which thaws and cooks food in a few minutes?

Entertainment preferences are important. Such factors as the amount of entertainment, the type, whether informal buffet or sit-down formal dinners and the number of guests will have a bearing on the type of kitchen that is planned.

The family will need to decide which major appliances must be worked into the kitchen plan and the new appliances to be added. An allowance must be made for the number of utensils and dishes as well as their storage.

The number of people who normally work in the kitchen must be provided for. Part-time help, a

cook, a catering service, relatives and child assistants are all factors in the design of traffic flow, storage and working areas.

BASIC KITCHEN PLANS

The next step is to choose one of the following basic arrangements and adapt it to fit the requirements you have listed above. Most kitchen plans fall into one of the five following arrangements:

One-Wall or One-Counter Kitchen

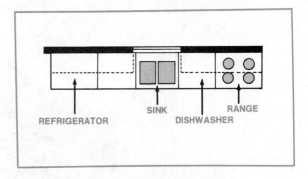

REFRIGERATOR   SINK DISHWASHER RANGE

One-wall kitchen, adaptable to a small home, cabin or apartment.

The one-wall or one counter kitchen, usually found in a house with limited space, works best for a small family. If your kitchen is in an apartment, condominium, cabin or retirement home, this is an ideal arrangement; however, once the length reaches three times the width, the plan is not feasible. It turns into a tunnel effect and requires too many steps for the cook. Planning a one-wall kitchen requires utilization of every inch of space. The sink should be located between the stove and refrigerator and counter space should be provided next to each appliance.

Household traffic must be routed around and away from a strip kitchen or work will be impossible. A pantry or broom closet will provide additional storage space. Linens, silver and china are stored in the dining area.

The addition of a piano-hinged table that folds up and out of the way provides informal dining. The table leg is hinged at the top to become a decorative wall sculpture when the leg is closed.

Build a piano-hinged table to fold into the wall of a cramped kitchen.

Corridor or Two-Wall Kitchen

The corridor or two-wall kitchen is a double version of the one-wall kitchen. The most efficient arrangement is to place the range and oven on one side and the sink and refrigerator on the opposite wall. This corridor kitchen is an excellent stepsaver, takes up little floor space and is easy to clean because of its simplicity. To prevent a household traffic problem try not to have a door at one end. Instead, add a pantry or utility closet at that end. Five feet of width between the two opposing counters are necessary for efficient working space.

U-Shaped Kitchen

The U-Shaped kitchen is an expanded version of the corridor kitchen which allows no thru-traffic, provides plenty of room for storage cabinets and the U-end permits a passthrough for food service to an outdoor dining area or to a family room. The two cabinet areas at the U-end which are formed by the right angles of the

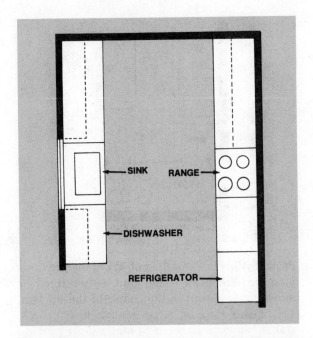

Galley, or corridor, kitchen arranged along two walls in a long narrow space.

Courtesy of the Masonite Corporation

The work counter also serves as room divider and buffet. Country kitchen decorating, copper hood over the range and old fashioned plate rack above the cabinets give an informal look complemented by plastic-finished panels which look like real wood. They clean easily and never need refinishing.

A ten-foot width at the base of the U is necessary to permit an efficient work triangle between appliances. A width larger than this usually results in the placement of chairs and a table in the center of the kitchen, thereby increasing steps around them for the worker and impeding the flow of traffic.

L-Shaped Kitchen

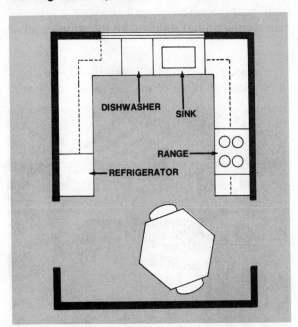

Well-arranged U-Shaped kitchen closed on three sides, providing a large amount of storage and counter area.

counters can be turned into usable storage space by installing revolving shelves in the under counter cabinets. The best place for the sink is at the end of the U.

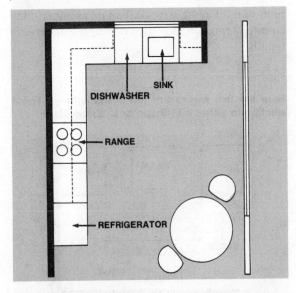

L-Shaped kitchen uses two walls with space for dining opposite work area.

Photo Courtesy: Courtesy of Masonite Corporation

Setting the sink at an angle in this small kitchen provides more work space. The plastic-finished mural, resistant to heat and moisture, substitutes for a window on this inside wall. It can be damp-wiped clean and installed over any solid backing with wallboard adhesive.

An L-Shaped plan places appliances and counters on two adjoining walls that meet at a right angle. It may seem logical to place dining table and chairs opposite the L, but these add traffic problems especially if there are also doors in this area. The L-arrangement works out well if the plan will allow at least six feet of uninterrupted counter space and an "L" leg at least eight feet in length.

Island Kitchen

Here are two versions of the island kitchen. These will fit into either a U-Shape or L-Shape plan.

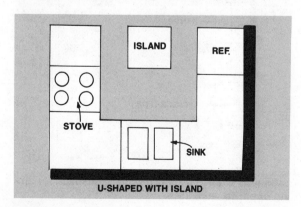

U-SHAPED WITH ISLAND

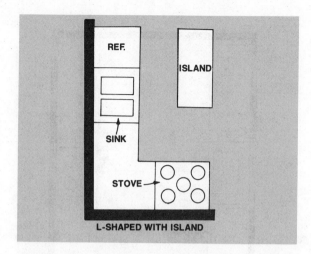

L-SHAPED WITH ISLAND

Basically this is a variation of any of the previous plans in which an island unit, either fixed or movable, is placed in the center of the kitchen. The island may be large enough to contain a sink, a range, a barbecue or may simply provide additional counter and storage space. A kitchen, which is dull and inconvenient in other respects, can become efficient and provide additional decorating opportunities with the addition of an island.

The surface of the island may be a large chopping block or piece of marble for the cook who

Courtesy of Masonite Corporation

Extra large chopping block island also has cabinet space below. The skylight brings in plenty of natural light in a windowless kitchen. Wall panels resemble natural wood but are a soil-shedding plastic surface. Even the decorative carved panels on the cabinet fronts are scrubbable.

specializes in pastry making. If the unit has a cooking surface, there may be added an overhead ventilating hood. Space above the island may be used for hanging cabinets or for large hooks on which to hang pans and utensils. Appliances which won't fit in the rest of the kitchen, a garbage compactor for instance, often will fit into the island. In a remodeling job where kitchen space is plentiful but existing built-ins cannot be moved easily, an island may be the solution.

PLANNING GUIDELINES

In working out a floor plan, first take accurate measurements of the appliances you now own and obtain measurements of appliances you plan to buy. Check with appliance stores and manufacturers for specifications. Beware of planning to the last inch and do not crowd too much into a small space. You should aim for approximately one hundred square feet of kitchen space. An overly planned kitchen may not provide room for small additions, or for replacing an old appliance with a larger unit.

Facing counters should have a minimum of four feet six inches between them. Plan to have counters twelve to twenty-four inches wide on both sides of a surface cooking area and on at least one side of the oven. Aim for sixteen inches of elbow space between a wall and any piece of equipment.

Locate doors to avoid traffic jams. Sliding, folding doors or bead curtain doors are good space savers.

Try not to place a refrigerator in the corner of an end wall. The door may need more than a 90 degree angle to open fully. Also avoid placing a refrigerator or wall oven at the end of a work counter if there is also a door there. A range should not be placed under a window, and a sink need not be. If the cook is left handed, remember to plan for this when buying and placing appliances.

Allow at least thirty-two inches minimum space for a person to seat himself or rise from a table. Another four inches is required to allow some-

one to pass behind the one who is seated. Allow twenty-four inches of elbow space per individual for eating.

KITCHEN CENTERS

Think of your kitchen as an area with four basic work centers. This will simplify your planning. The four centers are: SINK-DISHWASHER, RANGE-SERVE, MIXING-PREPARATION, and REFRIGERATOR-FREEZER. An optional fifth center is FOOD STORAGE.

Sink-Dishwasher Area

Nearly fifty percent of kitchen activities occur here. Some of the appliances which fit in are: dishwasher, disposer, trash compactor and drink-making equipment. Cabinet, bin, and drawer spaces are needed for vegetables and fruits which need no refrigeration, cleaning supplies, a wastebasket with lid, dish drainer and towels, colander, knives and a container for both plastic and paper bags.

Sinks

Sinks are available with right or lefthand drainboards, two drainboards, or no drainboard. If there is no drainboard, a dishwasher with a built-in counter top will provide a work area on

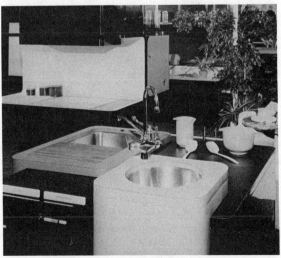

Courtesy of Frigidaire Division, General Motors Corporation

This island unit in a kitchen of the near future features dishwasher, trash compactor, two sinks, and a work area. Almost a kitchen in itself, it would be a good add-on in a remodeling job.

one side of the sink. At least three feet of built-in counter is needed on the other side. If yours will be a larger kitchen, consider sinks in more than one location. A second sink in a bar set-up, in an island in the center or near the back entrance for children to use are all convenient.

Of the most common types of sink, porcelain-on-steel is the least expensive sink, and enameled cast iron is the more durable. A variety of colors is available in either type. Both will show dark marks from metal cookingware and from fruit acids. Also the enamel on either can chip or craze.

Stainless steel is a first choice for sink durability. Water-spotting can be a problem if you live in a hard water area. For quiet use and fewer dents choose a sink of heavy gauge (thickness) steel.

Sinks are available with spray fixtures or faucet-dishwashers. There is a brush attachment on the regular faucet which dispenses water mixed with a detergent when a button is pressed on the handle.

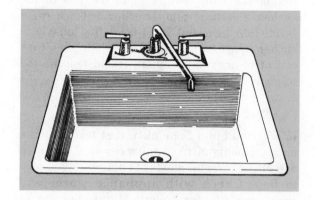

Single Porcelain Sink

Courtesy of Kitchen Aid Division, Hobart Manufacturing Company

Install an instant-hot extra faucet in an existing sink or adjacent counter, and you'll have teakettle hot water up to 190 degrees for making soup or drinks, heating or sterilizing baby bottles or getting a head start on cooking jobs. The two-quart tank if offset sufficiently to take up very little room below the sink. Faucet turns off automatically without a drip when the handle is released.

In deciding whether to install a single, double or even triple basin be sure to select a type which will permit washing large roasting pans and accessories from refrigerator and range.

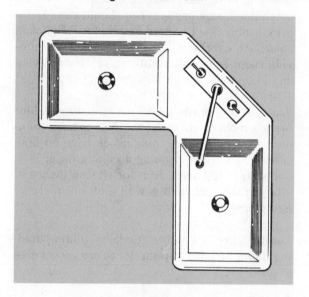

Double Stainless Steel Corner Sink

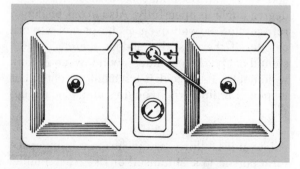

Stainless Steel Sink With Small Disposer Well

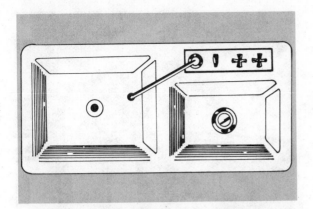

Regular Bowl Plus Small Bowl with Disposer

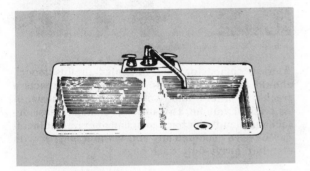

Double Porcelain Bowls With Disposer

Porcelain Drainboards With Single Bowl

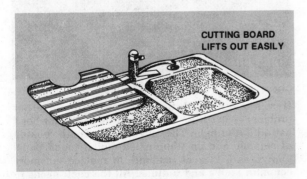

CUTTING BOARD
LIFTS OUT EASILY

Double Stainless Bowls With Vegetable Spray and Chopping Block Inset

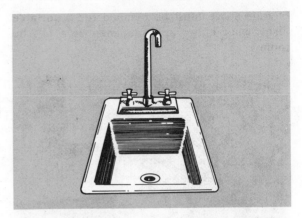

Stainless Bar Sink Unit Makes Good Additional Sink in a Large Kitchen, Useful For Flower Arranging

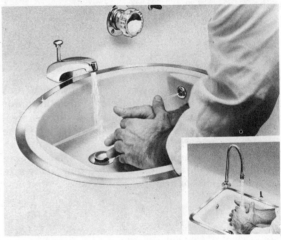

Courtesy of Qualco

No faucet is needed for this sink. An electric eye turns water off and on. If the electricity goes off there's a button to operate it manually. The sink comes in sizes and styles useful for a kitchen, bar, or washup area.

The newest sink on the market is an automated electric eye sink. Water at a preset temperature flows automatically when hands interrupt the self-contained eye beam, stops when hands are pulled from the flow.

Dishwashers

Dishwashers, either built-in or portable, can be obtained with or without a countertop surface. You can also get a portable which converts to a built-in dishwasher and compensates by needing no special plumbing connection or wiring. It also may be taken with the family to a new home.

897

Storage space must be planned for a portable dishwasher either in the kitchen or a nearby room.

Courtesy of General Electric Company

Is there room for a dishwasher? The owner of this portable model is shown enclosing it in a Philippine mahogany cabinet at one end of a dining area. Closed cabinet cuts out most of the noise when the machine is working. Shelves and cabinet top (with an inlay of ceramic tile) make a buffet-serving counter. Front panel fastens with four screws to facilitate repairs or eventual replacement with a new machine.

Food Waste Disposer and Compactor

A food waste disposer and compactor will handle all usual garbage problems. Any disposer will fit a standard four inch sink opening. Consult the building inspector before buying one. In some areas a disposer is mandatory, in others it is still illegal. A somewhat larger septic tank may be required if there is no hookup to a sewer connection.

The compactor reduces cans, bottles and paper to one-fourth the original bulk. Allow 24 inches depth and 18 inches width of cabinet space, depending on make. The compactor should be placed on the opposite side of the sink from the dishwasher. Most types operate from an ordinary household circuit, but one model operates on existing water pressure taken from any standard cold-water supply. Trash is deodorized by either an automatic built-in aerosol device or by spraying it manually.

A trash compactor, door mounted in this model, should be placed next to the sink. It compacts a week's trash for a family of four into one quarter of its original volume. This unit has a snap-release detachable handle for bag replacement or unloading. It can be used economically and without bags or with standard heavy-duty trash bags.

Courtesy of Frigidaire Division, General Motors Corp.

Here's another solution to that difficult corner problem — use it for the range. The ventilator-hood has a built-in light. The range has a smooth cooktop of ceramic and an illuminated digital touch panel known as a "visual readout" to replace the more common knobs and buttons. All the cook needs to do is press a finger lightly on a number and the range elements or oven will operate.

Range-Oven Center

A range-oven center will include a freestanding or built-in range with an oven either above or below the range, or a built-in surface unit with one or two wall ovens elsewhere in the kitchen. Most owners feel the self-cleaning feature in an electric oven is well worth having. Although the self cleaning cycle requires a great deal of electrical energy, this can be minimized by wiping up minor spills after each oven use, thus reducing the need to clean the oven to three or four times a year.

A gas-operated oven can be purchased with a continuous cleaning feature. The inside oven lining works catalytically to repel and char food spatters which can later be wiped up with a sponge. The cleaning job is not as thorough as the high-heat electric method, but since the process is continuous while the oven is in use for baking, no additional cost is involved.

Heat-proof surfaces, such as ceramic tile, are highly desirable on both sides of a range and on at least one side of the oven. If the oven is in a wall, a tile-covered surface could be supplied by installing a folddown or slide-in-the-wall

A hot spot of ceramic tile in a color which contrasts with the plastic-laminate counter around it will provide a safety area for pans removed from the range burners.

counter which could be pulled quickly into position when needed. If counters near the range will be surfaced with laminated plastic, it is wise to protect them from hot pans by adding an inset of ceramic tile near the range surface.

Colored tile on a board which hinges up, down, or pulls out from the wall, is a handy helper to build in near a wall oven.

Supply storage space and a cabinet near the range for skillets, pans and small tools used for cooking. Spices, often housed above the range, will keep their color and flavor better if stored in a cooler area of the kitchen. A pegboard or a hanging tool rack will place small items within reach of the range.

Consider the height of the cook when placing shelves, cabinets and the wall oven. Normally, the bottom rack of the oven should be 32 inches above the floor.

Refrigerator Center

A refrigerator center usually means one large refrigerator with freezer space to allow longer

899

storage (up to several months for some foods) of perishables. Kitchen space is too valuable to house a large freezer which is opened once a day or less. It is best located in a garage recreation room or utility store room.

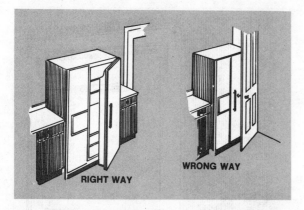

RIGHT WAY   WRONG WAY

Do not place the refrigerator next to a doorway where the appliance and kitchen doors can crash together when both are opened at the same time. Place refrigerator where there is a counter on the open side, and away from a wall on the hinged side to facilitate removal of shelves or bins for cleaning.

Try to place the refrigerator so there is a 15 to 18-inch wide working counter at the open side. Avoid placing it adjacent to a busy doorway. Check to see if the model you own, or plan to buy, requires air space at the side and the back, and whether the door must be able to swing

Courtesy of Frigidaire Division, Ford Motor Corporation

This refrigerator double duties as an entertainment and message center. There is a radio, recorder, and tape player which removes for use elsewhere, and plugs into a regular household circuit.

open to more than 90 degrees to allow shelves and bins to be removed for cleaning.

Space above the refrigerator which is not very useful for an ordinary storage cabinet, can house trays and flat baking sheets.

Food Preparation-Mix Center

A food preparation-mix center can be one large counter area or several smaller specialized types. Correct counter height will minimize stress. Put on work shoes, drop your shoulders, and then bend an elbow. Measure from elbow to floor, and subtract six inches, this will be the correct counter height for you.

If desired, undercounter knee space can be provided for sitting as you work. Look for an adjustable posture stool with a fold down back which will store under a counter.

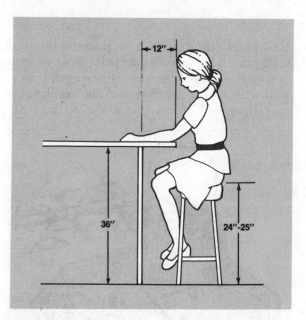

12″   36″   24″-25″

When planning a counter for working from a stool, allow 12″ of knee space, 36″ to the counter level. Buy a stool 24″ to 25″ high, depending on the height of the person using it.

A mix center for pastry making can be a counter with a marble top. The smooth surface remains cold, an asset when working with chilled dough. Marble now has a manmade counterpart called Corian which is a nonporous material that won't absorb grease and stains.

A pullout cutting board, adjustable to several heights, works well for many mixing jobs. It, plus a disappearing mixer shelf, supply a valuable work area. Mixer shelf hardware (available at your lumber yard or hardware store) is designed to swing a small appliance shelf up out of a cabinet and lock it securely at a comfortable working height. The unit is lowered and closed into the cabinet with a trigger release.

Courtesy of Long Bell Division, International Paper Co.

Slide-out chopping block adds to counter space and is about the right height for sitdown work. The dropdown door matches other cabinets and conceals the block when it is not wanted.

Courtesy of Flecto Company, Inc.

Homemade popup shelf houses a break-meat slicer, folds down and back into the undercounter cabinet when a catch under the board is released. The mechanism, available at any lumber yard, is easily installed by a do-it-yourselfer. Same device could be used for an electric mixer, eating counter or extra work space. Shelf is coated with a pour-on plastic imbedded with colored plastic flakes. It's impervious to water, resistant to stains, easy to clean.

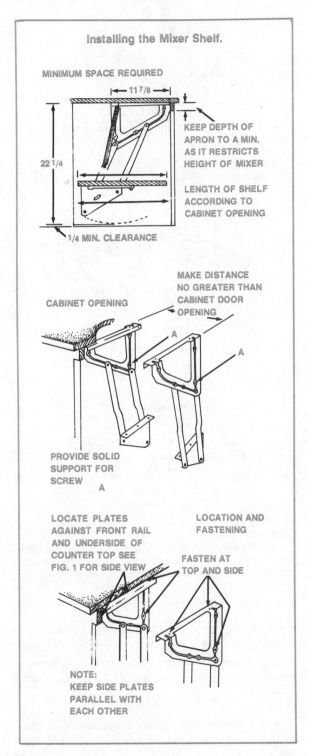

Installing the Mixer Shelf.

MINIMUM SPACE REQUIRED

11 7/8

22 1/4

KEEP DEPTH OF APRON TO A MIN. AS IT RESTRICTS HEIGHT OF MIXER

LENGTH OF SHELF ACCORDING TO CABINET OPENING

1/4 MIN. CLEARANCE

MAKE DISTANCE NO GREATER THAN CABINET DOOR OPENING

CABINET OPENING

A

A

PROVIDE SOLID SUPPORT FOR SCREW

A

LOCATE PLATES AGAINST FRONT RAIL AND UNDERSIDE OF COUNTER TOP SEE FIG. 1 FOR SIDE VIEW

LOCATION AND FASTENING

FASTEN AT TOP AND SIDE

NOTE: KEEP SIDE PLATES PARALLEL WITH EACH OTHER

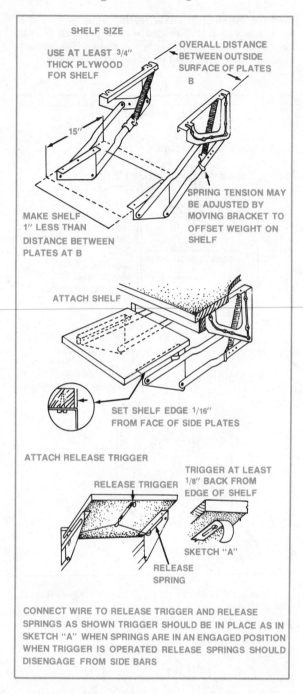

SHELF SIZE

USE AT LEAST 3/4" THICK PLYWOOD FOR SHELF

OVERALL DISTANCE BETWEEN OUTSIDE SURFACE OF PLATES B

15"

MAKE SHELF 1" LESS THAN DISTANCE BETWEEN PLATES AT B

SPRING TENSION MAY BE ADJUSTED BY MOVING BRACKET TO OFFSET WEIGHT ON SHELF

ATTACH SHELF

SET SHELF EDGE 1/16" FROM FACE OF SIDE PLATES

ATTACH RELEASE TRIGGER

RELEASE TRIGGER

TRIGGER AT LEAST 1/8" BACK FROM EDGE OF SHELF

SKETCH "A"

RELEASE SPRING

CONNECT WIRE TO RELEASE TRIGGER AND RELEASE SPRINGS AS SHOWN TRIGGER SHOULD BE IN PLACE AS IN SKETCH "A" WHEN SPRINGS ARE IN AN ENGAGED POSITION WHEN TRIGGER IS OPERATED RELEASE SPRINGS SHOULD DISENGAGE FROM SIDE BARS

A solution to the inadequate mix center problem might be to add a mobile island with slideout cutting board top and cabinet below to house spices, dry ingredients, and divided areas for pans.

Another handy spacesaving appliance is the built-in food center which consists of eight ap-

pliances (mixer, blender, knife sharpener, can opener, ice crusher, meat grinder, shredder-slicer and can opener) that work on one motor. The heavy duty motor installs beneath a counter or in a drawer. Individual appliances snap on to the motor unit without tools or attachments, take up less cabinet space and cost less than if each item were purchased separately with its own cord and motor.

Courtesy of Nutone Division, Scoville Housing Products

A compact built-in food center provides eight snap-in appliances all of which operate from a single built-in power unit. The solid-state switching dial offers six speeds.

Courtesy of Swanson Manufacturing Company

Install an automatic can opener in stud space, and it won't take up counter or cabinet room. Plastic-coated pegboard wall paneling needs no painting as the color is built-in.

Courtesy of Swanson Manufacturing Company

Another in-a-wall helper is a built-in toaster which takes up no space, except when it is folded out to toast four pieces of bread at once. Toaster shuts off automatically when unit is closed or can be unplugged as shown and lifted out to be used at the dining table.

If you already own a number of appliances which clutter the kitchen counter, you can plan a special appliance storage area. One suggestion is a long shallow cupboard at the rear of a counter with doors to conceal appliances until they are ready for use. One manufacturer makes a toaster and a can opener, shallow enough to fit into the stud space on the back wall of the counter. The toaster tips forward for in-the-wall use and shuts itself off when closed into the wall. This toaster can also be unplugged and lifted out for use at the dining table.

Food Storage-Pantry

A food storage-pantry area can be a walk-in room large enough to store several months' supplies of canned and dry foods or it can be a floor to ceiling set of shelves, one can deep, which occupies normally useable space behind a kitchen door. Search your plan for a space that may seem useless at first glance.

The plan will be more useful if it does not permit a deep cabinet as shallow shelves make foods easier to locate.

Shelves should be able to accommodate tall bottles as well as tiny cans of meat or baby food.

Courtesy of Masonite Corporation

Wasted space between stove and wall has been transformed into an efficient floor to ceiling pantry. Doors and sides are lined with 1/4″ plastic-coated pegboard panels. Shelves are also covered with soil shedding plastic-coated paneling laminated to hardboard.

Space behind a kitchen door is useless unless used for a pantry. It is one can deep to see everything at a glance. Shelves can be open, or add a door, or even two (allowing space for door knob) and use magnetic latches.

Four or five inches of space at the end of a row of cabinets or between cabinets is room enough for one or more pullout shelves that will stow away small bottles, spices and ordinary cans.

Measure a number of items now on your shelves. Enough space should be allowed to place or grasp the item easily. A pantry is a good place to store little-used appliances such as ice cream freezer, popcorn popper, fondue pan, provided you've planned extra high shelves to take the larger items.

Hobby and Specialized Centers

A kitchen office will need a desk, a chair that can be pushed under the desk when not in use, a

Courtesy of Swanson Manufacturing Company

Install a hide-a-way planning desk in the stud space, and space won't be sacrificed, because the unit is flush with the wall when closed. Next to it is a built-in ironing board with a cork pinup board on the back. Desk units, which come with metal shelves and dividers, can easily be installed by the home-owner.

shelf for a cookbook collection, pigeon holes for bills, recipe file and a telephone. A typewriter will not take up desk space when fastened to a popup shelf.

A barbecue requires storage space for charcoal, tools and rotisserie attachment. Indoors, a chimney or built-in ventilator is an essential to draw off poisonous fumes. A heatproof counter should be located adjacent to the grill.

A greenhouse or window garden can be installed. There are prefabricated glass roofed or all-plastic models which attach to a window or can be an extension of a wall.

Courtesy of Frigidaire Division: General Motors Corp.

For additional oven space a microwave oven will fit on a rolling cart. It requires only a 110-volt plug in and cooks food in a few minutes on paper or glass, with no messy oven to clean up afterward.

A laundry-ironing center need take up only a couple of feet of closet or wall space. There is a mini unit available which has washer on the bottom, dryer offset at the top so it doesn't interfere with the top-loading lid. Normal washer plumbing, dryer vent, and 220-volt hookup are required. One model has a 110-volt dryer. This 24 inch wide major appliance can become even more useful if you also buy the chopping block accessory which fits the washer top and becomes useable counter space.

You will need to allow sufficient space in front of a kitchen laundry to permit clothes sorting and to allow for normal traffic flow. (Diagram Y)

Add an ironing center by installing an ironing board in a 15 inch wide wall space. The unit can be recessed into wall stud space or surface mounted. One model is available in several lengths with a built-in light, automatic timer, electric outlet, sleeveboard, storage space for fabric finish and a safe landing spot for the iron. The back of the board, which is all you see when the unit is closed can be finished in a variety of ways. (Insert Illustration)

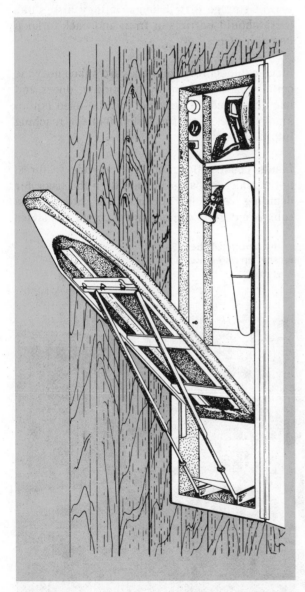

Fifteen inches of wall width and the depth of the studs are all the space necessary for this ironing center. This one comes with timer, light, sleeveboard, storage area for iron.

CHOOSING KITCHEN CABINETS

Don't economize on cabinets. Well built cabinets chosen for their efficiency will last the lifetime of the kitchen. When equipped with drawers, partitions, sliding shelves, bins, cup and towel racks and good hardware they make the difference between an efficient and a poorly planned kitchen.

Custom cabinets (those built especially for an individual) are too expensive for most homes. However, good stock cabinets can be bought at a lumber dealer or hardware store. Some dealers have a custom service available should you need to add one or two cabinets which match the stock items for a space unique to a specific kitchen design.

Courtesy of Long Bell Division, International Paper Co.

The irregularly shaped revolving shelf unit plus a door is divided and hinged so it won't bang a knee or interfere with work at the counter. It solves the problem of utilizing the space in this kitchen corner. The metal shelves will support a heavy load of canned goods.

The cabinet has a convenient divider arrangement to house awkward dishes. The pegboard divider could be used for hanging utensils.

It is more economical to buy well built cabinets minus the desired accessories and build or add your own later. Sliding drawers, cup racks, towel racks, small turntables and devices to stow paper goods are all available in hardware stores. Colors are integral, the plastic is easy to wipe clean and items install with a few screws. The accessories can easily be removed or changed.

Adjustable shelves, especially in base cabinets, permit storage of tall items. If they also slide, there should be rims at front and back to keep items in place.

Stock cabinets leave an awkward space near the ceiling. Close this up by building in doors and use this space for seasonal or little-used equipment. Allow space for a stepstool for reaching into high cupboards.

Inside construction and convenience features, not outside appearance, should be the basis for deciding which line of cabinets to choose. Most cabinet exteriors come in many colors and styles

Elegant hostess cabinet stores china when it is in place under the counter. When it's rolled out for use in dining or living room the drop-down leaves go up and convert it into a piece of fine furniture for serving food.

This kitchen cabinet is both a piece of furniture and an efficient small pantry with
shelves on the doors for small items that would be hidden if stored on ordinary shelves.

Courtesy of Long Bell Division, International Paper Co.

These ventilated plastic storage bins slide out for easy access to fruits and vegetables which do not need refrigeration but will be cleaned and prepared at the sink above.

Courtesy of Long Bell Division, International Paper Co.

Change your mind about your kitchen storage system and these shelves will change also. They can be adjusted for easy removal of the contents.

such as Colonial, French, Spanish, Old English or pop art. Many come prefinished in decorator colors, stained natural wood or surfaced with prints that so closely resemble wood it may be impossible to tell the difference. Some are available with either removable or reversible door panels.

Most cabinets will come without knobs or handles. This choice will be up to you. You can have pewter handles, cut glass, clear plastic types with real flowers or seeds imbedded in the plastic, simple wooden knobs or no handles at all, just fingerholds. Elaborate handles can come close to equaling the cost of the cabinets themselves.

Doors

Doors on cabinets are either sliding or hinged. Outward swinging doors should swing a full 180° for safety and convenience. Hinges should be heavy enough to support the door easily without a sag. Cheap hardware is no economy.

Courtesy of Arist'O Kraft, United States Cabinet Corp.

A sink doesn't need to be placed on a straight counter, as this arrangement shows. Fine wooden cabinets take away the antiseptic look. The flagstone floor is actually easy to clean vinyl put down in squares.

Sliding doors take up less space, and give the kitchen a better appearance than do swinging doors if they are left open; however, soil can accumulate in the track which is difficult to clean. Nylon or fiber track permits easy sliding with little noises.

Catches

Catches (two on all doors more than 24″ high) should come open easily but fasten securely at a touch. Magnetic catches are the most popular because they do not rely on friction to work well. Touch-latch catches require no door handle, rely on light pressure to swing the door open. Inexpensive cabinets usually have bullet-type friction catches with stiff action.

No matter what type of catch you choose or find on the cabinets you select, remember that the catch is only as good as its alignment. Catches on sample cabinets in a dealer's display will usually work well; however, the ones delivered to you may not be as satisfactory. This is one reason for buying from a reliable dealer or cabinet manufacturer who will guarantee the workmanship after the cabinets are installed.

Cabinet Material

Wood cabinets are the favorite. Cabinet fronts are made of every type of wood with natural, stained or painted surfaces. Backs and sides are ordinarily made of plywood or particle board. For painted cabinets, choose a semi-gloss

Courtesy of Masonite Corporation

Deep-textured barnside paneling gives a rugged cozy look to an efficient kitchen. The prefinished wall and counter panels, available in gray or brown, resist moisture and stains and can be applied over old walls or any solid backing. This kitchen is made more useful by having a work and serve counter in the middle of the room. Dutch door and plant shelves add country charm.

enamel which cleans well and doesn't have the highly reflective surface of glossy enamel. A natural or stained finish will scratch and dent over the years, but touchups are not difficult to blend in, and the dents may add to the charm. Some cabinets even come with antiqued and distressed finishes.

A well made wooden cabinet will not be bowed or warped, the door will fit neatly and close firmly, drawers will open and close smoothly, shelves will be thick enough to support heavy utensils and edges will be sanded and rounded so there will be no rough or splintered edges.

If you have patience, proper tools, and some carpentry skills, consider purchasing knock-down cabinets. These are unassembled pre-cut, sanded kits which contain all the parts, hardware and instructions for construction. These result in better cabinets because you can use more nails or screws, do a more thorough gluing job and do the hand sanding which makes all the difference in how the surfaces look and feel. They are also more economical as you save labor costs.

Steel cabinets with a baked-enamel finish are easy to wipe off with a damp cloth, last almost indefinitely and come in so many colors, or in a choice of wooden fronts, that they no longer have that hospital look which was produced by a kitchen with many glossy white cabinets. Look for these points when shopping for steel cabinets: drawer glides should be 18 gauge, but doors, sides and backs can be 22 gauge. (The lower the number the thicker the steel.) Insulated doors reduce the noise factor, as will rubber bumpers at the corners of the doors or near the catches. Buy from a well-established manufacturer and you will be better assured of obtaining a matching replacement should it become necessary.

Rust is always a problem with steel. A small crack between sink and cabinet will start invisible deterioration that cannot be repaired. Damp dishes on shelves will also wear away enamel and cause rust. Wax the shelves occasionally, or use shelf liners to reduce this problem. The best protection against rust is the manufacturer's guarantee that an anti-rust primer has been used

This airy, feminine kitchen, set up for a birthday party, doubles as a recreation area for children. All surfaces are easy to wash, including the vinyl floor which glows but never needs waxing.

underneath the primer and that both the prime and finish coat have been baked on.

Particle board cabinets surfaced on all sides with laminated plastic sheets (the same material you see on counter tops) are becoming more popular now that steel and all-wood cabinets are very expensive. Particle board is an extremely hard durable material made of wood chips which have been pressure-treated. Plastic sheeting, easy to clean and never in need of refinishing, comes in hundreds of colors, patterns, and

woodlike grains. Today's glues are so good it is extremely rare for the plastic surface to separate from the particle board. There is no rust and little chance of a warp problem with particle board.

Sizes of stock cabinets are standardized. Base cabinets are 24 inches deep and 34 inches high. The countertop will bring the height to 36 inches. The tall cook may want an extra inch of height, and this can easily be provided by placing cabinets on a recessed frame which will also give extra toe space.

910

Courtesy of Frigidaire Division, General Motors Corporation

If your kitchen can spare only two feet of space, there's room for a washer-dryer of this type. This model has a top loading washer. The dryer is available in either 110- or 230-volt model.

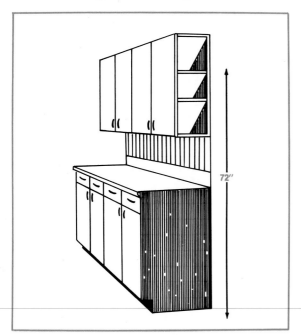

Wall cabinets should be placed 15 inches above the counter. This allows ample clearance for the mixer and other equipment used on the counter. The third shelf of wall cabinets should be no more than 72 inches above the floor for convenience in daily use. Cabinets for everyday dishes should be near either the sink or the dining area, and preferably accessible to both.

Wall cabinets vary from 12 inches to 36 inches high and are 12 inches deep. They are available in widths from 9 inches to 36 inches. An odd corner can be filled in with some useful item such as a sliding towel rack or open shelf for storing trays vertically.

The top shelf in a wall cabinet should not be higher than 52 inches from the floor for someone 5'2'' to 5'5'' tall, if the item to be stored requires two hands to place it on the shelf. For a light-weight item that can be placed or removed with one hand, the top shelf should not be more than 68'' from the floor. In base cabinets the space below 28 inches (about fingertip distances) should be kept for storing pots and pans that are rarely used. If seated work is planned at a mix counter, the top shelf of the wall cabinet should be only 64'' from the floor.

CHOOSING A COUNTERTOP

Choosing a countertop actually means selecting

several surfaces that will serve several different purposes. No one type of counter material will do all the jobs. Ideally a surface should be easy to clean, resistant to staining and scratching, able to stand heat, be easy to install, and not very expensive.

The answer to the problem, therefore, is to use several different materials. A good choice would be a large area of ceramic tile on both sides of the range and near the oven. The hottest pan directly off the range will rarely stain or crack ceramic tile, and if it does, usually one or two tiles can be inserted without replacing the entire counter. Buy a few extras of the ceramic tile pattern you choose and replacements should they be needed, will be available. Meanwhile they will serve as protective plates on a dining table or other delicate surface.

A home handyman can do a good job on a counter with ceramic tile by putting it down on a solid plywood surface with recommended adhesive and grouting it with one of the new plastic grout materials.

When economy is important, settle for several 12 x 12 inch tile inserts in a less expensive counter surface and place them at such strategic points as on either side of a range surface and near the wall oven.

Courtesy of Thermador Division, Norris Industries

This stainless steel hood not only gets rid of kitchen grime and smoke but the unit also contains a condiment shelf, a light, and two infra-red bulbs over the drop down stainless steel racks at each end of the hood. When food is cooked and placed on the shelves heat bulbs will keep food at eating temperature until serving time. Griddle unit in center of the range has a cover, adding to counter space.

Plastic laminate is an excellent and most often used material for counters. It comes in large sheets, is waterproof, almost stainproof, is soft enough to prevent dish breakage, absorbs noise and withstands relatively high temperatures. Knife cuts, scratches, and stubborn stains will show, however, but most can be avoided by strict use of a chopping block.

Marble, expensive and stain-absorbent, is preferred by the gourmet pastry cook because it retains its cold surface during the roll-out process. Man made marble (Corian) is elegant, available with marble graining and cannot easily be distinguished from the real thing. The big advantage is that Corian is a nonpourous surface which is easy to clean and it is easy for the do-it-yourself worker to cut and install. Removing stains and repolishing or cutting real marble is an impossible job for an amateur.

A chopping block counter, usually made of a very hard wood such as maple or cherry, is a good companion to the sink where vegetables can be cut and the waste easily pushed into the disposer. Stains and knife marks damage a chopping block, but scrubbing and oiling with vegetable oil will keep it usable. Periodically it can be sanded, deep stains removed with bleach, and then wiped again with vegetable or mineral oil.

One sink model comes with a chopping block insert which fits the top of one half of the sink bowl. Consider inserting a removable chopping block into a plastic laminate surfaced counter. The block could be turned over or replaced with a new unit when the old one became badly damaged.

Stainless steel is used occasionally for a counter top, especially near a sink. If the gauge is heavy enough it won't dent easily, won't rust, and will last forever. It's disadvantages are that hard water will spot it, it's noisy and dishes break easily when dropped on it.

Hardwood when finished with a heavy coating of polyurethane makes an elegant, but impractical, counter. Water will eventually blacken and rot it, and hot pans will ruin the appearance.

Hardwood counters are only for people who want to work hard to keep them beautiful.

WALL FINISHES

Paint is still a first choice, probably because newly developed dripless, odorless paints are inexpensive, wash easily and dry quickly. A semi-gloss type is best on kitchen walls even though it doesn't clean or resist soil as well as a glossy enamel. Glare, especially under artificial light, is less annoying and the appearance more pleasing.

If you are painting the kitchen yourself, be sure that dust, grease, carpenter pencil and chalk marks and mildew are removed. New lumber with black mildew on it will need to be primed with an anti-mildew paint. Unfinished wood must be smoothed with fine sandpaper both before and between coats. Even a hardboard which feels smooth should be sanded or fibers may rise in the wet paint. Nails should be countersunk and holes and cracks filled with spackle or putty and pre-primed. Hardware needs to be removed or covered with masking tape.

Paint can directions should be followed, including the use of the correct type brush or paint roller. Paneling is running paint a close second for kitchen walls. Plywood, hardboard, or gypsum board panels come in 4 x 8 sheets in many types of factory finished designs, colors, and real and simulated wood surfaces. Heavy soil cleans off easily, especially on those which are plastic-coated hardboards. Price range is from as little as three dollars a sheet to fifteen or twenty dollars for real hardboard.

Ask the dealer whether the type you choose is satisfactory for a kitchen. Some cannot stand up to steam or grease. If you do prefer a paneling which could not easily be cleaned or washed, one solution is to cover all problem areas, behind range, oven, oven sink, and in splash areas, just above counter surfaces with see-through transparent plastic, about the same thickness as window glass. The wood or plastic-coated paneling can be seen through the transparent plastic, so the kitchen has a coordinated look. One vinyl type is now available which is less expensive than an acrylic plastic.

913

Fabric for curtains and table cloth are the same colors and pattern as the floor. You can use this scheme if you live in an area where there is a floor fashion center.

Paneling also has the advantage of covering walls which have imperfections, cracks or damaged plaster. It's easy for the homeowner to cut with a fine-toothed saw blade and put into place with a waterproof adhesive. Use the type recommended by the manufacturer.

Wallpaper used in a kitchen should be washable. Most types have some degree of washability, but for a kitchen a scrubbable, plastic-coated type which is impervious to stains and can be scrubbed with a mild cleanser is necessary. Most wallpapers claim to be washable, but a type with a protein size or one with a protein size combined with plastic to make a plastic-bonded paper, is not durable enough for a kitchen. A few drops of water dropped onto the surface of a wallpaper sample will not disappear or soak in if the paper is truly scrubbable.

Wallpapering has become a good home project. Most amateurs find that the unpasted type (the paste must be mixed and applied to the back of the paper) is easier to handle than the prepasted type which only is soaked in water. The un-pasted type can be shifted easily if you find it needs re-positioning on the wall, whereas the prepasted type cannot be moved once it is put in place.

In remodeling a kitchen with rough cracked walls, a vinyl wallcovering is better to use than paper. Vinyl, either solid or backed with fabric or paper, is expensive but extremely durable and abrasion-resistant. It is flexible, moisture-resistant and unaffected by quick temperature changes.

Pegboard is a double-duty wall covering which is available in several thicknesses. It comes ready to paint or in pre-finished decorator colors which will blend with the rest of the kitchen. Pegboard covers most wall defects and at the same time provides flexible storage. Accessories are available in white plastic or metal which not only hang tools, but shelves as well. The surfaces of pegboard wash clean with a mild detergent. The factory enameled finish will last many years. An excellent spot for pegboard is the long strip of wall at the back of the counter surface and just below kitchen cabinets.

Brick, stone and their imitators are being used more today to give kitchens that warm feeling of

the past. However, they are best used on only one wall or in an area around a barbecue or fire-place, since they darken a room and are not easy to keep clean. A sprayed-on clear plastic finish will keep them from shedding dust.

An amateur can do a creditable job with natural materials, but if imitation stone or brick is used, the job is much easier. Even if you rub your hand across one of these man-made wall materials you will have difficulty distinguishing it from the real thing. Some are made from vinyl, but the most authentic looking ones are made of vermiculite, which won't burn and also have insulation value. Most are applied to the wall with an adhesive recommended or supplied by the manufacturer. Because these imitators are light-weight there's no stress on the supporting structure of the house.

FLOOR COVERINGS FOR THE KITCHEN

Choice of floor coverings ranges from durable expensive slate or marble to carpet, luxurious to the feet and the eye, but reasonably durable.

Carpet for the kitchen was an unheard of idea until recently when indoor-outdoor carpet was invented. These synthetic materials can be taken

Courtesy of Armstrong Cork Company

Pegboard, easy to damp-wipe, is a good substitute for cupboard space. Everything is in view and can be re-arranged to suit the cook. The work table has a heavy butcher block surface and handy knife racks at either end. The shine on the floor comes from a no-wax vinyl surface which is permanent.

Courtesy of the Ozite Corporation

Carpet squares make a soft, warm, noise deadening kitchen floor. These are impervious to moisture and spot resistant. If one or more get damaged or permanently stained only a few squares need be replaced. The brick cooking grill which is open to both kitchen and dining area also serves as a convenient heatproof counter for the oven.

A kitchen floor can have a cobblestone look without the problems of the real thing. This is a no-wax sheet flooring material. The open shelves, both above and below the counter next to the range, are a good idea. Cabinet doors would be in the way, and the one below the counter would be awkward and dark.

Interlocking octagons resemble ceramic floor tile, but are neither cold nor slippery because the material is seamless vinyl with a no-wax finish. Another good feature of this kitchen is the divided open cabinet below the sink area where awkward sized trays and pans can be stored.

up and washed with a hose or scrubbed right on the floor. The carpet is available in wall-to-wall sizes or in squares with a self-stick backing. In a kitchen area where spills and wear are heavy, the squares which become damaged can be shifted around or replaced one at a time. Design a floor pattern which makes use of different patterns and colors and any new squares which are added will blend in better than in a floor which is all one color. Patterned carpet will conceal stubborn stains. A very dark color is not a good choice because kitchen spills are often sugar, flour, or food bits which show up plainly. Carpet with a short shag surface will hide more spills than a smooth surface. When kitchen carpet wears out or becomes unusuable from stains, it can have a second life in the garage or workshop.

Kitchen carpet is not recommended for the family with a lot of children and animals or for the fussy housekeeper who wants an immaculate kitchen floor.

Vinyl, in sheet or tile form, is available in several kinds. Cheapest is roto vinyl sheet flooring which is color printed on a backing and coated with clear vinyl to protect the design. It gouges easily and will need to be replaced in a few years. Inlaid vinyl sheeting often available in widths to 12′, is a permanent flooring because colors run completely through the material. Cushioned vinyl sheet has a layer of vinyl foam under the surface vinyl to soften footsteps, muffle noise and give a warm surface. Many vinyls come in squares, either with a self-adhesive peel-off backing or requiring adhesive recommended by the manufacturer.

Linoleum, the earliest of today's many floor coverings, is still a good material. It is made of ground cork and linseed oil. Colors run through to the backing, making it a durable floor cover. It comes in widths up to six feet and in a wide range of colors which resist fading. Linoleum also resists grease and is reasonable in price. If you plan to lay the floor yourself do not be tempted by sheet material. Careless handling or a wrong cut can ruin an entire floor. Use the same material, but in tile form.

Rubber tile is no longer stocked by most stores.

While it is very durable, muffles sounds and is long lasting, grease stains show on rubber tile and it is expensive.

Cork tile is attractive but takes work to keep beautiful. Bright sun soon fades it from a rich dark brown to a washed-out tan. Heavy objects dent it, and soil tracked in from outdoors scratches the surface off, especially if the soil happens to be sand. Choose instead a vinyl cork tile with a plastic-coated surface. It is not as warm and bouncy as pure cork, but it looks better and is almost as resilient.

Asphalt tile, although a good choice if the kitchen floor will be on a concrete slab that is damp, has many disadvantages. Its noisy, hard to clean and brittle. Vinyl-asbestos tile costs a little more but is moisture and grease resistant and has resiliency. Marble, slate, brick, terrazzo, and ceramic tile make handsome kitchen floors but have several disadvantages in common. They are hard, cold, slippery, and expensive. All are extremely durable and fireproof, however. Mosaic tiles, still comparatively undamaged and their colors bright, survived the eruption of Vesuvius in 79 A.D.

A skillful homeowner with much patience can lay a slate, brick or ceramic tile floor. Marble and terrazzo require professional know-how and equipment. All types, with the exception of brick, clean easily and repel stains.

Seamless plastic floor, a newcomer, makes an attractive resilient kitchen floor. It is durable, decorative and almost maintenance-free. The homeowner can do the job for about 50 cents a square foot. Basically it consists of combining plastic chips with two or more coats of clear acrylic, epoxy or urethane plastic, depending on the brand he chooses.

Wood, once a floor favorite because more suitable materials had not yet been invented, is no longer considered practical for a kitchen. Should you decide to use wood, it must be sanded after the floor is down, then stained, and given a surface topping of several coats of polyurethane. It will look beautiful, won't need waxing, and will enhance the kitchen decor. But, as it is used, splinters and cracks will develop, water will damage it and the surface will need to be renewed at intervals.

KITCHEN LIGHTING

Shadow-free, glareless lighting throughout the kitchen will require general lighting in the ceiling plus area lighting at the sink, range, and work counters. A kitchen with cabinets of dark wood and wall materials such as brick and wood paneling will need considerably more artificial light than one which is painted a cheery yellow throughout.

If the kitchen is small, an ideal way to get even lighting is by making the entire ceiling a light source. The frame can be an egg crate of lumber that harmonizes with the rest of the room. Cut diffusing panels from a material such as white fiberglass-reinforced plastic and drop them into the sections of the egg crate. Allow one light socket for each 10 or 15 square feet of ceiling. If the ceiling must illuminate an area much larger than itself, allow one socket for each 4 to 5 square feet of luminous ceiling. Exact light intensity can be varied by choice of light bulb size.

Another way to bring even light into a kitchen is by installing a combination skylight-light fixture. The skylight, made to fit flush with the ceiling, can be a sandwich constructed of two pieces of the flat plastic. Between the two sheets, wire in a socket at either end of the rectangle. In the daytime soft, even light will come in from the sky. At night the two sockets, fitted with 100-watt bulbs will light an ordinary kitchen. The bottom of the two plastic sheets should be made to slide easily so panels can be washed or light bulbs replaced.

When purchasing a ceiling light fixture, avoid any made of clear glass or decorative features such as a protective grid in front of the glass. Elaborate fixtures collect grease and are difficult to reach for regular cleaning. Try putting in and taking out a bulb in the store. If the process seems even slightly involved, remember that it will be even more difficult to change a bulb when it is above your head.

Check to see if the fixture is ventilated to prevent fires caused by excessive bulb heat. Prescribed bulb wattage should be printed on the fixture. Be sure it is not exceeded.

A 100 watt bulb gives 15% more light than do three 40 watt bulbs, even though they add up to 120 watts. Long-life bulbs, though not as efficient light producers, are a good idea for hard to reach fixtures. Fluorescent lights save on energy and help to keep a cool kitchen. In normal use, they will last three to five times longer than incandescent lights. Choose a bulb which casts a warm light on the skin to avoid the ghostly, unhealthy look produced by an ordinary white fluorescent bulb.

Localized or area lights above the sink, range and counters can come from either a 100 watt bulb or two 20 watt fluorescent bulbs. A tubular showcase incandescent bulb, a very slender type, is a good choice for under-the-counter fixtures.

Courtesy the Westinghouse Electric Corporation

The newest of kitchen designs combines solar power with energy saving. Part of a house designed by the Ohio State University and the Homewood Corporation, the kitchen makes uses of presently available appliances chosen for their energy conservation abilities. The house uses an array of solar roof panels to provide energy for home cooling, home heating, and hot water heating.

When remodeling and adding a number of new lighting fixtures, the old wiring should be updated. Planning should include an expandibility feature to take care of future needs. If, for instance the purchase of a microwave oven is planned for a later date it would be best to include its separate circuit at the time of the remodeling.

Minimums established by the National Electrical Code recommend 3 watts to the square foot of room area. Kitchen outlets on 15- or 20-ampere branch circuits must be spaced no more than 12 feet apart, so that no point on the wall measured along the floorline will be more than 6 feet from an outlet. Outlets in the kitchen should be equally divided between 2 or more 20-ampere branch circuits. Many homeowners have each kitchen outlet installed on an individual circuit. This is an increase in cost, but it is a worthwhile

Remodel an old kitchen, or design a new one with old fashioned elegance, by putting in these stock cabinets which look as though they were made by hand. Then add the convenience of an island sink. Kitchen and dining area blend through use of continuous carpeting and matching cabinet work in both areas.

Courtesy of Long Bell Division International Paper Company

Antiseptic white has left the kitchen. This one is equipped with matching appliances in Chinese red, and the shag carpet is an orange-red tweed mixture which conceals crumbs and stains.

safety feature and virtually eliminates blown fuses.

Three-way and four-way switches are especially helpful in a kitchen where you may wish to switch lights off and on from an outside entrance, a garage or outdoor dining area. In kitchen work areas, receptacle outlets should be eight inches above the counter surface.

Multi-outlet raceway is another way to update the electrical system. It is a pre-wired strip, comprised of a two-part grounded metal channel,

which mounts on a wall like molding. The usual place to mount it is at the back of a counter, a few inches above the surface. Outlets are usually spaced about four to the foot.

KITCHEN CLIMATE CONTROL

Ventilation

Ventilating the kitchen gets rid of grease, smoke, odor and moisture. Moisture which isn't removed from the room makes its way inside walls and condenses there, damaging the paint and

Courtesy of Nutone Division, Scovill

Decorative range hood containing duct and powerful fan is well-adapted to trapping kitchen pollutants because of its funnel shape. This one mounted directly under the soffit takes up very little space.

loosening wallpaper or paneling. Over the years wooden framework may rot.

The Home Ventilating Institute recommends that kitchen air be changed at least 15 times an hour, a process that can be achieved only by mechanical means. Not only does the kitchen benefit, but all other rooms of the house. Problems such as dull windows and mirrors, grime on wallpaper and odor in draperies which are often blamed on the heating system or fireplace, are actually caused by poor kitchen ventilation.

A ducted fan, the best type, changes the air by pumping it outdoors through a vent in either a sidewall or the roof. A short duct, kept at full size all the way to the outdoors, is best. Ducting the fumes out of an island cooktop or a range on an interior wall may be difficult, but it is worth the trouble. The duct can even be run through ceiling joists or a cabinet if there is no other solution.

Ductless fans are easier to install, especially in an older house which is being remodeled, but they cannot get rid of dirt-laden air to the outdoors. Air is filtered, usually through replaceable charcoal filters, and sent back into the room.

Both ducted and ductless ventilating fans are built into range hoods. Often range hoods, identical in appearance, are available with a choice of the two types.

Four ways to provide kitchen ventilation are shown here. Ducted models are best. Non-ducted systems merely recirculate the air without removing soil and humidity. Prime location for the fan is above the range. Some ranges and ovens have their own built-in ventilating systems, with and without ducts.

Find out what capacity fan is needed by multiplying the length of the kitchen by the width and then by the height, all in feet. This gives you the cubic footage. Divide this figure by four and you will have the fan capacity needed to move the air of the room every four minutes, or fifteen times an hour. An even heavier fan, one which moves two cubic feet of air per minute for each square foot of kitchen floor area, is a real advantage if the kitchen is open to other rooms or your normal kitchen operations produce an unusual amount of vapor (canning, steaming or making jams and jellies).

The heavier the fan capacity, unfortunately, the greater the noise volume. Choose, then, a fan with a multiple-speed switch. You can run it at low speed when the cooking is light and turn it up to high only when dispeling offensive odors.

Ordinarily, the ventilating fan above the range or inside the range hood is enough. It should be placed no more than 30 inches above the burners. However, if the wall oven is in another part of the kitchen there is need for a second fan there.

Usually a fan contains a metal grid or decorative grill over the opening as a safety factor. Examine it to determine how easily it can be removed for

cleaning. Unless dust and grease are removed frequently, the fan can't do its job. There may even be a two-part grid which is put together with a number of screws. These will be difficult to remove as they become imbedded in grease or if they rust.

Courtesy of Nutone Division, Scovill Housing Products

This ducted ventilating fan mounts neatly into the ceiling above a range. The aluminum mesh filter can be dunked in a detergent solution to remove trapped grease. It takes removal of only one finger nut to pull the unit apart for regular cleaning.

One model has a permanent filter of aluminum mesh. It won't rust, keeps grease out of the fan blades and duct, can easily be removed for a dunking in detergent and warm water.

One new through-the-wall multiple speed fan takes both ease of cleaning and decoration into

Courtesy Nutone Division, Scoville Housing Products

A smooth panel snaps on to cover this ducted ventilating fan in a kitchen wall. The panel can be covered with redwood to match the wall, other decorative material, or even a picture.

account. The working parts are concealed by a rectangular brushed-steel plate placed so the air-intake occurs around the edges. The plate is attractive in itself, but it can also be covered by gluing to the face a piece of paneling or wallpaper which matches the rest of the wall. The panel clips on and can be removed and replaced without tools.

Although a range hood is an essential for ventilation and is required by some building codes, it also improves the appearance of the kitchen. It can match the range, be made of copper, stainless steel or add a period accent to the decor of the finish is antiqued or decorated with wrought iron. One unusual hood is a roll-out model mounted on nylon casters. The unit pulls out to do a thorough ventilating job over range and oven. The fan operates automatically when the hood is pulled out, shuts itself off when the hood is retracted.

Another solution for a kitchen where room construction will not permit installation of a range hood, is a high-capacity fan that mounts flush with the ceiling. It should be connected to a duct that discharges through the nearest outside wall.

All ventilating fans should be cleaned often enough to prevent grease-build up which could be a fire hazard. Blades and motor can be cleaned by wiping with a paper towel. Do not use water.

Ventilation through doors and windows is helpful, too. Small louvers at ceiling height will help ventilation. They will need to be the movable kind if your home is situated where the climate varies a good deal.

Never place a window above a range. If the unit is gas operated, a blast of air could extinguish the flame or a blowing curtain or sleeve on an arm, reaching to close or open the window, might catch on fire.

Heating

Heating the kitchen would not seem to be much of a problem with all the heat generated by cooking. However, walls are so completely covered with cabinets and appliances that it is difficult to find a place for heating. One solution is to use the toe space under the base cabinets for long slim grilles into which the warm air is ducted. Sometimes there's room for a radiator at the bottom of a base cabinet.

A radiant-heat system in which hot water runs through copper pipe in a concrete slab or under the floor gives even comfortable heat to the entire floor and heats the whole kitchen efficiently. During times of the year when the main heating system may be turned off, spot heating can be provided. One model is a combination heat-light-ventilating fan unit which installs neatly into a ceiling. It operates from a wall switch, and the three operating features can be used independently or together. One switch comes with an automatic timing device, both a safety and energy-saver.

One builder created a uniquely useful heating system in his kitchen by placing a radiator on the floor within a cabinet where dishes, as well as dry cereal and crackers are stored. One shelf also contains a dish drainer. When the heat is operating dishes are warmed, or dried, and the crackers are always crisp. A small rack was added to dry dishtowels and small laundry. The door to the cabinet slides and does not interfere with traffic. It is kept open whenever kitchen heat is desired. The heat flow is a good foot and floor warmer in winter.

Cooling

Cooling the kitchen may be more important to you than heating it. If your area has a hot summer climate, place the kitchen on the north or east side of the house. If you have a choice, orient the house setting to take advantage of prevailing breezes and place doors and windows to provide good cross-ventilation.

Plant a couple of deciduous trees and bushes which shade the room in summer and let sunshine in during the winter.

A wide roof overhang or eaves, movable shutters, and awnings all help to cool a kitchen. Louvered screens are a good idea. Try not to have a paved area near the kitchen as it will retain the heat long after the sun has gone down.

A high ceiling is cooler than a low-pitched one. Use shades or curtains in light colors. Some are available with an aluminum reflective backing to keep out heat. Choose a cool color scheme such as blue or green. The kitchen should be insulated and the roof of light-colored roofing material. If the roof is to be of tar and gravel, ask for white rocks instead of the usual gray.

A room air conditioner will satisfactorily cool a small kitchen whose plan is not so open that the unit will work too hard trying to cool other rooms nearby. It should be mounted in a hole cut through the wall, rather than in a window where it will reduce needed light and spoil the view. If using central air-conditioning, do not keep the ventilator in the range hood running any more than necessary or it will pump cool air out and put a strain on the air conditioner.

GETTING THE KITCHEN BUILT

The homeowner has the following choices in choosing a method of building a kitchen.

He can hire an architect. He will quote a fee, based on whether he is designing the whole house or just the kitchen. He will take the homeowner's ideas, sketches and budget allowance and work from them to produce a final blueprint. He will also contract with dealers, tradespeople and subcontractors for materials and work to be done. He will also see the job through to the finish.

A less costly choice would be to hire a professional kitchen designer. Find one by inquiring at a decorating shop, asking a dealer who handles appliances and cabinets or getting a recommendation from the local American Institute of Architects for the name of a kitchen planning architect.

A third choice would be to buy ready made blueprints from a kitchen designer, architect or from any of the home magazines, and then fit his own ideas into the plans he buys. Dealers, who hope to sell appliances and cabinets, may supply

kitchen blueprints free of charge. These are a help only if your kitchen ideas fit in with their desire to sell cabinets and building materials.

Finally, he can draw his own plans, have them blueprinted, act as his own contractor, do part or all of the work himself or subcontract the difficult jobs such as plumbing and wiring. Do-it-yourself methods cut costs as much as half, but they do require a lot of time. The easiest jobs for the home builder are: laying floor tile, putting in insulation or an insulated ceiling, painting, paneling, laying carpet tile, hanging wallpaper and removing and rebuilding any existing cabinets and furnishings if it is a remodeling job.

DRAW YOUR OWN REMODELING PLANS

You will need some graph paper and a metal tape measure. (A cloth one will stretch and you must be accurate to the fraction of an inch). Start at a corner and measure the room above counter height. Mark the dimensions on a rough sketch. The final ones can be transferred later to graph paper. You will need to measure doors, windows, door swingouts, thickness of walls, radiators, chimney, or any irregularities. Mark the location of electrical outlets, light switches and fixtures, plumbing, any existing air conditioning equipment and exhaust fan as well as wiring, pipes and ducts. To move these involves additional expense. Note items you intend to replace.

Consult the local building inspector as you make your plans in order to find out what the local building codes require of you in the way of permits and permissable changes.

Once you're satisfied with your plans, have them blueprinted and use them to obtain building permits and for use by sub-contractors as well as for your own building purposes.

BUILDING A NEW HOUSE

You probably will have purchased, or have had someone such as an architect or designer supply you with, blueprints which contain the basic measurements of all kitchen features. If all you have are the outlines of a kitchen with room dimensions, you can buy some graph paper and work out your own ideas and have them transferred to a blueprinted plan.

You will want to locate the kitchen centers such as the range, sink, food preparation and mix, food storage and any special spots such as desk or dining areas. You will need accurate measurements of appliances you now own as well as those you plan to buy.

Many sketches and changes will be necessary. Remember to allow adequate space for moving about, sitting and getting up from a table as well as room for doors and cabinets to swing out. Check traffic patterns and work area to see whether too many steps will be required.

Changing plans on paper can be tedious work but all changes should be made at this stage. Once the construction of your new kitchen is underway even a small change can be extremely costly.

Courtesy of Arist-O-Kraft

Stock cabinets such as these come in many kinds of wood and finishes. The units shown here are maple, and they are available in many sizes and shapes to fit your own plan. This kitchen shows an interesting use of modern materials. It features brick behind the range, tile on the wall, and wood on the floor, but they are all manmade. The brick is a washable plastic panel, lightweight and easy to install. The tile is a realistic washable wallpaper, and the wooden floor is no-wax vinyl.

CABINETMAKING

Experience in using hand tools and some knowledge of basic woodworking, particularly framing and making wood joints, are useful. In cabinetmaking, the real key to a successful job is taking one step at a time, and not being satisfied to move on to the next until the previous step is done perfectly.

The kitchen cabinets discussed are those that are hung on walls and rest on the floor. Floor-supported units are called base cabinets.

Base cabinets are often placed against a wall, but they may also be a peninsula or island units. A peninsula cabinet is one forming a right angle with a wall or with another base cabinet, extending into the middle of the kitchen for a distance of at least three feet. Any less than three feet would provide limited storage space and would not be worth the expense or effort of construction. An island cabinet stands by itself in the middle of the kitchen.

The term cabinet usually refers to storage units, and obviously this is what cabinets are used for, but base cabinets also have other uses. The tops of base cabinets are usually finished with a durable material, such as plastic laminate so they can be used as work counters. Other base cabinets support kitchen equipment, particularly sinks and built-in ranges.

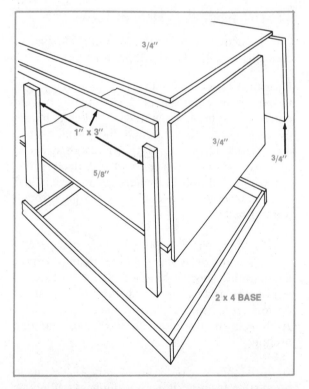

This drawing stresses the thickness of wood that will afford maximum strength. Base cabinets should be built on a 2" x 4" base to provide a 3 inch deep by 4 inch high toe space.

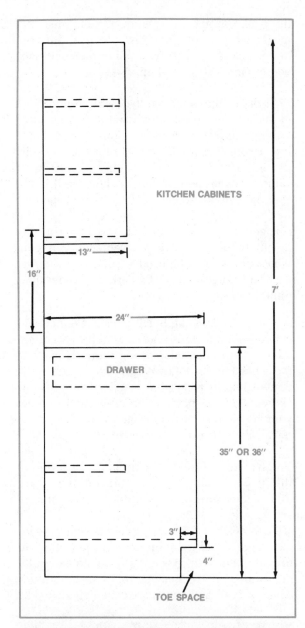

This drawing shows a view of a base and wall-hung cabinet installation. Dimensions provided are standard ones used by cabinet manufacturers. They should be altered to meet your needs.

For this article, it will be assumed that you have decided on a kitchen layout, that you know where cabinets are going to be placed, and that you know which base cabinets are going to be cut-out to permit the installation of a sink, range or dishwasher. The construction process now begins.

Where to Do the Job

You can build cabinets for your kitchen in one of two places: on-site (in the kitchen) or in the workshop, which will entail bringing the cabinets to the kitchen after they are built for installation. Each alternative has advantages and disadvantages.

Constructing cabinets in the kitchen involves more intricate framing. You have to build the frame out from the wall and ceiling or wall and floor and attach top, bottom, and face components.

Framing out a cabinet in the workshop involves less complicated construction. You basically have to make a box on which to attach exterior (facing) and interior (drawers and shelves) components. The cabinet is then carried to the kitchen and is either hung on the wall or placed on the floor and attached to the wall. In the case of peninsula and island units, the cabinet can be fastened right to the floor.

The big stumbling block to workshop construction is that you must be exacting in your measurements. It would be very frustrating to build a beautiful cabinet, take it to the kitchen and find that it is a foot too long or too short.

The advantages of building cabinets in a workshop outweigh on-site construction, and it is highly recommended especially if you are a beginner, to do the job there. In addition to the less complicated framing operation, workshop

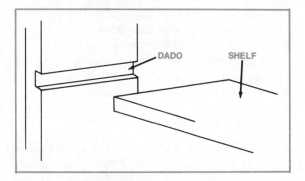

This is a dado joint. The cut-out (dado) in the end piece supports the shelf. Dadoes can also be used in drawer construction.

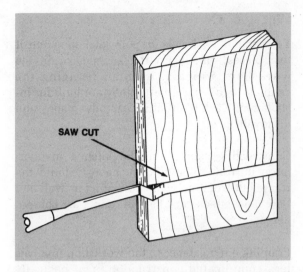

SAW CUT

Make dadoes by cutting the wood with a saw and using a chisel. Keep the chisel almost flat as it is tapped with a hammer. Shave off thin pieces. Do not cut too deeply.

construction of kitchen cabinets affords the following advantages: The kitchen does not have to be disrupted. Building cabinets for an entire kitchen can take a few weeks and doing the job on-site leaves the kitchen in disarray, limiting normal kitchen functions. Doing the job in the workshop allows ready access to tools. Furthermore, there may be floor-mounted power tools in the workshop such as a radial saw, that would make the construction task easier, but cannot be brought into the kitchen.

Building cabinets in the workshop allows the homeowner to fasten backings to them. Backs give the cabinets a more finished appearance and permit direct mounting to walls. Cabinets built on-site do not normally have backs. A back fastened to the type of frame necessitated by on-site construction leaves an air space between the cabinet and wall, which could become an area where condensation will develop.

Measure to be Sure

Cabinets have three main dimensions. The *width* is the measurement of the cabinet when viewed from the front. The *height* is the distance from the floor to the counter of a base cabinet, and from the bottom to the top of wall-hung units. The *depth* is the distance from the front to

the back. Be absolutely sure of your measurements. Make notes or draw pictures. Do anything necessary to refresh your memory once you get into the workshop.

Plan the cabinets to give the maximum amount of storage and work area without having them impinge on other functions. For instance, take into account where the refrigerator is going to be placed. If you plan on having a wall-hung cabinet above the refrigerator, be sure it is not low enough to prevent fitting the refrigerator beneath it. Decide on the capacity of the refrigerator you wish to install and measure its height before building the cabinet. Also plan what cut-outs will be needed such as where the sink and range will go. Be sure you know their dimensions.

Agencies such as the Small Homes Council and cabinet manufacturers have established certain standard dimensions for cabinets. However, these need not be followed to the letter. Alter the dimensions to meet your requirements insofar as your kitchen plan is concerned and to meet your homemaker's requirements insofar as her physical stature is concerned.

To give you a foundation from which to figure the size of your cabinets, the following are dimensions considered standard: Base cabinets are usually built 36 inches by 24 inches and as wide as desired. Countertops are normally 24 inches deep. Wall-hung units are usually built to provide 12 inch deep shelves. They are normally positioned 16 inches to 18 inches above a counter. Wall-hung units are usually installed 22

For adjustable shelves, attach shelving channels to each side of the cabinet, insert cleats and mount the shelf.

Another way to make shelves adjustable is to drill holes in end pieces that will accept shelf holders. This involves more work than mounting channels.

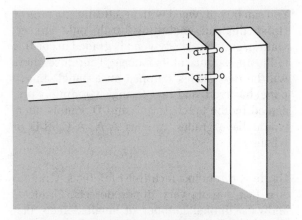

A dowel joint is formed by joining two pieces of wood together with wooden dowels and glue. Most cabinet makers employ the method, because it provides strength and a neat-looking finish.

inches over a sink and 30 inches over a stove. These are precautionary measures to prevent moisture and heat from damaging the cabinet and its contents. Wall-hung units may be dropped 12 inches below the ceiling to avoid the problem of putting storage space out of reach of the homemaker. This, of course, leaves an open space between the top of the cabinet and ceiling, which is a dust-catcher. It can be enclosed by framing out the space with 1 x 3 or 2 x 3 lumber and attaching drywall or some other paneling.

However, there is really no reason why cabinets cannot be built right to the ceiling and this hard-to-reach shelving area used for storing infrequently employed items. A kitchen step stool can be purchased that will overcome any problem and inaccessibility.

Buying Materials

It is recommended that you use plywood, except for trim pieces. However, to build cabinets with solid wood, use ash, birch, maple, oak or walnut if you desire a natural finish. Cypress and northern white pine are particularly suitable for painting.

Plywood is the main wood used in the construction of kitchen cabinets although recently a pressed material called flakeboard has come into wide use by cabinetmakers because of cost. It is best to use plywood as flakeboad does not give as attractive results.

Plywood is composed of laminated veneers. The grain of each layer is placed at a right angle to the layer next to it. Layers are glued and then pressed together under extreme pressure, making the board much stronger than a solid piece of lumber. Solid lumber may bend, warp and buckle, but plywood will not. Keep in mind that lumber used for cabinet doors, end pieces and drawer fronts must be selected not only on the basis of appearance, but mainly on the ability to withstand warping and shrinking. Plywood offers the strength to resist these problems. Furthermore, it won't split, as solid lumber often does, when you drive nails close to the edges.

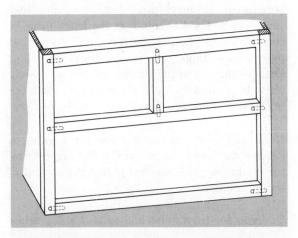

A typical front frame of a cabinet and places where dowels would be employed. Although one dowel is shown per joint, two should be used for maximum strength.

You can buy plywood with practically any type of finish desired, including birch, oak, cherry, walnut, and maple. Plywood is graded according to the appearance of its facings. Therefore, there will be two grades stamped on a panel since a panel has front and rear facings. Grading is presented by the letter A, B, C and D. Panels, then, would have grades such as A-A, A-C, B-D or whatever.

Grade A refers to a face free of defects. Grade B is a face having very minor defects. Grade C allows a limited number of small defects that will not show through when the board is painted. Grade D allows a significant amount of defects but these too can be covered with paint. The grading system has nothing to do with the strength of plywood. However, the better the grade, the more costly the panel.

Select panels having a grade A face and grade A or B back for cabinet doors and drawer fronts. Panels having a grade A or B face and grade C or D back should be for end pieces. Select what is called plyscord (grade B-D) for cabinet bottoms, tops that will be covered with plastic laminate or some other covering and backs. Plyscord may also be used for end pieces that will be mounted next to a wall. You can also use plyscord for shelves and dividers.

Selecting wood that is thick enough to provide sturdiness is very important. You can buy plywood in 4 x 8 sheets that are from ¹/₄ to ³/₄ inch thick in ¹/₈ inch increments. You must decide how thick you want components, but keep in mind that the thicker panels obviously provide greater strength and often eliminate the need for adding reinforcing pieces to the cabinet.

Generally, the lumber needed for making a kitchen cabinet is as follows. (The suggestions for thickness are those that give a cabinet maximum strength):

Wood for front stiles and rails: 1 x 3 lumber strips.

Wood for bottom and top pieces - for top, ³/₄ inch plywood; for bottom, ⁵/₈" plyscord.

Wood for end and back pieces - Use ³/₄" plyscord for hidden end pieces and for backing, better quality plywood for exposed end pieces.

Suggested: ³/₄ inch.

Wood for shelves - use ³/₄ inch plywood or regular shelving, which is available in sizes from 1 x 6 to 1 x 12.

Wood for hidden parts of drawers - sides, back and botton, ¹/₄ inch plywood; for drawer facings, use ³/₄ inch plywood.

Doors - use ³/₄ inch grade AA or grade AB plywood.

All lumber must be dry to avoid shrinkage problems. The best way to assure yourself of dry wood is to deal with a lumber dealer you know, or with one who has a reputation for being reliable. Reputable lumber dealers will discuss your project with you and give advice if you encounter a problem.

Generally, dry (and moist) lumber can be recognized by looking for the following: dry lumber is apt to possess small, brittle slivers and emits a hollow sound when rapped with the knuckles. Dry lumber is springier and weighs less than moist lumber. Moist lumber has a sharp odor and may feel damp.

Constructing the Frame

The frame of a cabinet is composed of solid pieces (end, top, bottom and backing) and a

The first step in constructing the front frame of a cabinet is to measure out wood exactly and cut each piece.

series of rails and stiles that separate various functional aspects of the unit. For example, a cabinet may be composed of sections for drawers and storage space.

To begin frame construction, first cut dados into end pieces and also into top and bottom pieces if you are sectioning the cabinet with dividers. A dado is a groove having a flat bottom and square corners. If made properly, dados provide a strong, snug seat for shelves. The need for additional reinforcement will not be necessary. Dados may also be cut into top and bottom pieces to accept dividers.

To make dados, the following procedures may be used; First, measure the exact location on each end piece where a shelf is desired. Be meticulous in measuring. The spot on one end piece must correspond exactly to the spot on the other end piece if the shelf is to be level. Next, measure the thickness of the shelving you will be using. Draw two parallel lines representing the thickness of the shelf at the indicated spot of the dado on each end piece. Use a carpenter's square for drawing the lines to assure they are perfectly straight. With each end piece marked off exactly, make saw cuts just inside each line across the wood to the desired depth of the dado. The depth of the cut should be approximately one-half the thickness of the end piece. For example, if the end piece is ³/₄ inch plywood, the depth of the saw cut should be about ³/₈ inch.

The most accurate way of making saw cuts is to place the board in a metal miter frame (box) and draw a box saw across the reference marks. Use the straight guide groove of the miter frame, not one of the angle guide grooves.

Now, complete making the dado with a paring, or finishing chisel. A paring chisel has a short blade which is held flat to the wood surface and is tapped gently with a hammer to produce a thin shaving effect. The result is a smooth, flat cut surface. Chisel blades vary in width from ¹/₈ inch to 1 inch, in ¹/₈ inch increments. Do not use a blade which is too wide. A word of caution: when using the chisel, make shallow shaving cuts. Do not cut deeply or dig the chisel into the wood.

When the dado has been shaved, smooth out the joint and its edges. Use a half-round cabinet rasp to begin with until you get a relatively smooth surface. Then complete the finish with a piece of medium grit sandpaper. The surface does not have to be absolutely smooth.

Cut the dado into the other end piece in the same manner. With both dadoes cut, place the shelving piece into the dadoes to see that it fits and is tight. The corners of the shelf can be beveled (rounded off) if you find it difficult to insert the shelf into the dadoes.

Dadoing provides permanent shelves; that is, shelves that cannot be adjusted, but must stay in place. Many homemakers prefer the advantage of adjustable shelves, and providing this is easy. Instead of making dadoes, purchase adjusting channels and screw them to the end pieces. Shelves are placed on metal cleats that are inserted into the channels. To change the position of the shelf, take the shelf from the cabinet, remove cleats from channels, place them into the holes that will give the desired height and lay the shelf on them.

Another type of joint that you should know how to make for cabinet construction is the dowel joint. It is used in fine cabinetmaking for ensuring strength and holding power where rails and

Measure and mark off where dowel holes are to be drilled in one piece and then in the other piece of wood. Holes in both pieces must match up exactly.

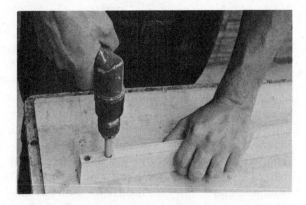

Drill holes, using a bit that is the same diameter as the diameter of the dowels being used.

Before gluing pieces together, see that dowel holes match precisely. Notice that grooved dowels are being used. They provide a better base for glue to take hold.

stiles are joined together. You can buy dowels in a lumber yard in several different diameters. For cabinet construction, sizes usually used are $3/8$ inch and $1/2$ inch. Get grooved dowels as they will provide a firmer grip when glued.

Generally, each end of a dowel should extend into the wood being joined about three times the diameter of the dowel. In other words, if you are using a $1/2$ inch dowel, and the width of the boards being joined permit, the dowel should extend into each board about $1^1/2$ inches. Also, for maximum strength, provide each joint with two dowels. This means that two dowel holes have to be drilled into *each* board.

Take plenty of time in preparing dowel joints. Make very sure that the holes in one board line up perfectly with the holes in the other. Use a

drill bit of the same diameter as the diameter of the dowel to drill out dowel holes. A practice used by professionals is to slightly bevel the edge of each dowel hole to provide space that will receive an extra amount of glue. This will result in a stronger joint.

After the dowel holes have been drilled, make a test assembly of the joint to see that everything lines up properly. If a hole doesn't match exactly with its corresponding hole, you can enlarge it slightly with a rat-tail file. The extra gap will fill with glue.

To complete the joint, mix a supply of casein or resorcinol glue, or use a ready-mixed white glue. Put glue into each dowel hole, insert the dowel and push the joint together.

Squeeze glue into each dowel hole. Use plenty, but there is no need to flood the area. After the boards are joined, wipe off any excess glue that may be forced from the joint.

Press the two pieces possessing dowels together firmly to assure tightness. Notice how sharp and neat a properly made joint looks.

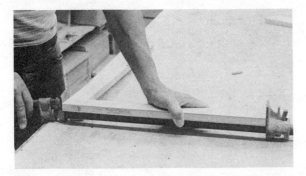

The joint should now be clamped with a pipe clamp. Pipe clamps are available in various sizes from a hardware store.

After becoming proficient at making dowel joints, you will be able to construct any type of cabinet front, even one that appears as intricate as this.

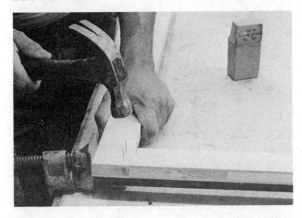

With the work clamped, hammer brads through the wood and into dowels to give the joint maximum holding power. Although three brads are seen, there are really four. One has already been hammered into place.

Now clamp the joint with a pipe clamp. Hammer $1/2$ inch or larger brads into each piece so the brads insert themselves right into the dowel. You will hammer in four brads. The result, when the glue hardens, is a joint that is about as strong as can be made.

Assembling

You should have ready for assembly the following components: A cabinet form consisting of rails and stiles that are joined together by dowels, end pieces that may or may not be dadoed, depending whether the shelves will be adjustable or nonadjustable shelves. A $3/4$ inch countertop for a base cabinet that has been built up to $1\frac{1}{2}$ inches by gluing and nailing 1 x 2 or 1 x 3 trim pieces around the perimeter. The buildup of the countertop is done to provide a suitable

firm surface for working. A base piece that can be an appropriate sized piece of shelving for gluing and nailing to the bottom of the end pieces, cabinet front and back piece.

In constructing a countertop, glue and nail or staple or trim pieces around the perimeter to build up the counter and provide a stronger counter. The buildup also facilitates finishing the edges with plastic laminate.

This is the face of the countertop which has been finished off with plastic laminate.

With the top resting firmly on the cabinet, the two are screwed tightly together from below. Use screws of a size that will provide maximum holding power, but make sure they aren't so long as to penetrate the countertop.

A top piece, if this is a wall-hung cabinet, of the same type of shelving used for the base piece. This, too, can be glued and nailed to the end pieces, cabinet front and back piece.

Important: If you are making a base cabinet, build it on a 2 x 4 frame to provide toe space.

To put pieces together, first hold end pieces in a vertical position and insert shelves into dados if dados are used. Hammer 8d finishing nails, spaced about 6 inches apart, through the end pieces into the shelves. Next, fit the front of the cabinet to the end pieces with glue and 8d finishing nails. Then, nail and glue the back to the assembled components. Turn the construction over, nail and glue the bottom piece in place.

If this is a base cabinet, glue and nail 1 x 2 or 1 x 3 trim pieces around the perimeter of the end pieces to serve as a base for the countertop. (The trim pieces nailed around the countertop must fit on the trim pieces nailed around the edge of the end pieces.)

Put the top of the base cabinet in place. Screw the top of the rest of the construction from below. Screws should be inserted through the trim pieces nailed around the perimeter of the cabinet front so they extend through the trim pieces nailed around the perimeter of the countertop.

Finally, countersink all finishing nails and fill holes with wood filler.

Important: If the cabinet is designed to accept drawers, do not install the countertop until drawer guides and rollers have been installed. Trying to do this after the countertop is in place is very difficult. It is suggested that metal guides and nylon rollers be used, which are easier than old-fashioned wooden guides. Follow installation instructions accompanying hardware.

Finishing a Countertop

Before the countertop is attached to a cabinet, it is suggested that you cover it with a plastic laminate. Plastic laminate has long been used as a work covering, because it resists scratching, grease, high temperature, impacts and moisture.

Determine the amount of material needed for the top and edges. Plastic laminate may be cut to size by scribing along cut-off lines with a sharp or pointed tool, such as a knife used for cutting drywall or an awl. Now, saw along the scribed line with a hand saw which has 12 to 15 teeth per inch. A power saw equipped with a plywood cutting blade may be used, but it doesn't afford the control that a hand saw provides.

Be absolutely sure that you scribe lines and cut the laminate with its finished side *up*. This will produce rough edges on the underside and not the top side. Rough edges can be smoothed off with sandpaper.

Cut and install edging pieces first. Then, install the top. Plastic laminate is applied to wood by spreading contact cement on both the backside of the material and on the wood surface. The fit must be exact the first time, because once the cemented surfaces come in contact with each other, it is very difficult to shift the laminate.

Making Drawers and Finishing the Job

There are several ways of making a drawer. The method illustrated employs dado and rabbet

A rabbet cut is nothing more than half a dado. It is made at the edge of a board in the same manner as a dado.

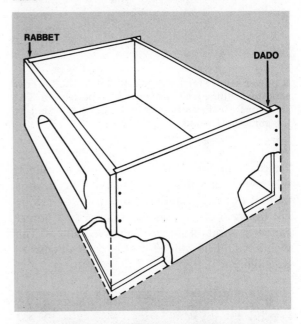

RABBET

DADO

This is one way of making a drawer. The bottom of the drawer may be fitted into dados in corresponding pieces, as seen here, or simply nailed to corresponding components. Dadoing provides a more permanent construction.

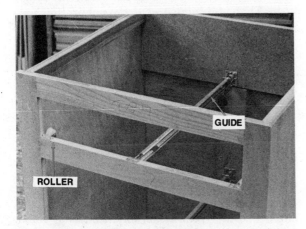

GUIDE

ROLLER

Drawers will operate easier and will not bind if metal drawer guides and nylon rollers are used.

cuts, which give the drawers a great deal of strength. Be sure to make precise measurements. The drawer does not have to fit snugly, but it should fit into its space with enough ease to allow easy opening and closing.

There are many varieties of doors and matching drawer fronts available for cabinets. Visit kitchen cabinet showrooms for ideas. Examining a professional job can also be a great help to you in building the cabinets.

A power sander facilitates work. But no matter how sanding is done, it should be done to perfection. The smoothest finish on the cabinet will be afforded by the smoothest wood.

When the cabinet is built, it must be finished. The most important step in finishing a cabinet, whether it is going to be painted or have a natural finish, is sanding. Don't ruin the job by not taking time to sand it properly. If a power sander is available, it will facilitate matters. The wood should be sanded until it is as smooth as possible.

You can make your own doors using ³/₄ inch plywood with the type of face desired such as birch, ash, oak, etc. This is especially suitable if you want a door with a simple, straight finish. However, if you want a door that is grooved or rabbeted, it is suggested that you visit a showroom that displays kitchen cabinets. Find what you like and order the door from the salesman. They will come precut, but not prefinished. Unless you are an exceptional craftsman possessing special tools, making doors is difficult.

While you are at the showroom, get some idea of the kind of cabinet hardware you would like. There are many varieties, including strap hinges, H-hinges and offset cabinet hinges. You also have a choice concerning the type of catches for your cabinet doors.

Hinges are usually sold with corresponding drawer pulls that match.

The last task is to attach the wall-hung or base cabinet to the wall. Preferably, find wall studs and screw the cabinet into studs which are normally placed 16 inches apart, center-to-center.

Kitchen Fixtures
[SEE KITCHEN DESIGN & PLANNING.]

Kitchen Wiring
[SEE ELECTRICAL WIRING.]

Knee-Wall

A wall construction usually found in attics is called a knee-wall. The term is derived from the appearance of the wall. There is a joint which angles the wall into the roof.

A knee-wall should be at least four feet high. The knee-wall studs are attached to a base plate which may be nailed to the subflooring or in some cases the floor itself. The knee-wall and the base plates should be of the same size lumber.

When building an attic knee-wall, the base plates should be nailed to the subfloor or joists with 16 penny nails. These base plates are the bottom foundation of the knee-wall.

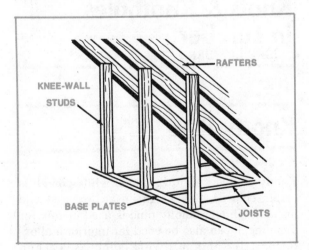

Knee-wall studs placed perpendicular to the subflooring.

After measuring the distance from the base plate to the ceiling beam above, cut the lumber in those dimensions to form the wall studs. Remember that *each* rafter must be joined to the base plate by means of a stud.

The stud should be toenailed to the base plate with 8 penny nails. Make sure the studs are level.

The area behind the knee-wall can be used for storage. If the knee-wall is paneled or closed in, a hinged door can be hung as an entrance to the area. *SEE ALSO WALL & CEILING CONSTRUCTION.*

Knife, Electric
[SEE ELECTRIC KNIFE REPAIR.]

Knives & Scrapers

Knives and scrapers are used mainly for smoothing wood and removing varnishes and

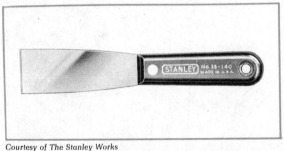

Courtesy of The Stanley Works

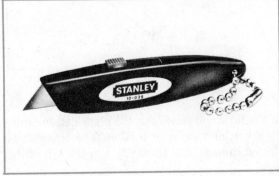

paints. The drawknife and putty knife are two of the most common knives and scrapers. *SEE ALSO HAND TOOLS.*

Knob & Tube Wiring

Knob and tube wiring, an antiquated wiring technique, is still in use in many homes. In this system, the wiring is fastened to the framework of the building with porcelain knobs. Porcelain tubes act as bushings to insulate the holes where wires pass through the framework. *SEE ALSO ELECTRICAL WIRING.*

Knockdown Sawhorse

For a small home workshop, a knockdown sawhorse might be the answer to the limited space problem. Collapsible sawhorses can be built out of solid wood or by using plywood.

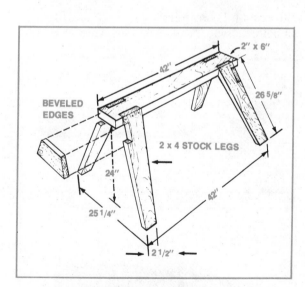

Solid Stock Sawhorse

In a solid wood sawhorse, the plans call for sturdy 2 x 4 inch strips of lumber. The crossbar is slotted causing it to fit tightly into the top of the legs.

A double railed sawhorse is built using ³/₄ inch plywood. It is locked together with 20d nails spliced into predrilled holes.

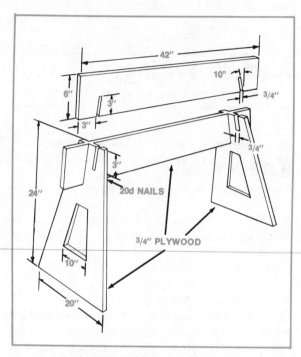

Plywood Knockdown Sawhorse

On both projects be sure of accurate measurements to insure proper fit.

Knots & Knotholes in Lumber
[SEE LUMBER.]

Knotty Pine

Knotty pine is a knotty grade of white pine. It is cream colored, lightweight, even textured and durable. Though knotty pine is used mainly for paneling, it can also be used for interior and exterior trim and millwork such as kitchen cabinets, doors and window frames. *SEE ALSO WOOD IENTIFICATION.*

Lac

Lac is the natural gum secreted by an insect called the lac bug found in India and near-by countries. Lac forms the base for shellac.

Lacquers

Lacquer is a clear finish which has as its base cellulose nitrate combined with other man-made materials. It comes in either brush or spray form and produces a hard finish, often used on floors. Lacquer will not change hue, but will intensify color and grain. Because lacquer requires some skill to use, it is less popular in home use than varnish or shellac. *SEE ALSO WOOD FINISHING.*

Ladder Jack

A ladder jack is an adjustable support that is suspended from a ladder by hooks that attach to the side rail. To form a scaffold using two ladder jacks, two ladders of the same size and a strong plank are needed. A ladder jack can also support a short, wide board to be used as a tray for holding various objects such as tools, paints or nails. *SEE ALSO SCAFFOLDS & LADDERS.*

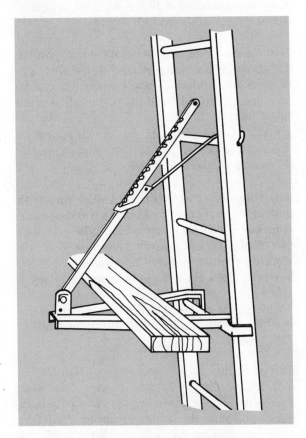

Ladder jack used as a tray.

Ladder jack used for making scaffolding.

Ladders
[SEE SCAFFOLDS & LADDERS.]

Ladder Safety

The safe use of a ladder requires that the ladder be used only for its designed purpose: a simple climbing tool.

Ladders should be inspected frequently for such defects as general wobbliness, loose hinges, loose rungs, cracked or split side rails or rungs, or defective latches (on extension ladders). If such defects are found, they should be repaired before the ladder is used again. These repairs should be made only by the manufacturer or a skilled craftsman. If the ladder cannot be repaired, it should be destroyed to prevent accidents.

Ladders should be carried parallel to the ground. This carrying position provides the greatest safety, since the ladder's forward movement can be seen and controlled. In addition, the ladder is not likely to catch in the ground or on passing objects. A ladder should not be dropped or deliberately caused to fall. The impact loosens joints and weakens the ladder.

Safe ways to set up or raise a ladder vary with the kind of ladder used. The safe working angle is precalculated for a stepladder. When the legs of a stepladder are separated and locked, a safe working angle is assured. An extension ladder, however, does not have preset angles. To get a safe working angle, the home craftsman must set the base of an extension ladder one-fourth of the working length of the ladder from the wall. (a $75\frac{1}{2}°$ slant).

The procedure for erecting an extension ladder is as follows: Brace the base so it will not slip. Facing the ladder, grasp the top rung with both hands and raise the ladder overhead. Walk forward, moving hands to lower rungs, until the ladder is perpendicular to the ground. Lower the ladder until it rests against the wall or roof edge. Make sure the base and top are firm and secure. Check the safe angle with a rough measurement of the base-to-wall distance.

Ladder safety demands the right ladder for the job and the right procedure for use. There are three classes of stepladders established by ladder manufacturers. These classes are identified by color-coded labels:

Type I   (a yellow label) is designed for heavy-duty use by contractors and industry.
Type II   (a blue label) is designed for reasonable service in commercial maintenance work.
Type III (a red label) is intended for general service around the home.

A Type III ladder is not intended for use by industry or commercial painters.

Extension ladders must have an overlap of the sections or the ladder will collapse at the joint. Ladders up to 37' long must have an overlap of 3' for safety. Longer ladders, generally speaking, require one foot of overlap for every twelve feet of working length (a 59' ladder needs 5' of overlap) until a maximum overlap of 5' is reached.

Safe use of a ladder involves a number of common sense precautions, such as the following:

Always climb and work facing the ladder.

Hold onto the ladder with at least one hand. If two hands are needed for a job, hook a leg around a rung.

Locate the immediate work area within easy arm's length of the centerline of the ladder, to prevent excessive leaning and possible unbalancing of the ladder.

Never stand on top of a stepladder. Use a ladder with sufficient height so that the home craftsman may stand two or three rungs from the top. The lower position provides greater balance and support.

Use an extension ladder that will extend (with safe overlap) at least 3 feet above the edge of the roof. Such an extension lessens the chance of the ladder slipping and provides adequate handholds for getting on and off the ladder.

Remove mud and grease from shoes and ladder rungs to prevent slipping and falling.

Make sure the legs of the stepladder are fully extended and locked to avoid collapse in use.

Never use a metal ladder near live electrical wires.

If the ground is soft, place wide boards or stone blocks under the legs of the ladder to prevent uneven sinking.

Do not store a ladder by leaning it against a wall. It should be hung by its side rails from a wall or posts. Horizontal storage will prevent sagging and warping of the ladder. To prolong the life of a ladder, do not store it in areas of high heat or exposed to the weather.

Prepared from information supplied by the National Safety Council and the American Ladder Institute.

Lag Bolt

A lag bolt or screw is a heavy duty screw with a square head that is primarily used as a wood screw. Available in lengths up to six inches, the screw is driven into the material with an adjustable wrench. *SEE ALSO FASTENERS.*

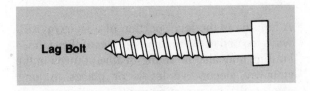

Lally Columns

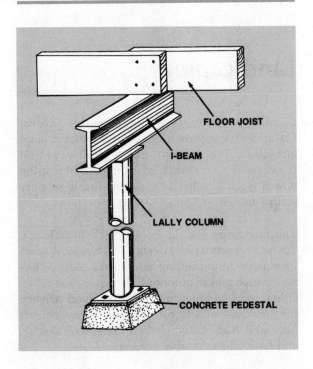

A lally column is a steel post, often concrete-filled, which provides support for beams and girders. *SEE ALSO FLOOR CONSTRUCTION.*

Laminate

Laminate is the process of pressing thin sheets or layers together to form a solid, single piece of material. Plastic laminates are generally used to protect and decorate floors, counter and tabletops, and are easily applied to plywood and chipboard surfaces. A laminate backing should be applied to boards that may warp due to moisture. Both the backing and the laminate coverings may be glued in place with contact cement. Laminate can be cut with a fine-toothed saw and smoothed on the edges with a plane, router or fine-toothed file.

Plastic laminates can be scorched and blistered by extreme heat, therefore hot objects like skillets and pans should not be placed directly on laminate coverings. Any chemical spills should be wiped up immediately to avoid staining or burning the laminate.

Plywood is the most common building laminate.

Laminated Beams & Arches

Laminated beams and arches are made of layers or plies of wood, usually softwood, glued together with a waterproof adhesive. These large structures, a product of modern construction, offer strength, versatility in shape, safety, natural wood beauty and endurance. The beams and arches are constructed and prefinished in industrial plants. The timbers are usually end-joined with a special hooked-scarf joint to permit the needed length. Straight or tapered beams are generally used in house construction while the more complex shapes, such as curves and arches, are used in commercial construction.

941

Courtesy of Southern Forest Products Association.

Laminated Beams

Laminated Floors

Laminated floors are constructed of compressed plastic layers that form one solid sheet. Laminated floors have become increasingly popular because they are durable, need little maintenance, are easily installed and come in a wide selection of colors, patterns and textures.

Before installing laminate, use paint remover and a scraper to clean the floor of any varnish, stain or paint. Smooth down the surface and, if necessary, replace portions of the damaged floor with particle board or plywood. Cut the laminate face up with a fine-toothed saw; if a circular saw is used, cut face down. Always saw the laminate $1/4$ inch to $3/8$ inch larger than necessary. Excess can be trimmed after the laminate is glued. Ap-

ply one coat of adhesive to the laminate back and to the floor with a clean brush. Allow both coats to dry before brushing a second coat on the laminate. Always follow manufacturer's directions for application and drying time. When the two coated surfaces touch, a bond is immediately formed. Therefore, be sure the sheets are positioned correctly before laying them down. Use a small hand roller to press the sheets for a satisfactory bond. Roll the center area first and move toward the edges, keeping the pressure even. A strip of laminate or metal may then be applied for a finished edge. SEE ALSO FINISH FLOORING.

Landing

A landing is the level portion of a stairway. Always located at the top and bottom of the stairs, a landing may also be found at abrupt turns in the stairway, decorative levels or places in long, steep stairs for a resting point. Landings can be large enough for plants or a chair and lamp arrangement or so small that they provide just enough space to stand. SEE ALSO STAIR CONSTRUCTION.

Landscaping

Landscaping involves changing the natural features of a section of ground to make it more attractive. Trees, lawn, drive, walkways and flowers are elements of house landscaping which work together to make the house scenery complete.

The landscape should be arranged to enhance the natural setting and design of a house. A good focal point in the setting is to have a patio or terrace which makes outdoor living space available. Other additions may include shade and privacy for the house and terrace, service areas for garbage and trash cans, clothes lines, tool storage and fruit and vegetable gardens.

For landscaping to be effective, it must be well planned. Family needs should be considered as well as existing conditions such as trees, shrubs, walkways and walls which may be used in final plans. *SEE ALSO LAWNS & GARDENS.*

Lap Joint

Full and half lap joints are commonly used in furniture construction for fitting crossrails in frames. Full lap joints are the strongest and easiest to form. Mark the depth and width of the crossrail on one end of the side rail. Carefully cut the waste from the sides with a hacksaw and chisel the base until it is level. The crossrail and side rail can then be joined and secured with glue.

The half lap joint requires cutting both the side and crossrails. Measure the width of the side rail and mark it on one end of the crossrail. Measure the depth of the crossrail and mark it on the side rail. Saw from the sides to the base of the joint in both the side rail and crossrail, and remove any waste with a chisel. Glue the two members

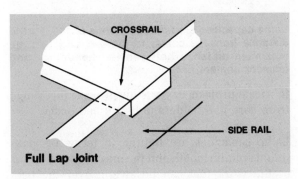

Full Lap Joint

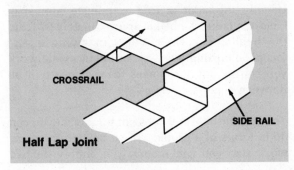

Half Lap Joint

together, let dry, then trim if necessary. *SEE ALSO FURNITURE MAKING.*

Larch Wood

Larch wood is a strong, heavy, coarse-grained wood. Its sapwood is yellow while the heartwood ranges from orange to reddish-brown. Because of its resistance to the effects of the soil, larch wood is used for telephone poles, railroad ties and mine timbers. Larch is also used in the construction of ships and barges.

The larch tree has ten to twelve species and is native to the cooler temperature zones. A portion of the city of Venice is reported to be built on pilings of European larch. *SEE ALSO WOOD IDENTIFICATION.*

Latex Paints

Latex paints are a significant improvement in painting. A dispersion of polymer in water, latex paint is popular because it is easy to use and care for. All latex paints may be thinned and cleaned up with water. They spread easily and evenly and dry very fast, usually in about an hour. They are known for their durability and lack of odor. Brushes or rollers may be used to apply latex paint. Because it dries so quickly, a wet rag should be kept at hand, to wipe up spills and drips as they happen. *SEE ALSO PAINTS & PAINTING.*

Lath

Lath is a building material attached to rafters, joists or studs as a support for slats, tiles or plaster. The lath may be made of narrow strips of wood or insulating board, steel or metal mesh or gypsum in sheet form. *SEE ALSO WALL & CEILING CONSTRUCTION.*

Lathe

The lathe is one of the few woodworking machines on which you can turn out a finished project. For example, work held between its centers might become a lamp base; a block mounted on a faceplate might become a salad bowl. Shaping, smoothing, and finishing are all done right in the machine.

Reactions to the lathe differ. Some people immediately operate the tool without regard for some basic considerations; others assume that a long period of apprenticeship will be required before they dare try an actual part or project. The latter approach is safer, but it should not be carried to an extreme. The truth is that a beginner can form a good piece of work immediately as long as he uses lathe chisels in a simple fashion. The professional uses a "cutting" action whenever he can whereas the learner should stay with a "scraping" action, a technique that enables him to use any chisel right from the start. In so doing, he can accomplish quality work. He can be immediately productive while taking an occasional crack at more advanced chisel usage.

General Characteristics

In concept, all lathes are the same. They differ in features, weight and capacity. The main parts include a *headstock* that is in a fixed position, a *tailstock* that is movable, and a *tool rest* that is adjustable. All parts are mounted on a *bed* or *ways*. The tool rest and the tailstock are movable laterally so they can be situated to suit the size of the work.

Spindle turnings are mounted between the headstock and the tailstock. Bowls, trays and the like are mounted on a *faceplate* that secures only the headstock. When work can't be mounted between centers and is too small to do on a faceplate, a *screw-center* can be employed. This too secures only to the headstock and is designed so small pieces can be worked. In addition, universal chucks, three-jaw chucks and holding devices that you can make yourself can be used with the lathe. Therefore, on a lathe you can

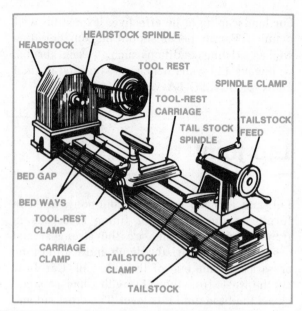

Basic parts of a woodworking lathe

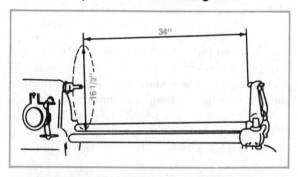

Lathe capacities are figured in terms of "A", 2 x the distance from the center to the bed and "B", the maximum distance between the headstock and tailstock centers.

fabricate projects or parts for projects that range from corn cob holders to heavy bed posts.

Lathe capacities are figured in terms of maximum spindle length and the maximum diameter of the work that can be swung over the bed. Usually, the latter is used to indicate lathe size. On a 12″ lathe, the bed is approximately 6″ from the headstock. Thus, you can swing a 12″ faceplate turning. The greater the faceplate work you can mount, the longer the distance will be between centers.

The spindle capacity does not limit what you can do in terms of a project. To go beyond the basic work size you can mount, you simply do two turnings and then join them. On many lathes you can do outboard turning. For such work, the workpiece is mounted on the outboard side of the headstock so the work radius is limited by the distance from the center to the floor. Therefore, even the lathe-size figure given in catalogs isn't a true picture of maximum work size.

Safety

Generally, the lathe is a safe tool. Of course, the usual clothing precautions apply. Half sleeves are good; long sleeves are fine as long as they don't flap and the cuffs are tight around the wrists. Follow the rules concerning handling chisels and hand position on the tool rest. Be extremely careful with speeds, especially when doing roughing operations. Wearing goggles is a good idea although they are more important for preliminary steps than they are for final sanding and finishing.

Check how secure the mounted work is before you start cutting and, occasionally, during the turning. Do this even more on softwood than on hardwood. Always spin the work by hand before you flick the switch. Keep all chisels sharp.

Adjustment

The one major lathe adjustment is alignment of the *spur center,* which is in the headstock, with the *cup center,* which is in the tailstock. How this is accomplished and maintained may vary from tool to tool, and you'll find instructions for doing it in the owner's manual. The important thing is for the points on the centers to meet when they are viewed from above (vertical alignment) and when they are viewed from the side (horizontal alignment). Since the spur center has a fixed position, any necessary adjustments are made by moving the cup center.

Speeds

The basic rule is to use slow speeds for large work and fast speeds for small work. On all jobs, speed changes should be made during the work. The lowest speeds are suggested for roughing operations. The rpm's move up as you get into the shaping stages. The high speeds are used for

final cuts and for finishing. The exception occurs when you get to maximum-size work. Actually, this restriction is more a safety factor than anything else.

You can get quite close to the suggested speeds if your lathe is equipped with a variable speed changer. In most cases, however, you'll be working with belts and will have to use specific speeds provided by the relationship between pulleys. Stay as close to the suggested speeds as you can. if you must (at least until you acquire good skills on the lathe), use a lower speed rather than a higher one.

At all times, let the action of the lathe and of the work be your best guide. If it's difficult to hold the chisel or if the work or the lathe vibrates excessively, it's a good sign that you are going too fast.

Centers

The drive center in the headstock has a point for centering the work plus spurs that dig into the wood. The spurs must always seat firmly in order for the wood to turn. It's a good idea to work on one of the spurs with a file, making a very small half-round shape or forming a bevel at one end. In doing this, if you ever have to remove a spindle turning from the lathe before it is complete, you'll be able to re-mate it with the spur center, placing it back in the original position.

The center in the tailstock can be plain or cupped. The cupped design is better because it provides more bearing surface and thus less chance for the mounting to loosen. With either one, you should check occasionally and tighten the fit if necessary. Many craftsmen use a tiny drop of oil on the dead center as a lubricant. However, don't overdo it since the oil can stain the wood. Paste wax works fine but don't use too much of it; just polish the point on the center.

The best method is to use a ball-bearing live center in the tailstock. The point on this turns with the work and, therefore, eliminates the loosening and burning problems you can encounter with a dead center.

Lathe

Faceplates

Faceplates come in different sizes, ranging from about 3″ up to 10″. They are always mounted in the headstock and make it possible to turn work that can't be mounted between centers. In this way you can do such work as bowls, trays, round boxes, and bases for spindles.

Screws are used to attach the work to the plate. Use screws that are heavy enough to provide security but not so long that you may cut into them when shaping the project.

The tool rest

The tool rest is an adjustable ledge on which you rest the chisel when you apply it to the work. It can be moved either laterally or vertically and will pivot so you have complete freedom of adjustment in relation to the work whether it is a spindle turning or a faceplate job.

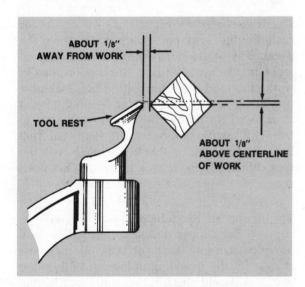

The theoretically correct position for the tool rest. It's not always possible to work this way, but stay as close to it as you can. Let the chisel play against the rest.

The ideal position for the tool rest is about ⅛″ away from the work and about ⅛″ above the work center line. It's a difficult position to maintain constantly unless you are doing work such as straight cylinders or tapers. Still, it's generally a good rule and should be remembered at least as a guide post.

Lathe chisels

A good set of chisels should include a *gouge*, a *skew*, a *squarenose*, a *parting tool*, a *spear point* and a *roundnose*. An ordinary butt chisel can be used in place of the squarenose; the skew, when placed on its side and used in a scraping action, will do many of the jobs performed by the spear point.

If you don't maintain a keen edge on the chisels, you'll be working under a handicap. Your best bet is to study the shape of the tool before you start using it. Keep a stone handy and, as you work, touch up the cutting edge occasionally.

Carbide-tipped tools are available in various sizes. The cutting edges are made of an extremely hard material that will hold sharpness much longer than steel. They can be used on wood but, more importantly, they make it possible to do freehand turning on metals and plastics at woodworking speeds.

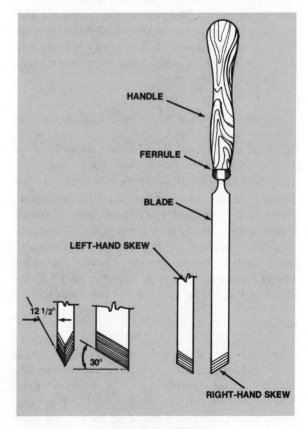

Typical lathe chisels.

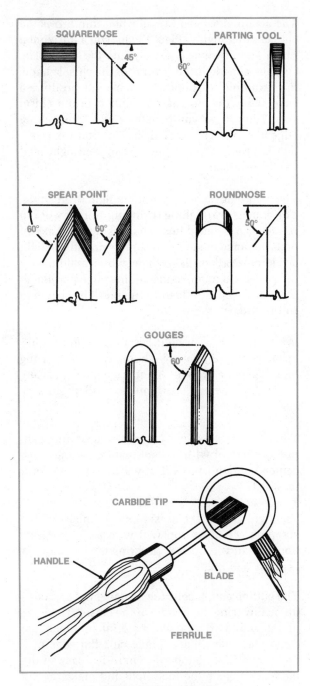

Typical lathe chisels.

This is the correct and safe hand and chisel position. Note how the index finger of the left hand rides the tool-rest ledge.

Hand positioning

The basic rule is to hold the forward end of the chisel in your left hand, the handle in your right hand. Don't use your left hand like a fist. Instead, rest the tool toward the tips of the fingers with your thumb gripping against the side or on the top of the blade. Your index finger should rest comfortably on the tool-rest ledge.

When you are making a cut that is parallel to the work, the index finger acts as a depth gauge. Both hands and the chisel move as a unit. For many types of shaping cuts, view the contact point between the chisel and the tool rest as a pivot. This point is just about maintained as the right hand provides the cutting action. On many types of scraping cuts, the tool is held at right angles to the work and simply moved forward.

Always feed the chisel slowly and steadily; don't force it and don't jab it into the work. Make the initial contact cautiously; then get a little bolder as you cut. You don't want to overdo it, but on the other hand, just rubbing the tool against the wood won't get you anywhere.

It's a good idea to keep tools so they are behind you or to one side to avoid reaching over the lathe. Don't check work for roundness with your fingers, especially on roughing jobs. Stop the lathe to check or rest the blade of the tool lightly on the turning wood. You can tell by vibration of the tool whether the work is approaching roundness.

Three actions of lathe chisels

Lathe chisels scrape, cut, or shear.

Scraping is the easiest and safest of the three and the best for the beginner to use. All the tools can be used in such fashion, but the technique is most applicable to the roundnose, the parting tool, the squarenose and the spear point.

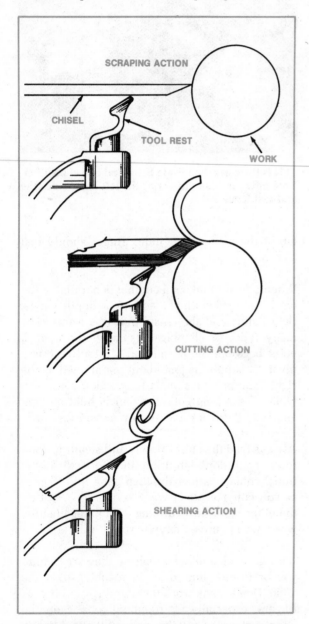

The three chisel actions. The beginner can do a fine job using the scraping action almost exclusively. In the meantime he can practice the cutting and shearing techniques.

The action gives good results and minimizes the chances of gouging. Place the tool on a horizontal plane and advance it slowly into the work. The cut that is made is the reverse of the chisel shape. For example, a roundnose tool will produce a cove. The cove size is not limited to the chisel size. You can, as you penetrate, pivot the cutting edge in a uniform arc. This has to produce a cove that is broader in its radius than a straight feed would produce.

The scraping action is not limited to shaping. The gouge for roughing (bringing square work to round) can be used in similar fashion. What you do is advance the gouge until it is making a slight cut (from $1/16''$ to $1/8''$); then, while maintaining the penetration, move the cutting edge parallel to the work. Repeat this until the work has come to full round.

When you do a straight scraping action with a spear point, you get a V-shape; with the parting tool, you get a groove. A squarenose, depending on the number of cuts you do, will produce a fillet or a band.

You can work faster if you start the scraping action of the tool with a point just below the work center line and move it upward as you move it forward.

You will never get as smooth a finish with a scraping action as you will with a shearing action, but all you need do to bring the work to par is apply sandpaper.

The cutting action calls for bringing the tool edge up by lowering the handle of the chisel. The edge of the tool will remove material in much the same way that a hand plane cuts the edge of a board. This is a situation where it's easy to dig the tool so, keep the feed light and make the cut slowly. Jabbing the chisel in suddenly or too deeply can wrench it from your hands. It's also possible to ruin the work by lifting large chunks of it.

The cutting action is something you should try after you have done enough with the scraping action to be really familiar with each of the tools. When you first try it, be cautious. Don't become bold until after you have done enough practicing to build up your confidence. A good cutting action should produce a finish that requires little touchup. This can vary from wood to wood. A grainy species will not impress so much and will require sanding even after a professional cutting action.

The shearing action can separate the expert from the amateur, not in terms of ultimate quality but in production speed. It's done best with the gouge and the skew.

It's an action that requires the tool edge to be moved laterally. It takes a consistent bite, removing a layer of wood from the surface of the stock. This varies, of course, since manipulation of the chisel in a shearing action is relative to the shape you must produce.

When first trying this technique, do it with a gouge on a roughing operation. Here, the tool is held almost on edge with your thumb behind it to keep it steady and to feed.

While each lathe chisel will do a category of jobs best, the overlap is so great that it's foolish to try to establish hard-and-fast rules. The tools work differently but the action you use, the feed angle, the cut direction, etc., influence the shape you get. A squarenose chisel or a spear point can produce a quality bead even though the skew might be the best tool to use for the job. The parting tool is basically for dimensional cuts, yet it is also very fine for shoulders, cleaning out corners and the like.

Practice with each chisel, trying to duplicate the shapes that will be described. Get the feel of each tool. You will soon develop proper handling techniques.

Applications

The gouge

This is a very versatile tool and may be used in any one of the three positions. Actually, in some applications, all three of the cutting actions come into play. It's the best tool to use for roughing operations. The scraping action works well enough, but you should try to graduate to the

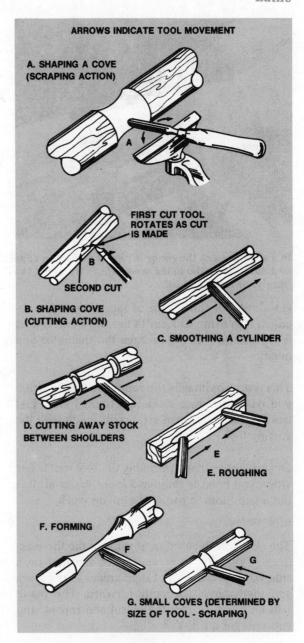

ARROWS INDICATE TOOL MOVEMENT

A. SHAPING A COVE (SCRAPING ACTION)

FIRST CUT TOOL ROTATES AS CUT IS MADE

SECOND CUT

B. SHAPING COVE (CUTTING ACTION)

C. SMOOTHING A CYLINDER

D. CUTTING AWAY STOCK BETWEEN SHOULDERS

E. ROUGHING

F. FORMING

G. SMALL COVES (DETERMINED BY SIZE OF TOOL - SCRAPING)

Typical applications of the gouge.

shearing action quickly. Here, the tool is held almost on its side and moved parallel to the work. The depth of cut is maintained by the index finger of the left hand as it rests on the ledge of the tool rest.

Start roughing cuts somewhere along the length of the stock and direct feed toward an end. Move the tool rest laterally until you've done the same

Lathe

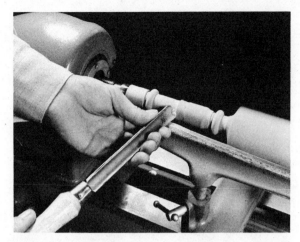

In a shearing cut, the gouge is placed almost on edge and moved parallel to the work. Don't try to cut too deeply, or feed too fast.

cut along the full length of the stock. Then re-adjust it to bring it closer to the work and repeat the procedure until you have the diameter you need.

This is approximately the routine to follow when you wish to reduce stock in a limited area. Just use the gouge between sizing cuts made with the parting tool.

Overall, the gouge is probably the best tool to use when you need to remove a lot of material. It is not a good tool to use on faceplate work.

The skew

The skew can be used in any one of the three actions. Typically, to scrape, place the tool on a side while you hold it at right angles to the work and then move it directly forward. The result will be a half-V. Flip the chisel and repeat, and you will get a full-V.

You can demonstrate a typical cutting action by holding the tool on its edge and then moving it forward. In this position the tool presents a sharp point to the work. It cuts fast and will leave a smooth finish. When you do this on the end of a cylinder or to square a shoulder, it's best to hold the chisel at a slight angle so that one of the bevels on the cutting edge will be flush against the work. When you work in this manner, you'll be using more than the point of the cutting edge.

Typical applications of the skew, an angle-pointed tool. Arrows indicate tool movement.

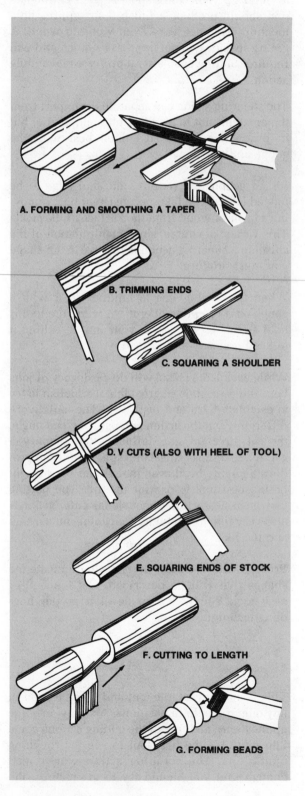

A. FORMING AND SMOOTHING A TAPER

B. TRIMMING ENDS

C. SQUARING A SHOULDER

D. V CUTS (ALSO WITH HEEL OF TOOL)

E. SQUARING ENDS OF STOCK

F. CUTTING TO LENGTH

G. FORMING BEADS

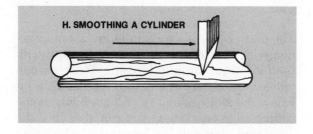

Probably the smoothest cut you can make in lathe work is with the skew in a shearing action, but it's one of the toughest to master. Overall, you should picture the cutting point as being near the center of the edge of the chisel and high on the work. You can start by placing a bevel of the cutting edge flat on the work so no cutting occurs; tilt slightly until the edge begins to penetrate. Then move the tool in parallel fashion. Don't try to cut too deeply or to feed too fast.

The skew is often used to do ball shapes and beads. This advanced technique is best started by resting the heel of the cutting edge of the center line of the form and then rotating the chisel in a 45° arc. Since you won't be able to achieve the full shape in one pass, you must imagine the final shape and direct the chisel along lines that, when repeated enough times, will result in the form you want.

The pro way to use the skew is in a shearing cut. This is probably the toughest lathe-chisel technique so take your time getting into it.

The skew is not the tool to use on faceplate work unless you limit it to a scraping action.

The roundnose

This is a very easy chisel to use because it is always used in a scraping action. To do a cove, just move the chisel directly forward. To enlarge the cove, combine a pivoting action with the forward feed. The sharper the tool, the faster you will cut and the smoother the results will be.

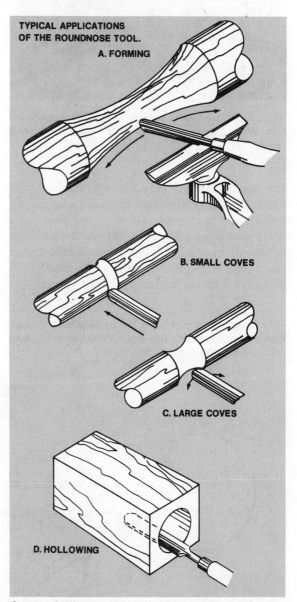

TYPICAL APPLICATIONS OF THE ROUNDNOSE TOOL.
A. FORMING
B. SMALL COVES
C. LARGE COVES
D. HOLLOWING

Arrows indicate direction of tool movement. The round nose tool is always used in a scraping action and is used on any concave shape.

The roundnose tool is always used in a scraping action. When you move it directly forward, you form a cove.

The parting tool

The parting tool is always used in a scraping action with the blade resting on an edge and with the feed action directly forward. The operation will go faster if you start with the handle a bit below the tool rest and raise it gradually as the cutting edge penetrates. You can also do it the other way: start with the handle on the high side and lower it as you go.

Quite often, the parting tool is held in one hand while the other hand grips outside calipers that ride the groove being formed. In this way, you'll know when you have reached the penetration you want on dimensional cuts.

When the cut is very deep, make slight clearance cuts on each side of the main groove to provide room for the body of the blade and thus prevent burning.

The roundnose is a very fine tool for faceplate work, especially when you are doing a hollowing operation. This occurs when you are forming a bowl or doing a round box. Situate the tool rest to provide maximum support for the chisel near the cutting edge even if it means the rest has to be situated inside the hollow being formed.

How to do sizing cuts with the parting tool. It goes faster if you start with the tool handle below the tool rest and swing up slowly as you cut.

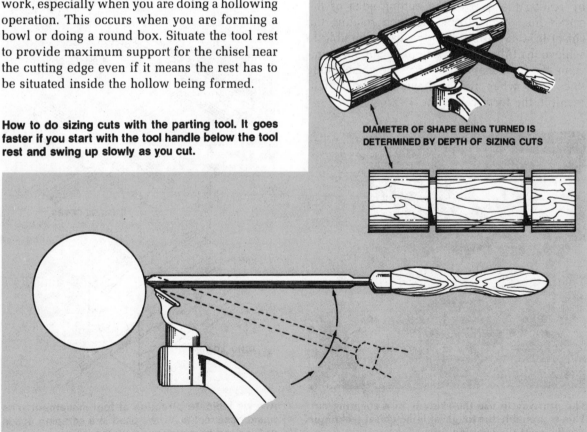

DIAMETER OF SHAPE BEING TURNED IS DETERMINED BY DEPTH OF SIZING CUTS

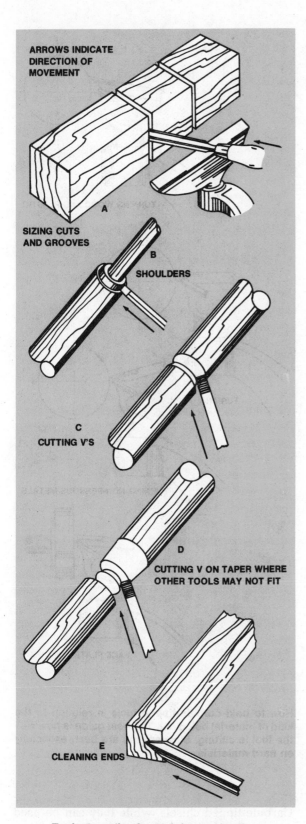

ARROWS INDICATE DIRECTION OF MOVEMENT

A

SIZING CUTS AND GROOVES

B

SHOULDERS

C

CUTTING V'S

D

CUTTING V ON TAPER WHERE OTHER TOOLS MAY NOT FIT

E

CLEANING ENDS

Typical applications of the parting tool.

The squarenose

Beginners will find the squarenose a very easy tool to handle. Keep it sharp, use it in a scraping action and feed it slowly, but steadily. When you move it directly forward, you form a fillet that matches the width of the chisel. Move it parallel to the work and you get a smoothing action. Feed it at an angle and you can form V's. Also, it's a very practical touchup tool for such operations as cleaning shoulders and smoothing convex forms.

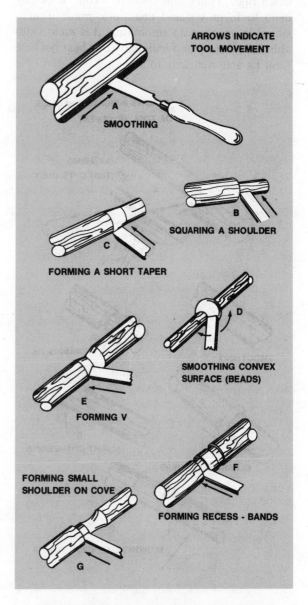

ARROWS INDICATE TOOL MOVEMENT

A

SMOOTHING

B

SQUARING A SHOULDER

C

FORMING A SHORT TAPER

D

SMOOTHING CONVEX SURFACE (BEADS)

E

FORMING V

F

FORMING RECESS - BANDS

G

FORMING SMALL SHOULDER ON COVE

Typical applications of a squarenose tool.

953

Lathe

Ordinary butt chisels can be used in place of the squarenose. If you are equipped with a set, you'll be well organized for this aspect of lathe work. You can choose a chisel width that is best for the job on hand. Use the widest chisel for smoothing jobs; use the narrowest one for touchup work such as cleaning shoulders.

The spear point

Often called a "diamond" point, the spear point is handy because its sharp point can produce clean lines, edges and corners. While it can be used to form V's and chamfers, mark dimensional lines, even do smoothing, it is most valuable for touchup applications. Your best bet is to limit its action strictly to scraping.

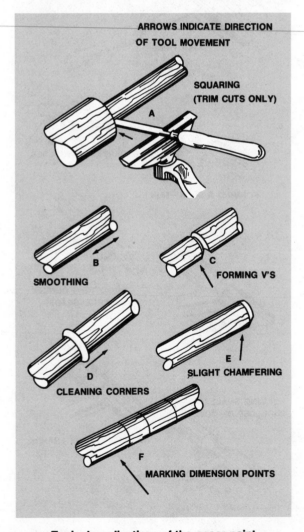

Typical applications of the spear point.

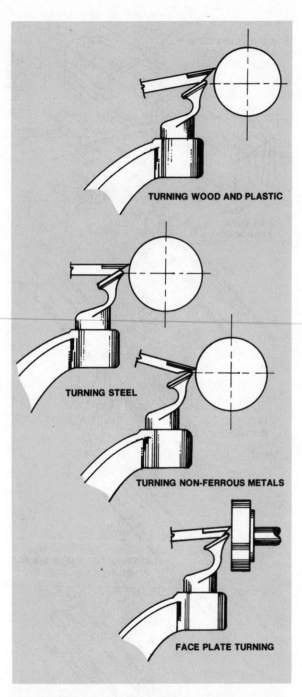

How to hold carbide-tipped tools in relation to the kind of material being cut. The best guide is how well the tool is cutting. Slow speeds are best, especially on hard materials.

The carbides

Carbide-tipped chisels, while they can be used on wood, are nice to have mostly because they

954

allow you to work on materials like metal and plastics at woodworking-lathe speeds. Most times, slow speeds are best, especially on hard materials. Waste should come off cleanly. Should the work begin to chatter or if you find you are getting a ridged surface instead of a smooth cut, it's a pretty good indication that the work is turning too fast, that you are feeding the tool too fast, or that you are trying to remove too much material in one bite.

The angle of the tool can help you do a better job with carbides. For wood and plastics, the tool handle should be slightly below the tool rest. For steel, keep it about level; for non-ferrous metals, raise it.

Tungsten carbide is very hard and will hold a keen edge for a long time, but it is quite brittle. Be sure that the cutting edges are protected; avoid banging them against hard surfaces.

Molding knives as chisels

If you own a molding head and an assortment of knives, you can have a lot of practical fun and do some fine work simply by making a handle for the knives so they can be used like lathe chisels. In fact, the technique is so intriguing that it pays to buy a few molding knives for the purpose even if you don't own a table saw.

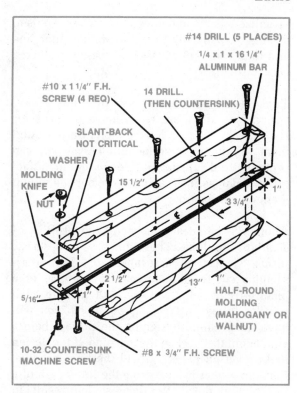

How to make a holder for the molding knives.

The knives are always used in a scraping action and with minimum feed. In some cases, where the shape you want is large, it pays to remove the bulk of the waste with a conventional chisel and then finish with a knife.

The idea will work on softwoods or hardwoods, but be especially careful on soft species. You will not get good results by forcing the cuts. The wood should scrape away in a fine dust. Working so fast that you lift chips is not good practice; in fact, you will ruin fine detail.

It's a good idea to practice on a scrap turning. Use a slow speed to start and move the knife directly forward. As it begins to cut, add a slight up-and-down action to the handle as you continue to penetrate.

Designing ideas

The worst thing you can do, unless you are just experimenting with chisels, is to start work on a lathe turning without any idea of what the result will be. Like the sculptor and his stone, you must

The larger the knife used, or the larger the shape made, the slower the feed. Always use a scraping action with a slight up-and-down motion to speed the cutting.

visualize what is in the wood. Your best bet is to do this on paper by first drawing a center line and then combining classic forms to produce a good design.

Those same molding knives previously suggested for cutting are ready-made patterns for layout work. All you have to do is trace around them. If you don't own molding knives, you can probably find full-size profiles in tool manufacturers' catalogs. You can cut these out and mount them on cardboard.

Another good idea is to study the profiles of standard moldings. These are based on classic forms. Collect an assortment of slim cross-sections cut from moldings. The catalog of a picture-frame supply house will include such profiles in sketch form. So equipped, you will have no problem designing the project before you mount the stock in the machine. If the design looks good on paper, so will the final product. Remember that just covering the full length of a turning with detail after detail seldom results in an item you will want to live with.

Spindle Turning

Mounting the work

Before you mount the work in the lathe, you must find the center of the stock at each end. If the stock is square, all you have to do is draw in-

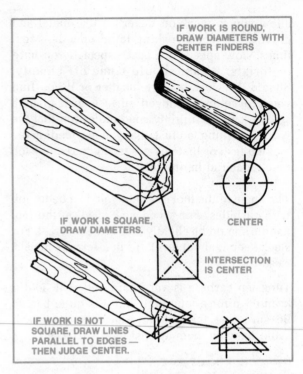

Methods to use to locate the centers on different shape materials.

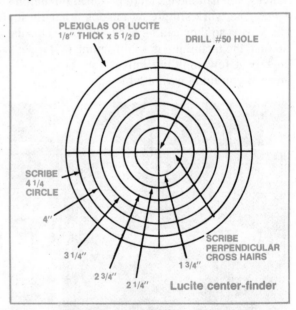

Another type of center-finder is made of clear plastic. Work is placed within the closest matching circle and a mark made through the tool's center-hole.

tersecting diagonals at each end. The point at which they cross gives you the center. When the work is not square, use the following trick. With

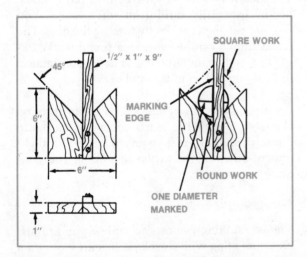

How to make a center-finder. Note that the tool can be used for square as well as round stock.

a pair of dividers or a compass, draw lines parallel to each edge of the material. Then, the center will be confined to an area small enough so that you can judge its location with reasonable accuracy.

When the wood is soft, you can use an awl to indent points for the centers. This is all you need at the tailstock end. The spur center in the headstock must be seated firmly. You can accomplish this by removing the spur center from the lathe and tapping it in place in the work with a mallet. Don't use a steel hammer. If the wood is quite hard, take the time to make shallow saw kerfs on the lines you have drawn to find the center.

To situate the work in the lathe, place it firmly against the spur center and lock the tailstock in place about 1" away from the opposite end. Then use the tailstock ram to bring the dead center into position. Don't bear too heavily, just make good contact. Often, this setting will loosen, so it should be checked frequently as you are doing the turning. A drop of oil or a spot of wax on the dead center will help. When the wood is very soft and you have much turning to do, it may pay to use a furniture glide at the dead-center end. The indention for the point on the center can be accomplished with a prick punch. Another idea is to nail a small block of hardwood on that end of the work.

Layout

After the stock has been turned down to the point where you are ready for actual forming, it should be marked to define particular areas. A simple way to do this is to use a ruler on the tool rest with the work turning at slow speed. Mark the dimension points with a pencil.

You can work in similar fashion with a flexible tape but with the work stationary. Make your dimension points about $1/2''$ long. When you turn on the machine, the marks will be visible enough so you can hold a pencil against the turning stock to complete the line.

When you have duplicate pieces to form, it pays to make a marking gauge like the one shown in the accompanying sketch. This gauge is a piece

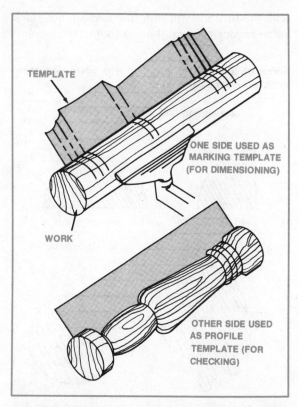

A profile template with one straight side can be used for checking the work as you go and for the initial marking as well. It is merely turned over as needed.

of wood with brads driven into one edge. You hold it against the turning stock and the brads mark the dimension points. This method is good to use for simple turnings.

For more complex turnings, you should make a full-size cardboard template of the project. The template provides a profile for checking the shape of the work as you go. The center-line, straight edge can be used for marking dimension points.

A trick you can use to make a turning to replace a broken part is to use the part itself as a template. Slice the part down the center on a band saw or with a handsaw to give you an accurate profile of the part you must shape. Place this on the stock and trace around it. Then, use a saw to cut into an adjacent side for dimension lines that match the profile. Cut to the full depth of each design feature; make kerfs on outer sides of all beads and other raised elements. You can then proceed

Lathe

with the turning, working first to clean out stock between designs and then to shape the details.

Some of the classic forms to use when designing lathe projects.

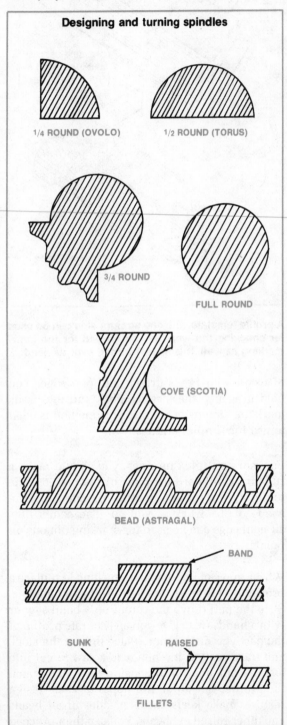

Designing and turning spindles

1/4 ROUND (OVOLO)

1/2 ROUND (TORUS)

3/4 ROUND

FULL ROUND

COVE (SCOTIA)

BEAD (ASTRAGAL)

BAND

SUNK   RAISED

FILLETS

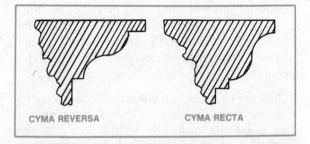

CYMA REVERSA   CYMA RECTA

A section cut lengthwise from a part to be replaced can be used as a readymade pattern. Place it on the stock and trace around it as shown.

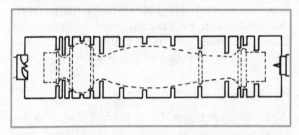

Try to visualize the finished turning inside the wood blank.

Slender work

Long, slender spindles require the support of a steady rest to keep the work from whipping and to avoid deflection under cutting pressure. Accessories to provide this support are available, but you can make a suitable one for yourself. This support is a V-block mounted on a platform that you can clamp to the lathe bed. Size the vertical block so the center of the V is on the work center line. Situate it as you go so the work is supported near the area where you are cutting.

Long work

No matter what the capacity of your machine, there is a limit to spindle lengths you can mount. For pieces longer than this limit, you simply turn separate parts and then join them. Do this by drilling holes in the mating ends and then using a dowel between them. Or you can form a tenon right in the lathe on the end of one of the pieces and drill a hole in the other.

Sanding

Final finishing is done by using sandpaper while the part is turning in the lathe. The normal sanding procedure which calls for a progression through finer grits should not be regarded as a hard-and-fast rule. There is no point starting with a very coarse paper if the turning is quite smooth to begin with. In most cases, a medium-grit paper will do, and even this should be used cautiously around small details.

For straight cylinders, long tapers and similar areas, the sandpaper can be wrapped around a smooth piece of wood. Another way is to hold a strip of sandpaper between your hands and to use it like a shoe-polish cloth.

A good way to get an extremely fine finish is to work with sandpaper until you are satisfied. Then, dampen the work with water but don't soak it. After it has dried, use fine steel wool to do the final smoothing.

Imaginative techniques

As it was suggested with using molding knives for shaping work, there is no law that says you must limit yourself to lathe chisels. Shaping operations can be done with wood rasps or files, rotary rasps in an electric drill, a hand plane, Surform tools, etc. Don't be a purist and shy away from this aspect of lathe work. In the final analysis, it's what you produce that counts.

Faceplate Work

Mounting the work

Draw lines from corner to corner on the square stock and from the intersection scribe a circle that is just a fraction larger than the diameter of

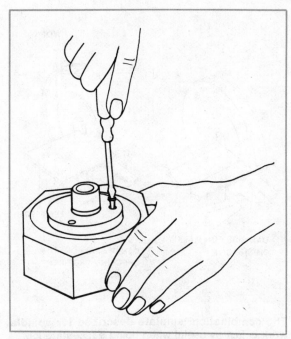

Use screws to attach the faceplate. These should be as heavy and as long as possible without creating interference for lathe-chisel cuts. Remove as much waste stock as feasible before mounting in the lathe.

the faceplate. After that, draw a second circle as a guide for rough cutting the blank stock to round on the band saw or jigsaw. The least you should do is remove as much of the waste as possible with straight saw cuts.

Use screws to fasten the faceplate to the turning block, but be sure to choose a size that will not interfere with chisel work. The general rule is to use the longest, heaviest screw. Do this in line with the base thickness of the finished project.

After you have mounted the work in the machine, spin it by hand to be sure you have clearance between the blank and the lathe bed.

Templates and marking

To find the center, turn the work slowly with a pencil resting on the tool rest. Touch the work lightly with the point and then move slowly toward the center. This will reveal the midpoint of the mounted work.

To scribe a circular dimension line, you can use dividers or a compass. Don't dig the dividers in

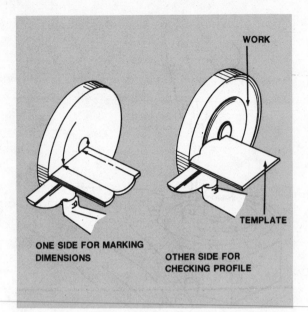

ONE SIDE FOR MARKING
DIMENSIONS

OTHER SIDE FOR
CHECKING PROFILE

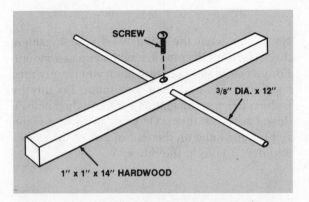

Easy-to-make gauge will let you judge the depth of
faceplate turnings. It's especially useful for deep bor-
ing jobs — a round box being a typical example.

**The combination template described for spindle
work is just as useful when doing a faceplate job.**

either the center point or where you are scribing;
a light touch is sufficient. To mark the perimeter
after you have turned the work to full-round, you
can use an ordinary marking gauge, or you can
do the job simply with your fingers holding a
pencil. In this case, your fingers would act as an
edge gauge. This kind of marking can be done
while you are turning the work by hand.

Templates are useful on faceplate work,
especially if you must turn out more than one
piece of the same design. Make the template so it
has a profile side and a straight edge. Carry the
main detail points of the design across to the
straight edge, and you will have a single template
that will serve for marking dimension lines and
for checking the shape as you work.

Depth gauge

You can easily make a depth gauge. It's nothing
but a hardwood block through which you pass a
dowel. The lockscrew will work if you just drill
an undersize hole for the screw to be used. Put a
drop of oil on the screw and drive it home so it
will form its own threads. This gauge is useful
for checking the depth of items such as bowls
and round boxes.

Chisel technique

This technique doesn't differ too much from
spindle turning, but you should use a scraping
action exclusively. The tool rest may be situated
in front of the work, at the edge, behind it, even
inside it. Be sure at all times that tool rest-to-
work relationship provides maximum support
for the chisel close to where you are cutting.

You'll find the roundnose a very useful tool,
especially for the bulk of the waste-removal
chore. Work will go faster if you set the tool rest
for the point of the chisel that is on the work
center line and if you drop the handle a little
below the tool rest. Don't use the gouge or the
skew, although it is not out of line to work with

Faceplate turning is the method to use when making
trays, bowls and the like. The roundnose tool is an
excellent choice for such jobs.

the latter if you limit the application, for example, to cutting lines with the point or cleaning out shoulders.

A faceplate-mounted, heavy block of wood can cause considerable vibration so start at lowest speeds. Speed up only as you lighten the load by removing waste and only as long as you don't cause excessive vibration. Typical faceplate turnings require more time than spindle work simply because a lot of material must be removed before you get to the actual shaping. Rushing the job can cause you to jab in the chisels.

Joining work

Quite often, it's necessary to join a spindle turning to a base that you form on the faceplate. Drill a center hole in the base and form an integral tenon on the spindle. Actually, you can drill a hole in each part and join them with a dowel.

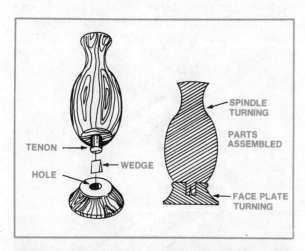

The tenon idea is good when joining a spindle turning to a base made on the faceplate. The wedge is optional but can provide a lot of strength.

Thin work

When work is too thin to mount on a faceplate, you can often get the job done by putting the blank on a nut and bolt that you then grip in a lathe-mounted chuck. When this procedure is not practical, glue the work to a piece of scrap that is thick enough to be faceplate-mounted. If you use newspaper between the pieces, you'll find they are not too difficult to split apart after

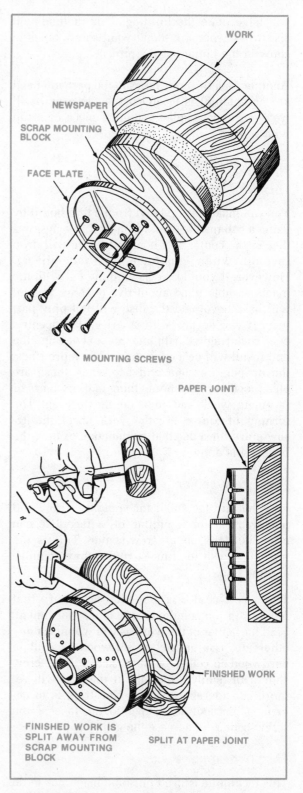

The technique of mounting faceplate work when screws are not desirable in the base of the project.

you have done the forming. This method will also work when you don't want screw holes to show in the bottom of the project.

Another idea (if screw holes in the part you need are acceptable) is to attach the piece you will work on to a faceplate-mounted piece of scrap with screws.

Special Techniques

The drinking cup trick

You can make a deep bowl from a thin board by using a collapsible drinking cup. If you jigsaw a disc in the center of a board, the disc will drop through when you have finished cutting. However, if you do the same thing but with the machine table tilted about five degrees, the cut will be a bevel and the disc will fall only part way. If you do this with a series of concentric cuts, each ring will jam into the next one and the end result will be a cone shape. The more rings, the deeper the cone will be. When these are glued together, you mount them like any piece of faceplate work and then do the turning. The turning, of course, is lathe work; check the jigsaw entry for a detailed explanation of how the beveling is done.

The screw-center

Jobs that are too small for spindle turning and not practical for mounting on a faceplate can often be done on a screw-center. This is the method to use for finials, round drawer pulls, and the like.

The screw-center is a special accessory that mounts on the spindle as any other attachment. Find the center of the work as you would for any other job. Use an awl in softwood or drill in hardwood so you can seat the screw. The screw should fit tightly, especially if the part will require considerable turning. One trick is to cement a piece of sandpaper to the face of the screw-center to increase the grip.

Outboard turning

This technique is used on some machines to do jobs that are too large to be done conventionally. It is straightforward faceplace turning except,

because of the work size, you must restrict yourself to minimum speeds. Manufacturers of machines that permit this operation usually list outboard turning stands as accessories. These are no more than supports for the tool rest. If you anticipate doing outboard turning occasionally, you can improvise a stand. Be sure the top-to-floor distance lets you place the chisel on the work center line. Don't push this kind of thing when cutting. Don't try to mount work so large that the tool motor must strain to turn it. If you wish to experiment with this technique, do so with softwoods. Let the heavier, harder woods come later.

Built-up sections

There are many lathe jobs that require a large diameter in limited area of the work. There are two methods you can use to facilitate such work. In one, you can use another woodworking tool such as the band saw or the jointer to reduce the stock in particular areas. In the other, you can add wood by gluing in those areas that require it.

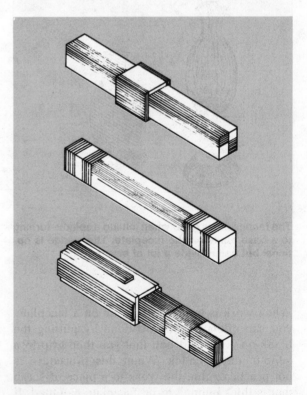

Building up blocks can result in fascinating results, by combining contrasting woods. A good glue job is essential.

The glue-on chore must be done with some precision. The joint should be invisible after the turning is complete. Unless you deliberately plan otherwise, the grain pattern and direction should be compatible. Getting these results calls for discernment, as well as a good glue job. Be sure that mating surfaces are flat and true before you apply the glue and the clamps. Don't rush; let the glue dry thoroughly before you mount the work in the machine.

This kind of thinking applies to faceplate work as well as spindles. To build up a thick blank, you can glue thin pieces together. To facilitate the removal of waste in the lathe, the glued-on pieces can be rings that you precut on a jigsaw or even with a sabre saw. If the project is to have sloping sides, play along with it by cutting rings of increasingly smaller diameter.

An interesting lathe procedure is to glue together blanks of contrasting woods. These can be simple or complex. After turning they become intriguing inlaid projects. Select wood for this technique to produce good contrast and similarity in degree of hardness. To experiment, try combining rosewood and maple, redwood and pine, birch and cherry, holly and walnut.

Split turnings

A common split turning is one that is halved after the piece is shaped to produce two identical half-columns. This can be accomplished with solid stock by cutting on the band saw after the turning is complete, or you can work with a paper-glue joint.

Another way is to make the blank by joining two similar pieces without using glue. This you can do by nailing the parts together at the extreme ends in areas that you know will be waste, even by using corrugated fasteners at each end of the pieces. The mating surfaces of the joint, whether you use glue or not, must be flat and true. The idea can be used not only for quarter-round molding, but also for half-moldings. This is not the method to use every time you need a short piece of molding, but it's a fine procedure when you need something special.

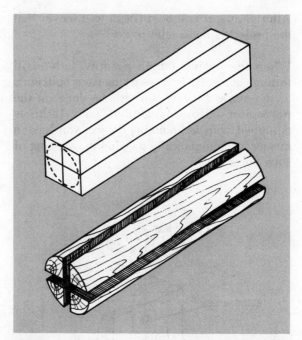

Gluing together four similar pieces and then separating them after turning will produce ¼ round moldings.

Drilling

There are several ways to do drilling in the lathe. In one, the chuck and bit are mounted in the tailstock. The bit is still and the work turns. Feed is accomplished by moving the tailstock forward or by using the tailstock ram. Such jobs are easier to do when the work is on a faceplate. In the second method, the drilling tool is in the headstock; the work is held against the center in the tailstock. Here the bit is turning and the work is still. The first method is preferred for faceplate work, the second method for spindles. Standard drilling rules apply. Use slow speeds for large holes; increase speed only for small holes.

Quite often when you need a center hole all the way through a project it's better to prepare for it before you turn the work. For this, you can use a kind of split-turning technique, running small center dadoes in each piece before you bond them with glue. Fill the hole at each end with a "key" so you'll have a solid area for the centers. After turning, hand drill through the keys to reach the square hole formed with the dadoes.

Lathe

After gluing, it will be difficult to discover that the project is not a solid piece.

When the project length permits, lathe-drill through center holes by working from both ends of the stock. Drilling can also be done on the perimeter of pieces; and if your lathe is equipped with an indexing device, you have a means for automatically gauging the spacing of such holes.

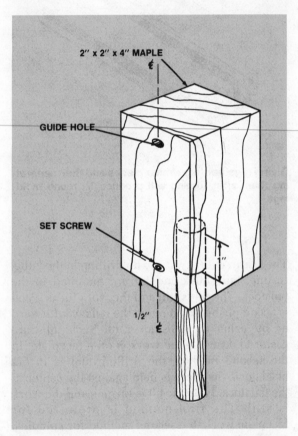

To drill horizontally on the perimeter of a job, make a guide like this.

Spiral work

The forming of spirals is usually classified as lathe work, but it's mostly a hand job with the lathe used as a holding device after the stock has been turned to full-round.

The layout can be done precisely by dividing the total length of the spiral into equal spaces, each one about the diameter of the stock. The next

Spirals are listed as lathe jobs but the truth is, it is mostly hand work. The lathe is not much more than a holding device. Follow these instructions to do precise spiral-layout work on true cylinders and on tapered ones.

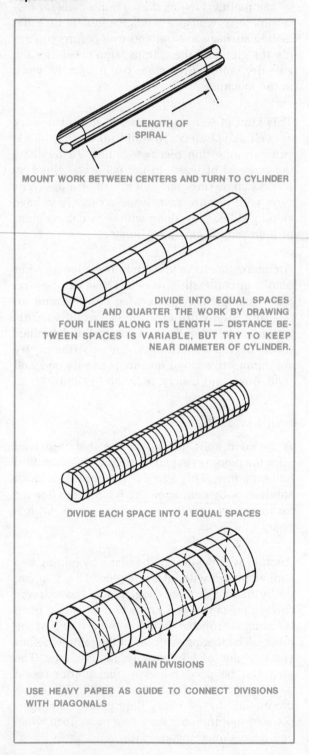

LENGTH OF SPIRAL

MOUNT WORK BETWEEN CENTERS AND TURN TO CYLINDER

DIVIDE INTO EQUAL SPACES AND QUARTER THE WORK BY DRAWING FOUR LINES ALONG ITS LENGTH — DISTANCE BETWEEN SPACES IS VARIABLE, BUT TRY TO KEEP NEAR DIAMETER OF CYLINDER.

DIVIDE EACH SPACE INTO 4 EQUAL SPACES

MAIN DIVISIONS

USE HEAVY PAPER AS GUIDE TO CONNECT DIVISIONS WITH DIAGONALS

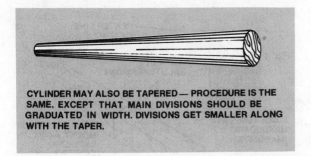

CYLINDER MAY ALSO BE TAPERED — PROCEDURE IS THE SAME, EXCEPT THAT MAIN DIVISIONS SHOULD BE GRADUATED IN WIDTH. DIVISIONS GET SMALLER ALONG WITH THE TAPER.

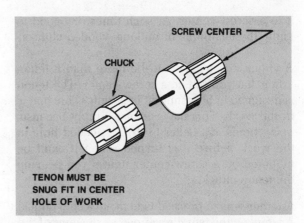

SCREW CENTER

CHUCK

TENON MUST BE SNUG FIT IN CENTER HOLE OF WORK

A simple chuck is a tenon design that is mounted on a screw center. Used if more conventional methods fail.

step is to draw four lines along the length of the stock. These should run from common perpendicular diameters at each end. What these lines do is divide the cylinder into four equal ¼ rounds. Next, divide each of the spaces into four equal parts and, using a heavy piece of paper as a guide, mark diagonals across each of the small spaces.

You can also work in fairly good fashion without all the layout by using a long strip of paper immediately. The paper can have parallel sides or can be tapered. This paper is wrapped around the cylinder in spiral fashion, and the spiral line is marked by following the edge of the paper with a pencil.

Actual work is started by using a handsaw to cut the spiral line to the depth you want. As a depth gauge, you can make a mark on the saw or clamp a wood block to it. Work on the cut line with a round or square file, depending on how you visualize the final product. In essence, the initial file work opens up the groove you cut with the saw.

Then you can work with a flat file to shape the sections between the grooves. A rasp will speed up the job, but it's best followed by a smoother cut file before you get to the sandpaper chore, which is the final step. It's possible to have the work turning as you do the sanding, but you must be very careful to follow the spiral as you hold the sandpaper in shoe-polishing-cloth fashion. Start the spiral at slow speeds; increase the speed as you become confident.

Working with chucks

Sometimes it's not possible to hold work between centers, mount it on a faceplate, or secure

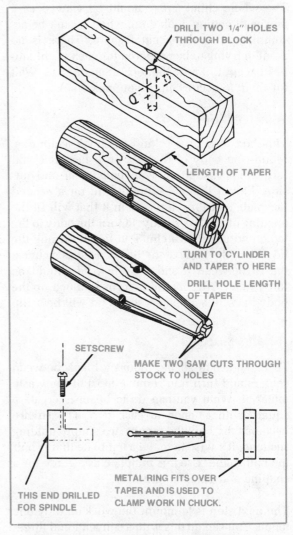

DRILL TWO ¼" HOLES THROUGH BLOCK

LENGTH OF TAPER

TURN TO CYLINDER AND TAPER TO HERE

DRILL HOLE LENGTH OF TAPER

SETSCREW

MAKE TWO SAW CUTS THROUGH STOCK TO HOLES

THIS END DRILLED FOR SPINDLE

METAL RING FITS OVER TAPER AND IS USED TO CLAMP WORK IN CHUCK.

How to make a split chuck. Use maple stock.

it to a screw-center. At such times, it's good to know the technique of making wooden chucks.

A chuck doesn't have to be more than a tenon affair that you put on a screw-center. The tenon is designed to be a snug fit in a center hole that is in the work. This makes sense simply because, many times, it's better to drill a needed hole in the work before it is turned. Then it can't be mounted on a screw-center unless you provide the tenon-chuck.

Another way to proceed is to make a split chuck. A tenon on the work is gripped by the jaws of the chuck because of the ring that forces them together.

The whole chuck area should be viewed as a means of getting a job done when it can't be accomplished in the usual fashion. There is no point in trying to be prepared for such eventualities except to know the techniques to use. Wait for them to occur before you make tools.

A box with fitted cover

This box also uses a kind of chuck technique. Mount the body of the box on a faceplate and turn it to the shape you want both inside and outside. Mount the stock for the lid on a second faceplate and form a recess in it that will fit the opening of the box's body. Return the body to the lathe and use it as a chuck to finish turning the lid. When the body of the box is used as a chuck, the fit between it and the stock lid should be fairly tight. After the lid is formed, touch up the body lip with sandpaper so the lid will be a slip fit.

A ball shape

To make a ball shape, mount a blank between centers and turn it to remove most of the waste material. What you can do to begin is create a square with a tenon at each end. The square becomes the ball; the tenons are simply holding sections. It's wise to make a template that is half the ball shape. Use this template as a guide for a shaping and smoothing device.

The next step is to mount the work on only one tenon. You can do this with a conventional three-jaw chuck or by making a special wooden one.

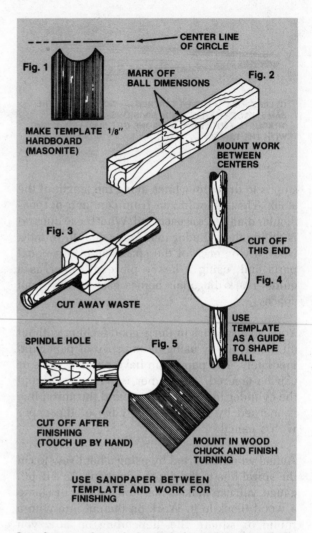

Step-by-step through the technique of turning a ball-shape. Here, a wooden chuck is used for the final steps but a conventional chuck may be used.

Cut off the outboard tenon and work to achieve the final shape of the ball. The last step is to use the template as a touchup device by placing fine sandpaper between it and the ball shape. Use a light touch and do the final finishing by hand holding the sandpaper.

After you are satisfied with the shape, separate the ball by using a parting tool or a skew in a cutting action and touch up the cut end by hand with sandpaper.

Ring work

A variety of techniques can be used to do ring work, and the choice will usually depend upon

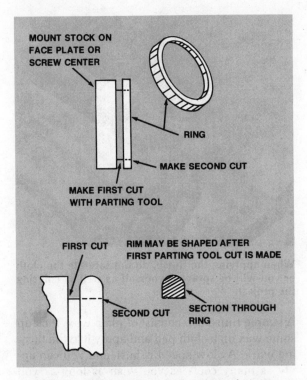

**MOUNT STOCK ON
FACE PLATE OR
SCREW CENTER**

RING

MAKE SECOND CUT

**MAKE FIRST CUT
WITH PARTING TOOL**

FIRST CUT   **RIM MAY BE SHAPED AFTER
FIRST PARTING TOOL CUT IS MADE**

SECOND CUT   **SECTION THROUGH
RING**

The two steps required for a simple ring cut.

the cross-section profile desired. For example, for a ring with a square cross-section, mount a blank on a faceplate and turn it to full-round with the diameter to match the O.D. of the ring. Make one cut with a parting tool on the edge of the turning. Its depth should be a bit deeper than the cross-section of the ring when viewed from the front. Make a second cut, again with the parting tool, on the face of the stock. Make the second cut to meet the first one; and when the two cuts meet, the ring will fall off onto the shaft of the chisel. The rim of the ring can be shaped before you separate it from the body of the faceplate-mounted stock.

If the cross-section of the ring is to be a true circle, then you must use a combination of faceplate turning and chuck turning. Start the job with faceplate-mounted stock and turn half of the ring shape. Make a chuck with a recess that will provide a snug fit for what you have done. This can then be pressed into the chuck, and the final half circle of the ring can be formed.

All chuck work of this type requires an accurate dimension in the cavity that holds the work. If

you make a mistake, it's often possible to compensate by wrapping a strip of masking tape around the ring to make it fit snugly.

A project like a circular picture frame or a one-piece circular molding that may be used to edge a flat tray can be done in this fashion. Mount the work on a faceplate and recess it to form a rabbet. Shape the perimeter as you wish. Then make a chuck to fit the rabbet diameter and shape the work on the opposite side. View the original rabbet cut, in the case of a picture frame, as the recess that holds the glass. If you are making a tray, simply cut a disc that fits inside the turning.

Ovals

The major factor in this process is a layout that you do on the ends of the stock after you have turned it to true round. Your best approach is to make a template that locates the true center plus two "off centers" that are on a common diameter. It's a good idea to draw a "ridge" line on the work. Once you have this line, it's easy to position the template to mark the common off centers.

Mount the work on one of the off centers, and turn it as you would normally until the cut nears the ridge line. Be careful when positioning the tool rest. One side of the work will come closer to you than the other; the off center makes it possible to cut on just one side of the diameter. You'll find after this operation that one side of the stock is oval while the other side remains round. Shift to the second off center and repeat the operation. Use sandpaper to remove the ridge line.

Offset work

In this type of work, parts have a projection that is not uniform about a center line. You can find this on leg designs that end in a right angle departure from the spindle. The cabriole leg is another good example. Lathe turning can be applied to part of the project either before or after the overall shape is established. The turning is done on the true-center portion of the work — either in an overall or limited area. In the case of the cabriole leg, you can turn a round foot after the part has been bandsawed to shape.

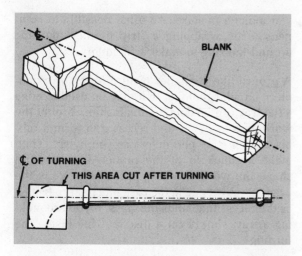

Typical part that calls for offset turning. Note that the center for lathe mounting ignores the projection of the work.

When applying the finish, do not saturate the cloth or you will be spraying yourself as well as coloring the project.

This is not a difficult chore, but you must be aware that the off-center portion of the project can be a hazard. Always be sure, after you have set the tool rest, that you hand turn the work to check clearance. When you start cutting, keep your hand clear of the projection area. The work is unbalanced, so you are bound to get more vibration than you would from a symmetrical piece. Start at very low speeds. Increase the speed only if results indicate that you can do so without danger to yourself or to the work.

Finishing

To get to a final smoothness, work through progressively finer grits of sandpaper. The grit you start with must be judged on how smooth the project is to begin with. A very coarse paper may be completely out of line since all you will be doing is creating scratches you will have to remove with other paper. On lathe work, it's often possible to start immediately with a fine paper. Be careful around fine details since excessive sandpapering can destroy them.

When you are satisfied that the wood is smooth enough, dampen it slightly with water. Don't soak it. Let it dry and then do a final smoothing with fine steel wool. Some craftsmen use a handful of fine shavings to do this. It does bring out a degree of shine; but whether you use chips or steel wool, this is just a step before application of color or clear finish.

A simple finish can consist of plain wax. Pick up some wax on a cloth pad and apply it to the turning work. A slow speed is best, and you can apply as many coats as you wish as long as you allow sufficient drying time between the applications. After the part is evenly coated, polish with a clean, lint-free cloth.

Apply stain in similar fashion. Don't saturate the cloth, or you will be spraying yourself as you color the wood. Remember when you do this kind of thing in the lathe that finishing materials require just as much drying time as when they are applied with a brush. Rushing the procedure will do more harm than good. Overall, it's best to apply any finish in a diluted state; the heavier the material you are using, the slower the speed should be.

Shaping attachment

With a lathe, you have the makings of a shaper. With a chuck spindle for mounting a shaper adapter, plus one or two easily made jigs, you have an efficient setup for producing decorative edges or doing such functional chores as forming tongue-and-groove joints. There is little a conventional shaper will do that can't be done here. You can even set up for horizontal drilling and routing.

You need a chuck spindle and a shaper adapter. The type of spindle depends on your lathe. If it

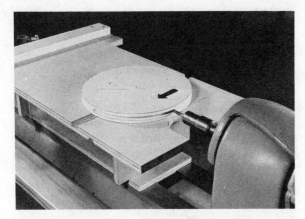

Rout circular edges by using the pivot method. The pivot, a nail driven through the work into the table, should be on the spindle centerline. Position the work, move the jig to engage the cutter, lock the jig, and turn the work to complete the cut.

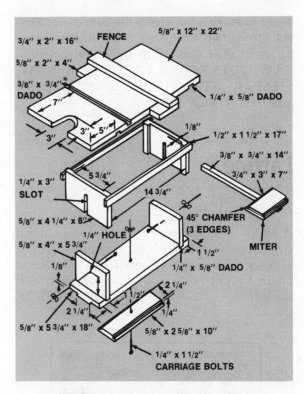

Construction details of the horizontal jig.

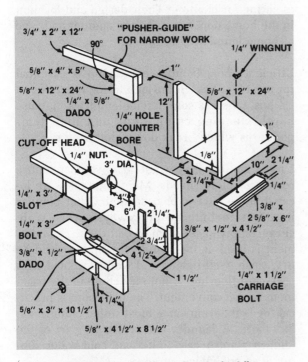

Construction details of the vertical jig.

has a straight, unthreaded spindle, you can use a shaper adapter that mounts directly on the spindle. If the lathe has a tapered hole, then you will need a tapered spindle chuck.

Most lathes will provide a high speed of about 5,000 rpm's. This speed level will do for shaping even though a higher speed is better. Don't use special pulleys to provide higher speeds unless

you are sure the lathe is built for it. To compensate for speed that is less than ideal, slow up on feed rates and take small cuts.

The vertical jig is essentially a shaper table that stands on edge. The fences do the same job as a regular shaper fence but, in this case, they also support the work. On long jobs, stand at the side of the table and feed the work across. On small work, position your hands so they are never directly over the cutter.

The fulcrum pins in the vertical table make it possible to shape freehand against collars. There are limitations here because of the lathe bed and the fence slide bars but not enough to restrict most common jobs. If you wish, attach the slide bars with screws instead of glue. Then they can be removed to facilitate a particular operation.

A horizontal jig can handle larger work more easily. Also, it changes the work position in relation to the cutter, and this feature increases the variety of shapes you can get from a single cutter. More important, is that you can use a miter gauge to move work across the cutters, facilitating cross-grain edge cuts. *SEE ALSO BAND SAW; BENCH GRINDER; DRILL PRESS; JIG-SAW; JOINTER; RADIAL ARM SAW; SHAPER; STATIONARY BELT & DISC SANDER; TABLE SAW.*

Lattice

A lattice is an arrangement of wood or metal strips, bars or rods made by crisscrossing them to form a network. In some cases, a lattice is made by cutting out a panel of plywood, hardboard, etc. *SEE ALSO MOLDING & TRIM.*

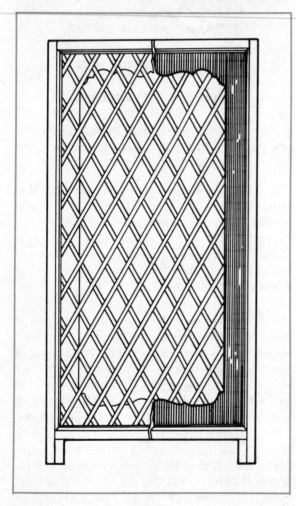

Lattice

Lauan Wood

Lauan wood is widely used as a surface veneer on flush doors and plywood paneling. Classified as an exotic wood, lauan wood is an open-pored, inexpensive, middle-toned wood that can be finished with or without stain. *SEE ALSO WOOD IDENTIFICATION.*

Laundry Rooms

Laundry rooms all function to provide a means of caring for clothing. Their design and location in the home depends upon the amount and type of home laundering required.

Efficient home laundry equipment is essential for most families. Home laundering is gentler on clothes, whereas commercial laundries may use harsh cleaning compounds and high temperatures which break down cloth fibers.

Large families may want to devote an entire room to laundry needs. Many laundries are located in the kitchen or basement. Other popular locations include an entryway, garage wall, closet, empty guest room or bathroom. If a basement is used as the laundry room, it should be dry, clean, well-lighted and well-ventilated with easy care flooring. A laundry chute to the basement is also convenient. The bathroom is practical for laundering since most soiled clothes collect there. A laundry center can be part of the kitchen plan. Access to hot and cold water supply is an advantage here.

If a family requires six or seven wash loads a week, a central clothes-care center is needed. This center should include a washer, dryer, ironing board and sewing machine. A good arrangement provides storage for out-of-season clothing.

Comfort is important in a complete center. The area should be well-lighted and should contain an ample amount of electrical outlets for appliances. An exhaust fan will help to control odors as well as the temperature and humidity.

LAUNDRY APPLIANCES

Newer washers and dryers offer more flexibility for better results in laundering. Laundry practices may need revision to make the best use of new appliances.

Washers and dryers are made larger today to handle more clothes in a single load. Larger washers however use more water and detergent and other laundry aids. It may be necessary to supplement the hot-water supply with an extra tank for the laundry center.

Water temperature selector switches allow a choice of wash and rinse water temperatures for many clothes-load types. Water level controls allow small loads to be washed at a water and detergent savings. Agitation and spin speed selectors give vigorous or gentle action for both normal and special loads. For fully-programmed washer controls, a button for the type of wash load is selected, and the proper temperatures and speeds will automatically be used in the cycle.

Dryers should have lint filters which are easily located and emptied. Depending on the type of clothes to be dried, various temperatures and fan speeds may be chosen. Some dryers, which have sensors, stop when clothes are dry. A drying rack may be located inside the appliance to make it easier to dry such items as canvas shoes without tumbling.

Sinks, which should be included in fully-equipped laundry facilities, are helpful in soaking out stains, pretreating badly soiled laundry loads, for dyeing and for mixing starch solutions.

Families with small wash loads and limited space need compact washers and dryers, which offer the basic features of larger models. Washer-dryer combinations solve space problems and use less water and detergent.

In planning space, it is more efficient to arrange appliances so that a step-by-step laundry process can be completed in minimum times.

Lavatory

A lavatory or bathroom sink is a plumbing fixture designed to supply water for hand washing, face washing, shaving, light laundry and similar tasks.

Lavatories are made of one of four materials: vitreous china, cast-iron, stainless steel or plastic. Vitreous china is produced by combining and casting minerals and clay, then glazing and kiln firing the resulting fixture. Of the four materials, vitreous china possesses the greatest strength. A cast-iron bowl is covered with baked-on porcelain enamel. While this enamel coating shows stains and scratches easily, the metal surface of a stainless steel bowl does not. The plastic lavatory is not widely used.

Courtesy of Eljer.

The oval, flush-mount lavatory completes the patriotic scene.

Lavatories are available in round, oval, rectangular or triangular shapes. This variety of shapes gives the homeowner flexibility in designing a bathroom.

971

Courtesy of Eljer

The square, uni-rim lavatory adds a sleek, modern look to this bathroom.

The pedestal model is probably the oldest type of lavatory. In addition to the pedestal, there are four methods of mounting a lavatory. A wall-hung lavatory extends from the wall. Supported in a cabinet, the flush-mount lavatory rim is even with the surface of the counter. The uni-rim fixture protrudes above the counter surface; the under-counter lavatory sets below cabinet level. The style of mounting and shape of bowl can be fitted to the individual preference or need. The style of mounting and bowl shapes are also determined by available or needed space and bathroom style.

Courtesy of Eljer

The under-counter lavatory lends to the decor of the room.

Although most lavatories are equipped with a drain and a hot-and-cold water system, many bathroom sinks are also equipped with an overflow drain as a safety feature. Faucet designs and new attachments are developed annually. Sprayer attachments and lotion soap dispensers are two of the newest faucet fixtures. Before installing any of the faucet fixtures, check the local dealers for the latest feature that may complement the lavatory that has been chosen. *SEE ALSO PLUMBING FIXTURES.*

Courtesy of Eljer

The wall-hung lavatory fits into the corner of the western style bathroom.

Courtesy of the Kohler Company

The uni-rim lavatory has side mount faucets, soap dispenser and sprayer attachment.

Lawnmowers

With only seasonal maintenance in Fall and Spring, a mower can be kept in top condition and at its cutting best. Combine equipment care tips with the tips for better and safer mowing and you will improve your lawn while preserving your mower investment.

FALL MAINTENANCE

Fall is the time to put a mower in shape for winter. By *winterizing* a mower, years can be added to its life and a costly repair bill may even be saved. Certainly, it will guarantee a quick start and full power the next spring.

Since you will be working with gasoline and oil, choose an outdoor area far from open flames and smokers, where fumes can readily dissipate and an oil spill will not be disastrous. Running water from a garden hose will further ease the chore, especially if the mower is caked with pulp and debris below-deck.

Most likely hardware, which has become loosened by vibration, will need to be tightened. A tool kit, tablespoon, fresh can of oil (usually SAE 10W-40) and some absorbent rags should be kept handy.

Before clean-up chores can be done safely, the mower's tank must be rid of fuel. Fuel dumping is dangerous because a stray spark, struck as the mower is turned over, could ignite the fuel with catastrophic consequences. Play it safe and let the mower use up its fuel as it was intended — through the engine. Start the mower, throttle down to a low speed as soon as it is warmed up, and keep the mower in its normal position while running.

Of course, if the mower is equipped with a washplug, you can hook a garden hose (without the nozzle) to a plastic cap in the mower housing. Turn the water on to moderate pressure for at least two minutes. The whirling blade of the running mower will forcibly distribute the water on the housing inner surface loosening and safely flushing out the accumulated grass clippings within.

If the mower lacks a wash-out plug, a water stream from the garden hose can be directed into the discharge chute. Do so only from a safe distance and keep your face, hands, body and the hose well out of line with the chute. Take care not to splash water up into the air cleaner or onto the hot exterior surfaces of the engine. After the flushout is finished, all fuel must be used up before continuing.

Do not leave a mower running for any reason and *do* discourage children and nosey pets from coming close, until the fuel runs out. When the engine quits, remove the spark plug wire from the spark plug and coil it back for safety.

Gasoline contains sticky varnishes and waxy residues, so it is vital that the slight amount remaining in the tank after the engine has sputtered to a stop is removed. If this is not done, the gum formed by evaporation of the residual fuel in winter will find its way into the fuel line and carburetor with the next spring's first refueling. There could be enough to clog the fuel system which means hard starting, hard work in cleanup or much expense at the local service shop.

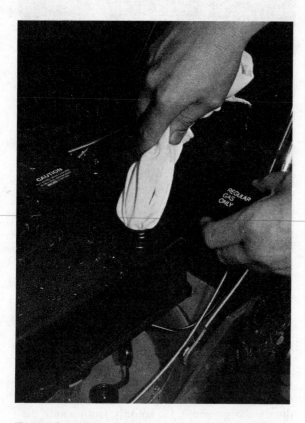

To get the left-over fuel, wrap an absorbent cloth around a small-diameter dowel stick and insert it into the fuel tank, through the screw-top opening. Work the cloth-padded tip end around the tank bottom to sponge up the fuel that clings to corners. Discard the gas-soaked cloth, away from fire, smokers and sparks.

If the mower is four-cycle engine powered, this is the time to drain the oil from the crankcase. Place a shallow pan on the floor and tilt up the mower so that gravity will pull the warm, thinned oil and its suspended contaminants right out of the engine. Be sure to drain the crankcase completely because the sludge that clings to the bottom of the crankcase will poison fresh oil by releasing carbon and tiny metal particles it holds captive. Replace the crankcase cap after the mower is completely empty of oil and fuel.

At this point, engine parts are much too hot to handle, so now is a good time to clean up the underdeck and check the mower's blade. By the time these steps have been completed the engine should have cooled to the touch.

Even though the underdeck area has been flushed with water as a preliminary, the pulpy accretions of the summer's mowing may have to be scraped off. Both a scraper (try a putty knife) and a wire brush may be needed to clear the dried grass pulp from the machine. It is smart to recheck the spark plug wire and make sure it is safely tied up before proceeding. Next, turn the mower on its side. Do not balance the machine on its grass chute or plastic carburetor cover. This would fracture one or more mower parts.

With the machine in a stable position, start cleaning the under-deck surface. Long even strokes with the putty knife will soon pare away any stuck-on grass below-deck. In corners and tight spots, clean away grass with the wire brush. Flush the undersurface periodically with water from the garden hose to wash away debris and soften any residual material.

Check the blade's condition. A bent blade may cause vibration and power loss. A dull blade will tear and injure the lawn. An out-of-balance blade is dangerous and can hurt both you and the mower.

To check for a bent blade, place a straight-edge, such as a yardstick, across the bottom of the housing. Align the blade below the stick and make sure that the blade tips are within an equal distance of the yardstick. Next, check the blade by measuring the distance from blade tip to the housing edge, then rotate the blade until the opposite tip is under the stick. If the two tips do not measure within approximately $1/8$ inch of each other, relative to the housing edge, blade replacement is in order.

If blade condition warrants it, loosen and remove the nut holding the blade to the motor shaft and remove the blade to the bench. Sharpen the blade at the original angle and be sure to press out the nicks and dents that stones and roots have inflicted. Reinstall the blade after rechecking its balance and sharpness. Of course, if the original blade of the mower is beyond repair, buy a new blade. The cost of a new mower could be saved.

While the blade is off, if it is a 2 cycle mower, take the time to clean away power-robbing carbon deposits from the mower exhaust parts behind the muffler plate. The muffler plate is usually held to the mower housing by four nuts. Remove it and pull the starter rope slightly until the piston covers the exhaust parts. Using a $3/8$ inch diameter dowel stick, insert the dowel into the mower parts and turn to loosen carbon deposits. Remove the dowel, place the mower in an upright position and pull the starter rope vigorously several times to blow the loosened carbon from the exhaust parts.

Set the machine aright on its wheels before tackling the clean-up of the engine. First, check the carburetor's airway, and be sure to clean the engine air cleaner. Generally, this will be an oiled polyethylene filter. Wash the filter element in a detergent and water solution and squeeze dry. Re-oil the filter by applying five teaspoonfuls of engine oil to the sides and open ends of the filter element. Squeeze to distribute oil, as well as to remove excess oil, and reinstall in engine air cleaner.

Next, use a soft brush and cloth to clean away debris from the engine exterior and upper deck.

Pay particular attention to air-cooling fins of the engine. Any dirt, leaf or grass residue act as insulators, retarding heat transfer from engine to air.

If the mower is a self-propelled type, take time to remove the cover-ups from the drive mechanism to get out clippings, check parts and lubricate, if necessary. In a belt-driven model make sure that the belt is in good condition and free of any gummy or oily residue.

To get the grit off all surfaces before applying lubricants, apply a strong detergent car wash and hose down. Avoid flushing water into the carburetor air cleaner. Wipe the machine down using an old towel.

Lubrication

Mower owner manual contain specifics, but these are applying two or three drops of oil behind the wheel bolts. Spin the wheel afterwards to distribute oil to bearings.

For easy operation, apply a drop or two of oil to the inner member of each control cable. Do so from the top and gravity will do the rest. Likewise, apply a drop or two to the pivots of control handles to smooth their operation.

A light film of oil is the best corrosion-proofing that can be given a mower's engine interior. To apply, remove the spark plug and pour two tablespoons of 10W-40 oil into the cylinder. Crank the engine several times to allow oil to coat the cylinder walls and piston.

Now install fresh oil in the crankcase (if it is a four-cycle machine). Simply lift out the dipstick and pour in the required lubricant (typically, 10W-40) to the FULL mark of the dipstick. (Do not skip this step. If the crankcase is left dry and oil is not added in the spring, the engine will ruin in only minutes of operation.)

Ignition

While the spark plug is out of the engine, clean away carbon deposits from the housing and plug tip. If the center electrode of the plug appears rounded, file it flat. A plug with square-edged electrodes fires more reliably than a worn plug with rounded electrodes. Check and reset the gap, as necessary. If the plug can not be easily cleaned, replace it. Either way, install the plug in the engine, but do not connect the plug wire.

If it is a mower with conventional magneto ignition and a drop in power is noticeable, hardstarting or missing, the ignition breaker point set may need replacing. Generally, points start pitting after about 50 operating hours. Since this entails dismantling of the magneto assembly, a professional might be able to do a better job. However,

if the handyman has the skill and specific details at hand, it is a job he can tackle himself. If the mower bears the words *Solid-State Ignition,* there are no breaker points, eliminating an annoying periodic maintenance task.

Courtesy of Lawn Boy

Electric-Start Mowers

The power pack starting battery should be charged for 48 hours before off season storage. This can be done with the battery in place on the mower, using the plug-in charger supplied by the manufacturer. Do not leave the battery on charge beyond the recommended period. Leave the battery disconnected from the mower wiring after taking the battery off charge.

Final Inspection

Go over the mower carefully. Tighten any loose hardware and be sure to replace any lost pieces. Bagging chutes and grass deflectors are now commonly made of plastic. If any such part is cracked or broken, do not take chances — replace it.

Also, be sure to carefully inspect the bag to determine its future serviceability. Sun, moisture, sagging loads and flying shards take their toll on catcher bags. Especially check the zipper and that part of the bag which joins the chute. Mend torn or abraded areas, if possible, or replace the bag.

Storage

Be sure to choose a dry area for storage, to reduce chances of rusting. To keep the rubber-tired wheels of a mower from flattening, block under the housing to raise the wheels off the floor, with four bricks or scraps of wood. A plastic drop-cloth may be used to cover the mower and keep it clean.

SPRING MAINTENANCE

Remove the mower from its place of storage and thoroughly inspect it. If no parts are damaged or lost, check the crankcase oil level (if it is a four-cycle engine) and top up, if necessary. Fill with *regular* gas. (Premium contains benzene which can swell and ruin carburetor parts in small engines.)

Connect the spark plug wire to the spark plug, set the choke control and pull the starter.

Let the mower run for a few minutes so that you can check by ear the way the engine is performing. If the mower skips or misses even after warm-up is completed, the carburetor air filter, spark plug or breaker points may be at fault. The handyman can tackle these or the mower can be taken to the nearest authorized repair station for a tune-up.

SAFE MOWING TIPS

All power mowers, whether electric or gasoline, should be used with due consideration for their hazards. Some tips on operating power mowers follow.

Know how the machine works before attempting to run it; keep it out of inexperienced hands.

Check for cracks, replace any defective parts, and tighten loose nuts and bolts before each use.

Never mow a wet lawn.

Rake away loose stones, etc., before you start.

When starting the motor, stand clear of the discharge opening and be sure that you have a firm footing. With a cord-powered electric model, be sure the switch is off before you plug in the cord (first at the outlet, then at the mower) so that the blades will not start rotating before you are ready; and when you have finished, remember to switch the mower off, not just unplug the cord.

Never leave a mower running unattended.

Keep bystanders well away and see that the discharge is never pointed toward them.

Wear shoes wherever you use a lawn mower.

Mow across any slope if possible, starting at the top.

Stop immediately if the machine starts shaking excessively, and check for loose parts and (on a rotary mower) for an unbalanced blade. Dynamic unbalance can occur if a blade gets bent; it can be detected by revolving the blade slowly and noting whether its tips come opposite the same point on the housing. A bent blade is best replaced, since it may break in use if merely straightened. Static unbalance, which may result from uneven sharpening, can be detected by poising the blade (when it is off the mower) seesaw fashion on the edge of a ruler that bisects the center hole. To correct static unbalance, grind some steel from the heavier end of the blade.

With an electric mower, use only a brightly colored cord that stands out against the grass so you will not accidentally mow over it. It must be of a gauge suitable for the amount of current it will handle and of the three-wire type. Never use the mower unless the cord is properly grounded through a grounded outlet.

Courtesy of Janco Greenhouses, J.A. Nearing Co., Inc.

Lawns & Gardens

Are you thinking of fixing up one or two areas or doing over the whole yard? In either case you need to know just how difficult it is, how much time you can give it and what it will cost. Remember there are alternatives at every step. For instance, in fixing up the lawn you can patch the poor areas, reseed and fertilize all over or dig up the whole lawn and lay a long-lasting, beautiful turf. The important thing is to take on only what serves your purposes, and modify suggestions in order to meet your needs.

LANDSCAPING

Almost every homeowner has some sort of site problems: too long and narrow, dead-flat and square, rocky and steep or an oddly shaped lot.

Look clearly at the whole picture — your family needs, how you use the house and yard (or would like to), your style of living, the kind of house you have and how it sits on its site.

Landscaping, even a small bit at a time, takes careful planning. As the work progresses, you will find even the hard work enjoyable if you do it in easy stages. Landscaping does not have to be done all at one time. You can spread a big job out over several years if necessary and enjoy the changes that take place. This also gives you many opportunities to modify your plan as you learn.

Low-maintenance features are essential for most of us. For example, ground cover instead of grass on banks and under trees takes little attention year after year. Wood decking or concrete in hard play areas, gravel in service areas, and hardy lanscape plantings that can stand neglect will spare time and expense. Then, you can con-

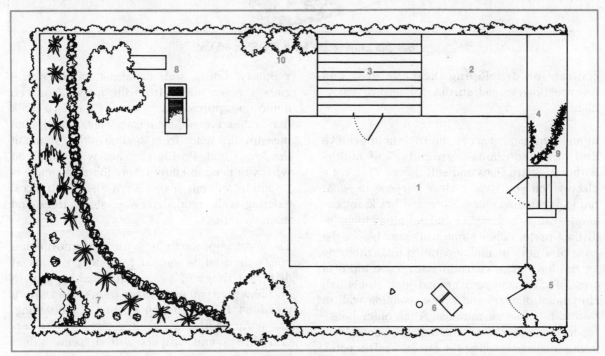

Landscaping a long, narrow lot can be effective if it is well planned.

1. House
2. Garage
3. Patio and door to garden
4. Service area with trellis rose
5. Hard-play surface
6. Low gate to side garden with small plantings and lawn chairs
7. Flowers and shrubs
8. Cook-out center
9. Evergreen screen
10. Tall hedge, slender evergreens.

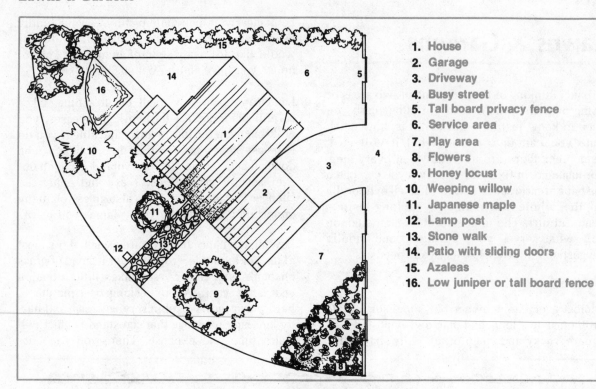

1. House
2. Garage
3. Driveway
4. Busy street
5. Tall board privacy fence
6. Service area
7. Play area
8. Flowers
9. Honey locust
10. Weeping willow
11. Japanese maple
12. Lamp post
13. Stone walk
14. Patio with sliding doors
15. Azaleas
16. Low juniper or tall board fence

Sample Landscape for a Pie-Shaped Lot.

centrate on developing the patio area and favorite flowers and shrubs for leisure enjoyment.

In any landscaping work the trick is to achieve unity between house, grounds, and neighborhood. Sharp lines and soft lines both have a place when you have a clear purpose in separating or melding areas. Stone and brick, for example, can give character and definition to an indistinct place. A low stone wall seen below the crest of a hilly mound separating a neighboring lot can have great charm; however, on top of a crest, it can make your ground look embattled. Horizontal planters and a low retaining wall in front can define an entrance. A tall older house can take on new charm with new horizontal lines in the landscape facing the street. Traffic paths invite the use of attractive paving materials with plantings.

MAKING THE PLAN

First make a rough, but accurate, map of your property on graph paper. Show the outlines of your house with window and door openings, the property lines, and distances of important glass vantage points from the house. You can determine approximate grades by staking a chalk line taut and level (use a carpenter's level), then measure the space from the line to the ground at the lower end. Profile sketches will show you what you need to know where the slope angle is important in your plans. Show street entrances, existing walks and driveway, steps, trees and major plantings.

The most important single piece of information you will need is sun and shade positions at different times of year. This enables you to decide where you want shade trees — and where you don't. It lets you plan a patio for sunbathing, or one for cool, shady seating; know where certain shrubs and flowers will succeed; select kinds of grass; and decide where you will want overhead shelter. On your property map, sketch in where shade from house and trees will fall at midmorning and midafternoon. Do not overlook winter sun positions. An evergreen that should give year-around beauty may look poor if shaded by a neighbor's house for three to four months. Also, winter sun positions may allow you to bring container plantings inside for continued pleasure if you have not shaded a large glass area with an immovable outside overhang.

When you discover all the possibilities in your property you will have to make choices, deciding that some things are not possible, while others are top objectives. This will help you simplify the plan and choose materials and plantings with intelligent restraint.

At this stage it is important to collect specialized information from building materials sources, growers and horticulture associations, mail-order houses and the government. A list at the end of this entry will help. You will find materials that are new to you, methods that will save you years of trial and error, and prices with which you can accurately budget the project.

PAVE OR PLANT GRASS?

No surface is maintenance-free. Grass needs cutting, watering, feeding, and weed-control, but it

also gives natural drainage — a major asset on any property. Paving may create drainage problems that can affect the house unless runoff is accurately provided. The initial cost for paving of any sort is greater than for grass. Cost of repairs and maintenance are about equal. Most homeowners find that both are needed in the right places.

High-traffic places — walks, steps, patios, and service areas — need secure footing, of course. Flagstone or brick, concrete or wood rounds,

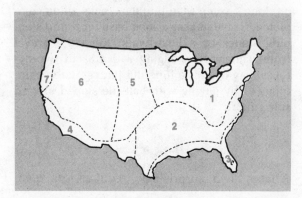

	Choose the Right Grass for Your Situation			
Grass	**Lawn Use**	**Mowing Height**	**Area**	
Bent Grass, Colonial	rich soil, constant moisture, 4-6 hrs. sun, tolerates lt. shade	$1/2'' - 3/4''$	1, 6	
Bermuda	rich, moist soil, full sun, tolerates salt spray	1''	2, 3, 4	
Bluegrass, Kentucky	rich, loamy soil, well drained. Full sun in northern tier, tolerates some shade farther south. Mix with annual ryegrass for banks and hills; drought-resistant. Requires frequent feeding.	2''	1, 5, 7	
Fescue, red	grows in heavy shade (less than 5-6 hrs. sun) as well as in sun. Mixed with bluegrass makes fine, all-purpose lawn	2'' - 3''	1, 7 northern 2	
Fescue, tall	athletic fields	2'' - 3''	1, 7 northern 2	
Ryegrass, annual	banks and hills for sod-holding, rapid growth. In South, for second seeding as winter grass	2''	2, 3, 4	
Ryegrass, perennial	sunny locations; often mixed with finer grasses as a sun shade	2''	2, 3, 4 and elsewhere in mixture	
St. Augustine	full sun or shade, stays green in winter in Gulf area	1'' - 2''	2, 3, 4	
Zoysia	shade and sun	under 1''	2, 3, 4 northern coastal area	

crushed stone or gravel, timber for garden steps, are attractive with any style of architecture. In landscaping you can repeat here and there a texture of material that was used on your house, or select one that contrasts with and relieves it, such as a brick or stone terrace or wall with a clapboard house.

You can lay some paving materials yourself, saving a good part of the cost. Level four inches of crushed rock or small gravel topped with two inches of sand for laying dry paving with brick or stone. Sweep sand into the cracks when completed. Gravel makes a good base for round stepping stones or a boardwalk. Keep the gravel from scattering by edging with treated two-by-fours. Lay drainage for solid paving with drainpipes or by edging with half-tile sloped toward safe runoff.

Making and Keeping a Lawn

A large lawn, surprisingly, requires less atten-

tion than a small grass area because flaws are less conspicuous. Whether you are restoring an old lawn, rebuilding it, or planting the first lawn on a new homesite, you should have your soil tested to make your efforts worthwhile.

Send soil samples (four cubic inches each) from principal lawn areas to your county agriculture station or state agriculture college for a complete analysis. Enclose a note saying what you intend to plant and what has been grown there before. Ask also for recommendations as to soil amendments and amounts needed to condition your soil. The report returned to you should give the pH factor, represented on a scale from 0 to 14, with seven the neutral condition between acidity and alkalinity. Most grasses and plants grow best in slightly acid soil, between pH 5.5 and 6.5. The report should also tell you the soil conditions in respect to nitrogen, phosphorus, and potassium content. Healthy soils need some 16 elements in balance, but these are the large factors essential to plant life. Fertilizers are commonly rated by

Well-fed lawn on house property next to an unfed neighboring lawn shows what difference fertilizing makes even with a top-grade grass.

Courtesy of O.M. Scott & Sons

content of these three elements, as 10-6-4, a generally good mixture containing 10 percent nitrogen, 6 percent phosphorus, and 4 percent potassium compounds.

The simplest lawn repair is to cut out dead and diseased spots with an edging tool, loosen the soil to about six inches deep, mix in an inch of peat and fertilizer each, and sow lawn seed of a suitable and hardy variety that will grow in your difficult places. Aerate the lawn with a hand aerator. Also remove crabgrass and other lawn-choking weeds, spread seed lightly over the entire lawn, and sprinkle with topsoil to give the seed a good chance to germinate. Keep seeded areas moist until grass shoots are two or three inches tall; then water more deeply twice a week until the grass is mature. Lawns should be watered to a depth of two inches at every watering, for light watering encourages shallow root growth. A small glass jar or rainfall measuring tube set on the lawn will give you an idea of how much water has been given. The average sprinkler with good coverage puts down about an inch of water per hour.

If spots of grass disease show on your lawn, they should be treated promptly with the correct fungicide. To control weeds in following seasons, treat the lawn with appropriate weed-control products in early spring before new growth appears.

To overhaul an old lawn or plant the first lawn on a new site, there is an important preliminary operation. Stick in a spoon spade two feet deep to see what kind of soil you have. If the site has been filled with building rubble and only a thin layer of topsoil, you have a major problem, for nothing will grow well there except weed. The best solution is to scrape off and mound the layer of topsoil and bring in a bulldozer to remove at least a foot of the rubble fill; then have suitable topsoil brought in and leveled to the correct height, maintaining drainage slopes at a slight grade.

Windsor bluegrass lawn is a beautiful carpet leading to this snug home.

Courtesy of O.M. Scott & Sons

If the topsoil is four to six inches deep, peel off the old lawn in strips, saving as much soil as possible. With a rotary tiller (these can be rented) run through to the depth of the topsoil to break up the earth to a depth of six inches and rake out all large stones and root. Spread an inch of peat and an inch of well rotted manure or garden compost, plus conditioners indicated by your soil test. The peat will temporarily reduce the nitrogen content of the soil, and whenever it is used an additional supplement of nitrogen should be added to compensate. Both peat and manure in the soil provide good moisture retention and porosity; the manure provides slow-release nutrients and acts to free natural soil qualities for use by plants. With a cart-type spreader add fertilizer that approximates the recommendation in your soil-analysis report. Use the tiller again to stir the ingredients into the soil and break up the earth finely, running it in a crisscross direction. Rake the ground level, and with a light roller crisscross the soft earth, pushing it before you to avoid leaving deep holes from your step, and do this until only light footprints appear.

If you are laying sod, soil preparation suggested above is equally necessary. Be ready to lay the sod as soon as it is delivered, and lay it in staggered strips so that joints do not coincide. Use a chalk line pegged at opposite ends of the area to keep straight rows. Fill cracks between strips with topsoil, then tamp down with a sod tamper or by jumping on a square board until every bit of the sod is in firm contact with the soil. This is necessary to make sure the roots are covered. Last, water it down with a fine spray and water twice weekly until growth is about 4 inches tall.

To seed, rake *lightly* across the rolled earth to make small furrows. Use a wheeled seeder set according to directions on the seed label. It is important not to seed more densely than the grower recommends for the roots of each type need a certain space for growth and strength. After seeding, rake across your little furrows very

Courtesy of O.M. Scott & Sons

Grass in the round helps to relax a busy traffic area at this residence.

lightly in crisscross directions to let the seeds fall into the earth. Wet lightly and evenly with a fine spray mist until the surface is moist (dark colored) and continue until growth is two or three inches tall. You should see tiny blades appear in about five days, depending on climate and the seed type. You can buy inexpensive cheesecloth at the feed store to protect the area from birds, wind, heavy rain and sun. Remove the cheesecloth when blades are two inches tall, carefully lifting the cloth off to avoid uprooting.

Early fall is the best time to plant a lawn, when grass root growth is vigorous and weeds are failing. Spring seeding is less favorable due to strong sun in late spring when the grass is tender and crabgrass infestation before the grass roots are strong enough to take over. About a month after grass shoots appear you can apply the first feeding at half strength, mixed with a high-quality weed control. Do this on a still day so that nearby plants are not ruined by the weed-killer.

Mow new grass when it is three to four inches high. Generally, the higher grass is cut, the stronger it will be. It is particularly important not to cut grass closely that is infested with crabgrass and other strong weeds, because that gives the weeds a better chance. The Department of Agriculture recommends mowing lawn grass with a slow-motion blade because the powered rotary blades, turning at very high speed, shred the blade instead of making a square cut.

Sprinkler systems tend to result in a poor lawn over a period of time. Not only is the homeowner tempted to water too frequently, drowning the grass and inviting mildew and other fungi, but when the piping is installed a rotary tiller cannot be used to overhaul the lawn. The owner must only patch and repair. The same problem results when electric conduit is laid under lawns.

Planting on Hills and Slopes

For grades under 30° either grass or ground covers will do. For steeper grades, consider how to hold the soil while also making it attractive as a landscape feature. Recent Department of Agriculture studies indicate that ground moisture [and therefore topsoil] is best retained by furrowing rather than terracing; but this would not apply to very steep grades. The vertical side of a terrace step brings roots into contact with dry, hot retainers in summer, and frigid in winter. Earth furrows hold moisture and house roots better, resulting in less dieoff. Planted with ground-holding varieties, they blend into the landscape, where wood, stone, or brick terrace retainers usually become a focal point. You certainly could employ both as the grade changes. Large rocks well embedded can be most attractive.

CHOOSING TREES

The relationship between trees and house is intimate, and the size and character of trees can affect your home's appearance fundamentally. Trees in scale with the house and lot are generally easy to live with. Contemporary low-profile houses seem to invite trees that grow to 25 or 30 feet at maturity, although on a large lot a ranch-type house can take on a distinguished homestead look with towering forest trees bordering a clearing near the house. Flowering, light-limbed trees such as the dogwood along borders and the horizontal-topped mimoza near a patio or porch are attractive plantings for a standard house.

Trees that should be on every list for the small yard or garden nook are the Japanese maples, with various leaf colors and fine form; the threadleaf maple, one of the most beautiful, with low, spreading, reaching, elbowed limbs; the paperbark maple, with straight, slim trunk and fine skin; the canoe birch, slender and light-feathered, which often is planted in stands of two, three, or four with roots joined, striking white in the dooryard or property corner; the blue spruce, geometric and unique in color and the English yew, ideal for topiary shaping at any size. If you like flowering fruit trees with edible fruit, try to find the orange *Poncirus trifoliata;* its fruit can be used in marmalade, ripens in September-October, and for an orange it has an unusual northern range.

How to Plant a Tree

1. Make the hole large enough for the root ball plus ample space for fertile soil added around it.

2. Set the root ball so that the base of the tree is level with the ground. Fill new soil beneath to hold it at that level.

3. Stakes will support tree until roots take over and abundant new growth appears on limbs.

4. Fill the hole with friable soil, firming it with your feet around the root ball. Cut cord holding burlap before covering the hole. You should leave a shallow basin at the top to collect rainfall for the roots.

5. Wrap the trunk with tree wrapping available at garden centers. This keeps bark-eating animals and insects from destroying the young tree.

Trees	Average Height (feet)	Spread (feet)
Arborvitae	35	35
Canoe Birch	20	14
White Birch	45	30
Red Cedar	40	12
Flowering Crabapple	18	18
Dogwood	18	18
Colorado Fir	80	40
Hawthorn (Rose of Sharon)	15	15
American Linden	70	40
Globe Locust	22	25
Honey Locust	30	25
Saucer Magnolia	25	20
Star Magnolia	14	14
English Maple	35	35
Japanese Maple	12	12
Red Maple	30	40
Sugar Maple	60	40
Mimosa	20	20
Black Oak	50	50
Pin Oak	30	35
White Oak	65	65
Lombardy Poplar	40	10
Blue Spruce, Koster	20	12
Weeping Willow	35	35

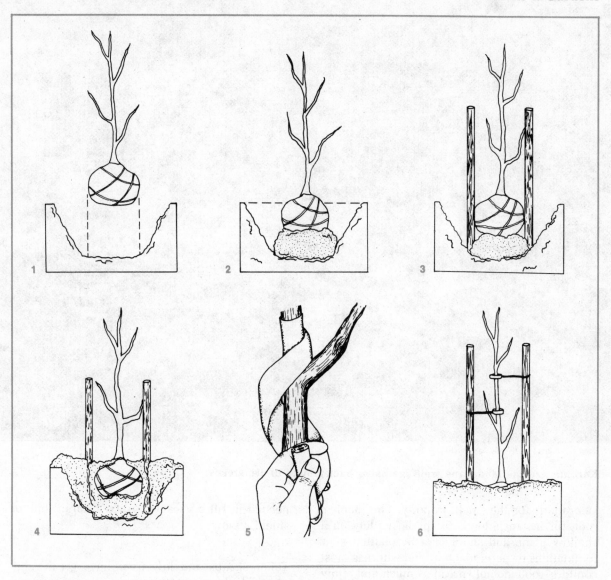

6. Use sections of inner-tube or garden hose to cushion wire supports around tree. Water the tree immediately until water appears at top. Then water well twice weekly until the tree is on its own.

Every yard should have at least one big tree, for shade on the house is valuable. Since the disaster to the great elm, we look for a substitute until a cure for Dutch elm disease is found; perhaps the scholar tree or pagoda tree as it is sometimes called, is the nearest in size and shape to the elm, with large, economical habit, refined compound leaves and tiny flowers in midsummer. If you worry about the broad-branching of maples over roof and chimney, look at the Newton Sentry, a sport of the sugar maple, with superbly narrow form, ideal along the lane or as the family tree that does not take over the whole garden. For the large lot, consider the silver linden the most dense shade tree. Sometimes very light shade cools an afternoon over the patio and garden; that is the place for the honey locust, which, besides, has a compact root system. You can even grow flowers in its shadow.

A tree's hardiness, spread, shape density and root habit, as well as height, are prime con-

Karume azaleas landscape well against a background of evergreens.

siderations for the small property. The maple's root, for instance, tends to spread widely on a shallow plane and should not be planted near foundations or perennial borders, whereas most conifers' roots do not spread as much and allow close planting. The branch spread, incidentally, is ordinarily smaller than a tree's root spread. You can judge and plan accordingly:

SHRUBS FOR LANDSCAPING, PRIVACY, AND CLIMATE CONTROL

The homeowner's timesaver is the hardy shrub. Small flowering tree forms never fail to add sparkle with blossoms in spring and early summer, brilliant leaf colors and berries in fall and early winter. Evergreen shrubs give outdoor life and color twelve months around. Shrubs are versatile, for most are easily dug up and moved or planted in containers to be placed wherever needed to fill a vacancy, grace a harsh line, or shield a view.

Taller shrubs and low trees have great value planted close together as a sunscreen and windbreak near the house, modifying the temperature toward the house by five to ten degrees. This is a great asset in fuel savings. Noise control is another boon from such planting, damping busy street sounds.

The key to using shrubs in the yard and as architectural features, as with trees, is economy. Many are tempting when you see them in the nurseries and growers' catalogs, but space and form urge careful choice of a few types well placed on the average lot. A handsome shrub placed at the focal point near the front door can be spoiled by planting other varieties too near.

988

Courtesy of Brooklyn Botanic Garden, Osborne Section

The Japanese garden for a pool.

Do not overlook the chance to customize your property by imaginative placement of shrubs as a neat sentinel at the street entrance such as the Greek juniper or more slender, taller Irish juniper Hibernica, with a small mushroom night light at its base; a spreading shore pine, weeping forsythia, or double-file viburnum to protect the patio; rounded and spreading forms for a casual border or filling an awkward corner; hydrangea, flowering raspberry, and pepperbush for full-sun positions; low-lying dwarf evergreens to soften entry steps. Your own ideas will begin to materialize when you look at your house and yard from this viewpoint, then visit the nursery and go through the catalogs.

Dwarf Evergreens and Conifers

These are among the most useful plants we have. As a group they thrive in cool climates with plenty of rain, but many varieties such as the dwarf and Italian cypress, the Greek juniper, and several that originated in Japan do well in warm climates. With minimum care they are attractive looking in any season. Euonymus 'Emerald Gaiety' has a light twinkle in sunny locations, a darker hue in shade. These evergreens respond well to shaping and their size is quite easy to control. Ask your nursery dealer for suggestions about what types grow best in your area and will suit the situation you have in mind.

A carpet juniper grows well among rocks for green gracefulness near an entry, on an embankment, between large trees, or in a rock garden. Japanese holly, a relatively dwarf plant growing to four feet in time, is very compact, tolerates shade, and needs trimming only once or twice each summer. The gowdy spruce has the shortest needle among dwarf conifers and is an attractive accent plant that will not screen architec-

989

Rock garden brings bulb blooms, perennials and evergreens into delightful harmony.

tural features such as a step that must be seen, or a turn in the walk. Some dwarf conifers are true miniatures that delight the eye and are charming in close quarters, such as in an entry or door-step planter. The dwarf Canadian hemlock and Hinoki cypress dwarfs are only eight to ten inches tall when almost twenty years old. If you want to start your own Bonzai, you will probably succeed with a blue Atlas cedar or one of the short needled pines or junipers such as 'Nana.' Best of all for this is pyracantha.

Evergreens do need watering, feeding, and most need sun to stay in good color. They are a healthy group, however, and require relatively little attention.

PLANTS IN CONTAINERS

You will be surprised by what you can do with top specimen plants in containers. Dress up the

patio or entry by using a pair of floribunda roses covered with blossoms grown in containers. Then, while they are resting, bring in a bird-of-paradise plant, camellias or rhododendron in top form. Some varieties produce abundant bloom when tightly planted (much closer than seed instructions advise); big-trumpet petunias, wax begonias and impatiens do this. Of course, they have to be fed well and the soil aerated, good drainage be provided and deadheads kept picked and stems clipped to branch more, but this goes for all container-grown plants.

Stacking containers in receding steps is a good way to show a mass of bloom in a small space. For larger plants, use caster platforms sold with the big containers so you can wheel them to the proper spot when they are in bloom.

Gardening in containers is the perfect solution for people in mobile homes. You can always

990

have your favorites with you. Just pack them into the home when you have to move, and in a new location add fast-growing annuals to fill in for a quick and easy garden highlighted with your impressive container plants.

FLOWERS FOR FUN

It is easy to grow successful flowers. Before you start, ask this question: Do you really want an easy garden, or a more ambitious one with its periodic triumphs and splendid cut flowers for the house? Perhaps you can have both if you concentrate on one or two specialities you will enjoy and be proud of.

An easy flower garden can be planted with perennial plants from the local garden shop that almost take care of themselves, such as bearded iris, daylilies, lily of the valley, phlox, long-lasting bulbs and hardy flowering bushes such as lilac. For variety and bright spots of color in the easy way, buy plants of annuals such as zinnias and marigolds, petunias, pansies and geraniums.

There is an enormous variety available, both in form and color, to suit any plan or pattern you want to carry out. Annuals are especially easy to grow in containers of small size, for they are mostly shallow rooted. To plant annuals the earth should be finely broken up to about six inches, but preparation is less demanding than for planting perennials.

Perennials deserve the time and attention you give to preparing the ground, for they will beautify your grounds for years to come. Depth of digging actually depends on the species, but one foot is a useful average for preparing a perennial bed where you will have a mixture of plants. For average home soil of sandy loam, mix in two inches of peat moss and two inches of compost or well-rotted manure, and consult your soil-test report on what your soil needs for good production. In clay soil, increase the amount of peat moss and break up finely to make the soil porous. Certain perennial species have particular requirements; the grower will list these on the package or tell you what they are. Most perennials are hardy and reliable bloomers. The

A planter beside the fence helps break the monotony.

Courtesy of California Redwood Association

Courtesy of Janco Greenhouses, J. A. Nearing Co, Inc.

most popular of all are roses, iris and daylilies (hemerocallis). Other colorful varieties are shasta daisies, hollyhocks (good near fences and walls) and the chrysanthemums. There is a great variety of mums, all reliable flowers in the fall when most others have passed, and if you will nip the tops as they grow strongly in mid and late summer, you will make their branches multiply for more bloom. To get a banked, long-lasting fall display, nip the plants in front shorter and more often than those in the rear.

Starting plants from seed is fun and gives the gardener a great sense of accomplishment when his seedlings turn out to be strong, healthy plants

with good bloom. Annuals and many perennials are relatively easy to grow from seed. Some can be planted directly in the ground when danger of hard frost is past. Others should be started early indoors, the strongest small seedlings picked out and transplanted into peat pots to be set in the ground at the right time.

Tulips, daffodils, hyacinths, scilla (intense small blue) and most other spring-flowering bulb species are easy to grow and have the virtue of dying down to make way for alter planting of annuals near the surface. They can also be planted among shallow-rooted perennials that rise later in the season. However, bulbs need care in dig-

Courtesy of Janco Greenhouses, J. A. Nearing Co, Inc.

ging the hole at the right depth, spacing the right distance apart, and putting some bulb food in the bottom of the hole and feeding again during the blooming period to keep plants strong for many repeat performances. The tulip, for one, is rather short-lived, a bulb producing for about four years. Spring bulb flowers are effective either planted in massed, formal shapes, or naturalized in mixed planting under trees, in slopes and around large rocks. The gladiolus is breathtaking when grouped formally and bulbs inserted at ten-day intervals for continued and changing bloom; this species must be dug up each year before fall for resting and replanting the next season. The clump-rooted varieties such as iris and daylilies reproduce rapidly and can be raised each third or fourth year to be divided and replanted.

Home-Grown Roses

Growing roses is great fun with splendid returns. Most popular and most admired are the great hybrid tea roses with free-blooming fence ramblers probably a close second.

Roses need five or six hours of full sun, but are tolerant of periods of bad weather. Plant them, preferably, at least six feet from shrub roots and twelve feet from the drip line of trees. A south

993

and east exposure grows the best roses, in a place where the air flows freely and without reflected heat from walls.

If there is a secret to success in growing roses, it is thorough preparation of the soil. If soil drainage is poor, with clay, marl, or hardpan under the topsoil, dig on the deep side. In any case, roses cannot survive in extremely moist soil. If the water table is high (you will find out when you dig), lay gravel in the lower third of a deep hole and raise the bed several inches above surrounding ground.

Mix the dirt from the hole with about six inches of peat moss and six inches of well-rotted manure or compost. A handful of bone meal or a little less superphosphate for strong root growth is the only supplement wanted during the first season. In following years, feed roses in sandy soils more than those planted in clay soil or heavy loam because nutrients leach out faster in sand.

How to Plant Bare-Root Roses

1.   Lay out bed with at least twenty-four inches between bushes, thirty inches between larger varieties. Stagger individual locations so that flowers will be displayed and bushes can be cared for. Beds should have no more than three across so that you can reach all plants. Preliminary, of course, is to prepare ground as described in text. When planting several roses or a long bed, dig the entire area and grade it, then open single holes when roses arrive for planting.

2.   Soak the roots in a large bucket for one hour to as long as overnight, depending on moisture in plant when it arrives. Cover the roots with mud to help them hold moisture during the planting

operation. Water should cover bud union and base of canes. Bud union is the knotty knuckle where hardy root stock is grafted to great bloom varieties. Prune canes to remove dead wood, which looks dry, brown-gray, and lifeless. Live wood will be green or show green signs of life such as bud starts. Make cuts one-quarter inch above live bud-breaks or leaf joints (crescent-shape marks on cane). Cut off entirely dead canes flush at source. Trim root ends a bit at a time until you see white centers, indicating life. Main plant life comes from root ends. Also remove ailing canes that show brown or black canker blotches on sides; cut back until cross-section is clear green-white, with no brown or tan spots. Paint all cane cuts or scrapes immediately with tree-wound dressing.

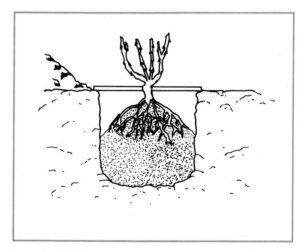

3.   Dig the hole 18 inches wide and from 24 to 36 inches deep. Fill the bottom half with prepared soil mix (see text) and root food, leaving a cone shape on which to spread the roots. Set plant so that the bud union is at the center of the hole and

level with surface. Where winter temperatures frequently go to -10°, set the bud union two inches below ground level.

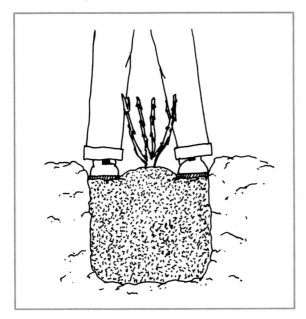

4-6. Fill the hole to about six inches from the top, stuffing the mix with your fingers around the roots and under the bud union. Press the mix down *firmly* with your feet, then fill to the brim with water and let it settle. Make sure there are no spaces around the roots and bud union. Fill in the remaining soil and water down again. Then mound moist soil over the stubby canes until only the tops show. You can use a plastic or asphalt collar to hold the soil in place. The mound is needed to keep winds and sun from drying out canes before new growth starts.

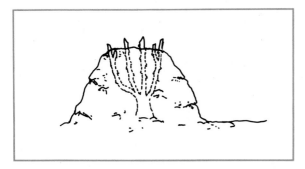

Experienced gardeners usually buy bare-root plants from reliable mail-order growers. But local garden shops sell potted rose plants with a tight earth ball on the roots, ready to slip into the hole if you need extra rose in midseason. The bare-root plants usually last longer, are stronger, and produce more and better blossoms.

Planting should be done in the late fall or when the ground opens in the spring. When new shoots appear through the soil mound and cold winds subside, remove the mound bit by bit as the ground warms until the bud union is exposed. This aids basal shoots to break from the bud union to form strong new growth.

When leaves appear, start a regular weekly or biweekly spray schedule, but use sprays (or dust) at one-quarter recommended strength until after first bloom appears, then increasing the dosage enough to control insect and fungus problems that may appear. Many successful rose-growers use a mixture consisting of diazinon or Isotox for insects with folpet for black spot and mildew, and benlate for mildew. Together, they do a very reliable job without leaf burn or high toxicity. When spraying, use the finest mist you can get and concentrate on the base of the plant, the canes, and the underside of leaves.

Where to Plant Roses

Hybrid teas are bedding rose bushes that can be used singly or in small groups for garden highlights, or in long beds devoted to a number of varieties, where you can control conditions (including the original preparation of the soil) better. The same is true of tea roses, hybrid perpetuals, polyanthas, floribundas and miniature roses. The smaller varieties are excellent in small, single-file beds along walks. The shorter hybrid teas such as Chrysler Imperial and the floribundas such as Oregold and Gene Boerner make superb container plants, although they take longer to get started than the same plants in open ground.

Shrub roses mound and sprawl in a casual form in an open space; they lend themselves to a casual boundary planting or to separate a lawn from a steep drop-off. Ramblers make good ground cover on banks or along fences, and can be trained up posts. Climbing roses include climbing forms or other great blooming types, and can be trained to grow on house pillars and

Four stages of blossom, from bud to full bloom, are seen in the hybrid tea, "South Seas."

A climber can be planted anywhere along a trellis or fence.

doorways, tall fences and trellises. Tree roses (or standards, as they are known) include many of the great species grafted to fine upright trunks, and often produce the best flowers.

Winter protection for roses is necessary in deep cold regions, but from the lower half of Zone Six southward it is a matter of opinion and experience, not omitting the microclimate of your own garden. Mr. George Ohlhus, chief rosarian for Star Roses, reports that in the southeast corner of Pennsylvania where their fields are located, they have experienced more dieback of rose canes when plants are hilled over the winter, possibly caused by rot from alternate freezing and thawing of the small earth mound.

Some of the top-rated roses in the United States, as determined by the American Rose Society, are listed here by type, size, and color:

> ### Hybrid Tea
>
> Charlotte Armstrong, tall, deep pink
> Chicago Peace, medium, pink blend
> Chrysler Imperial, medium, dark red
> Electron (not sized), deep pink
> First Prize (not sized), pink blend
> Fragrant Cloud (not sized), orange-red
> Miss All-American Beauty
>   (not sized), medium pink
> Mister Lincoln, tall, dark red
> Peace, medium, yellow blend
> Royal Highness, medium, light pink
> Swarthmore, tall, pink blend
> Tiffany, medium, pink blend
> Tropicana, medium, orange-red
>
> ### Grandiflora
>
> Camelot, medium, medium pink
> Carrousel, medium, dark red
> Montezuma, medium, orange-red
> Queen Elizabeth, tall, medium pink
>
> ### Floribunda
>
> Betty Prior, medium, medium pink
> Europeana (not sized), dark red
> Gene Boerner (not sized), medium pink

PRUNING

The reason one gardner has attractive plants

while another has poor ones under the same conditions may be pruning or the lack of it. Woody plants and trees especially need clear form and strong new growth to stay healthy, produce abundant bloom and leaf and look attractive. Pruning should be done at planting time and at least seasonally, usually after a blooming period or before new growth starts at the beginning of the season. Beware of heavy pruning after leaves fall to avoid severe dieback over the winter.

Decide how your plant should look and prune to shape it in that form. Hedge plants set close together can be pruned or trimmed to direct upright growth. Individual plants may reach full grace and strength by pruning for free-flowing form and open center. Roses and many other flowering shrubs need open centers and space between branches to let in light and air, but branch length should be pruned to produce good bloom. Root pruning can control the size of fast-growing shrubs and trees; dig down about a third of the way in from the ends of the branches with a sharp spade.

A common mistake is to prune out new shoots on woody plants such as the lilac, guarding the old growth as the lifeblood. The vitality is really in the root, which has set up new slender shoots to produce abundant leaf necessary to life. The tough old growth produces fewer and fewer leaves, and blossoms only at the farthest tips, eventually rotting and breaking from lack of chlorophyll production and open sap lines. When such plants begin to look toppy and bloom is reduced, cut out old wood close to the root joint, paint the wound, and let new shoots in the right positions develop in the form you want.

Cutting blossoms is an important form of pruning. How you cut them determines the future shape of the plant. Cutting blooms often results in more prolific bloom and saves plant energy spent in trying to make seed from the bloom head.

PLANTS THAT GROW IN SHADE

Tree-lovers and those who like to have a naturalized landscape value plants that will

Courtesy of Jackson and Perkins Company

A rose garden in a small home landscape is entirely practical.

grow well and bloom in shady places. There are really two kinds of shade, however, and plants respond differently in them: deep shade and open shade. Some varieties of the following will grow in shade:

Dwarf conifers: Honoki, or false cypress; common spruce or Norway spruce; white spruce, Canadian spruce; all hemlocks.

Broad-leafed evergreens: rhododendron, mountain laurels and hollies, barberry, cherry laurel, abelia, andromeda, camellia, cyrilla.

Shrubs: azalea, glossy abelia, red and black chokeberry, sweet pepperbush, cotoneaster, honeysuckle, witchhazel, oakleaf hydrangea, black alder, privet, rhododendron, St. Johnsworth, highbush blueberry, viburnum.

Bulbs (listed in order of blooming through the season): crocus, snowdrop, winter aconite, eranthis, anemone, chionodoxa, bulbous iris, scilla, wood hyacinth, Spanish bluebell, Canada lily, Turkscap lily, amaryllis, daylily, caladium, hosta, colchicum, cyclamen, fall crocus, most Dutch bulbs.

Annuals: phlox, impatiens, wax begonia, coleus, balsam, browallia, calendula, English daisy,

Courtesy of Janco Greenhouses, J. A. Nearing Co, Inc.

lobelia, lupine, myosotis, sweet alyssum, thunbergia, vinca.

Many ground-cover plants, many vines, ferns, and primroses (primulas) also grow in shade. The big majority of shade-tolerant plants may do well in light or medium shade, but fewer in deep shade.

USEFUL GROUND-COVER PLANTS

Ground covers are used because the homeowner prefers them to grass, or because they are a more attractive plant in certain situations than others or because they grow better in some situations, such as on banks and in shade and under trees, where other plants grasses will not survive.

Any low-growing plant you like can be used as ground cover. Many homes have rambling roses covering banks; they are excellent and attractive soil-holders. Spreading miniature evergreens

are often used in limited areas. Sometimes conifers seed themselves and spread. Lily-of-the-valley is a fast spreading ground cover, however, walking on it breaks the plants, though it does not kill them.

Ground covers of particular value include pachysandra, English ivy, Virginia creeper, carpet bugle, St. Johnsworth, candytuft, myosotis, prostrate juniper, blue phlox, periwinkle or myrtle (Vinca minor), the Max Graf rose and several other rose varieties.

THE GREEN GARDEN

The garden without flower-head blooms of prominence, but with interesting, attractive and often colorful leaf is in great popularity now, as it was in the Romantic and early Victorian periods of the 19th century. Plants in this group have great character and in microcosm hold immense in-

Courtesy of Janco Greenhouses, J. A. Nearing Co., Inc.

terest for the horticulturist. Some easy-to-find types include the ferns, coleus caladium, cacti, hosta, mosses, Japanese andromeda, fatsia, bergenia, the large-leaf begonias, and arrowhead. More exotic varieties are being imported by the hundreds from the southern hemisphere and tropical areas. Many of them need careful protection from cool temperatures.

GARDEN STRUCTURES

If you have not thought about a greenhouse, the idea may seem ridiculous, out of the question. But fact is, many serious gardeners who have a small property have built lean-to greenhouses that are completely successful and inexpensive. Heavy-gauge plastic can be attached to aluminum channel stock from building suppliers, or heavier sheet plastic can be used, as well as glass. A number of lean-to and self-standing greenhouse structures are for sale by mail order.

The most important garden structure for the serious gardener is a cold frame. It consists of a foot-deep base dug in the ground lined with cinder on the bottom, peat and sand above; at ground level you install a frame that slants toward the winter sun, about six inches high at the south end, a foot or more high at the north. On top, glass or plastic covers the frame; an old storm window or door will do. Here seedlings are raised long before planting time, ready to be set out when the weather permits. Other plants that cannot survive winter outdoors are hardened off here for planting again in the garden. Tomato plants, hardwood cuttings, and flowers of all descriptions can be hardened for the growing season when you prop open the lid on warm spring days, close it against frost at night. This gives you a much longer growing season in the garden for plants handled this way.

A potting table is one of the most useful things

1001

Courtesy of Janco Greenhouses, J.A. Nearing Co., Inc.

you can provide yourself, for here you not only have free work space for handling potted and container plants, but also a place to separate seedlings for planting in the ground and handle cut flowers and vegetables before taking them into the house.

A garden tool center is the natural location for the potting table if you have space for it. Perhaps your space is a corner of the garage, or in the house service area. Provide yourself a place where you can keep the lawn mower, trimmer, other garden tools and fertilizers and insecticides. Insecticides should be kept safe from children and pets.

Garden Tools

The basic tools you will need to maintain any garden are a hoe, a rake, a shovel, heavy shears, lightweight clippers, trowels, and a fertilizer spreader. Perhaps the most important of all is the spoon-type spade, for it slides more easily into the ground than any other, and a quality design makes it easy to remove a full load with it. The five-prong fork is more useful than ones with fewer tines. When you get a trowel, buy two: a narrow one for small spaces and bulb-digging, and a big one of cast metal for general use. As you become more interested in gardening, you will want to add other, more specialized tools.

INFORMATION THAT WILL HELP YOU

Places to Write

Brooklyn Botanic Gardens, 1000 Washington Avenue, Brooklyn, New York, 11225, has the best information program of all American botanical institutions, including a large series of booklets on specific subjects written by top experts in their fields. Booklets cost $1.50 each, but general information is free.

American Horticultural Society, 1600 Bladenburg Road, N. E., Washington, D. C., 20002.

Garden Club of America, 598 Madison Avenue, New York, New York, 10022.

Government Printing Office, Washington, D. C., Pamphlets.

Associations

American Begonia Society, Mrs. Virginia Barnett, 1213 South Mullender Avenue, West Covina, California, 91790.

American Camelia Society, Mr. Joseph H. Pyron, Box 212, Ft. Valley, Georgia, 31330.

American Daffodil Society, Mrs. Robert F. Johnson, 2537 West 89th Street, Leawood, Kansas, 66206.

American Dahlia Society, Mr. Edward B. Lloyd, 10 Crestmont Road, Montclair, New Jersey.

American Gesneria Society, Mrs. Thomas Neel, 6504 Dresden, Indianapolis, Indiana, 46227

American Hemerocallis Society, Mrs. Lewis B. Wheeler, Box 28786, Memphis, Tennessee, 38128.

American Iris Society, Mrs. Clifford W. Benson, Missouri Botanical Garden, 2237 Tower Grove Boulevard, St. Louis, Missouri, 63110.

American Peony Society, Mr. C. Dan Pennell, 107 West Main Street, Van Wert, Ohio, 45891.

American Rhododendron Society, Mrs. William Curtis, Route 2, Box 105, Sherwood, Oregon, 97140.

American Rock Garden Society, Mr. Richard W. Redfield, Box 26, Closter, New Jersey, 07624.

American Rose Society, P. O. Box 30,000, Shreveport, Louisiana, 71130. Ask for "Handbook for Selecting Roses" and *What Every Rose Grower Should Know. The American Rose* magazine, published by the Society, is a major source of information about methods and new developments for every section of the United States.

National Chrysanthemum Society, Inc., 8504 Laverne Drive, Adelphi, Maryland, 20783.

National Tulip Society, 55 West 42nd Street, New York 36, New York.

North American Gladiolus Federation, 234 South Street, Elgin, Illinois, 60177.

North American Lily Society, North Ferrisburg, Vermount, 05473.

Catalogs From Outstanding Growers:

Armstrong Nurseries, Inc., P. O. Box 473, Ontario, California, 91761 (roses, gladiolus, miniature fruit trees, full-size peach trees, grapes).

W. Atlee Burpee Company, Box 6929, Philadelphia, Pennsylvania, 19132 (flower and vegetable seed, hedges, ground covers, vines and climbers, shrubs, shade and ornamental trees, berries, gardening equipment).

Cooley's Gardens, Silverton, Oregon, 97381 (bearded iris).

P. De Jager , Sons, Inc., South Hamilton, Massachusetts, 01982 (tulips and all other bulbs).

Jackson & Perkins Company, Medford, Oregon, 97501 (roses, strawberries, grapes, dwarf fruit trees, flowering trees).

Kimbrew Roses, Wills Point, Texas, 75169.

Henry Leuthardt Nurseries, Inc., E. Moriches, New York, 11940 (dwarf fruit trees, espalier [trained] fruit trees, grapes, berries).

Nor'east Miniature Roses, 58 Hammond Street, Rowley, Massachusetts, 01969.

George W. Park Seed Company, Inc., Greenwood, South Carolina, 29647 (flowers, vegetables, grasses, shrubs, vines, herbs, gardening supplies).

John Scheepers, Inc., 63 Wall Street, New York, New York, 10005 (flower bulb specialists).

Schreiner's Gardens, 3625 Quinaby Road, N. E., Salem, Oregon, 97303 (bearded iris).

Star Roses, the Conard-Pyle Company, West Grove, Pennsylvania, 19390 (roses, perennials, holly, spirea, hydrangea, azalea).

Stokes Seeds, Inc., Box 548, Main Post Office, Buffalo, New York, 14240 (vegetables and flowers, garden supplies)

Tillotson's Roses, Brown's Valley Road, Watsonville, California, 95076 (specialists in old, rare, and unusual roses).

Gilbert H. Wild and Son, Inc., Sarcoxie, Missouri, 64862 (peonies, iris, daylilies).

Martin Viette Nurseries, Northern Boulevard, East Norwich, New York, 11732 (perennials, shrubs, trees, and evergreens).

Botanical Gardens, Arboretums and Display Gardens to Visit:

Los Angeles State and County Arboretum, 301 North Baldwin Avenue, Arcadia, California.

Denver Botanical Gardens, 909 York Street.

Henry Francis Du Pont Winterthur Arboretum, Wilmington, Delaware.

United States National Arboretum, Montana Avenue and Bladensburg N. E., Washington, D. C.

Gifford Arboretum, University of Miami, Coral Gables, Florida.

Flamingo Groves Tropical Botanic Garden, 3501 South Federal Highway, Flamingo, Florida.

Founders Memorial Garden and Living Arboretum, Athens, Georgia.

Foster Park Botanical Garden, 45 North School Street, Honolulu, Hawaii.

Garfield Park Conservatory, 300 North Central Park Avenue, Chicago, Illinois.

Lincoln Park Conservatory, 2400 North Stockton Drive, Chicago, Illinois.

Lilac Arboretum, Ewing Park, Des Moines, Iowa.

Jungle Gardens, Avery Island, Louisiana.

Arnold Arboretum, Harvard University, Jamaica Plain, Massachusetts (near Boston).

Botanic Garden of Smith College, Northampton, Massachusetts.

Walter Hunnewell Arboretum, 845 Washington Street, Wellesley, Massachusetts.

The Nichols Arboretum of the University of Michigan, Ann Arbor, Michigan.

Anna Scripps Whitcomb Conservatory, Belle Isle, Detroit, Michigan.

University of Minnesota Landscape Arboretum, St. Paul, Minnesota (near Excelsior).

Botanical Garden of the University of Minnesota, Minneapolis, Minnesota.

Missouri Botanical Garden, 2315 Tower Grove Avenue, St. Louis, Missouri.

New Jersey Agricultural Experimental Station Arboretum, Rutgers University, New Brunswick, New Jersey.

Cornell Plantations, Cornell University, Ithaca, New York.

Brooklyn Botanic Garden, 1000 Washington Avenue, Brooklyn, New York.

The New York Botanical Gardens, Bronx Park, New York, New York.

Planting Fields Arboretum, Oyster Bay, Long Island, New York.

Eastman Park Arboretum, Rochester, New York.

The Coker Arboretum, University of North Carolina at Chapel Hill.

Eden Park Conservatory, 950 Eden Park Drive, Cincinnati, Ohio.

Hoyt Arboretum, Portland, Oregon.

Longwood Gardens, Kennett Square, Pennsylvania.

Botanical Garden of the University of Pennsylvania, 38th and Spruce Street, Philadelphia, Pennsylvania.

Phipps Conservatory, Schenley Park, Pittsburg, Pennsylvania.

Texas A & M Arboretum and Trial Grounds, College Station, Texas.

Finch Arboretum, 3404 Woodland Boulevard, Spokane, Washington.

University of Washington Arboretum, Lake Washington Boulevard, Seattle, Washington.

Alfred L. Boerner Botanical Garden, Whitnall Park, Hales Corner, Wisconsin (near Milwaukee).

Memorial Rose Garden, Prescott, Arizona.

Tucson Rose Garden, Tucson, Arizona.

AA Gladiolus Trial Garden, Jonesboro, Arkansas.

Municipal Rose Garden, Berkeley, California.

Balboa Park Rose Garden, San Diego, California.

Palomar College Cacti Garden, San Marcos, California.

Bellingrath Gardens, Mobile, Alabama.

Simpson Park Tropical Garden, Miami, Flordia.

Cypress Gardens, Winter Haven, Florida.

Piedmont Park Rare Trees Arboretum, Atlanta, Georgia.

Tanglewood Park, Winston-Salem, North Carolina (roses, azaleas, shrubs, wild flowers).

Wade Park Herb Garden, Cleveland, Ohio.

Lawn Sprinklers
[SEE LAWNS & GARDENS.]

Lawn Tools
[SEE LAWNS & GARDENS.]

Layout Tools

Before a carpenter can begin any project, he needs the proper tools for laying out squares, angles, circles and curves and for measuring depths.

The carpenter's square, also known as a framing, rafter or steel square, is the most useful and important of all squares. Its flat L-shaped body has marked graduations and special tables on its body and tongue for measuring and dividing lengths, widths and angles. Try squares can be used for marking right angles across lumber and checking joints and corners for squareness. The combination square has a handle that can slide to any point along the length of the blade. Because of this, the combination square can be used as a marking and depth gauge and can double as a straightedge, level and plumb. Sliding T-bevel, or bevel square, is used primarily for checking and transferring angles from one wood surface to another during beveling.

Levels are for checking horizontal and vertical surfaces for trueness. The 24-inch aluminum-frame level has one horizontal vial in its center and the vertical vials are at either end of the level.

The line level is for use in construction work for checking alignment over long distances. A nine-inch torpedo level can be used for leveling in small areas.

The folding rule is useful in measuring boards longer than the blade length of a square. Most of these rules fold out to be six feet long, but 12 foot length styles are available. The tape measure, like the folding rule, is six to 12 feet long, but because of its flexibility is more useful for measuring round areas.

The marking gauge is used somewhat like a ruler for making cutting lines, but it is much more accurate than a ruler because it can be locked into the desired cutting length.

Depth gauges are used for measuring the depth of holes for screws, nails, dowels, etc. in wood and metalwork.

Wing dividers resemble and are used like a compass for marking circles, arcs, dividing lengths and transferring measurements to other wood or steel surfaces. These are useful tools for scribing tile to fit irregular wall lines.

A plumb bob is used to measure the plumbness of a wall for checking door frames and in placement of paneling.

The chalk line, used in construction work, is for forming straight lines over a long distance when no other means of measuring will do. One of the most common uses for the chalk line is in measuring across floors for laying tile. *SEE ALSO HAND TOOLS.*

Leader

A leader, also known as a downspout, is a metal or aluminum pipe running vertically along the outside of a building to carry rainwater from the gutter or eave trough to the ground or a drain. *SEE ALSO GUTTERS & DOWNSPOUTS.*

Lead Float File

Lead float files come in flat and half-round forms and are used on lead, aluminum, brass and other soft metals. *SEE ALSO HAND TOOLS.*

Lead, Sealing Pipe Joints

Lead is a metallic element used to form a seal in pipe joints. It is ordinarily used on cast-iron joints.

Since lead has to be molten for use in sealing, an iron pot suspended over a blowtorch should function as the receptacle during the melting process. Although the lead must be heated just a few minutes beyond melting, it will burn the packing substance if it becomes too hot. Necessary equipment other than the iron pot includes an iron ladle for dipping the molten lead and a heavy pair of gloves to handle the hot la-

dle. By briefly holding the ladle in the flame of the blowtorch to remove any trace of moisture, dangerous spattering will be prevented. Be exceedingly careful with the molten lead since it can cause serious burns.

Lead is normally poured over a packing or caulking substance such as oakum, and it is pliable enough just after hardening to be spread with a caulking tool around the edges of a joint. *SEE ALSO PLUMBING MATERIALS.*

Leaf Blowers

Leaf blowers reduce the problem of raking leaves by blowing them into one pile. This machine consists of a blower and housing assembly, gasoline engine and a carriage with handles. The leaf blower is operated by pushing it like a lawnmower with the air shaft facing the leaves. By moving in a spiral-like pattern, leaves, twigs and sticks will be blown closer together each time and eventually form a pile. Although the leaves still have to be burned or removed, the leaf blower quickly cuts down the raking process. *SEE ALSO LAWNS & GARDENS.*

Leaf Guards

Leaf guards are screens which slip under the lowest row of shingles on a house roof and cover the eave trough or gutter to keep it free from debris. Leaves and other debris which collect in gutters not only clog them but contribute to corrosion. Leaf guards, used properly, prevent particles from entering the system and allow water to pass through effectively.

One type of leaf guard is an aluminum gutter screen which is easy to install and can be cut with a regular pair of scissors. One end inserts into the gutter lip; the other under the roofing. An aluminum sheet, designed with little rows of louvers, is another leaf guard which has tabs that clip into the gutter lip.

Uncovered gutters may require a cage-type of strainer in the downspout opening to prevent clogging or a ¼ inch cone-shaped mesh screen may be inserted into the top of the downspout opening to permit free water flow. An aluminum strainer is another type of guard which is pressure-fitted over the downspout to keep out leaves and twigs. *SEE ALSO GUTTERS & DOWNSPOUTS.*

Cage-type Strainer

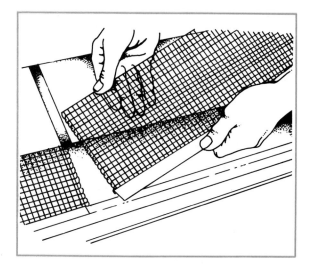
Aluminum Gutter Screens

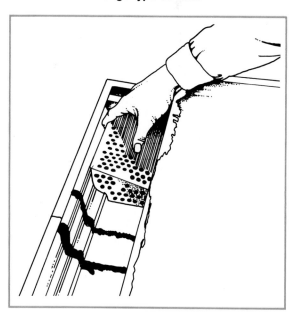
Aluminum Strainer

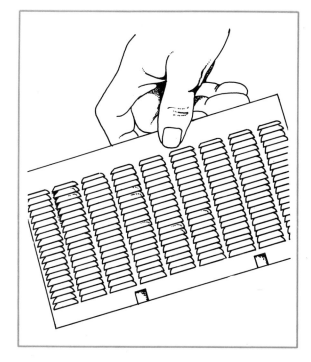
Rigid Aluminum Leaf Guard

Leaks In Wall
[SEE PIPE LEAKS.]

Leaky Faucets
[SEE FAUCET REPAIR.]

Leaky Pipes

[SEE PIPE LEAKS.]

Leather Adhesives

Leather adhesives fall into five major categories depending on what type of material the leather is being adhered to.

Contact cement glues leather to acoustic tile, ceramics, fabrics and cloth, hardboard, leather, metal, plaster, drywall, hard rigid plastic, laminated plastic, rubber, rubber floor tiles and sheeting, stone and wood.

Rubber base cement is best for gluing leather to bricks, cork, glass, china, pottery, vinyl, paper, hardboard, soft flexible plastic and plastic floor tiles and sheeting. Although rubber base cement can be used on hard rigid plastic, contact cement is recommended.

Carpet and polystyrene foam can be glued to leather with a latex base adhesive. It is best to use a contact cement when attaching fabrics and cloth to leather, but a latex base adhesive is also good.

Although a contact cement can be applied, plastic cement is best for gluing leather to metal. Plastic cement can also be used to adhere glass, china and pottery to leather, but an epoxy adhesive is recommended. *SEE ALSO ADHESIVES.*

Ledger

A ledger is a strip of wood that is horizontally attached to the face of a framing member such as a stud or girder. The ledger is used as a support for horizontal framing members, mainly floor joists. *SEE ALSO FLOOR CONSTRUCTION.*

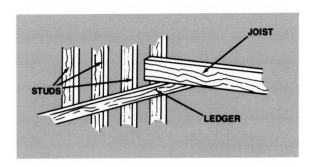

Leisure Time Home

[SEE VACATION HOMES.]

Let-In Brace

A let-in brace is a piece of lumber, usually a 1 x 4 or 1 x 6, set into a stud so that the brace is flush with the surface. After nailing the brace temporarily in place and marking its position on the studs, make side cuts in the studs and remove the cut wood with a chisel. After the stud is notched to receive the let-in brace, nail the brace permanently in place. *SEE ALSO WALL & CEILING CONSTRUCTION.*

Level

Levels are used to determine whether a surface is level (horizontal) or plumb (vertical), and some models can be used to check a surface angle. Levels are made of wood, metal, aluminum and other alloys and can be as long as six-and-one-half feet. Vials made of plastic or glass are filled with fluid and set into the body of the level to protect them from chipping and breaking. When the air bubble is in the center of the vial, the surface is either plumb or level. The vials that check level surfaces are parallel with the level; the vial that determines plumbness is at one end of the level at a right angle to the long edges. Rarely is an angle vial in the same level with level and plumb vials, but when it is, it will be at the opposite end of the plumb vial. The angle vial can determine angles from 0° to 90°.

A 24-inch aluminum-frame level with six vials is usually in the correct position for taking a reading. Torpedo levels have three vials and is best for working in tight areas because of its short body. The line level is a single-vial tool for checking alignment across long distances. By hooking it onto a line, attaching each end of the line tightly to objects at either end of the distance to be leveled, foundations, garden walls and fences may be checked. *SEE ALSO HAND TOOLS.*

Level Transit

A level transit is used in surveying and in measuring long distances prior to construction. Mounted on a tripod to provide a stable base, the level transit has the advantage of a telescope that can be moved up and down in a vertical plane. This is useful in measuring vertical angles, in determining the plumbness of a wall and in the operation of aligning a row of stakes. *SEE ALSO HAND TOOLS.*

Lifesaving Techniques
[SEE FIRST AID.]

Lifting

Lifting, if not done properly, can result in a painful back injury. If possible, use rollers such as poles or pipes to roll heavy objects. If the object is too awkward, a block and tackle or dolly can be used to transport it. Another person's aid can lessen the strain of a heavy object. Whatever method is used, the basic rule for avoiding back injuries is to bend at the knees not the back. A certain amount of bending will be necessary, but the maximum lifting power should come from the legs not the back. *SEE ALSO SAFETY.*

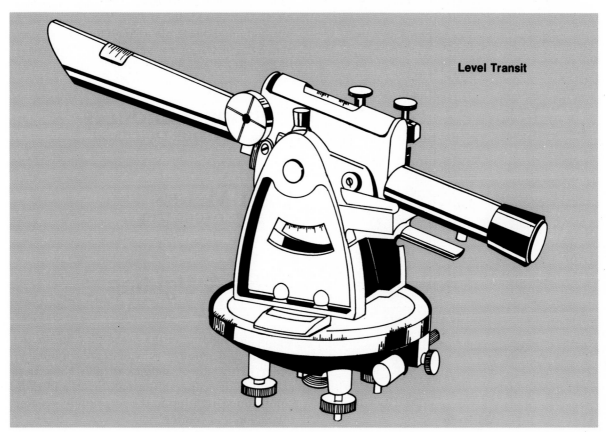

Level Transit

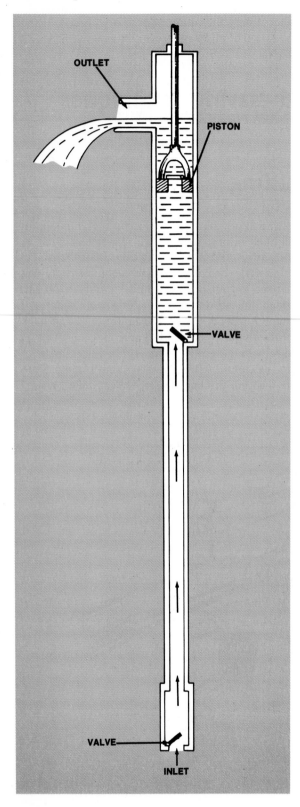

OUTLET

PISTON

VALVE

VALVE

INLET

Lift Pump

Lift Pump

A lift pump is the simplest of the suction pumps. Since this pump operates by only a smooth-bored iron cylinder, a leather-rimmed piston and a handle to move the piston, no electricity is needed. Therefore, it is frequently used at camping and summer cottage areas.

A spout extends from the top of the cylinder and a pipe from the bottom of it reaches into the well water. Generally, the lower end of this pipe has a foot valve. This attachment allows water to enter the pipe without allowing it to flow out.

As the piston is drawn from the bottom of the cylinder, it sucks water and, at the same time, opens the valve located in the bottom of the cylinder. This pushes the water in the pipe up and out of the spout. The weight of the water in the pipe closes the cylinder valve. As the piston goes down, its one-way valve opens and lets water up through the piston. When the piston hits bottom and starts to ascend, the valve closes above the piston so the water will be forced out. *SEE ALSO WELL PUMP SYSTEMS.*

Lighting, Outdoors
[SEE OUTDOOR LIGHTING.]

Light Meters
[SEE PHOTOGRAPHY.]

Lights & Lighting

Lights and lighting in the home play an important role in decorating as well as contributing to better living. Room settings display their best effects with proper illumination. In addition, conditioned lighting helps to provide greater relaxation and comfort.

Courtesy of Sterling Lighting, division of NUTONE

Recessed lighting with proper distribution can provide overall illumination and prevent the need for table fixtures in a family room.

Depending on a room's decor, many types of lighting have been designed to achieve specific results. General illumination, specific task lighting and decorative lighting are basic types to consider.

The delicate look of fine porcelain is a charming eye-opener in room settings.

This traditional candle cluster is covered by a Flemish-lipped bowl of clear glass with a brass finish, useful for general illumination.

Cornice, valance, luminous ceiling panels and wall bracket lighting provide general illumination and are usually for fluorescent tubes, although the less economical incandescent bulbs can be used. *Cornice lighting* is used to direct light downward to cover a wall, to accent draperies or bring in light over drapes at night for daylight effects. It is fastened to the wall or ceiling at ceiling height and is good for rooms with low ceilings.

Valance lighting is also fastened to the wall, but at window height. It may be designed to direct light downward, or upward when the top is open, and reflect on the ceiling as well as on the wall below. It may be softened with a glass or plastic cover. If the valance is ten inches or closer to the ceiling, closing its top will eliminate an overbright ceiling. Valances are built the width of a window with several inches of overage on each side.

Luminous ceiling panels may be installed in different sizes and are economical and modern. Luminous ceilings are versatile enough to fit any room in the home. They require no special type of ceiling material. However, installing fluorescent channels and plastic luminous panels will cost more than a standard fixture. *Luminous wall panels* may be installed in narrow hallways or other small areas to make them appear wider. Luminous ceiling and wall panels may also be used in areas such as recreation rooms to make them appear as outside walls.

Wall bracket lighting is very versatile. It may be used for general illumination, specific task lighting and decorative lighting. Its mounting height depends upon how it will be used. A wall bracket over a bed should be about 30 inches above the mattress. If used to light pictures or murals, wall brackets are placed about 6 inches above the top edge. Depending on the subject covered, a wall bracket varies in length.

This tri-colored trestle duplicates carved wood and is attractive over a dining room table or in a family game room.

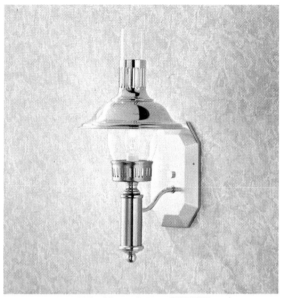

This lacquered metalware fixture is perfect for lighting a hall or entranceway.

Vanity mirrors become more useful with shadow-free lighting which also provides general bathroom illumination.

Wall bracket lighting combined with overhead recessed panels, provides adequate task and general lighting for the bath.

Soffit lighting is preferred in kitchens, bathrooms and laundry rooms, since it utilizes overhead space and throws light directly over a counter or onto a mirror. *Cove lighting* is a type of supplemental light extended along a wall close to the ceiling. It is recommended only for rooms with white ceilings since it directs all light upwards.

Wall Bracket

Cornice

Luminous Ceiling Panels

Valance

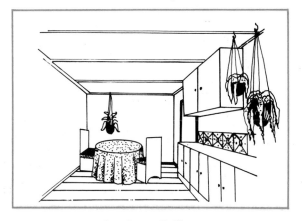

Luminous Ceiling

Bookcase lighting or lamp light provides good conditions for reading, sewing or viewing television. A lamp has several requirements for controlling light glare and to provide upward light for better overall illumination. A lamp should be placed so that the bottom of its shade is at eye

Luminous Wall

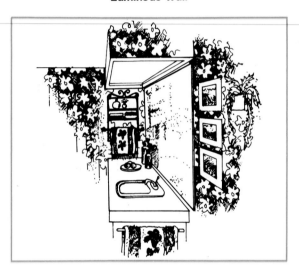

Soffit

Cove

level of the person seated. If too high, it may cause glare in the user's line of vision. The bright inner surface of the shade should never be visible to the user. All lamps contribute to general illumination in a room. A room bathed in soft light is more comfortable to be in since it prevents sharp contrasts of light and shadow.

Besides the conventional floor and table lamps, there are chain-hung lamps that can be mounted on the ceiling and plugged into a wall outlet. Light tracks are a cross between portable and built-in lights. The track is permanently built into the ceiling, but its fixtures come in various types and may be clipped onto the track anywhere.

Courtesy of Lightcraft of California, division of NUTONE

This chain-hung fixture with the look of wrought iron is very fitting for a typically Spanish design.

In selecting lighting, keep the entire room setting in mind and choose equipment that contributes to an overall system. Place sources of light where they are needed, adding others to create balance and a decorative scheme. Five or six portable lights are needed for a large living room; three for bedrooms. Artful use of accent lighting can be an element of decoration by emphasizing an art object, a picture, a planter, a brick wall or a mural.

Fixtures in room edges may provide both general and task lighting. Chandeliers may be used in living areas over baby grand pianos, sofas or other appropriate large pieces of furniture. Since ceilings are lower in today's homes than in older ones, many people think chan-

deliers are impractical except over dining areas where there is no danger of running into them. However, new fixtures have been designed with this in mind so that modified versions, still retaining traditional designs, are available. Some are made to fit snugly against the ceiling so that even the smallest homes may attractively use chandeliers of proper proportions in the scaled-to-fit models.

Courtesy of Lightcraft of California, divison of NUTONE

Modeled after the gaslights often used in restaurants, this chandelier offers generous illumination without glare.

Courtesy of Lightcraft of California, division of NUTONE

Consistently turning out light beams, this crystal chandelier creates a look of sophisticated style and elegance.

Fluorescent lights, because they produce softer light than incandescent bulbs, do not require as much shading to shield the eyes. Fluorescents are the closest to true daylight. Their light is not as concentrated or as sharp in shadows as some other types and they supply two or three times more illumination than an incandescent lamp using the same wattage.

Fluorescent lamps are usually in long straight tubes which vary in length and diameter, according to their ratings in watts. These lamps also come in circular tubes. The short tubular types are good for wall lights in bathrooms or for desk lamps.

Fluorescents come in colors, also. In fluorescent tube colors, deluxe warm white (WWX) and deluxe cool white (CWX) are most frequently used in homes. Warm white enhances warm colors and flatters complexions. Cool white is preferred if blues or greens are dominant in the color scheme.

Courtesy of Lightcraft of California, divison of NUTONE

A Tiffany-inspired pendant in pop-art design is versatile as well as eye-catching.

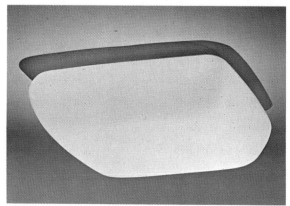

Courtesy of Lightcraft of California, divison of NUTONE

Soft, non-glare light fixtures, with simple lines, are functional for bathrooms and kitchens.

Good lighting means control of glare. Unshaded lamps do not produce good lighting. Use bulbs of ample wattage with a proper shade to focus light without allowing direct light to fall upon the eyes.

Courtesy of Lightcraft of California, divison of NUTONE

Squares of solid brass encircling a crystal jewel boldly enhance a simple decor.

Courtesy of Lightcraft of California, division of NUTONE

An old-world design with panels of hammered glass may provide an artful accent for almost any setting.

A photo light meter can be used to read various lamp wattages in determining the best light to use in certain conditions. The amounts of light are measured in foot-candles. The reading should be made on neutral gray cardboard since different colors used in rooms have different reflective factors. The best formula found may be repeated throughout the house by using various bulbs to get the same meter reading as before.

Enough light means an adequate amount of light to enable a person to see easily and quickly. Though the eyes are adaptable to low light

Courtesy of Lightcraft of California, division of NUTONE

Courtesy of Lightcraft of California, division of NUTONE

A polished type chandelier has both simplicity and good looks to make it blend with traditional or contemporary decor.

The striking set of finishes seen in this chandelier, compliment old-style decor in various traditional settings.

levels, most homes have less light than is preferred. Lighting authorities of the Illuminating Engineering Society have determined minimum amounts of light needed for different tasks.

Primary sources of light should have bulbs shielded in some way, except for see-through lamps and chandeliers. These often have dimmers or under-the-shade devices to provide comfortable viewing. These diffusers may be bowls of milk glass or plastic, plastic diffusers or refracting bowls. Select lamp shades with white lining.

A functional study lamp has standards set by the Illuminating Engineering Society. An adequate

amount of light for one is 70 foot-candles. Light should be distributed upward allowing low contrasts around the task. Light shining through a shade should be limited, from 50 to 150 foot-lamberts (the measurement of brightness) for eye comfort.

A table lamp should supply a minimum of 100 watts; 150 watts is better. For prolonged usage, table and floor lamps need 200 or 300 watts.

Select bulbs of the right size to fit the equipment. Information on the sleeves or jackets in which bulbs are packed, lists initial lumens and bulb life as well as wattage.

LIGHTING FOR THE HOME

Recommended Foot-Candles (Measured by Light Meter)	
Seeing Task	**Primary Task Plane**
Dining	15
Grooming, Shaving, Make-Up	50
Handcraft	70
Ordinary seeing tasks	70
Difficult seeing tasks	100
Very difficult seeing tasks	150
Critical seeing tasks	200
Ironing	50
Kitchen Duties	
Food preparation and cleaning, involving difficult seeing tasks	150
Serving and other non-critical tasks	50
Laundry Tasks	
Preparation, sorting, hand wash	50
Washer and dryer areas	30
Reading and Writing	
Handwriting, reproductions, poor copies	70
Books, magazines and newspapers	30
Reading Piano or Organ Scores	
Advanced (substandard size)	150
Advanced	70
Simple	30
Sewing	
Dark fabrics	200
Medium fabrics	100
Light fabrics	50
Occasional, high contrast	30
Study	70
Table Games	30

Lumen refers to light output or the initial efficiency of a bulb. A 40-watt fluorescent bulb equals 2,080 lumens while a 40-watt incadescent equals 450 lumens. Lumens increase as wattage increases. While a 100-watt bulb produces 1700 lumens, a 200-watt bulb produces 3900 lumens. Long-life bulbs are not as bright as comparable standard bulbs. Where they are the primary source of light, a higher-wattage bulb will compensate for reduced output.

Linden Wood

Linden wood is a soft but firm, straight-grained, light colored wood. Long ago the soft inner tissues were used as an antiseptic for binding and healing wounds. The inner bark of some species is cultivated by the Russians for cordage fibers, paper and cloth. A favorite of wood carvers, linden wood is used in the production of piano keys, luggage, cabinets, venetian blinds and excelsior.

Linden wood is a species of the American linden or basswood. *SEE ALSO WOOD IDENTIFICATION.*

Linear Foot

Linear foot, or running foot, is a standard measurement of length instead of volume (board foot) or surface area (width, thickness). In the home it is used for measuring molding, trim, furring strips, railings, etc., where length is the only consideration.

Line Level

The line level is a small, single-vial level used in construction work for checking the alignment between two points over a long distance. Its body, generally round in shape, has a hook at each end curved in the opposite direction from the other. To use the line level, first tie a cord tightly to objects at either end of the distance to

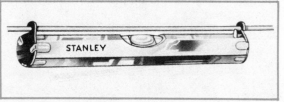

Courtesy of The Stanley Works

Line Level

be measured. Then, using the line level's hooks, place the line level on the cord. When the bubble in the vial is centered, the distance between the two points is level. Adjustments in the height of the cord may be necessary before the line level will register level. *SEE ALSO HAND TOOLS.*

Lineman's Pliers

Lineman's pliers, also called square-nose pliers, are fixed pivot pliers. The pivot gives them far superior cutting power to slip-joint pliers. The cutting edge runs more than half the length of the jaws that have flat surfaces suited for gripping wire and flat metal. Lineman's pliers can cut soft metals such as copper, brass, aluminum, but will be damaged if forced to cut harder materials. *SEE ALSO HAND TOOLS.*

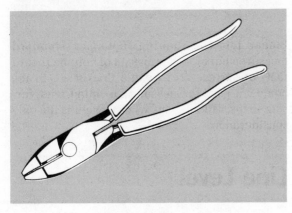

Lineman's Pliers

Lineup Punch

A lineup punch is used in woodwork for aligning holes of two separate pieces of material for

Lineup Punch

fitting. Made of steel, metal or other alloys, the lineup punch has a long body that tapers at one end to a flat punching head. *SEE ALSO HAND TOOLS.*

Lining-Up Bar

A lining-up bar (sometimes called a jimmy bar) is designed for close-quarter prying, nail pulling and aligning jobs. The average length of this bar is 16 inches. A lining-up bar is very useful in metal work because one end has a long slim taper for lining up bolt and rivet holes. *SEE ALSO HAND TOOLS.*

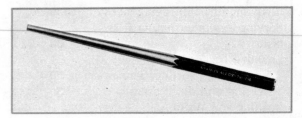

Lining-Up Bar

Link Surface Wiring

Link, or sectional, surface wiring, a form of surface wiring, is made in sections for forming a circuit on the exterior of walls and is used primarily with plug-in receptacles. Link wiring sections are approximately one foot in length and may be either rigid or flexible according to the need. Starting sections plug into an outlet receptacle. These sections may be rigid for smooth wall contact or flexible where the new circuit is going to run close to the outlet receptacle. The blank sections may be either flexible for following corners or rigid for straight runs. The receptacle section holds three outlets that may be placed anywhere along the length of the link wiring circuit. There are screws for fastening the sections to the wall. Link surface wiring is a quick and easy way of updating or adding to a household circuit. *SEE ALSO ELECTRICAL WIRING.*

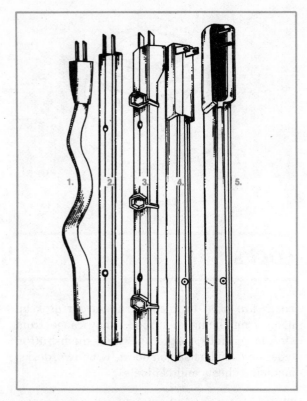

1. **Flexible Starter Section** 2. **Blank Section** 3. **Outlet or Receptacle Section** 4. **Rigid Horizontal Section** 5. **Rigid Vertical Section**

Linoleum Knife

Linoleum knives have a sharp, curved blade with a wooden handle and are used for cutting linoleum. *SEE ALSO HAND TOOLS.*

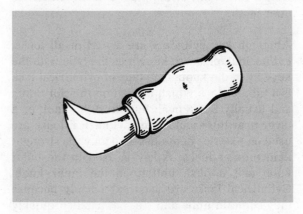

Linoleum Knife

Linseed Oil

Linseed oil is extracted from the linseed, an oilseed also known as flaxseed. This liquid ranges in color from golden yellow to brown and is classified as a drying oil because it becomes thick and hard when exposed to air. It is used in the manufacture of paints, varnish, ink, oilcloth and linoleum.

Linseed oil is manufactured in several grades including raw, refined, boiled and blown. Raw oil is the slowest drying of all the grades. The refined grade is raw oil from which all undesirable solids have been removed. Boiled linseed oil dries faster than either the raw or refined because certain chemicals, called driers, are added to the oil while it is hot. The blown grade dries to an even tougher film as the result of having air blown through the hot oil. *SEE ALSO PAINTS & PAINTING.*

Lintel

A lintel is either a wood, metal or masonry support placed over an opening for bearing loads over chimneys, windows or doors. *SEE ALSO WALL & CEILING CONSTRUCTION.*

Liquid Sandpaper

Liquid sandpaper is a solvent used to clean surfaces. Applied with a cloth that is rubbed over the old surface, liquid sandpaper is usually rubbed on enameled or varnished surfaces to prepare them for repainting. It makes the surface tacky so that a new coat of paint will adhere. *SEE ALSO ABRASIVES.*

Living Room
[SEE DECORATING.]

1023

Load-Bearing Wall
[SEE BEARING PARTITION.]

Local Building Codes & Ordinances
[SEE BUILDING CODES.]

Locking-Plier Wrench

Locking-plier wrench, also known as a vise grip or plier wrench, is used primarily for the loosening of rusted nuts and studs. This can be done whether the work surface is flat or round. With a squeeze, the jaws, either flat or curved, can be locked into position. With a light touch of the finger, the lock can be released. *SEE ALSO HAND TOOLS.*

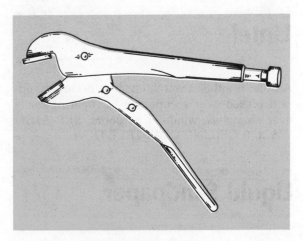

Locking-Plier Wrench

Locknuts

A locknut is a special type of nut which locks itself when it is tightened. It may be designed to grip the bolt shaft firmly or may contain unthreaded fiber inserts *SEE ALSO FASTENERS.*

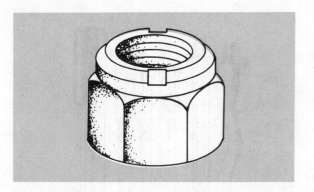

Locknut

Locks

Locks are used to keep intruders out or keep items from being disturbed. They range from simple padlocks to complicated push-button types and can be used on doors, windows, desks, medicine chests and cabinets.

The three basic residential door locks are mortise, rim and cylindrical. A *mortise lock* is installed in a hole or slot in the edge of a door at least $1^3/_8$ inches thick. The mortise lock has a spring-loaded latch and a dead bolt, which may be activated by turning a knob or using a key.

A *rim lock,* also known as a night lock or night latch, is often used in addition to a mortise lock. The rim lock is positioned on the inside face of the door and may have a dead bolt or spring-loaded latch. The strike plate is mounted on the door jamb.

Although key cylinders are a part of all locks, *cylindrical locks* are known as the type with the keyway in the knob. One type of cylindrical lock is a tubular lock which is used on interior doors and usually has a push button in the knob or a lever near the escutcheon. Cylindrical locks are used on exterior doors because they are stronger than tubular locks. A key is used in the outer knob and a push button on the inner knob. Cylindrical locks are used extensively because they come in units and can be installed quickly and easily.

Courtesy of the Kwikset Sales and Service Company

A lockset with cylinder deadlock and key-in-knob lock.

For best protection, dead-bolt type locks should be used. They can be opened only with a key and will deter a burglar from using a flexible card which can often open other types of locks.

Courtesy of the Kwikset Sales and Service Company

A typical cylinder deadlock.

Sliding glass doors can be secured with a keyed lock or keyed wedge lock. A metal bar or large dowel or broom handle may be placed in the channel where the door slides to keep the door closed.

Windows may be secured with a lock placed on the meeting rail of a double-hung window. A small lock may be placed on one side of the window with an additional strike on the upper sash to allow the window to be opened a slight amount for ventilation even though the window is locked.

Garage door locks often consist of spring-loaded bars, a crank handle and outside keyhole. The bars are latched into slots in the door rail tracks.

One of the latest innovations in locks is the push-button controlled lock. In large office buildings where keys may be easily lost or duplicated, push-button locks are an excellent means of security. The bolt is operated when the correct combination of numbers is punched in the correct sequence. In residences, push-button locks eliminate the need for keys, and combinations can be changed easily.

Courtesy of the Presto-Matic Lock Company, Inc.

A push-button lock eliminates the need for keys.

Locust Wood

Locust wood is a durable, strong close-grained hardwood. The two varieties of locust are black locust and honey locust. Because its heartwood is very resistant to the ill effects of the soil, the black locust wood is used for fence posts. The honey locust has little commercial value and is used as an ornamental tree. *SEE ALSO WOOD IDENTIFICATION.*

Lodge
[SEE VACATION HOMES.]

Log Cabin
[SEE VACATION HOMES.]

Long Bend

A long bend is a cast-iron soil pipe fitting designed to join pipes at corners or to curve pipe around obstacles. One side of a long bend is much longer in length than the other side. *SEE ALSO PIPE FITTINGS.*

Long Bend

Long Shank Straight Bit

A long shank straight bit is used in a router when a deep cut is desired. It is used primarily for general purpose jobs in which the longer shank is necessary to accomplish the depth of cut desired. Long shank straight bits are commercially made of high speed steel in limited sizes. *SEE ALSO ROUTER.*

Long Turn Elbow

A long turn elbow is a steel pipe fitting. It has internal threading at both ends and has a longer, more slender curve than the other elbow fittings. *SEE ALSO PIPE FITTINGS.*

Long Turn Elbow

Long Turn Y

A long turn Y is copper, fiber, steel or cast-iron soil pipe fitting. It can be distinguished by a branch which enters at an angle to the main lines. The connecting side inlet for the branch on the long turn Y has a much longer length than the normal Y branch. *SEE ALSO PIPE FITTINGS.*

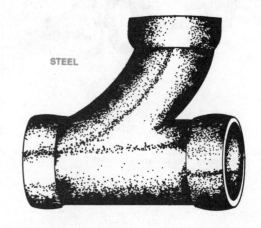

STEEL

Lookout

A lookout is a short wooden roofing member which is placed between the outer end of a rafter and the outside wall frame. The lookout is usually obscured from view, and is used as a support for the under side of an overhanging portion of a roof. *SEE ALSO ROOF CONSTRUCTION.*

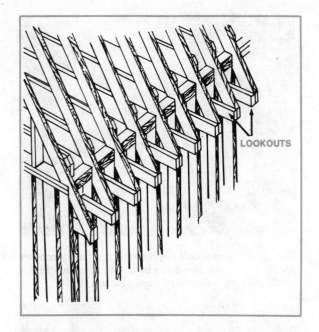

LOOKOUTS

Loops, Wire

Loops at the end of bare or stripped wire provide the contact to terminal screws necessary for the completion of a circuit. With a wire stripper or jack knife, strip about one inch of insulation from the wire and make the loop by twisting the end of the wire into a semicircle with a pair of utility pliers. Loosen the terminal screw, hook the wire loop around it and tighten the screw. *SEE ALSO ELECTRICAL WIRING.*

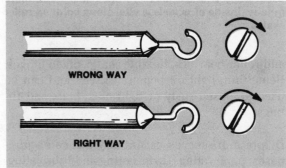

WRONG WAY

RIGHT WAY

Courtesy of Sears, Roebuck and Company

Semicircular loop is formed on wire end to provide for terminal screw connection. Loops must be attached according to direction in which screw is tightened.

Loose Fill Insulation

Loose fill insulation is a material that is installed in the walls, ceilings or floors of a structure to prevent the transfer of heat or sound. It is manufactured in both granule and fluffy forms, applied in bulk form and sold in sacks or bales. Loose fill insulation is generally used in spaces between studding members, and can be applied to a horizontal surface to produce any needed thickness. This type of insulation may be poured or installed by hand and is usually blown into the walls of an older building, an advantageous method of installation since a minimum of wall boards must be removed for the procedure. Loose fill insulation may be composed of several different materials, including rock, glass, wood fibers, redwood bark, cork, wood pulp, gypsum or sawdust. *SEE ALSO INSULATION.*

Loose Fill Insulation

Louver

A louver is a type of window or opening containing wood or metal horizontal slats which are angled to prevent the passage of rain, snow or sunlight, but allow ventilation. A louver is also a single slat in a louvered opening, fence, shutter or door. In a louvered fence, however, the boards are vertically arranged and are used only to restrict vision. *SEE ALSO FENCES & GATES.*

Louver Doors

[SEE VENTILATION, HOME.]

Low-Profile Floor Frame

A low-profile floor frame is a type of modern house construction in which the floor frame and foundation are constructed so that the distance between the floor line and grade (or ground level) is reduced to a minimum. Basically, the floor plates are set into the foundation instead of resting on the top of the wall. *SEE ALSO FLOOR CONSTRUCTION.*

Low Slope Roof

Low slope roofs generally have a pitch of $1/6$ or less, and require extra applications of certain materials to make them water and windtight. The felt underlayment should be doubled and, in extremely cold areas, cemented together from the eave up to the roof point, approximately two feet inside the interior wall line. Use shingles with factory applied adhesives and cement the tabs down. *SEE ALSO ROOF CONSTRUCTION.*

Lubricants

Lubricants can add years to the lives of household appliances. Lack of lubrication can cause an appliance to stick, bind, bend, break, rust or produce annoying squeals, squeaks and groans. The most dependable way to insure that the needed lubrication jobs really get done is to compile a checklist for use at regular intervals.

You will need a variety of lubricants as a single can of oil is not enough. *Lightweight household oil* will be the lubricant most often used for blenders, mixers, fans, small appliances, light motors and for moving parts on hand tools. It can also be used on guns, reels, bicycles, skates, house and car door hinges, office machines, ball

Use light oil on small appliances, light-duty motors. Avoid overoiling and mess by using a broomstraw to guide oil into holes hard to see or reach.

Light-oil small toys every month or two if heavily used. They will last longer, work better—and more quietly. Inside of wheels is vital oiling point on roller skates.

and roller bearings, flexible shafts, piano hinges. Being thin, light oil penetrates well and can be used to loosen rusty or tight nuts, bolts and fittings.

Dripless oil serves essentially the same purposes, penetrating, rustproofing and lubricating. It is recommended for concealed body squeaks, door hinges and handles and many other spots on a car. This kind of oil may come with a snorkel tube, like a miniature soda straw, for very precise application.

For lasting lubrication and quiet action, pull hinge pin, remove old paint or rust with steel wool, then oil lightly before putting back.

Don't forget the clothers dryer. Heavy oil is the safe lubricant for heavy motors, large appliances, since light oil can break down under heavy service.

Heavyweight oil comes in small household cans with spouts. It may be bought more economically as No. 10 to 30 motor oil and used in a refillable oil can. Such cans may have the added convenience of a pressure trigger or a flexible spout for forcing oil into difficult places. Oil bought in bulk may also be used in a small sprayer to coat areas or to lubricate surfaces not otherwise reachable. Heavy oil is required for motors and blowers on large appliances, except those with factory-sealed lubrication, since light

oil used for such heavy service will tend to break down and gum up the moving part. A tool may be lightly coated with heavy oil for protection when it is to be stored away.

Multipurpose grease or white lubricant serves some of the purposes of light oil, but has specialized jobs as well. Use it in casement and jalousie window channels, on door-closer shafts, hinge pins, shaft locks, sliding doors of showers and medicine cabinets. This or heavy grease will lubricate heavy sliding doors, such as those in barns and garages. The lighter variety should be used for interior folding and sliding door tacks, or substitute a small amount of vaseline.

Grease sticks offer in a convenient and durable form the characteristics of paraffin and wax. They are useful on both wood and metal parts that slide. These clean sticks that are used like a crayon prevent sticking, squeaks, wear and rust by forming a tough adhesive film. Applications include windows, doors, drawers, screens, storm windows, bicycle chains, typewriter carriages, casters, chair swivels, zippers, overhead garage doors, firearms, fishing tackle, tools, musical instruments, strike plates, latches. Grease sticks are also recommended for use on rubber parts requiring a surface lubricant, such as rubber seals on car locks.

Stick-lube moving parts of windows and doors every six months. Or use light oil on metal parts, candle stub or paraffin cake on wooden ones.

Lubricating sticks and silicone sprays are the handiest, cleanest, most lasting products for easing wood and metal drawer slides. Paraffin, candle, and vaseline are satisfactory, too.

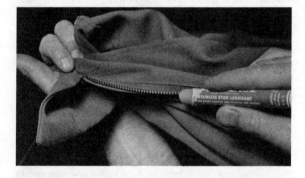

The action not only of closet doors but of some of the things stored behind them can be improved with stick lubricant. Lubricated zippers slide better, are less likely to break.

Puff powdered graphite from a flexible plastic spray pencil (or squirt graphited lock fluid) into latches while turning lock in and out to spread lubricant.

Graphite is cleanest lubricant for garden tools, doesn't collect dirt and grit as oil does. In colloidal suspension it penetrates better than in powder form.

Graphite is most often useful in the form of graphite-in-oil, which may be sold as lock fluid. It is a specialized lubricant to prevent and correct lock failure caused by sticking and freezing due to dust, dirt, moisture or corrosion. With its penetrating base, it flushes out dirt and metal bits. It seeps into remote working parts and depositing on them an extremely light graphite film. Graphite-in-oil contains a rust inhibitor and, by helping to seal out moisture, provides protection against freezing. Where only the lubricating qualities of graphite are wanted, it can be used in the form of a small puff tube of powdered graphite.

Penetrants come in forms primarily for loosening tight or rusted nuts and other metal parts, or in types that emphasize lubricating qualities. These products have widespread uses of their own. It is good practice to use one of them routinely where some corrosion protection and lubrication is wanted, but a conventional lubricant would be messy or has been tried and found ineffective. Squeaking swivel chairs, found impervious to oiling and spraying with silicones, have been silenced, and surprising results can be accomplished with old shower heads.

Silicone sprays are effective on metal and are a first choice where wood needs lubrication, as with door and drawer slides. They can be such effective friction reducers that care must be taken in using them near floors. Overspray from coating render an area of floor dangerously slippery underfoot. When using a silicone spray, it is wise to mask the floor area first with newspaper.

Penetrating solvents and oils in spray cans serve also to clean and free from rust machinery that has been stored outdoors or in damp buildings.

Use a penetrating lubricant to protect and drive out moisture from electric motors, radios and electronic equipment, chrome and metal parts of cars.

Specialized lubricants should be kept on hand where much shop work, such as automobile maintenance or woodworking is performed. A lithium grease, sold in cans and pails up to 35 pounds for marine, shop and farm use, can also be obtained in tiny tubes for general household use. A silicone lubricating compound, also obtainable in small tubes, prevents sticking and freezing of weatherstripping, trunk seals, hood bumpers, window channels, V-belts in cars and elsewhere. There is a lubricating dressing for fan and V-belts, in aerosol package, a snorkel-equipped aerosol lubricant for auto chokes and a tube-packed lubricant just for speedometer cables.

LUBRICATION RULES

A regular lubrication checklist, kept with lube supplies, will help to prevent breakdowns due to lack of lubrication. The list should include manufacturers' specifications where applicable, such as when and where to lubricate the furnace fan. The lube chart can be made part of a maintenance plan that includes such related chores as changing or cleaning furnace filters and those in ventilating fans.

The first rule of lubrication is: do it before it is needed. By the time squeaks, binds, rattles or failures occur, some permanent damage may have been done.

A good second rule is: clean it before you lubricate it. Besides making for a more effective general maintenance program, this means you can lubricate more effectively.

Follow directions supplied by the manufacturer. This may call for making the maintenance manual that came with the product a part of your lube chart, or noting pertinent information from it. If you no longer have the instructions, try to get a new copy by writing to the manufacturer so you will have specific instructions regarding how often to lubricate.

Use the appropriate lubricant. Light and heavy household oils usually are not interchangeable, although for some intermediate-duty conditions either may be used, with light grease as an alternative.

Do not overlubricate. The greater part of the time, a couple of drops is enough and very excessive lubrication can cause real damage.

Lumber

Lumber is wood (a log) that has been cut and planed into uniform thickness, width and length. Lumber can vary in color, grain, odor, strength, durability and weight according to the tree from which it was cut and the manner in which it was sawed from the log and seasoned. These different characteristics determine how it will be used. Because lumber is wood, it is both firm and fibrous, solid to the touch but porous to air and moisture, and stiff and strong, yet easily shaped.

CUTTING LUMBER

Logs are sawed lengthwise to produce lumber; the larger logs sawed along four sides and the smaller logs along two sides. The bark and the rounded sides of the log, called slabs, are re-

moved and the edges made parallel before the boards are cut. The slabs, along with the edges and trim, are ground into chips for chipboard. The outer parts of the log have fewer knots so this "clear" or "knot-free" lumber is cut into planks from one to three inches thick. Toward the center of the log, the oldest part of the tree, there are more knots so this portion is cut into the heavy planks and beams used in construction work. This green lumber is then sorted according to species, sizes and grades.

Logs can be sawed into lumber either by plain-sawing or quarter-sawing. To quarter-saw, the log is first cut into quarters lengthwise, then the lumber is cut at right angles to the annual rings producing lumber with a vertical end grain. If the wood being cut is hardwood, the lumber is said to be quarter-sawed; if softwood it is called vertical or edge grain. Quarter-sawing is difficult and expensive, but lumber sawed this way swells and shrinks less in width and is not as subject to warping.

Plain or flat-sawing is used more often and is cheaper because the log is sawed straight through lengthwise. With this method, the an-

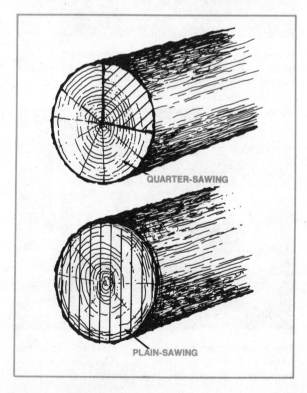

QUARTER-SAWING

PLAIN-SAWING

nual rings form an angle of less than 45 degrees with the surface of the board. When the angle is less than 45 degrees, this technique is called plain-sawed if applied to hardwoods and flat-grained if it is softwood.

HEARTWOOD & SAPWOOD

Wood can be classified depending on its closeness to the bark. The outer or newer layers are called sapwood and the inner or older core is called heartwood.

Initially all the wood in a tree carries sap and is sapwood, but as the tree gets older and larger the inner sapwood becomes inactive and usually turns darker because of the presence of gums and resins. This inner sapwood becomes heartwood (center rings), or wood that does not carry sap. Heartwood can be harder and stronger than sapwood (outer rings) and in some cases is more resistant to decay.

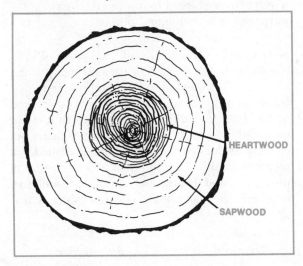

HARDWOOD & SOFTWOOD

Lumber comes from both hardwood and softwood tress. Hardwoods come from broadleafed, deciduous trees such as oak, maple, birch, walnut and mahogany. Softwood lumber comes from evergreen or needle bearing trees such as pine, fir, cedar, redwood and spruce. Hardwoods are more expensive than softwoods but are stronger, last longer and produce a better looking result. Softwoods, however, are easier to work with and to finish.

In the home, hardwood takes the form of molding, doors, floors, furniture and cabinets while softwoods are used in general construction for exterior trim, framing, siding, subflooring or fencing. Hardwoods can be softer than some of the softwoods or vice versa, and their uses may be interchangeable since there is no degree of hardness that separates the two categories.

SEASONING

Since half of the weight of a tree may be moisture (sap), lumber must be dried or seasoned before it is used to prevent excessive shrinkage and the resulting warping and splitting. As the wood loses its moisture and air takes its place, lumber becomes lighter in weight, but harder and stronger. To reduce this moisture, lumber can be either air-dried or kiln-dried.

In air-drying, lumber is stacked in layers with wood strips in between so air can circulate around each board, but this method is slow and can cause warping. In addition, water can collect around the boards causing permanent ingrained marks in the wood. The lumber also dries out on the ends faster than in the middle so the ends must be protected with paint or pitch. In kiln-drying, the lumber is placed in an oven or kiln where temperature and humidity can be controlled, reducing the seasoning time to days instead of months.

Eventually a balance is reached between the moisture remaining in the wood and the water vapor in the air.

With changes in humidity, there will be corresponding changes in lumber's moisture content and therefore its dimensions. This is the reason doors, windows and drawers swell and then stick during humid, wet weather. Lumber with a moisture content of from 15 to 19 percent is practical to use. In heated structures, the moisture content will eventually be reduced to about 8 percent. The greatest change in moisture content occurs during the first heating season after construction.

DEFECTS

A defect in or on wood reduces its strength and

durability. Defects determine lumber's usefulness and may or may not detract from its appearance. For instance, knots may add to the appearance of pine paneling. An irregularity that detracts only from appearance is called a blemish. Below are listed some of the common defects.

Knots: Knots are actually the branches that were cut or broken off and enclosed by the growing trunk. A knot could also be any other deep damage done to the bark that has been absorbed into the tree with time. All trees form knots at their center but eventually more knot-free layers form around the outer parts of the tree as the smaller side branches fall off. Knots may weaken depending upon their size, type and location. Knots do not have as much weakening effect on large, thick pieces as they do on smaller planks, but if they are at all loose they will eventually fall out.

Splits & Checks: Splits and checks are lengthwise cracks in the wood fiber along the grain and across the annual growth rings. Checks are due to shrinkage or excess exposure to heat and sun as the wood seasons. Splits are man-made tears. Splits and checks usually occur at the ends of lumber and it is best to cut them off to prevent further splitting.

Shakes: Shakes are separations between the annual growth rings and along the grain. If they occur at the lumber ends, they can be cut off.

Warp: Warping results from bad seasoning (improper stacking, for example) and causes the wood to twist or bend out of shape. It can be corrected by wetting the affected lumber and placing a weight opposite the concave surface until the board is straightened.

Blue Stain: Blue stain is a blue-black discoloration caused by mold-like fungi that thrive on moisture. It does not affect the wood's strength though it is not desirable in appearance.

Wane: Wane is a defect characterized by bark or a lack of wood at the corner or edge of a piece of lumber.

Decay: Advanced stages of decay result in wood that is spongy and crumbles easily. It is caused by the disintegration of the wood fibers due to fungi. Less advanced stages of decay are hard to recognize.

Holes: Holes in lumber are caused by insects, worms or handling equipment.

ORDERING LUMBER

Lumber is sized as it comes from the saw and this rough unfinished measurement is called the nominal size. It retains this size designation even after it has been surfaced (or planed) and dried, which actually reduces it in size. Though the actual or dressed size is less than the nominal size as a result of the seasoning and surfacing, the handyman is charged for the nominal size for the purposes of ordering and billing.

For example, a rough-sawed 2 x 4 piece of lumber will measure $1\,^5/_8$ x $3\,^5/_8$ after surfacing. If the exact size is essential, order the lumber milled from the next larger size and have it dressed down. This procedure will cost more so it might be simpler to make original measurements according to the actual size of lumber or instead, measure lumber first and then proceed with the project. Listed below are some representative nominal sizes and their corresponding actual size.

Nominal Size	Actual Size
2 x 4	$1^1/_2$ x $3^1/_2$
1 x 12	$^3/_4$ x $11^1/_4$
1 x 6	$^3/_4$ x $5^1/_2$
1 x 10	$^3/_4$ x $9^1/_4$
2 x 6	$1^1/_2$ x $5^1/_2$
2 x 8	$1^1/_2$ x $7^1/_4$

The length of lumber usually runs as listed with the actual length being the same as the nominal length. Most lumberyards stock lumber in standard sizes starting with 8' lengths that increase by 2' up to 24'. If a 7' piece of lumber is needed, the charge will be for 8' because lumber is cut slightly longer to allow for trimming to the exact size. With plywood, hardboard, asbestos board and other manufactured boards, the listed size is the actual size.

Since lumber must be planed smooth on one or more sides and edges to be usable for most woodworking projects, planing is designated by the abbreviations S1S, S2S, S1E, S2E and S4S, For example S1S means "Surfaced 1 Side", S1E, "Surfaced 1 Edge," and S4S, "Surfaced 4 Sides." For use around the house, order lumber S4S.

BOARD FEET

Both hardwood and softwood lumber is sold and priced by the board foot. A board foot is equal to the amount of wood in a board 1 inch thick, 12 inches wide and 12 inches long. To figure board feet, multiply thickness (in inches) X width (in inches) X length (in feet) and divide by 12. Use the nominal thickness and width.

Using this formula a 2 x 6 x 12' piece of lumber would contain 12 board feet, but a 1" x 6" x 12' piece would equal only 6 board feet.

Molding and trim, poles, dowels, furring strips and railing are sold by the linear or running foot since length is the only consideration. Plywood and wallboard are sold by the square foot, usually in 4' x 8' panels.

GRADES OF LUMBER

Lumber sizes and grades, for the most part, are determined by the U.S. Department of Commerce's American Lumber Standard PS 20-70. Grading rules established by major lumber associations combine both PS 20-70 and the National Dimension Rule. The National Dimension Rule provides a standardized listing of lumber sizes, grade names, grade descriptions, and moisture content requirements. Such a standardized rule eliminates many formerly confusing and overlapping grade names and descriptions, and assures a stabilized lumber sizing system.

Lumber is classified into two general areas: Framing and Board. Within each classification area, a series of subclassifications is established separating lumber into a variety of grades. The two major classifications are divided as follows:

(Grade classification information supplied by the Western Wood Products Association)

Framing Lumber

Category	Grades	Sizes
Light Framing	Construction, Standard, Utility, Economy	2" to 4" thick 2" to 4" wide
Studs	Stud, Economy	2" to 4" thick 2" to 4" wide
Structural Light Framing	Select Structural No. 1, No. 2, No. 3, Economy	2" to 4" thick 2" to 4" wide
Appearance Framing	Appearance	2" to 4" thick 2" and wider
Structural Joists and Planks	Select Structural No. 1, No. 2, No. 3, Economy	2" to 4" thick 6" and wider
*Decking	Selected Decking Commercial Decking	2" to 4" thick 4" and wider
*Beams and Stringers Posts and Timbers	Select Structural No. 1, No. 2, No. 3	5" and thicker 5" and wider

*Not included in National Dimension Rules.

Board Grades

Category	Grades
Selects	B & Better — 1 & 2 Clear C Select D Select
Finish	Superior Prime E
Paneling	Clear (any select or finish grade). No. 2 Common selected for knotty paneling. No. 3 Common selected for knotty paneling.
Siding (Bevel and Bungalow)	Superior Prime
Boards	No. 1 Common No. 2 Common
Sheathing and Form Lumber	No. 3 Common No. 4 Common No. 5 Common

Lumen

A lumen is a measure of light equal to one candle power. *SEE ALSO LIGHTS & LIGHTING.*

Magnetic Door Catch

Magnetic door catches are used primarily on kitchen and bathroom cabinets to stop and hold a door in a closed position. On double doors, this is done by installing two square metal plates on the inside of the doors in the upper corners above the handles or knobs. A rectangular plate containing two magnets is then installed so that the magnets are perfectly aligned with the metal plates. In most cabinets, this plate is concealed under trim or a shelf. On a single door, install the metal plates side-by-side so that they strike the magnets evenly. When the door is pushed, the magnets attract the plates and hold the door closed. *SEE ALSO KITCHEN DESIGN & PLANNING.*

Magnetic Hammer

The magnetic hammer is used for tacking when an item, such as upholstery, is held with one hand and tacked with the other. On one end of the hammer's head is a thin slit which forms a two-pole magnet. This holds the point of the tack out on the hammer face. As the hammer is swung, the tack is driven.

A magnetic tack hammer or a billposter's hammer has a straight head and is tapered at each end. An upholsterer's hammer has a longer head and is curved down at each end, which allows tacks to be driven into a sofa seat near the back without hitting it. *SEE ALSO HAND TOOLS.*

Mahogany Wood

Mahogany wood is a porous, warp resistant, medium strength, exotic hardwood. Its sapwood ranges from white to light brown and the heartwood varies from pale to deep reddish-brown. The pattern figure can be described as ribboned or striped.

Once used for its fever-curing extract, mahogany is now used for carving, solid and high grade furniture, boat construction and cabinetmaking. It is excellent for veneering because the consistent quality and even grain makes thin slicing possible. Because there are other woods very similar to mahogany, most genuine pieces have a label or tag from the Mahogany Association. *SEE ALSO WOOD IDENTIFICATION.*

Main Switch

The main switch disconnects the power to all the branch circuits in a house. The main switch is usually located in the service entrance panel, along with the fuses or circuit breakers that individually protect the branch circuits.

There are several types of main switches, depending upon whether they are in a fuse or circuit breaker box. In a fuse box, the main switch is not a switch in the sense that it is operated by flipping a handle or lever. Instead, two cartridge fuses are mounted with clips on a block of insulating material; when the block is pulled out of the box, everything is disconnected. If this pull-out fuse block is inserted upside down, the power still remains off.

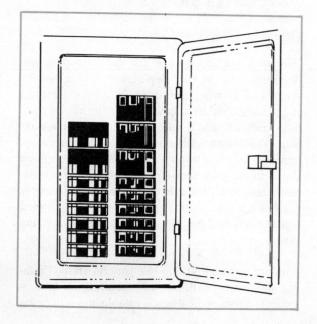

In a circuit breaker box there is usually a main circuit breaker switch, similar in appearance to an "on-off" wall switch, that can be flipped to "off" to shut off the household current. Circuit breaker boxes, although they are more expensive than fuse boxes, are being used increasingly in modern house wiring.

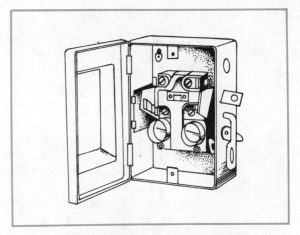

Main Switch With External Handle

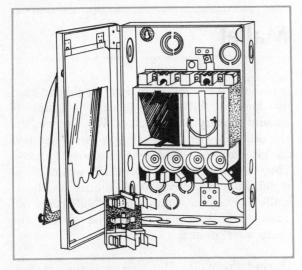

Fuse Box With Pull-Out Fuse Block

The simplest type of main switch is enclosed in a small metal box. The box is equipped with an external handle which is moved up or down to shut off current. This main switch is found in older homes or is used for very small installations.

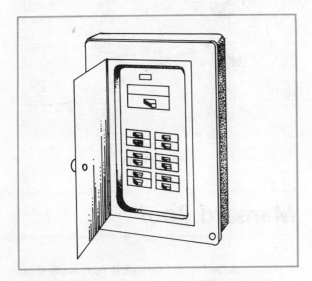

Circuit Breaker Panel With Main Switch At Top

Both fuse and circuit breaker boxes vary enough in design to warrant caution when attempting to shut off the power. The handyman should consult an electrician or power company representative if in doubt about the location of the main switch and the procedure for shutting off all household current. *SEE ALSO FUSES & CIRCUIT BREAKERS.*

Maintenance, Motors
[SEE MOTOR CARE & MAINTENANCE.]

Main Water Supply Valve

The main water supply valve in most homes is the primary water shut-off for the house. Also called a gate valve, it is placed directly after the main water line that comes through the foundation wall. It must be located at the lowest area of the plumbing system. Because gate valves offer very little resistance, they are used where the water flow is most important. This valve is the only one which will open to the same size pipe as the one used to connect it to the water line. For this reason, the water pressure does not decrease and a large flow of water is permitted through the valve.

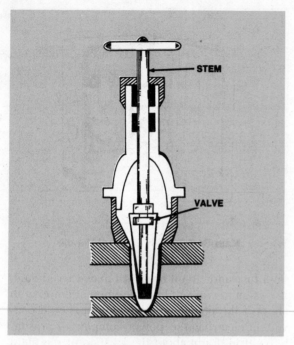

Main Water Supply Valve

Installing a gate valve is relatively simple since it can be placed in any position, with either end connecting to the inlet or outlet pipes. However, in cold climates, the valve's stem should be set upright so that its bonnet will not remain filled with water. If, after draining the lines, the bonnet is full of water, a freeze-up might cause it to crack.

Because the valve is sealed by fastening metal against metal, it becomes worn quickly and eventually loses its watertight quality. If the valve is fastened on sand or grit, its movable disc may be damaged easily. The complete valve will have to be replaced if the disc wears out. *SEE ALSO PLUMBING SYSTEMS.*

Male Adapter

The male adapter is a copper tube fitting with external threading. The external threading of the male adapter is joined with the internal threading of the female adapter to connect copper tubing. *SEE ALSO PIPE FITTINGS.*

1038

Male Adapter

Mallet

A mallet is a hammer with a barrel-shaped head that has two flat striking faces. The handle is usually hickory or fiberglass. Wooden mallets are used for striking plastic- or wood-handled chisels, gouges, wood pins and small stakes. They are also used to form and shape sheet metal without marring it. A rubber or plastic mallet is used for setting stones. Mallets are not designed to drive nails or screws or to strike sharp metal objects.

Discard any mallet if the striking surface is split, dented or damaged, and cannot be restored to its original condition by dressing or grinding. If only the handle is damaged, replace it with a new handle. *SEE ALSO HAND TOOLS.*

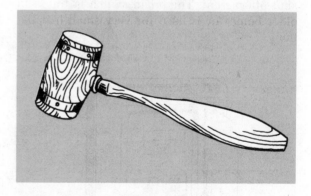

Wood Mallet

Mansard Roof

A mansard roof is a four-sided roof with each side having two slopes. The upper slope is usually flat and the lower slope almost vertical. The mansard roof, when augmented with dormer windows, provides additional space and a more economical use of the attic area. *SEE ALSO ROOF CONSTRUCTION.*

Mansard Roof

Mantel

A mantel is the ornamentel beam, stone or arch placed above a fireplace. Since it is not an essential structural feature, many types of fireplaces do not have a mantel. If one is built, it serves mainly as a display shelf and may be extended across an entire wall. It is usually designed to tie the fireplace into the room decor. *SEE ALSO FIREPLACES.*

Maple

Maple is a pale-colored, fine-grained, even-textured heavy hardwood used extensively in furniture making both for the reproduction of antiques and in the construction of contemporary designs. Its smooth, strong surface wears slowly without splintering and can withstand constant buffeting so it is ideal for flooring, shelves, benches, counters, cabinets or even boatbuilding. In the home, maple might take the form of furniture, kitchen woodenware, bowling balls, billiard cues and components of pianos and other stringed instruments. It is usually stained red-brown or yellow-brown.

Maple is popular with home craftsmen because it is an excellent wood for turning on a lathe and its fine texture is well-suited to painted or enameled finishes. Maple is not, however, as easily glued as some softer woods because of its hard, small-pored surface. *SEE ALSO WOOD IDENTIFICATION.*

Marking Gauge

A ruler type device, which has a sharp pin located at one end of a metal or wooden beam and a head that slides up or down the beam, is called a marking gauge. This tool is used for making lengthwise lines parallel to the planed edge of a board and for notching material that goes around pipes. To use the gauge, mark off the desired distance, set it with the adjustable head and tighten the thumbscrew. Then place the head on a smooth surface and as it is moved, a pin will scratch the surface to make a line. *SEE ALSO HAND TOOLS.*

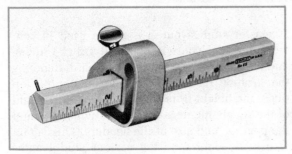

Courtesy of The Stanley Works

Marking Gauge

Marking Tools
[SEE MEASURING & MARKING TOOLS.]

Marquetry

Marquetry is a decorative inlay on furniture that consists of thin pieces of wood, ivory, metal or shell combined to form a design that is then veneered to a surface such as a table top.

Mash Hammer

Mash hammers, also called drilling hammers, weigh from two to four pounds are used with star drills much the same way as a chisel for cutting holes in masonry. *SEE ALSO HAND TOOLS.*

Masonry
[SEE BRICK & STONE WORK; CONCRETE; CONCRETE BLOCK.]

Masonry Tools
[SEE CONCRETE & MASONRY TOOLS.]

Master Stud Layout

A master stud layout is a device used in construction, and consists of a full scale drawing made on a 1 x 4 or 2 x 4 straight board, denoting the location of the sole plate and double top plate, the height from floor to ceiling, the height of the rough openings (doors and windows) and the position and size of the headers. This layout is used to determine the various stud lengths used in the construction. In multi-level or split-level structures, a separate master stud layout is usually made for each level. *SEE ALSO FRAMING.*

Mastics

Mastics are a type of adhesive used to bond floor, wall or ceiling tiles and wall or ceiling paneling. Mastics come in two basic types: synthetic latex, a water-base adhesive, and rubber resin which consists of synthetic rubbers in solvents. Both types provide a good bond to concrete, ceramic tiles, hardboard, asphalt, textiles and leather. Some types of mastic are used as protective coatings for thermal insulation or waterproofing. *SEE ALSO ADHESIVES.*

Measuring Electricity

Electricity is measured in kilowatt hours, which consist of watt-hours, volts, amperes and electrons. Washing machines and dryers are usually operated by 240-volt electrical outlets; light bulbs are measured in watts; lamps by amperes, all of which are powered by electrons, or electrical current. Volts, amperes and electrons form watt-hours and 1,000 watt-hours equal one kilowatt hour which is the unit of measure on a meter. *SEE ALSO ELECTRICITY.*

Measuring & Marking Tools

Measuring and marking tools are used for measuring and marking long, straight lines and angles in carpentry, furniture making, concrete construction, etc. The more conventional of these tools are levels, squares, rules and gauges. *SEE ALSO HAND TOOLS.*

Measuring Pipe
[SEE PIPE MEASURING.]

Medallion

A medallion is a decorative piece that is either raised or carved in bas relief. It is commonly found on doors, pediments, furniture and sometimes as inlays for floors.

Medicine Cabinet
[SEE BATHROOM DESIGN & PLANNING.]

Meeting Rail

A meeting rail, also called checkrail, is the bottom horizontal rail of the upper sash and the top horizontal rail of the lower sash of a double-hung window. Usually both rails are slightly beveled to insure a tight fit and correct location for the window latch. *SEE ALSO DOUBLE-HUNG WINDOWS.*

Metal Gutters

Metal gutters are normally preferred over most other types of rain-carrying equipment because of their effectiveness and durability. Metal gutters come in four styles: galvanized steel, unfinished aluminum, enameled galvanized steel and enameled aluminum.

The oldest and most popular type of metal gutter is galvanized steel. Unfinished ones must be primed with rust-preventive primer, then painted carefully every two to three years to cover all exposed parts. Unfinished aluminum gutters and galvanized steel ones can be color-matched to the house. They should not be painted when they are new, however, since both must oxidize for about six months before paint will stick. In an area where gutters are exposed to salt and chemicals in the air, the oxidation time is shortened.

Aluminum gutters are more expensive than galvanized steel, but are advantageous because they will not rust and corrode. Aluminum forms a natural protective coating of its own. Galvanized steel gutters have stronger resistance to dents but, because of their weight, are more difficult to install than aluminum.

Finished steel and aluminum gutters have a baked-enamel protection like an automobile finish. Prefinished gutters are preferred for new installation. They are less apt to corrode and are more attractive than brush-painted types.

Never combine steel and aluminum gutters and downspouts. Corrosion and decomposition of chemicals will result when they come in contact. *SEE ALSO GUTTERS & DOWNSPOUTS.*

Metal Painting
[SEE PAINTS & PAINTING.]

Metalworking Tools

Metalworking tools are a combination of some tools commonly associated with woodwork and those designed specifically for working with metal. These usually include tools for measuring, marking, drilling, cutting, punching, sawing, chiseling and smoothing.

Stock is measured with a steel rule. The more common ones are 6, 12 and 24 inches long and should have graduations divided into sixty-fourths of an inch for accurate measuring.

For truing corners, most metalworkers prefer to use a combination square because of its versatility in squaring, leveling and making angles. After corners have been squared, a steel-pointed scriber is used for marking the cutting lines.

The wing divider has two steel legs and is used like a compass for measuring distances and laying out circles and arcs.

Hacksaws, with their strong steel alloy teeth, are designed for cutting metal. Hacksaws have a reinforced spine to prevent crimping, and its blades are interchangeable so that a fine, medium or coarse cut may be achieved.

Before a hole can be drilled in metal with either a hand or power drill or a drill press, a prick or center punch should be used to form an indentation to keep the drill bit from sliding on the surface. Prick and center punches are available in different point sizes so that the indentation will match the size of the drill bit.

To assemble a metal project, nuts, bolts, dies and taps are needed. The tap makes the internal threads so the bolt can be driven into the metal. The die cuts external threads which is useful in making or repairing bolts.

For shearing, cutting, rounding and grooving metal, use the flat, diamond point, cape and round nose chisels. These will enable you to shape the metal and remove excess stock.

Files are for the smoothing and shaping jobs that a chisel cannot do. Flat and half-round files with a single or double cut are two of the most common in metalwork.

Cloths coated in natural or man-made abrasives are available in varying degrees of coarseness for the final smoothing and polishing of metal projects.

Vises are used to hold metal for shaping, smoothing and cutting. Select one designed for metalwork, as there are vises for use only with wood. *SEE ALSO HAND TOOLS.*

Meter

A meter is an instrument used for measuring the quantity or flow rate of gas, water or electricity. An electric meter measures electricity in kilowatt hours, while gas is gauged in cubic feet and water in gallons.

Meter Socket

The meter socket houses and protects the electric meter. A basic feature of the service entrance, the meter is usually located on the outside of the

house. Wires leading from the utility pole to the service entrance are connected through the meter socket so that once the meter is installed by the power company, the meter will reflect the usage of power in the house.

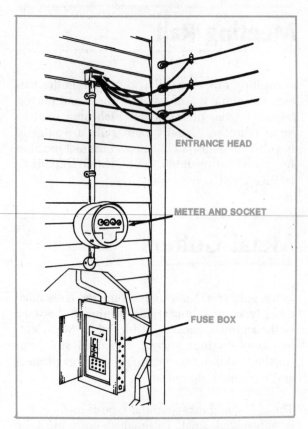

Meter socket and meter at service entrance.

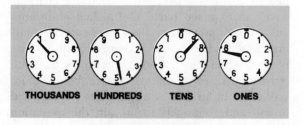

Reading a meter.

As electricity is "sold" in kilowatt hours, the dials of the meter will show electrical consumption in kilowatt hours. Read the meter from left to right in thousands, hundreds, tens, and ones. For instance, if the first dial of the meter shows a six, the second a five, the third a nine, and the fourth a seven, the meter shows that 6,597 kilowatts of power has gone through the meter. *SEE ALSO ELECTRICAL WIRING.*

Metric Equivalents

The metric system is the universal language of measure to which the United States will be converting in the near future. The metric system is a logical, related system of measurement based on the decimal system, or the number ten. With the metric system, measures of length, area, volume, temperature, weight and other amounts are coordinated to facilitate computations. It is actually simpler and more precise than the non-related system of measurement used now. For ordinary purposes, familiarity with the metric unit of length-meter, volume-liter, and weight-gram is sufficient since the metric units for time (second, minute, hour) and electricity (kilowatt) are the same as used now. A comparison of the old system of measurement and the metric system is presented below.

Meter: about 1.1 yards
Liter: about 1.06 quarts
Gram: about the weight of a paper clip

The common prefixes used with the basic units are:

Milli: one-thousandth (.001)
Centi: one-hundreth (.01)
Kilo: one thousand times (1000)

For example:

1000 millimeters = 1 meter

The Major Metric Equivalents

100 centimeter = 1 meter
1000 meters = 1 kilometer

Length

Inch	=	2.54	centimeters
Foot	=	.305	meter
Yard	=	.914	meter
Centimeter	=	.3937	inch
Meter	=	3.28	feet
Meter	=	1.09	yards
Mile	=	1.6	kilometers

Area

Square inch	=	.000645	square meter
Square foot	=	.0929	square meter
Square yard	=	.836	square meter
Square Centimeter	=	.155	square inch
Square Meter	=	10.764	square feet
Square meter	=	1.196	square yards
Hectare	=	2.5	acres

Volume & Capacity

Cubic inch	=	16.4	cubic centimeters
Cubic foot	=	.028	cubic meter
Cubic yard	=	.765	cubic meter
Cubic Centimeter	=	.061	cubic inch
Cubic meter	=	35.31	cubic feet
Cubic meter	=	1.308	cubic yards
Teaspoon	=	5	milliliters
Tablespoon	=	15	milliliters
Fluid ounces	=	30	milliliters
Cup	=	.24	liter
Pint	=	.47	liter
Quart	=	.95	liter
Gallon	=	3.785	liters
Liter	=	2.1	pints
Liter	=	1.06	quarts

Weight

Ounces	=	28	grams
Pound	=	.45	kilogram
Kilogram	=	2.2	pounds

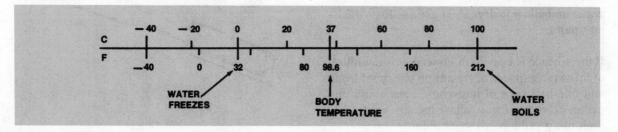

Under the metric system, temperature is measured in Centigrade degrees. A Centigrade thermometer is divided into 100 degrees with 0 degrees freezing and 100 degrees the temperature at which water boils. To convert from a Fahrenheit temperature to a Centigrade, multiply the Fahrenheit temperature by 5/9 and then subtract 32 from the result. To go from Centigrade to Fahrenheit, multiply the Centigrade temperature by 9/5 and add 32. A comparison of the two thermometers is shown.

Mildew Removing

Mildew is a fungus that thrives in warm, moist, dark places. It may be mistaken for dirt on house paint and often occurs in basements.

To solve a mildew problem in a basement, first make certain there is adequate ventilation and no water penetration. The understructure should be examined after a heavy rain. Openings around small pipes should be filled with oakum, and concrete mix can be used around large pipes. Cover sweating pipes.

The growth of mildew on paint is a problem in all areas of the country except possibly in the western desert areas. If linseed oil has been applied to the wood for finishing, mildew may be particularly prevalent. Mildew also grows faster on soft paints than on enamels.

If the surface is only slightly mildewed, apply paint with a mildewcide in it, such as pentachlorophenol or bichloride of mercury.

Wash a medium-mildewed surface with a solution of three tablespoonfuls of trisodium phosphate per gallon of water. Rinse with clean water and allow to dry. Then use a mildew-resistant paint.

If the surface is heavily mildewed, use a solution of three tablespoons of trisodium phosphate, one and one-half cups of household bleach and one gallon of water. Rinse, allow the surface to dry, then use a mildew-resistant paint.

Mill Bastard File

Designed originally for sharpening blades in sawmills, the mill bastard is also useful in knocking burrs from machine knives, axes, shears, circular and ice saws. Mill bastards taper in both width and thickness and are made with a single cut for a smooth finish in polishing and lathe work. The term "bastard" defines the coarseness of the file and is not a type of file. *SEE ALSO HAND TOOLS.*

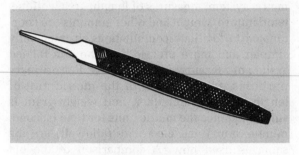

Mill Bastard File

Mill Chisel

The largest chisel, called the mill chisel, is rarely used in a home shop. It has a total length of 16″ or more and its blade length ranges from 8″ to 10″. The width of the blade ranges from 1″ to 2″. A mill chisel is used for heavy work. *SEE ALSO HAND TOOLS.*

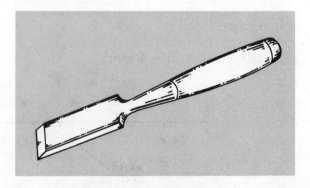

Mill Chisel

Millwork

Millwork refers to products manufactured from lumber in a planing mill or woodworking plant. These lumber products can either be standard items such as doors and windows or be made to special order. Other millwork includes molding and trim, cabinets, stairway parts, face frames, mantels, shutters, etc. *SEE ALSO MOLDING & TRIM.*

Mineral Fiber Shingles

Mineral fiber shingles or asbestos cement shingles are made from asbestos fiber and portland cement. Formed under high pressure, mineral fiber shingles are resistant to decay, fireproof and unaffected by ice, snow or salt water. Mineral fiber shingles are available in rectangular, square and hexagonal shapes as well as a variety of textures and colors.

Mineral fiber shingles are hard and rigid. Because of this feature, nail holes are prepunched at the factory. Galvanized needlepoint nails are recommended. Special equipment is a must for cutting the shingles. Most dealers have shingle cutters in the store for the convenience of their customers. These cutters have a nail punch for cutting additional holes. Shingles can be hand cut by scoring a line with a chisel or drift punch along a straight edge. After the shingle has been placed over a piece of wood, sharply rap the shingle along the scored line. To make a hole or irregular cut, punch holes along the line of the portion to be cut, and then break it away. A drift punch is well suited for this job because it cuts clean and does not split the shingle.

Mineral fiber shingles can either be placed over 30 pound felt or old roofing. When shingles are placed over old roofing, two inch nails should be used instead of the 1¼ inch nails normally used. *SEE ALSO ROOFING MATERIALS.*

Mineral Fiber Siding

Mineral fiber siding or asbestos cement siding is asbestos fiber and portland cement molded into sheets under pressure. It is prefinished with a baked, long-lasting coating. The siding is resistant to decay, fireproof and unaffected by salt air, ice or snow.

The siding comes in units or shingles, usually 24 inches wide and 12 inches deep. Sold in squares, each square covers 100 square feet of surface. Available in a variety of textures and colors, mineral fiber siding may have either wavy or exposed joint lines. *SEE ALSO SIDING.*

Miter Box

A miter box is a slotted wooden box or a one-sided metal platform that guides a saw at the proper angle to make a miter joint. The wooden box has 45° slots cut into its two opposite sides which act as saw guides. The one-sided metal platform has an adjustable metal guide into which the saw is inserted. The metal guide can be set at any angle from 30° to 90° to provide a greater variety of miter joints.

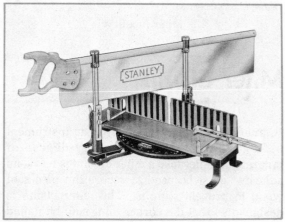

Courtesy of The Stanley Works

Metal Miter Box and Saw

Miter Box Saw

Miter box saws, when used with a miter box, are better than power saws for cutting accurate miters at angles from 30° to 90°. These saws can be 24-inches to 30-inches long, generally have 11 points per inch for fine cutting and a reinforced steel spine to prevent flexing. Miter box saws have a straight top edge, a square, blunt tip and a solid body. Unlike most saws, miter box saws are held horizontally and cut parallel with or across the grain. *SEE ALSO HAND TOOLS.*

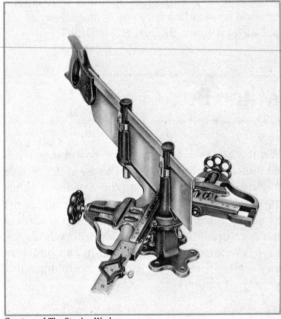

Courtesy of The Stanley Works

Miter Box Saw

Miter Clamp

A miter clamp or corner clamp is an instrument used to temporarily secure any degree of mitered joint. Because a mitered joint is weak, an adhesive must be used to secure the pieces of wood to prevent slipping. The miter clamp is designed so that the corner joint may be nailed or screwed for additional strength while the clamp is in place. *SEE ALSO HAND TOOLS.*

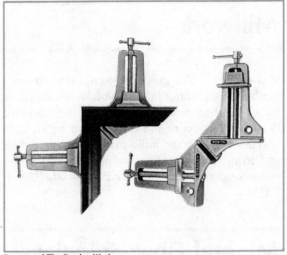

Courtesy of The Stanley Works

Miter Clamp

Miter & Miter Joints

A miter is most commonly a butt joint with beveled ends. Miter joints are frequently used in furniture construction for making chests, tables, picture frames and cabinets. Most miter joints are formed by cutting the ends of the members to be joined at 45 degree angles with a back or miter box saw and joining them together. Gluing is the simplest and probably most popular way of joining the two members. If brads are used, clamp the corner of the joint in a padded vise to prevent the hammer from knocking the joint out of line. Another method of joining is to apply glue to dovetail-shaped slots cut in the joint and insert veneer pieces. When the glue dries, the veneer may be trimmed and planed. A splined miter joint is made by cutting a slot in each member and using a plywood strip the same width as the joint to act as a reinforcement between the miter. Dowels may also be used to join a miter.

To cut the angles required for a miter joint, use a miter box. This will insure accurate, consistent work throughout the project. Miter boxes may be either purchased or built in the home workshop. Use a miter gauge when cutting miters with a table saw. *SEE ALSO FURNITURE MAKING; WOOD JOINTS.*

Miter Square

A miter square is used for marking miters, checking right angles in corners or joints and as a straight-edge. The miter square's blade is usually six- or eight-inches long and has a handle four- or five-and-one-half-inches in length, with one edge of the handle set at a 45° angle. This is its main difference from a try square. To check boards for warps with a miter square, set the blade across the board and slide it along the board's length. Light will appear beneath the blade where the board is warped. SEE ALSO HAND TOOLS.

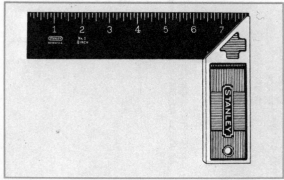

Courtesy of The Stanley Works

Miter Square

Mixers
[SEE FOOD MIXER REPAIR.]

Mixing Concrete & Mortar
[SEE CONCRETE.]

Mobile Home Construction

Construction of a large mobile home is clearly the job for a highly skilled home craftsman. However, the construction of a tandem-wheel travel trailer, one that may also serve as a small mobile home, is within the capabilities of the average home craftsman.

Detailed plans and component kits are available from several companies. These plans and kits greatly simplify the building of your trailer. The trailer plans discussed here may be obtained from Glen L Recreational Vehicles, Bellflower, California.

Mobile Home Construction

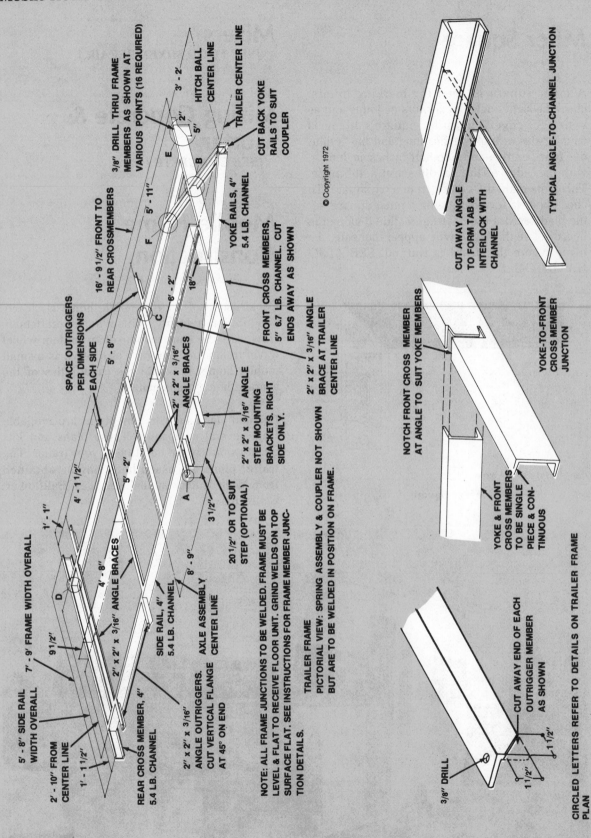

3/8" DRILL THRU FRAME MEMBERS AS SHOWN AT VARIOUS POINTS (16 REQUIRED)

HITCH BALL CENTER LINE

3' - 2"

2"

5"

TRAILER CENTER LINE

CUT BACK YOKE RAILS TO SUIT COUPLER

© Copyright 1972

YOKE RAILS, 4" 5.4 LB. CHANNEL

16' - 9 1/2" FRONT TO REAR CROSSMEMBERS

SPACE OUTRIGGERS PER DIMENSIONS EACH SIDE

5' - 11"

F

E

B

5' - 8"

C

6' - 2"

18"

FRONT CROSS MEMBERS, 5" 6.7 LB. CHANNEL. CUT ENDS AWAY AS SHOWN

2" x 2" x 3/16" ANGLE BRACES

2" x 2" x 3/16" ANGLE BRACE AT TRAILER CENTER LINE

5' - 2"

4' - 11 1/2"

2" x 2" x 3/16" ANGLE STEP MOUNTING BRACKETS. RIGHT SIDE ONLY.

1' - 1"

7' - 9" FRAME WIDTH OVERALL

9 1/2"

2" x 2" x 3/16" ANGLE BRACES

D

4' - 8"

8' - 9"

SIDE RAIL, 4" 5.4 LB. CHANNEL

AXLE ASSEMBLY CENTER LINE

A

3 1/2"

20 1/2" OR TO SUIT STEP (OPTIONAL)

TRAILER FRAME PICTORIAL VIEW: SPRING ASSEMBLY & COUPLER NOT SHOWN BUT ARE TO BE WELDED IN POSITION ON FRAME.

5' - 8" SIDE RAIL WIDTH OVERALL

2' - 10" FROM CENTER LINE

1' - 1 1/2"

REAR CROSS MEMBER, 4" 5.4 LB. CHANNEL

2" x 2" x 3/16" ANGLE OUTRIGGERS. CUT VERTICAL FLANGE AT 45° ON END

NOTE: ALL FRAME JUNCTIONS TO BE WELDED. FRAME MUST BE LEVEL & FLAT TO RECEIVE FLOOR UNIT. GRIND WELDS ON TOP SURFACE FLAT. SEE INSTRUCTIONS FOR FRAME MEMBER JUNCTION DETAILS.

TYPICAL ANGLE-TO-CHANNEL JUNCTION

CUT AWAY ANGLE TO FORM TAB & INTERLOCK WITH CHANNEL

YOKE-TO-FRONT CROSS MEMBER JUNCTION

NOTCH FRONT CROSS MEMBER AT ANGLE TO SUIT YOKE MEMBERS

YOKE & FRONT CROSS MEMBERS TO BE SINGLE PIECE & CONTINUOUS

CUT AWAY END OF EACH OUTRIGGER MEMBER AS SHOWN

3/8" DRILL

1 1/2"

1 1/2"

CIRCLED LETTERS REFER TO DETAILS ON TRAILER FRAME PLAN

1048

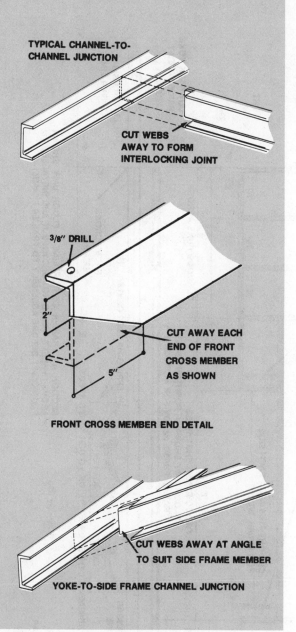

TYPICAL CHANNEL-TO-CHANNEL JUNCTION

CUT WEBS AWAY TO FORM INTERLOCKING JOINT

3/8" DRILL

2"

5"

CUT AWAY EACH END OF FRONT CROSS MEMBER AS SHOWN

FRONT CROSS MEMBER END DETAIL

CUT WEBS AWAY AT ANGLE TO SUIT SIDE FRAME MEMBER

YOKE-TO-SIDE FRAME CHANNEL JUNCTION

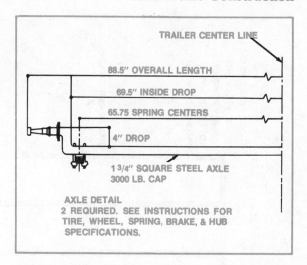

TRAILER CENTER LINE

88.5" OVERALL LENGTH

69.5" INSIDE DROP

65.75 SPRING CENTERS

4" DROP

1 3/4" SQUARE STEEL AXLE 3000 LB. CAP

AXLE DETAIL
2 REQUIRED. SEE INSTRUCTIONS FOR TIRE, WHEEL, SPRING, BRAKE, & HUB SPECIFICATIONS.

Diagonal measurements of the frame should be identical.

All running gear (axle, springs, spindles, wheels and tires) should be a minimum 4500 pound capacity. The tandem springs are connected to a center rocker arm hanger. The axle is mounted above the springs.

In order to make the home possible to be mobile, a 4500 pound minimum capacity coupler should be installed on the tongue. A jack stand should also be included in the coupler assembly. Twin safety chains of 5000 pound breaking test load should be fastened to the tongue.

Brakes, either hydraulic or electric, should be installed on the spindles of both axles. Surge brakes must not be used; they are inadequate for a trailer of this weight.

FLOOR

The trailer floor is built on a framework of 2 x 2 lumber. The underside is covered with $1/4$ inch exterior plywood, and the top with $5/8$ inch exterior plywood. Use a sawing jig when cutting stock for the framework to prevent errors in the length of duplicate parts.

Assemble the framework using 16d nails. Install the $1/4$ inch bottom covering, coating all mating areas with plastic resin glue, and fastening the plywood with 1 inch cement coated nails on 4 inch centers. Use the installation of the plywood to true the framework.

TRAILER FRAME

The trailer frame may be built from either standard structural steel or formed sheet metal sections. If the home craftsman is not an experienced welder, it is recommended that the frame be assembled by a metalworking shop.

The optional skid guards are recommended particularly if a holding tank is installed in the rear of the trailer. Make sure that when constructed the frame is not twisted or out of plumb.

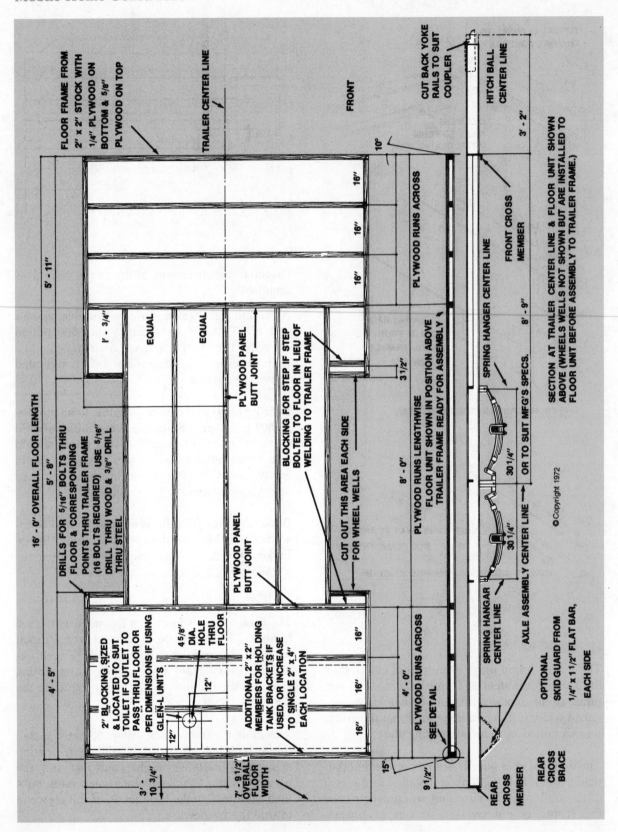

FLOOR FRAME FROM 2" x 2" STOCK WITH 1/4" PLYWOOD ON BOTTOM & 5/8" PLYWOOD ON TOP

TRAILER CENTER LINE

FRONT

CUT BACK YOKE RAILS TO SUIT COUPLER

HITCH BALL CENTER LINE

3' - 2"

16"

16"

16"

PLYWOOD RUNS ACROSS

FRONT CROSS MEMBER

SPRING HANGER CENTER LINE

10°

5' - 11"

1' - 3/4"

EQUAL

EQUAL

PLYWOOD PANEL BUTT JOINT

BLOCKING FOR STEP IF STEP BOLTED TO FLOOR IN LIEU OF WELDING TO TRAILER FRAME

3 1/2"

8' - 9"

OR TO SUIT MFG'S SPECS.

16' - 0' OVERALL FLOOR LENGTH

5' - 8"

DRILLS FOR 5/16" BOLTS THRU FLOOR & CORRESPONDING POINTS THRU TRAILER FRAME (16 BOLTS REQUIRED) USE 5/16" DRILL THRU WOOD & 3/8" DRILL THRU STEEL

PLYWOOD PANEL BUTT JOINT

CUT OUT THIS AREA EACH SIDE FOR WHEEL WELLS

8' - 0"

PLYWOOD RUNS LENGTHWISE FLOOR UNIT SHOWN IN POSITION ABOVE TRAILER FRAME READY FOR ASSEMBLY

30 1/4"

30 1/4"

© Copyright 1972

SECTION AT TRAILER CENTER LINE & FLOOR UNIT SHOWN ABOVE (WHEELS WELLS NOT SHOWN BUT ARE INSTALLED TO FLOOR UNIT BEFORE ASSEMBLY TO TRAILER FRAME.)

4' - 5"

2" BLOCKING SIZED & LOCATED TO SUIT TOILET IF OUTLET TO PASS THRU FLOOR OR PER DIMENSIONS IF USING GLEN-L UNITS

4 5/8" DIA. HOLE THRU FLOOR

12"

ADDITIONAL 2" x 2" MEMBERS FOR HOLDING TANK BRACKETS IF USED, OR INCREASE TO SINGLE 2" x 4" EACH LOCATION

12"

16"

16"

16"

SPRING HANGER CENTER LINE

AXLE ASSEMBLY CENTER LINE

OPTIONAL SKID GUARD FROM 1/4" x 1 1/2" FLAT BAR, EACH SIDE

3' - 10 3/4"

7' - 9 1/2" OVERALL FLOOR WIDTH

4' - 0"

PLYWOOD RUNS ACROSS

SEE DETAIL

15°

9 1/2"

REAR CROSS BRACE

REAR CROSS MEMBER

1050

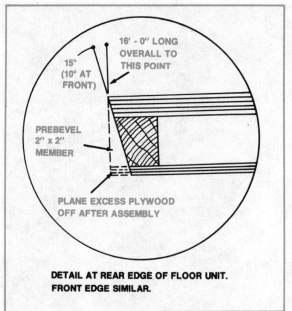

15°
(10° AT
FRONT)

16' - 0" LONG
OVERALL TO
THIS POINT

PREBEVEL
2" x 2"
MEMBER

PLANE EXCESS PLYWOOD
OFF AFTER ASSEMBLY

**DETAIL AT REAR EDGE OF FLOOR UNIT.
FRONT EDGE SIMILAR.**

Construct the wheel wells of exterior plywood with wood blocking at the corners. Be extremely careful in the layout and cutting of the wells because they must be watertight. Well interiors may be faced with fiberglass or sheet metal. Optionally, the wells may be fabricated of welded sheet steel.

Insert wheel wells in floor frame, flush with bottom. Glue and nail in place. Coat entire underside of floor with plywood sealer, followed with several coats of exterior paint,

Turn the floor over and place on metal frame. Completely insulate the floor with batt insulation. Check the floor plan for the possible underfloor routing of any portions of the plumbing and electrical systems. Apply the upper flooring of $5/8$ inch plywood. Fasten the floor to the frame with

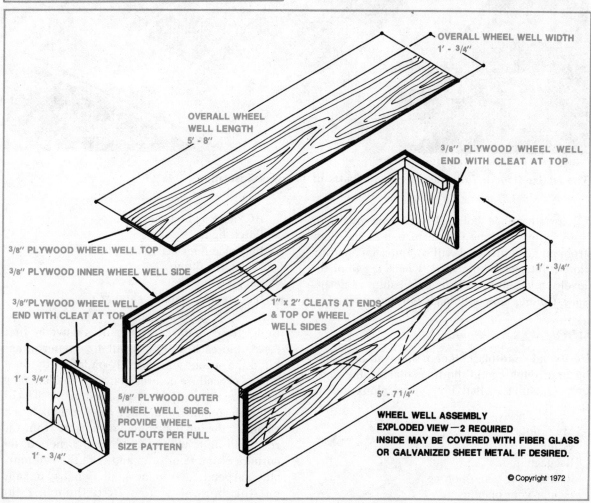

OVERALL WHEEL WELL WIDTH
1' - 3/4"

OVERALL WHEEL
WELL LENGTH
5' - 8"

3/8" PLYWOOD WHEEL WELL
END WITH CLEAT AT TOP

3/8" PLYWOOD WHEEL WELL TOP

3/8" PLYWOOD INNER WHEEL WELL SIDE

3/8"PLYWOOD WHEEL WELL
END WITH CLEAT AT TOP

1' - 3/4"

1" x 2" CLEATS AT ENDS
& TOP OF WHEEL
WELL SIDES

1' - 3/4"

1' - 3/4"

5/8" PLYWOOD OUTER
WHEEL WELL SIDES.
PROVIDE WHEEL
CUT-OUTS PER FULL
SIZE PATTERN

5' - 7 1/4"

**WHEEL WELL ASSEMBLY
EXPLODED VIEW —2 REQUIRED
INSIDE MAY BE COVERED WITH FIBER GLASS
OR GALVANIZED SHEET METAL IF DESIRED.**

Courtesy of Glen L Recreational Vehicles

The trailer floor is fully insulated with batts of fiberglass insulation.

⁵/₁₆ inch carriage bolts, driven from the floor side. Note: Any possible distortion in the floor from an absolute level will complicate construction of interior cabinetwork. Check the floor for level while bolting to frame, and shim as necessary. Countersink bolt heads wherever possible.

SIDEWALLS

Verify side and placement of sidewall openings by first roughing out the floor plan on the floor unit. Openings called for by the plans are as follows:

    Main door
    Windows
    Baggage door
    Refrigerator vent opening
    Heater vent opening

AC electrical entrance
Porch light
Entrance door access handle
Water fill fitting
Range hood vent
Blocking for bath or shower pan

Build front and rear units of sidewalls first. Assemble each unit on a full size pattern, then build the second unit directly on top of the first. Such a procedure insures that right and left sides are identical. Complete assembly of the sidewalls on the trailer floor. Snap a chalk line to establish the top plate line. Position the front and rear wall units with their bottom corners at the corners of the floor unit, and with the reference stud perpendicular to the chalk line. Lay out and cut the bottom plates. Drill them for the

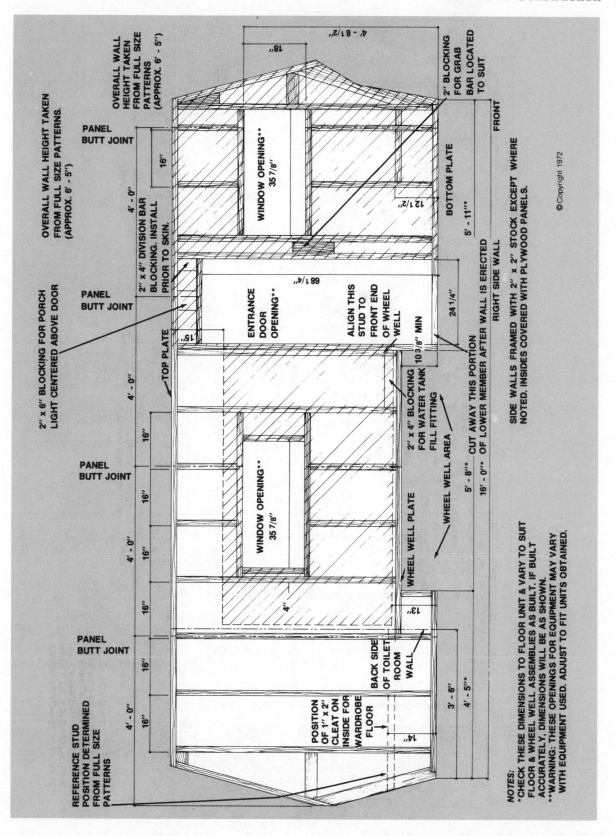

NOTES:
*CHECK THESE DIMENSIONS TO FLOOR UNIT & VARY TO SUIT
FLOOR & WHEEL WELL ASSEMBLIES AS BUILT. IF BUILT
ACCURATELY, DIMENSIONS WILL BE AS SHOWN.
**WARNING: THESE OPENINGS FOR EQUIPMENT MAY VARY
WITH EQUIPMENT USED. ADJUST TO FIT UNITS OBTAINED.

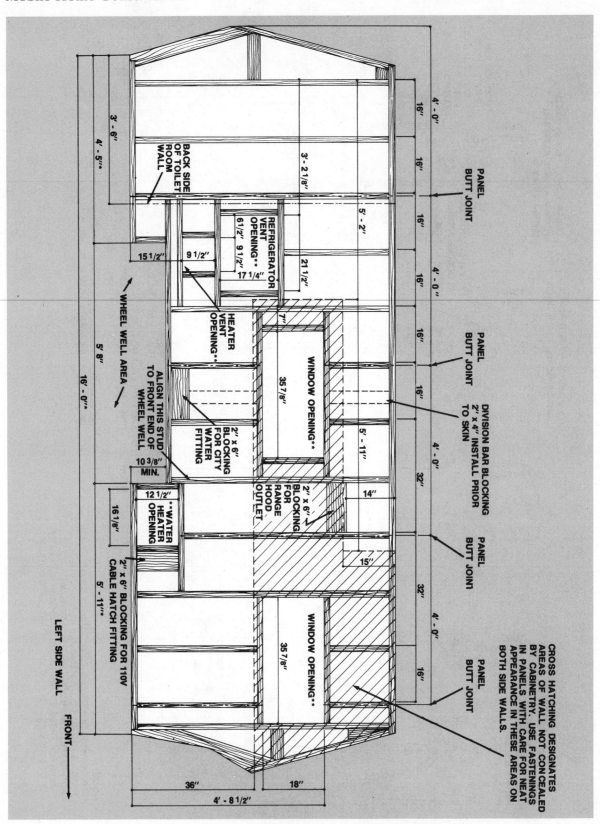

Courtesy of Glen L Recreational Vehicles

Before assembling walls, a rough layout of the trailer plan is made on the floor. This layout makes possible changes easier.

necessary mounting bolts or screws. Lay out and cut the necessary studs, and other wall members. Use sawing jigs to insure that all identical members are identical. Assemble the wall framework using 16d nails. When one wall is built, construct the other directly on top of it. While the openings may vary, the procedure will make sure that the wall dimensions will be identical.

The interior surfaces of the finished walls are covered with decorative plywood. Openings are then cut for windows and doors.

After the walls are framed they may be removed from the floor with care, and their interior surfaces covered with 3/16 inch interior plywood. Plywood areas that will be exposed should be fastened with glue and finishing nails. Plywood areas concealed by cabinetry should be fastened with glue and 1 inch ring nails, since the ring nails have additional fastening strength.

After all exterior walls and interior partitions have been framed and surfaced, the trailer floor should be checked for level. (If the floor is level, a plumb bob, builders level, or try square may be used to correctly align all interior construction. If the floor is not level, there is no true vertical to use for alignment.) After the floor is leveled, the sidewalls should be erected. Glue should be spread between the floor and the bottom plate, then the mounting bolts and screws tightened. Use diagonal braces as needed to hold the wall in place.

The first sidewall has been erected and braced. Note jack leveling floor.

PARTITIONS

All interior partitions are constructed of 1 x 2 framing members covered with interior plywood or plastic laminate. Such sheathing is not required in areas that are not visible, such as closet interiors.

Note: Corner beading (also known as welting or

Mobile Home Construction

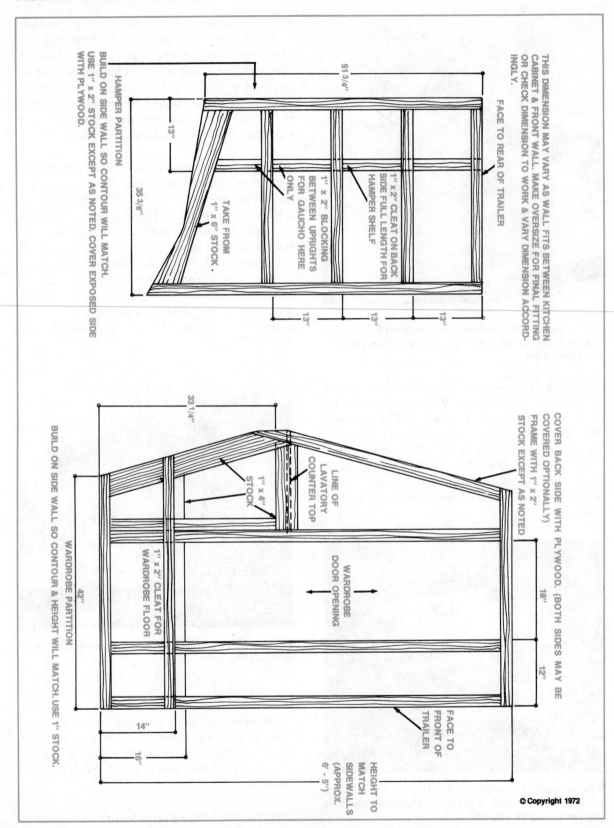

THIS DIMENSION MAY VARY AS WALL FITS BETWEEN KITCHEN
CABINET & FRONT WALL. MAKE OVERSIZE FOR FINAL FITTING
OR CHECK DIMENSION TO WORK & VARY DIMENSION ACCORD-
INGLY.

FACE TO REAR OF TRAILER

51 3/4"

13"

35 3/8"

HAMPER PARTITION

BUILD ON SIDE WALL SO CONTOUR WILL MATCH.
USE 1" x 2" STOCK EXCEPT AS NOTED. COVER EXPOSED SIDE
WITH PLYWOOD.

TAKE FROM
1" x 6" STOCK.

1" x 2" BLOCKING
BETWEEN UPRIGHTS
FOR GAUCHO HERE
ONLY

1" x 2" CLEAT ON BACK
SIDE FULL LENGTH FOR
HAMPER SHELF

13"   13"   13"

COVER BACK SIDE WITH PLYWOOD. (BOTH SIDES MAY BE
COVERED OPTIONALLY)
FRAME WITH 1" x 2"
STOCK EXCEPT AS NOTED

33 1/4"

1" x 4"
STOCK

LINE OF
LAVATORY
COUNTER TOP

WARDROBE
DOOR OPENING

WARDROBE PARTITION

BUILD ON SIDE WALL SO CONTOUR & HEIGHT WILL MATCH. USE 1" STOCK.

1" x 2" CLEAT FOR
WARDROBE FLOOR

42"

14"

16"

18"

12"

FACE TO
FRONT OF
TRAILER

HEIGHT TO
MATCH
SIDEWALLS
(APPROX.
6' - 5")

© Copyright 1972

1056

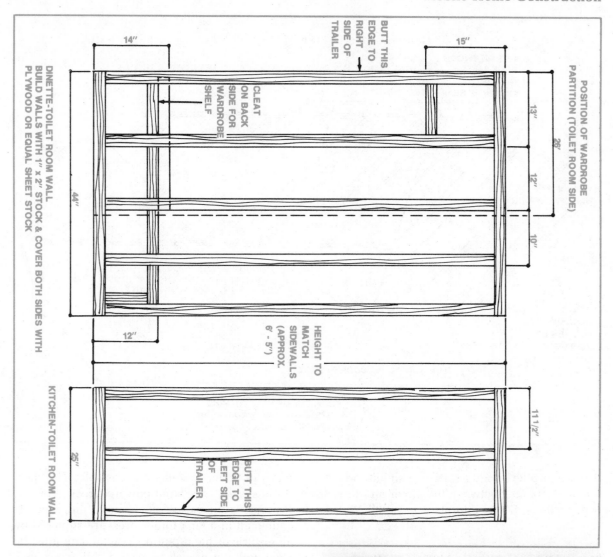

DINETTE-TOILET ROOM WALL
BUILD WALLS WITH 1" x 2" STOCK & COVER BOTH SIDES WITH
PLYWOOD OR EQUAL SHEET STOCK

14"

BUTT THIS EDGE TO RIGHT SIDE OF TRAILER

CLEAT ON BACK SIDE FOR WARDROBE SHELF

POSITION OF WARDROBE PARTITION (TOILET ROOM SIDE)

15"

13"

12"

10"

26"

44"

HEIGHT TO MATCH SIDEWALLS (APPROX. 6' - 5")

12"

KITCHEN-TOILET ROOM WALL

25"

BUTT THIS EDGE TO LEFT SIDE OF TRAILER

11 1/2"

gimp) is to be used in all interior corners. The welting serves a double purpose: concealing seams and sealing possible dust and air leaks.

Partitions should be securely fastened to the trailer floor. In areas that are not visible, inside closets for example, a floor cleat may be used. In more visible areas, carriage bolts extending through the entire floor unit should be used.

FRONT AND BACK WALLS

These walls are built in two sections. The sections should be prefabricated and then fastened to the trailer. Be particularly sure to use welting in the seam between the sidewalls and the front and back walls.

Courtesy of Glen L Recreational Vehicles

The back walls of the trailer are assembled on the ground before being put in place. Clamping the wall in place will simplify the final assembly.

1057

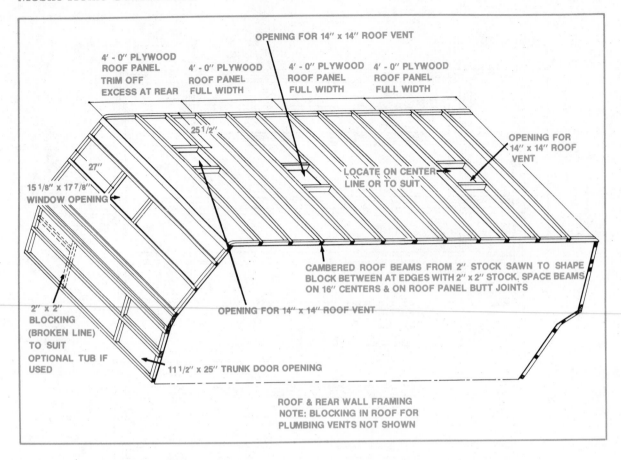

OPENING FOR 14″ x 14″ ROOF VENT

4′ - 0″ PLYWOOD ROOF PANEL TRIM OFF EXCESS AT REAR

4′ - 0″ PLYWOOD ROOF PANEL FULL WIDTH

4′ - 0″ PLYWOOD ROOF PANEL FULL WIDTH

4′ - 0″ PLYWOOD ROOF PANEL FULL WIDTH

OPENING FOR 14″ x 14″ ROOF VENT

25 1/2″

27″

LOCATE ON CENTER LINE OR TO SUIT

15 1/8″ x 17 7/8″ WINDOW OPENING

CAMBERED ROOF BEAMS FROM 2″ STOCK SAWN TO SHAPE BLOCK BETWEEN AT EDGES WITH 2″ x 2″ STOCK. SPACE BEAMS ON 16″ CENTERS & ON ROOF PANEL BUTT JOINTS

OPENING FOR 14″ x 14″ ROOF VENT

2″ x 2″ BLOCKING (BROKEN LINE) TO SUIT OPTIONAL TUB IF USED

11 1/2″ x 25″ TRUNK DOOR OPENING

ROOF & REAR WALL FRAMING
NOTE: BLOCKING IN ROOF FOR PLUMBING VENTS NOT SHOWN

A piece of pine or other softwood should be cut to fit the opening between the upper and lower wall sections. Screw into place using 3″ No. 14 screws.

PLUMBING, WIRING, AND INTERIOR JOINERY

The roof cannot be put on the trailer until the basic plumbing and wiring have been roughed in, and the interior cabinets installed.

Plumbing

The water and gas (LPG) supply systems must conform to state and local codes. The suggestions that follow are therefore only general guidelines.

The water tank is located directly over the wheels under the dinette. A full tank of water weighs a great deal, therefore the tank should not be repositioned during building. Several types of water systems are possible. The most basic system is a hand-powered rocker pump. Pressure systems are not vented; the water is contained in a tank under pressure supplied by an electric or hand pump. A metal tank must be used with a pressurized system. All water lines should be either galvanized or copper pipe, and copper tubing. The main runs should be 1/2 inch pipe, with 3/8 inch tube leads to the various fixtures. As protection from freezing, a drain should be installed in the tank or the lowest part of the system. Fittings may also be installed to connect a camp water supply to the trailer system.

The waste drain and vent system may use plastic pipe and fittings. The most useful system would have the waste from the toilet go to a holding tank, while the sink, shower, and lavatory drains are connected to a drain outlet. When in a camp with a sewage connection, all facilities are connected to the camp system. When in an area

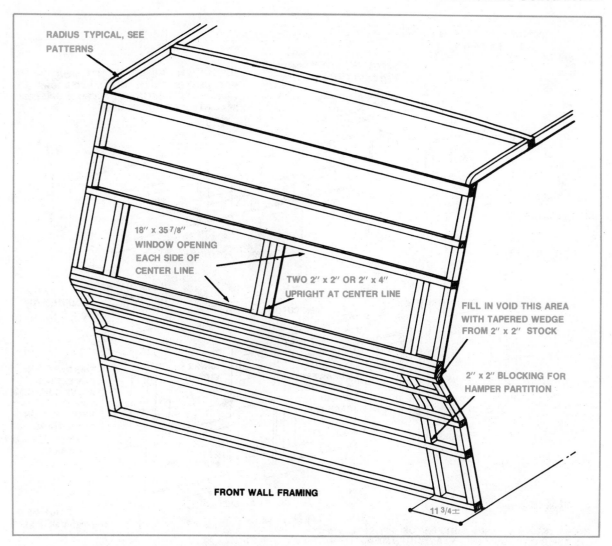

RADIUS TYPICAL, SEE PATTERNS

18" x 35 7/8"
WINDOW OPENING
EACH SIDE OF
CENTER LINE

TWO 2" x 2" OR 2" x 4"
UPRIGHT AT CENTER LINE

FILL IN VOID THIS AREA
WITH TAPERED WEDGE
FROM 2" x 2" STOCK

2" x 2" BLOCKING FOR
HAMPER PARTITION

FRONT WALL FRAMING

11 3/4

without sewage connections, the sewage is kept in the holding tank and the drain wastes are caught in a bucket. Most plans suggest a variety of possible drain systems. Any drain/vent system must conform to local plumbing codes.

Liquid petroleum gas (LPG) is usually contained in 2 5-gallon capacity tanks on the tongue of the trailer. The tanks are connected to a regulator (a device that controls the pressure of the gas entering the trailer system). A flexible hose or copper tube connects the regulator to the trailer piping system. A manifold to carry gas to all fixtures should be formed from 5/8 inch copper pipe or 1/2 inch black iron pipe. Lines to the appliance from the manifold should be 3/8 inch copper tubing. For safety, the gas lines should be type K or L copper tubing with flared fittings. Ferrule or slip-fit fittings *must not* be used. In addition, the tubing should be supported and protected from abrasion. The gas line supplying the gas refrigerator should have the entrance hole into the refrigerator compartment sealed air tight. If this is done, any gas leak in the refrigerator compartment will be vented outside.

Wiring

Electrical systems in a mobile leisure home can be a problem. The most practical arrangement is a group of 12 volt lights run off the car or a trailer battery, plus an adequate group of AC fixtures and convenience outlets that could be used in a camping facility with AC outlets.

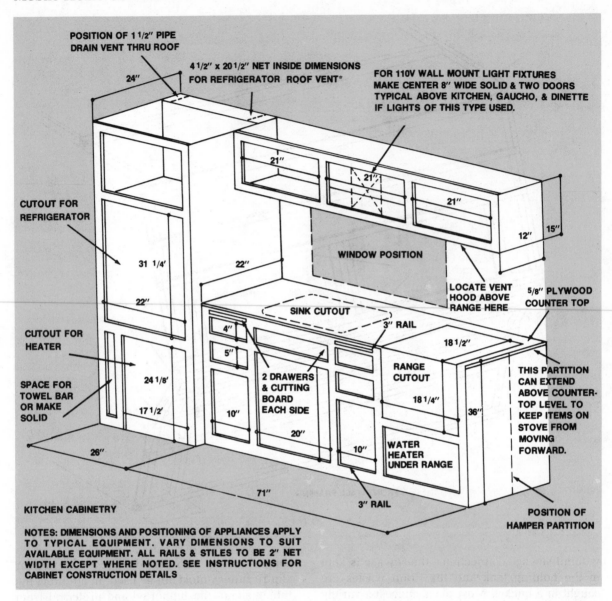

POSITION OF 1 1/2" PIPE
DRAIN VENT THRU ROOF

24"

4 1/2" x 20 1/2" NET INSIDE DIMENSIONS
FOR REFRIGERATOR ROOF VENT*

FOR 110V WALL MOUNT LIGHT FIXTURES
MAKE CENTER 8" WIDE SOLID & TWO DOORS
TYPICAL ABOVE KITCHEN, GAUCHO, & DINETTE
IF LIGHTS OF THIS TYPE USED.

CUTOUT FOR
REFRIGERATOR

21"

21"

21"

12"   15"

WINDOW POSITION

31 1/4'   22"

22"

SINK CUTOUT

LOCATE VENT
HOOD ABOVE
RANGE HERE

5/8" PLYWOOD
COUNTER TOP

CUTOUT FOR
HEATER

4"

5"

3" RAIL

18 1/2"

SPACE FOR
TOWEL BAR
OR MAKE
SOLID

24 1/8'

17 1/2'

10"

2 DRAWERS
& CUTTING
BOARD
EACH SIDE

20"

RANGE
CUTOUT

18 1/4"

36"

THIS PARTITION
CAN EXTEND
ABOVE COUNTER-
TOP LEVEL TO
KEEP ITEMS ON
STOVE FROM
MOVING
FORWARD.

26"

10"

WATER
HEATER
UNDER RANGE

71"

3" RAIL

POSITION OF
HAMPER PARTITION

KITCHEN CABINETRY

NOTES: DIMENSIONS AND POSITIONING OF APPLIANCES APPLY
TO TYPICAL EQUIPMENT. VARY DIMENSIONS TO SUIT
AVAILABLE EQUIPMENT. ALL RAILS & STILES TO BE 2" NET
WIDTH EXCEPT WHERE NOTED. SEE INSTRUCTIONS FOR
CABINET CONSTRUCTION DETAILS

The DC, or battery, system is divided into two major groups: the running lights, the brake, backup, tail, clearance, and directional lights required by law, and the interior lights for illumination. Since DC systems are vulnerable to voltage drop (loss of voltage causing dimming of lights) in longer runs, extreme care should be taken to use wire of adequate size. The minimum size that should be used is No. 16 stranded copper wire. All circuits should be fused, and should be led to a central connection on the tongue. A generous bed of putty or sealant should be provided for all exterior fixtures.

These fixtures should also be securely fastened to wooden blocking beneath the aluminum skin.

The AC, or residential power, electrical system is one that must be made in close compliance with state electrical codes. In general practice, mobile leisure home AC systems will consist of 2 15-ampere circuits. A 15 ampere circuit is usually classified as a circuit of 8 combined fixtures (light plus a convenience outlet) on which the fixed appliances (refrigerator, heaters, etc.) draw no more than 5 amperes. The service entrance should be accessible. All wiring should

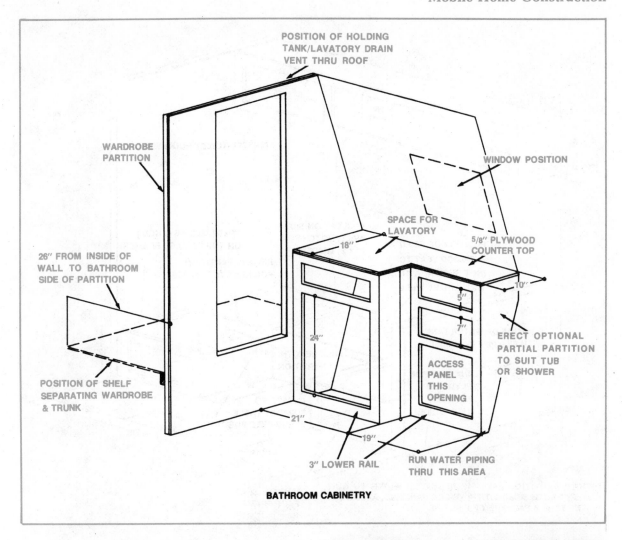

POSITION OF HOLDING
TANK/LAVATORY DRAIN
VENT THRU ROOF

WARDROBE
PARTITION

WINDOW POSITION

SPACE FOR
LAVATORY

5/8" PLYWOOD
COUNTER TOP

26" FROM INSIDE OF
WALL TO BATHROOM
SIDE OF PARTITION

18"

10"

5"

7"

24"

ERECT OPTIONAL
PARTIAL PARTITION
TO SUIT TUB
OR SHOWER

POSITION OF SHELF
SEPARATING WARDROBE
& TRUNK

ACCESS
PANEL
THIS
OPENING

21"

19"

3" LOWER RAIL

RUN WATER PIPING
THRU THIS AREA

BATHROOM CABINETRY

be taped, stapled, and otherwise fastened in place to prevent fraying. Wiring is frequently run through wall cabinets for both concealment and protection.

Interior Joinery

The cabinets for the mobile leisure home can be made of 1 x 2 stock with dowelled joints, and plywood facing. Base wood for counter tops should be ⅝ inch plywood or particle board faced with plastic laminate, linoleum, or other desired material. Specific details for needed cabinets are contained in the plans.

ROOF CONSTRUCTION

The roof is constructed in 4 foot segments. The

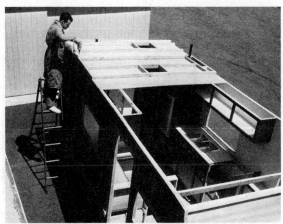

Courtesy of Glen L Recreational Vehicles

The roof is put on in 4 foot segments. Interior cabinetry, plumbing, and wiring is virtually complete at this stage.

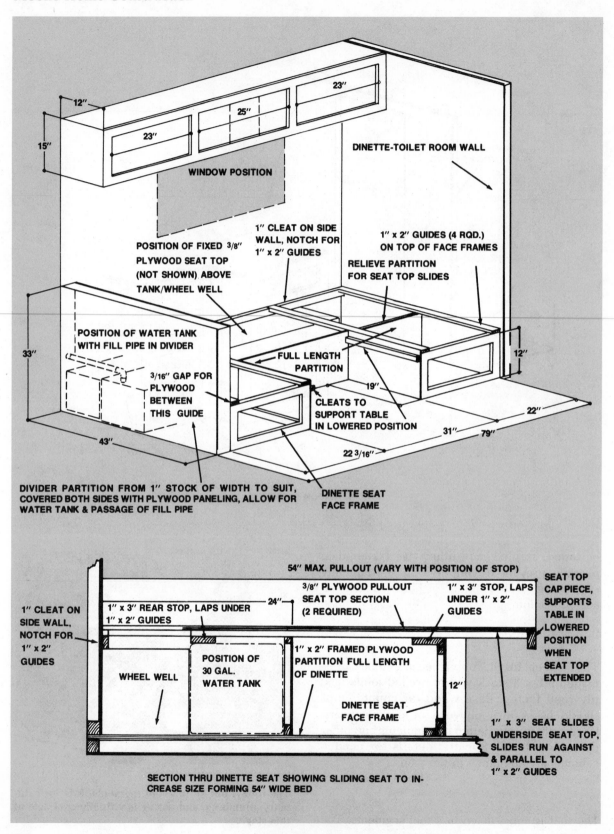

12″

15″

23″

25″

23″

WINDOW POSITION

DINETTE-TOILET ROOM WALL

POSITION OF FIXED 3/8″ PLYWOOD SEAT TOP (NOT SHOWN) ABOVE TANK/WHEEL WELL

1″ CLEAT ON SIDE WALL, NOTCH FOR 1″ x 2″ GUIDES

1″ x 2″ GUIDES (4 RQD.) ON TOP OF FACE FRAMES

RELIEVE PARTITION FOR SEAT TOP SLIDES

POSITION OF WATER TANK WITH FILL PIPE IN DIVIDER

33″

3/16″ GAP FOR PLYWOOD BETWEEN THIS GUIDE

FULL LENGTH PARTITION

19″

12″

CLEATS TO SUPPORT TABLE IN LOWERED POSITION

22″

43″

31″

79″

22 3/16″

DIVIDER PARTITION FROM 1″ STOCK OF WIDTH TO SUIT, COVERED BOTH SIDES WITH PLYWOOD PANELING, ALLOW FOR WATER TANK & PASSAGE OF FILL PIPE

DINETTE SEAT FACE FRAME

54″ MAX. PULLOUT (VARY WITH POSITION OF STOP)

3/8″ PLYWOOD PULLOUT SEAT TOP SECTION (2 REQUIRED)

1″ x 3″ STOP, LAPS UNDER 1″ x 2″ GUIDES

SEAT TOP CAP PIECE, SUPPORTS TABLE IN LOWERED POSITION WHEN SEAT TOP EXTENDED

24″

1″ CLEAT ON SIDE WALL, NOTCH FOR 1″ x 2″ GUIDES

1″ x 3″ REAR STOP, LAPS UNDER 1″ x 2″ GUIDES

WHEEL WELL

POSITION OF 30 GAL. WATER TANK

1″ x 2″ FRAMED PLYWOOD PARTITION FULL LENGTH OF DINETTE

DINETTE SEAT FACE FRAME

12″

1″ x 3″ SEAT SLIDES UNDERSIDE SEAT TOP, SLIDES RUN AGAINST & PARALLEL TO 1″ x 2″ GUIDES

SECTION THRU DINETTE SEAT SHOWING SLIDING SEAT TO IN-CREASE SIZE FORMING 54″ WIDE BED

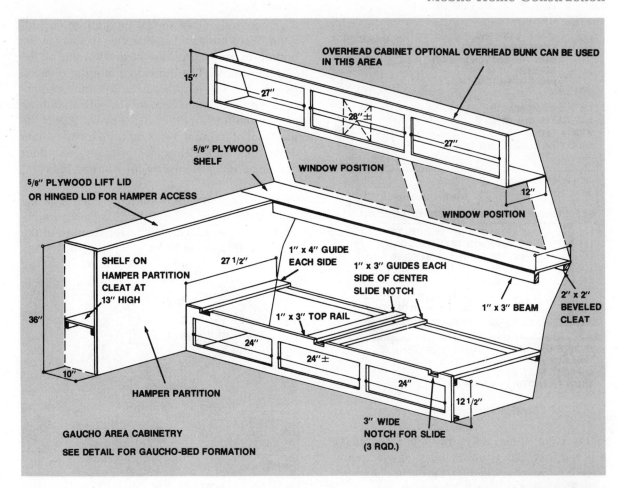

OVERHEAD CABINET OPTIONAL OVERHEAD BUNK CAN BE USED IN THIS AREA

15"

27"

28"±

27"

5/8" PLYWOOD SHELF

WINDOW POSITION

12"

WINDOW POSITION

5/8" PLYWOOD LIFT LID OR HINGED LID FOR HAMPER ACCESS

SHELF ON HAMPER PARTITION CLEAT AT 13" HIGH

27 1/2"

1" x 4" GUIDE EACH SIDE

1" x 3" GUIDES EACH SIDE OF CENTER SLIDE NOTCH

1" x 3" BEAM

2" x 2" BEVELED CLEAT

36"

1" x 3" TOP RAIL

24"

24"±

24"

12 1/2"

10"

HAMPER PARTITION

GAUCHO AREA CABINETRY

SEE DETAIL FOR GAUCHO-BED FORMATION

3" WIDE NOTCH FOR SLIDE (3 RQD.)

openings for all roof vents are spaced between the 16 inches o.c. roof beams. The beams are cut with a curve to shed water. Either cut a plywood template, or use the first beam cut as a model for the rest. Panel nails should not be used on ceiling work, as they tend to pull through the work. Use either drive screw nails or chrome screws to fasten the ceiling. The roof should be completely insulated with batt insulation.

INSULATION

Insulating the walls will make the mobile leisure home easier to heat and cool. Batt insulation is laid between the floor joists, and between the roof beams, as already described. Blanket insulation, 1/2 inch thick, is stapled to the sides of the trailer before the aluminum skin is applied.

ALUMINUM COVERING

The aluminum covering will require assistance

Courtesy of Glen L Recreational Vehicles

Blanket insulation is stapled to the outside of the trailer. It is held back from the edges of window and door openings. Note also the dividing bars that are used in applying the aluminum skin.

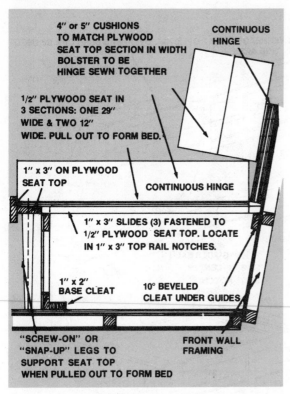

4" or 5" CUSHIONS TO MATCH PLYWOOD SEAT TOP SECTION IN WIDTH BOLSTER TO BE HINGE SEWN TOGETHER

CONTINUOUS HINGE

1/2" PLYWOOD SEAT IN 3 SECTIONS: ONE 29" WIDE & TWO 12" WIDE. PULL OUT TO FORM BED.

1" x 3" ON PLYWOOD SEAT TOP

CONTINUOUS HINGE

1" x 3" SLIDES (3) FASTENED TO 1/2" PLYWOOD SEAT TOP. LOCATE IN 1" x 3" TOP RAIL NOTCHES.

1" x 2" BASE CLEAT

10° BEVELED CLEAT UNDER GUIDES

"SCREW-ON" OR "SNAP-UP" LEGS TO SUPPORT SEAT TOP WHEN PULLED OUT TO FORM BED

FRONT WALL FRAMING

Section Through Gaucho

to be installed properly. The sides should be covered first. The general pattern of coverage is front laps over back and top laps over side. Such a lapping arrangement will lessen the chance of leakage.

Courtesy of Glen L Recreational Vehicles

The first aluminum skin panel is inserted in the divider bar. The panel is trimmed to shape after being fastened in place.

An upper side piece should be the first one applied. Place the panel so that the lap seam at the bottom of the siding just clears the top of the window frame. Tap the siding into the division bar. Fasten the aluminum with 1 inch cement coated nails 12 inches apart. The side aluminum is trimmed flush with the framework. Apply the panels of aluminum, working from top to bottom down the side. Allow for window and door openings. Indicate cutouts for running lights.

The metal for the top is started at the top of the front window and is carried across the top as one continuous sheet. The top metal should lap the side skin to prevent leaks.

Courtesy of Glen L Recreational Vehicles

A mallet is used to insure a close lap of the roof skin over the side skin. This joint will eventually be covered with a putty-bedded drip molding.

The following bill of materials lists the required material to build the 20' trailer. Due to variations in methods of construction and options of the builder, cabinets and partition materials are not noted. All listed lumber should be free of knots and imperfections that may weaken the structure. White fir is suggested as it is both light in weight and does not tend to split. Douglas fir is listed for points of stress. Other lumbers of similar properties could, however, be substituted. All lumber listed as to width and length is lumberyard size. All lengths are listed to provide material for trimming to the required length. All floor and wheel well plywood is listed as an exterior type. The exposed veneer panels may be of AB or AC grade with the "A" face always being the exposed surface.

MATERIALS LIST

LUMBER	AMOUNT	SIZE	TYPE
Wheel well cleats	36 lin. ft.	1"x2" stock	Pine
Floor framing	14	2"x2"x8"	White fir
	2	2"x2"x16'	White fir
Roof beams	6	2"x6"x8'	Doug. fir
Front wall framing	11	2"x2"x8'	White fir
	1	2"x4"x8'	Doug. fir
Rear wall framing	8	2"x2"x8'	White fir
	1	2"x4"x8'	Doug. fir
	1	2"x6"x8'	Doug. fir
Roof blocking at edges	8	2"x2"x8'	White fir
Side wall framing	2	2"x2"x16'	White fir
	40	2"x2"x8'	White fir
	2	2"x4"x8'	Doug. fir
	2	2"x6"x8'	Doug. fir

PLYWOOD:

	AMOUNT	SIZE	TYPE
Floor frame covering	4	1/4"x4'x8'	Ext. Doug. fir
	4	5/8"x4'x8'	Ext. Doug. fir
Wheel wells	1	5/8"x4'x8'	Ext. Doug. fir
	1	3/8"x4'x8'	Ext. Doug. fir
	1	3/8"x2'x8'	Ext. Doug. fir
Roof, front, and rear walls	8	3/16"x4'x8'	Interior to suit
Side walls	9	3/16"x4'x7'	Interior to suit

*Scrap plywood may be utilized for interior joinery.

FASTENINGS:

		SIZE
Screws	300	3" no.14
Screws	64	1-1/4" no.8
Ring Nails	1600	1"
Ring Nails	600	2"
Drive Screw Nails	200	3/4"
Corrugated Fasteners	100	5/8" no.5
Carriage Bolts (with nuts and washers)	24	5/16"x5'

Courtesy of Glen L Recreational Vehicles

The top skin is clamped in place with a 2 x 4 while it is being stretched into proper position.

FINISHING TRIM

After the skin is installed, drip molding bedded in putty tape should be installed. This drip molding should be fastened with 3/4 inch No. 8 hex head screws with washers. Windows and doors should be installed next, also bedded in putty tape to prevent leaks.

After the exterior is completed and weathertight, completion and installing interior equipment and trim can be done at the home craftsman's pleasure. *SEE ALSO KITCHEN DESIGN & PLANNING; PLUMBING SYSTEMS; WIRING SYSTEMS, ELECTRICAL.*

Molding & Trim

Molding and trim is the light woodwork used in the finish of a building or house around openings (doorways and windows), on walls and at the intersection of floors, ceilings and walls. It softens and ornaments square edges and right angle joints.

Molding and trim can divide rooms or surfaces into smaller areas, create interest and variety and add depth to flat surfaces. Generally molding is used for ornamentation, to conceal joints, to reduce maintenance in heavy use areas and to give a room or building a more finished appearance.

Most moldings and trims are wooden strips of various widths and thicknesses sold by the lineal foot. On their face, they are a combination of curves, convex and concave surfaces, etching or scrollwork.

Monkey Wrench

The monkey wrench was the first of the adjustable-type wrenches, but it has largely lost out to the handier and smaller adjustable wrenches. As a result, it is hard to find anything but the finest-quality, highest-priced monkey wrenches on the market, made only for plumbers. It has an advantage over other adjustable wrenches because its parallel jaws open much wider than adjustable wrenches of comparable size. *SEE ALSO HAND TOOLS.*

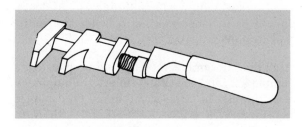

Monkey Wrench

Monolithic

Monolithic is a masonry term referring to structures made without joints. This structure is poured and cast as a single unit. *SEE ALSO CONCRETE.*

Mortar

Mortar is a mixture of cement, sand and occasionally lime. Used wet, it is a bonding ingredient for brick or stonework. *SEE ALSO CONCRETE.*

Mortar Joints
[SEE BRICK & STONE WORK.]

Mortar Mixing
[SEE BRICK & STONE WORK; CONCRETE.]

Mortar Tools
[SEE CONCRETE & MASONRY TOOLS.]

Mortgage

A mortgage is a long-term loan. To acquire a mortgage, a person uses a house, car or some other item of value as a security that the money will be repaid. If the person fails to repay the loan at a fixed rate of interest within a specified length of time, the lender can foreclose and sell the mortgaged item to defray the loss.

There are three types of mortgages: A *conventional* loan does not involve any federal agency, the *FHA mortgage* is underwritten by the Federal Housing Administration, and the *VA mortgage* is underwritten by the Veteran's Administration and is available to veterans of World War II, the Korean War and post-Korean service.

Mortise & Tenon Joint

A mortise is a depression or socket in one object which is used to house another object called the tenon. The tenon fits into the mortise resulting in a mortise and tenon joint.

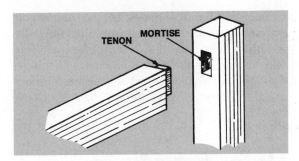

A mortise and tenon joint.

Mosaic Pebble Paving

Mosaic pebble paving is the effect produced by emplanting different sized and colored pebbles into a cement base. This craft is not exceptionally difficult and can reflect the personal tastes of the home craftsman. Any design is readily acceptable from the traditional Spanish arabesque to modern abstract designs; the ingredients are simple sand, portland cement and pebbles.

The only expense incurred with mosaic pebble paving is for the cement and the sand. The pebbles can be found at any beach, in the bed of quickrunning streams and rivers and along the graveled sides of mountain slopes.

When pebble hunting, the best types of rock for this particular project are round, oval egg-shaped and flat round to flat oval. The latter rocks will be particularly useful set on edge to achieve linear proportions. Color is significant. Black or dark stones will make good background while white and lighter stones will achieve highlights.

A project can be as big as a person's ambitions. It is suggested, however, that a novice begin with a simple border for a sidewalk or driveway, using, perhaps, a traditional frieze design. Or maybe a beginner could make an inset for a patio or barbeque area. The amount of pebbles available will certainly have direct bearing on the finished size of the project. Allow 5 to 10 percent overstock to take care of mistakes and miscalculations.

SKETCHING THE DESIGN

Once enough pebbles are obtained and some idea of the final design is determined, it is time to sketch the project. Make a shallow box the dimensions of the project and fill with sand. Once the sand is in the box, hose it down and tamp firmly. Then begin to push the stones into it to establish the design.

When the design is complete, it can be transferred to the finished project by pouring the mortar in small sections and moving the stones one at a time to keep the pattern identical.

SETTING THE PEBBLES

The way the stones are set into the cement produce the overall effect. The background is produced by putting the round and oval rocks in patterns. The flat stones are usually set on edge to form lines. A tweed effect can be achieved by placing flat rocks, edge up at 45° to 90° angles. Color here is of major concern as well as texture.

The only rule to follow in pebble design is to integrate it with the immediate surroundings. For example, French *fleur-de-lis* patterns would not be appropriate for strongly Spanish architecture.

MAKING THE CONCRETE BASE

After the design is finalized, begin the permanent construction by laying a cement base. Dig out a recess in the proper dimensions to a depth of about 9 inches (Make sure it slants slightly away from the house or other nearby structures for drainage.) Put 4 inches of porous material in the 9 inch recess and tamp until it is solid. Set up forms for the base and mix the concrete. Use the standard measure for good cement which is one unit portland cement, three units aggregate, and two units of sand. Make sure that sand and aggregate is clean. Wash it off with the hose if necessary.

Before laying the concrete mixture over the porous material, wet the drainage base so that the drainage material does not extract the moisture from the cement too quickly.

Lay the cement and level it by using a 2 x 4 dragged in a zig-zag motion over the surface. Then cover it with wet sacks or building paper to prevent over-rapid drying. In the summer this will take about two days; in winter or cooler weather allow three or four.

When the cement is dry enough to stand on but is still damp, it is ready for the mortar. Make sure that the concrete is not completely dry. If it is the mortar will not adhere well to the base. Mortar should be spread on the base in areas small enough to complete before the mortar sets up. Plan ahead and decide where a logical stopping point will be with the pattern you have selected. A break will be anywhere that a section does not overlap. If it is necessary to stop for the day before the project is complete, cover the surface with the wet sacks or the building paper.

MIXING THE MORTAR

Mortar can be purchased pre-mixed, all that needs to be added is water. But the same ingredients that are used in concrete are used in mortar; sand and portland cement. Use a ratio of 2:1; sand:cement. Add the water slowly until the desired thickness is achieved. Another alternative makes use of lime putty to retard over-rapid drying. The ratio for this formula is 3:6:1; cement:sand:lime putty.

Keep the area small when applying mortar. The consistency should be somewhat like that of sticky oatmeal. Remember, if it is too thin, the pebbles will sink to the bottom of the mortar; if it is too thick the mortar will not accept the stones. With a little practice the handyman can achieve the correct proportions.

Make the mortar at least $1/2$ - 1 inch deep. This will allow the stones to sink for better adhesion. Use damp rocks as the moisture will help strengthen the contact. Lay out only as much mortar much as can be done in one session. The surface should be kept as level as possible to avoid pools of water and ice in bad weather.

FINAL TOUCHES

Once the mosaic is complete, cover it with wet sacks or wet building paper. Let the cement and mortar cure for a week to 10 days, then finish by scrubbing with a mild solution of hydrochloric acid to remove the stains and porous lumps. Wash this solution off with the hose and a broom and the project is complete. *SEE ALSO CONCRETE.*

Motor Care & Maintenance

Many electric motor problems may be eliminated by care and maintenance. Motors do not need excessive oiling. Some types do not require oiling at all, while others require only a few drops. SAE 20 oil is used on motors of $1/6$ horsepower and more. Use a very thin oil on motors of less horsepower.

Cleaning the motor is an important part of maintenance. An air pressure hose or vacuum cleaner works well to keep dust from clogging vital motor parts. Use a soft brush on small electric motors, such as those found under phonograph turntables.

Although cleaning and light oiling increases the life span of electric motors, there are other, more complex maintenance jobs. These include replacing numerous parts and repairing or replacing electric cords. *SEE ALSO ELECTRIC MOTORS.*

Motorcycles, Minibikes & Trail Bikes

A motorcycle is a motorized bicycle. Excluding the heavy, high-horsepower "hog" or "chopper" racing machines, these motorized two-wheelers fall into these general classes: street or trail bikes, minibikes, and motorscooters. Motorcycles are used for basic transportation, for mountain and woods trail riding and for hunting and camping transportation.

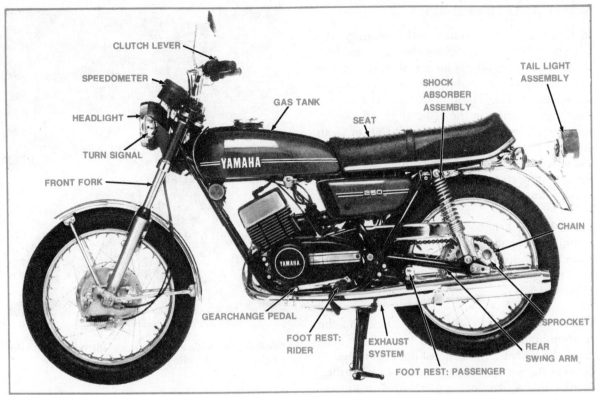

CLUTCH LEVER

SPEEDOMETER

HEADLIGHT

TURN SIGNAL

FRONT FORK

GAS TANK

SEAT

SHOCK ABSORBER ASSEMBLY

TAIL LIGHT ASSEMBLY

CHAIN

SPROCKET

REAR SWING ARM

GEARCHANGE PEDAL

FOOT REST: RIDER

EXHAUST SYSTEM

FOOT REST: PASSENGER

Courtesy of Yamaha International Corporation.

FRONT BRAKE LEVER

REAR VIEW MIRROR

TACHOMETER

FRONT BRAKE CALIPER

FRONT BRAKE DISC

HUB

RIM

SPOKE

KICK STAND

KICK STARTER

Courtesy of Yamaha International Corporation.

A typical street/trail motorcycle illustrates the standard equipment and parts of a modern cycle.

STREET AND TRAIL BIKES

In terms of sales demand and versatility, the most popular motorcycles are the street and trail bikes. The street bike is an excellent solution to the transportation problem in today's energy-conscious world. These bikes are known for their light weight (in the 150-200 pound range), relatively inexpensive price (about $300 to $500) and excellent gas mileage (an average of nearly 100 miles to the gallon). Most popular models are foreign imports, although American firms are making small machines to meet the competition.

Trail bikes are basically modified street machines. For greater power, an oversize rear sprocket is installed. Deeply lugged tires are used to provide traction in gravel, mud, sand and off-road trails.

Increased clearance between the tires and the fenders helps prevent dirt and brush from jamming the wheels. The exhaust outlet is raised to prevent drowning out the engine while fording creeks. Spark arrestors are included in the exhaust system as a safety feature on forest trails. The crank case and engine are protected from rock, stump and root damage by skid plates added to the bottom of the frame. The engine has relatively low compression to lessen the chance of overheating during prolonged or heavy use. Most trail bikes have some sort of carrier on the rear fender for gear, game or a passenger.

Courtesy of AMF Harley-Davidson Motor Company, Inc.

A trail bike provides sturdy off-road transportation for the camper or outdoor sportsman.

Courtesy of AMF Harley-Davidson Motor Company, Inc.

Minibikes provide an economical introduction to the world of motorcycling.

MINIBIKES

In addition to trail bikes, sportsmen have also been making increasing use of the second type of motorized two-wheeler: the minibike. These vehicles with their pipe frames, small, wide tires, and miserly fuel consumption provide reliable low-cost transportation for the sportsman both on and off the road.

The average minibike weighs about 125 pounds, costs about $300, and will get better than 130 miles per gallon from its 5 horsepower motor. Its small size and simple disassembly enables it to be carried in the trunk of a car, the back of a station wagon, on bumper racks or on car top racks with ease.

Several companies offer minibikes in kit form, and at a very low cost. One of these kits offers a front wheel ski for winter use.

MOTOR SCOOTERS

Motor scooters, the third type of motorized two-wheeler, are less familiar sights than street bikes on the streets of the United States. However, motor scooters in large numbers are a familiar sight to any traveler in Europe.

A motor scooter differs structurally from a street bike. It has small, wide wheels and, rather than a gas tank, a footboard in front of the driver. The scooter's engine is placed farther beneath the driver's seat to gain room for the footboard. The board enables the scooter driver to step onto his machine rather than clamber across the machine to occupy the riding position.

An average motor scooter weighs about 200 pounds, costs about $600, and will get about 100 miles to a gallon of gas. Its small size and maneuverability make it excellent city transportation.

PREVENTIVE MAINTENANCE

Whatever class of motorcycle a person may own, proper care through preventive maintenance (minor tune-ups, minor body work, regular oiling and greasing) will do much to keep it in top condition.

Proper tools make preventive maintenance easier. Some tools are sold with the cycle; others are available in optional kits designed for specific models; others are bought off the shelf from equipment companies. A well-equipped home workshop should include the following tools:

Allen wrenches, one set
Adjustable wrenches, 6, 10, 12 inch.
Impact wrench, electric or air driven
Torque Wrench
Box Wrenches, or box/ crescent combination wrenches, 12-point, 1 set
Ratchet wrench and sockets, $^3/_8''$ drive
NOTE: if foreign bike, wrenches and sockets will probably need to be metric.
Pliers, regular, needle-nose, vise-grip, snap ring
Screwdrivers, flat blade and Phillips, assorted sizes.
Timing light
Timing tester ("buzz box")

Feeler gauges, 2 sets (1 flat, 1 wire)
Electric drill, $^3/_8''$
Set of high-speed drills
Soft tip mallet or hammer
Catch pan for oil changes
Wire cutters
Files, flat, rattail, triangular
Flexstone

Additional items found in such a workshop may include touch-up paint, tubes of silicone sealant, contact cleaner, light penetrating oil and a liquid "lock-tight" fastener, to secure nuts and bolts. NOTE: Such a collection of equipment would have been gradually gathered over a period of several years, not in one afternoon's seige of tool buying. Buy only the tools needed and used.

Perhaps the most important item a home shop can have is not mentioned on the above list: the shop manual for the cycle. In order to do proper and correct maintenance on a cycle, the shop manual is a must. Despite many similarities among all cycles, each model has specific repair information and tuning specifications that general articles, such as this one, cannot provide. The shop manual for a specific model gives the specifications needed for a good maintenance program.

Despite the need for a shop manual to do an accurate servicing job, professional cycle mechanics do consider certain servicing sequences important for reliable, safe cycle performance. These sequences cover the following areas: wheels and tires, brakes, suspension, drive chain, clutch, battery, ignition, fuel system, valve adjustment, lubrication and tightening and general body maintenance.

Wheels and Tires

Inspect tires frequently for breaks and signs of unusual or excessive wear. Check air pressure often. Consider switching front tire with rear for even wear. Test wheels for loose spokes by striking each spoke gently with a wrench or screwdriver. A dull sound rather than a "ping" means tighten. Broken spokes should be replaced.

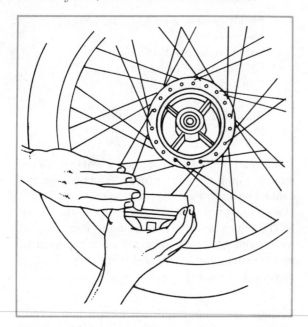

Check brake linings every 5000 miles. Remove glaze gently with emery paper.

Brakes

Normally, front brake levers and rear brake pedals shouldn't have more than $1/2''$ free travel. Adjust to the specifications in the shop manual. Pull the wheels every 7,000 miles and inspect the brake linings. If worn to the rivets (or to the drum if bonded linings), replace. If merely glazed, use emery cloth or armature paper to remove the glaze. NOTE: Don't use sandpaper to deglaze drums.

Suspension

The suspension system of a motorcycle is designed to permit the vehicle to travel under control as the wheels respond to the irregularities of the street or trail. The system must not only smooth out bumps for rider comfort, it must also keep the wheels in contact with the ground for driver control.

Periodic checks of bushings and seals on shock absorbers, swing arms and forks are an important part of preventive maintenance. Fork oil should be changed about once a month in an off-road machine, about every two months for a street machine.

To check a suspension system, push down on one end of the bike. If the bike bounces back too quickly, the shocks may be worn. If the machine depresses too easily, both springs and shocks may need attention.

Drive Chain

After a period of use, the drive chain of a motorcycle will "stretch" as metal wears away from the working surfaces. Although a drive chain must have some play in it (see shop manual for limits), a loose chain will damage both the cycle and itself with vibration, slap and whip. A loose chain may be tightened by moving the rear wheel back in its adjustment slot. Also, a link or two may be removed to shorten the chain. If the chain has stretched more than 3% of its original length, however, it should be replaced. If not, it may damage or destroy the sprockets. Chains should be inspected for cracked links often and when found, replaced. When replacement is necessary, attaching the new chain to the old while the latter is still on the cycle is an easy method of replacing a worn chain. Walk the joined chains through, and the old chain threads the new onto the sprockets. All chains, new or old, need frequent lubrication for proper operation and rust prevention.

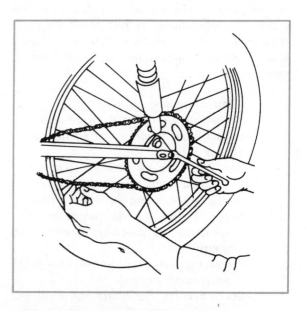

The drive chain is adjusted by a special nut on the rear fork. Chain tension should always be checked with the rider sitting on the cycle.

Clutch

Usually, a clutch adjustment is a simple task. For most cycles, the procedure is as follows: Uncover the capped port over the clutch. Inside is a lock nut with an adjusting screw in the center. Unlock the nut, turn the screw just until resistance is felt, then holding the screw in place, tighten the lock nut. Replace the port cap. Precise instructions on adjustment are found in the shop manual.

Battery

A battery that has been unused for any length of time should be checked for electrolyte level and charge. If charging is needed, use a trickle charged with an ampere-hour rating the same or less than the battery. Check all battery terminals and cables. Replace cables which have frayed or cracked insulation. Sand or wirebrush battery terminals until they are clean of corrosion. When reconnecting the battery cables, all connections must be tightly fastened.

Ignition System

A motorcycle engine, like all gasoline engines, requires a strong spark from the spark plug. Check the plug by removing it from the cylinder, reattaching the plug wire, and grounding the plug on the cylinder head. NOTE: Placing the plug on the cylinder head should provide sufficient ground, assuming a metal-to-metal contact between the plug and the head. Use the ignition to turn the engine over and look for a spark from the plug. If there is no spark, or a very weak spark, examine the plug for damage or fouled points. Also check the electrical wiring of the cycle for cracks, broken connections or frayed insulation. Check breaker points for pitting. If they need cleaning, use a flexible abrasive device. After filing, insert an ordinary business card between the points and twist until the card comes clean. Don't pull the card through the points; shreds of paper might be left to foul them.

The gap for some breaker points is precisely adjusted with a feeler gauge, while others do not have a precise setting. The shop manual will provide the needed specifications.

Timing is set by lining up the flywheel mark (sometimes labeled "F") with the stationary pointer on the crankcase. The breaker points should be just open as the marks line up. Some manuals recommend a timing light or a "buzz box" to set the points.

The timing on many cycles is set by lining up a flywheel mark with a stationary pointer.

Fuel System

Motorcycle fuel systems are usually simple — gas flows from the tank into the carburetor by gravity. The carburetor itself is sensitive, and should be checked, cleaned and adjusted regularly. Periodic checks of the cleanliness of the air filter, fuel strainer and fuel line will keep the engine supplied with the proper amounts of air and fuel. Adjust the idle setting of the carburetor to manual specifications after checking the air and fuel passages.

Valve Adjustment

Engine valves should be adjusted at least once every 1500 miles. Valve adjustments are made with the engine at Top Dead Center (TDC). On some engines, TDC is obtained when a mark on the flywheel is aligned with a mark on the crankcase (some flywheels stamp this mark "T"). The adjustments specified in the shop manual are made with a feeler gauge. On two-stroke engines, carbon deposits should be cleared from the exhaust ports.

Locks, Leaks and Lubrication

The vibration of operation, if continued long enough, could literally shake a motorcycle apart. Frequent inspection of all bolts and nuts on the machine is essential for safety and good maintenance. With the exception of the head bolts, which must be torqued to precise measurements, all other bolts and nuts should be fastened as tightly as practical. The use of a commercial adhesive on each fastener will lessen loss possibilities.

Maintain a constant inspection for oil leaks that seem more than the usual seepage. A silicone sealant will help in making most gaskets air or oil tight. Most cycle shops will be able to recommend useful sealants.

Use the shop manual to make sure that grease or oil is applied to every lubrication point. Use a hand gun only; a pressure gun could ruin seals.

Body Maintenance

Since paint protects the metal of the motorcycle against rust and corrosion, keep a constant watch for scratches or worn places. Touch them up with matching spray paint or a clear sealer.

Relatively small nicks and dents do not have to go to the shop for repair. Plastic, steel or aluminum putties can be used to fill dents. When dry, all three products can be filed, sanded and painted.

TROUBLESHOOTING YOUR ENGINE

By using a logical, orderly approach and common sense, a person should be able to discover and repair most of an engine's running problems. And even if the problem can't be fixed in the home workshop, you're still money ahead as home troubleshooting means less time in the cycle shop.

Throughout any troubleshooting, take nothing for granted, and try the easiest things first. For example, is the ignition turned on? Is there gas in the tank? Was anything done to the engine just prior to the problem? Was a part replaced? Were the points adjusted? Check the work.

An engine depends on three things to operate properly: carburetion, compression, ignition. Start troubleshooting in that order.

Disconnect the fuel line at the carburetor, holding a rag under the line. Check for water. Does the fuel run freely? If not, check for a blocked fuel line or a fouled gas tank. If the fuel flow checks out, disassemble the carburetor. Using a clean work area, lay out the parts in a logical sequence to make reassembly easier. The cycle manual is indispensable for this type work. Clean all parts with gasoline and air dry. Check each moving part for wear. Is the float needle worn, causing flooding and hard starting? (Wear is shown by a ridge around the tip.) Replace the needle, if necessary. Next, check the slide for excessive wear. Examine the idle jet (also called pilot jet). If the adjustment must be screwed all the way down for a smooth idle, it's probably worn. Replace it. If the carburetor passes inspection, reassemble and mount it back on the engine, using a new gasket.

Check compression next. Attach a compression gauge, open the throttle and kick start the engine to get a reading. One hundred pounds is usually the minimum effective reading. A low reading on a 4-stroke engine can mean bad rings, a bent or burned valve or a blown head gasket. Low compression on a 2-cycle engine indicates either possible ring or head gasket problems, or pressure loss in the crankcase. Check the seals. Next, choke the engine, turn it over, and then remove the spark plug. Is it wet? If not, there is no vacuum (check the troubleshooting program).

Troubleshooting the ignition starts at the spark plug. Unscrew it and, with the lead still connected, hold the base close to the engine head. (Be careful to insulate yourself). Kick start the engine. No spark or a weak one could mean a bad switch or a grounded wire. Check the troubleshooting program for other symptoms and remedies.

If you suspect the coil, disconnect the magneto-to-coil wire at the coil. Make a tester out of a cycle light bulb and bulb holder. Connect the wires in series between the disconnected wire and the chassis. Kick turn the engine. If the bulb lights, everything is functioning up to the coil. Try a substitute coil in the circuit and see if it solves the problem.

Check the points for foreign matter. Are they badly pitted? Replace them. Metal built up on either of the points means condenser problems. Replace it, and the points, too, if they can't be filed and cleaned.

If the points have just been replaced double check your work. Occasionally, points are installed with the spring on the wrong side of the mounting insulator grounding out the points. Recheck gap and timing, too.

If there is a CDI (capacitor discharge ignition) magneto system on the bike, a multimeter is needed to test it. This instrument is not too expensive to buy, and it's handy for tracing a variety of ignition and electrical problems. If you don't want to buy one, remove the CDI unit and have it checked at a cycle shop.

TROUBLESHOOTING PROGRAM

Engine Does Not Start or is Hard to Start:

1. Is ignition on?
2. Is there fuel in the tank?
3. Does fuel flow into the carburetor?
   If yes, continue to 4.
   If no:

Probable Cause	Repair Needed
Fuel line clogged or damaged	Clean or replace
Fuel strainer clogged	Remove and clean
Fuel tank petcock clogged	Remove and clean
Tank air vent clogged	Remove and clean
Flow stopped at float needle	Remove and clean
Float setting too high	Reset float level

4. Is there a good, hot spark at plug (at kickstarter speed?)
   If yes, continue to 5.
   If no:

Probable Cause	Repair Needed
Faulty plug under compression	Replace plug
Ignition timing off	Adjust timing correctly

If spark is weak:

Probable Cause	Repair Needed
Bad spark plug	Replace
Incorrect spark plug gap	Adjust to factory specs
Bad spark plug cap	Replace
Damaged or cracked high tension wire	Replace
Dirty contact points	Clean and adjust
Bad condenser	Replace
Bad ignition coil	Replace
Bad exciter coil in magneto	Replace
Low charge in battery	Charge to full capacity

If there is no spark:

Probable Cause	Repair Needed
Shorted or fouled spark plug	Replace
Dirty or wet contact points	Dry and clean with flexstone
Blown fuse	Replace with new one
Disconnected wire	Locate and reconnect
Bad condenser	Replace
Incorrect point gap	Adjust to correct gap
Short in the wiring harness	Repair or replace
Contact points installed wrong	Correct
Kill button shorting out	Repair or replace
Ignition coil failure	Replace
Bad ignition switch	Repair or replace
Magneto exciter coil failure	Replace
No charge in battery	Charge to full capacity
Battery will not hold charge	Replace
CDI unit failure	Replace

5. Check engine compression (at kickstarter speed and with throttle open). Does engine fail to start even though compression is sufficient?

Probable Cause	Repair Needed
No fuel entering engine because of air leak between carburetor and engine	Repair air leak
Too much fuel entering because float level is too high	Adjust float
Dirty air cleaner	Clean or replace
Carburetor slide backwards or sideways	Install correctly

Exhaust port or muffler carboned	Clean out
Crankcase seals leaking	Replace

6. Is compression insufficient?

Probable Cause	Repair Needed
Loose spark plug	Tighten
Loose head bolts	Tighten to correct torque specs
Leaking head gasket	Replace
Warped cylinder or head	Resurface or replace
Worn piston rings	Deglaze cylinder and replace rings
Rings stuck in lands on piston	Clean or replace
Incorrect tappet clearance	Adjust to manufacturer's specs
Bad valve seating	Regrind and reseat
Bent valve	Replace
Valve seized in valve guide	Replace both
Incorrect valve timing	Retime correctly
Badly worn cylinder	Rebore to next oversize
Holed or burned-away piston	Replace

Engine RPM Increases But Speed Does Not:

Probable Cause	Repair Needed
Clutch slippage	Adjust or replace clutch plates

Engine RPM Will Not Increase Smoothly:

Probable Cause	Repair Needed
Bad spark plug	Replace
Ignition timing incorrect	Adjust to correct timing
Dirty air cleaner	Clean or replace
Clogged gas cap breather	Clean
Clogged fuel line	Clean
Water in carburetor	Clean out entire fuel supply
Improperly tuned carburetor	Adjust jet correctly
Clogged exhaust pipe or muffler	Clean
Improper tappet clearance	Reset clearances
Leaking valves	Regrind and reseat

Engine Does Not Run Smoothly at Low RPM:

Probable Cause	Repair Needed
Improperly gapped spark plug	Replace
Dirty or sooty spark plug	Replace
Ignition timing advanced	Adjust to correct timing
Dirty contact points	Clean and adjust
Improper pilot air screw adjustment	Adjust
Carburetor pilot jet plugged	Clean with compressed air
Improper tappet clearances	Reset clearances
Defective or discharged battery	Replace or recharge

Engine Does Not Run Smoothly at High RPM:

Probable Cause	Repair Needed
Fouled spark plug	Replace
Improper spark plug gap	Adjust to correct gap
Pitted contact breakers	Replace
Clogged fuel line or gas tank breather	Clean
Dirty air cleaner	Clean or renew
Ignition timing retarded	Adjust to correct timing
Clogged main jet	Clean with compressed air
Choke closed	Open it
Carburetors not synchronized	Synchronize
Carburetor float level	Reset to proper level
Oversize main jet	Install correct main jet
Jet needle positioned too high	Lower clip notch in needle
Automatic advance stuck	Repair or replace
Faulty condenser	Replace
Faulty coil	Replace
Charging system not operating	Repair or replace
Bad crankcase seals (2-stroke)	Replace
Incorrect tappet clearance	Reset clearance
Weak or broken valve springs	Replace
Broken rings	Replace
Valve timing incorrect	Retime

Engine Overheats:

Probable Cause	Repair Needed
Spark plug too hot	Install colder plug
Too-lean air/fuel mixture	Adjust carburetor for richer mixture
Low-grade or stale gasoline	Change to fresh premium gasoline

Improper ignition timing	Set to correct timing
Carbon in combustion chamber	Clean out all carbon
Oil level too low	Add oil
Automatic advance sticking	Repair or replace
Brake dragging	Adjust brakes
Clutch slippage	Adjust or replace if necessary
Drive chain too tight or dry	Adjust and lubricate

Engine Stops As Though Key Were Turned Off:

Probable Cause	Repair Needed
Out of fuel	Fill
Spark plug bridged	Clean or replace
Fuse blown	Replace
Clogged fuel system	Clean
Plug wire shorted or came off	Replace
Broken or shorted contact point	Replace

Engine Stops as Though Brakes Were Applied:

Probable Cause	Repair Needed
Seized piston	Rebore and replace
Seized crankshaft	Rebuild or replace
Seized transmission gears	Replace
Seized bearings	Replace

Engine Stops Gradually:

Probable Cause	Repair Needed
Loose spark plug	Retighten
Partially clogged fuel system	Remove and clean
Blown head gasket	Replace
Loose cylinder head	Tighten securely
Bent or burnt valve	Replace
Holed piston	Replace

Motor Mounts

Motor mounts are devices for supporting and stabilizing motors. The mounts are usually bolted to the motor and a level surface, or mounting plate. This is then bolted on a foundation known as a mounting block. Motor mounts come in a variety of sizes. Examples of motor mounts are automobile motor mounts which are thick rubberized blocks, and generator motor mounts, L-shaped steel wedges attached to the bottom of the generator. *SEE ALSO ELECTRIC MOTORS; SYSTEMS, AUTOMOTIVE.*

Motors
[SEE ELECTRIC MOTORS.]

Motors, Fractional Horsepower
[SEE ELECTRIC MOTORS.]

Motor Types
[SEE ELECTRIC MOTORS.]

Mounting Blocks
[SEE MOTOR MOUNTS.]

Mounting Plate
[SEE MOTOR MOUNTS.]

Mowers, Power
[SEE LAWNMOWERS.]

Mufflers

A muffler is the device on a car which deadens the noises of the exhaust gases. Quality mufflers will be galvanized or specially treated to prevent rust and acid corrosion, and will have enough baffles to handle noise emissions from the car. A muffler too small for the vehicle can cause back pressure which could result in burned-out valves, engine power loss, excessive strain on the entire system or a plugged muffler. A plugged muffler is caused by a build up of carbon deposits from exhaust fumes. Even though this is a rare problem, it can occur, especially when the exhaust pipe is bent or dented and impeding proper expelling of fumes. A good muffler will last several years before it burns out or needs replacing. *SEE ALSO SYSTEMS, AUTOMOTIVE.*

Mulch

Mulch is a protective covering of organic material used in gardens and flower beds. The main advantage of using mulch is that the covering retards the growth of weeds and slows the evaporation of water from the soil. In addition, it stops erosion since the force of wind and rain is cushioned by the mulch before it reaches the soil. In this way, it also prevents mud from being splashed on foliage and fruits causing rot. It is particularly useful in the growing of strawberries, tomatoes, and cucumbers.

Mulch also provides good insulation. In the summer it keeps the soil cool and moist; in winter it lessens the chance of a hard freeze by raising the soil temperature. By having a layer of mulch, the need for soil cultivation is reduced also, this means there is less need for digging and hoeing around plants which might damage those with delicate, shallow root systems. Finally, when the gardener is through with the mulch, it can be plowed under to provide the soil with basic nutrients while it improves the soil structure.

Mulches have a few drawbacks which should be mentioned. If it is not readily available, it is very expensive to buy; it can be a fire hazard, especially when the mulch is of pine straw and hay; and it provides excellent housing for snakes, rodents and insects.

Anyone can get mulch from a simple compost pile that can be constructed at home. Add leaves, grass clippings, vegetable remains such as potato peels, bean and pea hulls, stems from shrubs and corn husks. Anything organic in the kitchen that is not used in food preparation can be tossed into a compost pile. Most leaves and raw vegetable material are high in carbohydrates, but low in nitrogen. Therefore, it may be advantageous to add some nitrogen-rich fertilizer to the compost before spreading it on the garden. It will also help the compost to decompose. Watering the pile at regular intervals will also help the decomposition. Shovel garden soil into the compost as well as wood ashes to achieve an adequate alkaline level.

The most important item to remember is to keep the compost pile watered. If the bin is packed more solidly around the edges than it is in the center, the moisture will be less likely to run off. It will collect in the middle and help decomposition. *SEE ALSO LAWNS & GARDENS.*

Mullion Casing

A mullion casing is a slender bar or pier that forms a division between panels or units of windows, screens or similar frames. It is generally nonstructural. *SEE ALSO MOLDING & TRIM.*

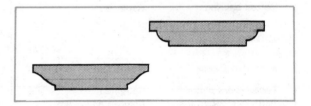

Multi-Bore Bit

The multi-bore bit is used with a power drill and comes in two types. Both are used to conceal screws and are wider at the top of the shank than at the tip. One type, however, also provides a recess for a plug to totally hide the screw. Multi-bore bits come in a variety of sizes, and the home handyman will probably want to obtain more than one. *SEE ALSO HAND TOOLS.*

Multi-Outlet Plug

The multi-outlet plug, a two-pronged plug with three or more slot faces, is used to increase the capacity of an ordinary duplex outlet receptacle. Designed for small appliances such as toasters, radios, or lamps, it increases the number of outlets on a circuit without having to install new outlet receptacles or use extension cords. Since a multi-outlet plug should not be used permanently, it is better to initiate a new circuit or replace the existing outlet with a four-way receptacle. *SEE ALSO PLUGS & CORDS.*

Multi-Outlet Wiring System

The multi-outlet system is surface wiring available in metallic or plastic channels mounted on the surface of walls for installing an additional circuit. The multi-outlet strip is made of flexible plastic and has no predetermined limit of receptacles. The wire running under the lip of each edge makes contact with prongs on the receptacle clip. Install the strip, then determine the number of receptacles needed for the area and simply clip them into the channel. This type of surface wiring is permanently connected to an existing outlet. Remove the receptacle cover and connect the wires of the strip to the terminal screws of the outlet. Lead the strip cable from the bottom of the receptacle and replace the receptacle cover.

The metallic channel, or raceway, has several advantages over other types of surface wiring. The wires are installed in a metal channel with a snap-on cover, allowing for easy adjustment and/or replacement of receptacles. Switches, outlets and fixtures may be installed into the channel itself. To install metallic raceways, the channel circuit may be directly connected to the house circuit by leading a length of BX cable

from the inside-the-wall wiring through a small hole in the wall and knockout in the channel. All of these connections are spliced and soldered. After inserting the wiring into the channel, fasten it to the wall surface with special screws and snap on the cover. Note: The desired size of the channel is determined by the number of circuits desired, as this channel ranges from one circuit to as many as four or five in one area or room. *SEE ALSO ELECTRICAL WIRING.*

Multi-Purpose Bench

Many bench ideas can be adapted from these general plans. Here we provide two variations of the same plan, one with a 1″ x 2″ top, the other with a 2″ x 2″ top. Simply remember when building long sections of benches that it is a good idea to place legs or supports about every four feet for stability and load requirements.

The overall effect of the bench or benches that you build can be varied in the type of materials used, not only in the lumber species but in the difference between rough and finish grades. Finish lumber serves well for both indoor and outdoor use. However, if the bench is used outdoors, especially to display potted or tubbed plants, the rough lumber gives a more rustic effect.

Start by cutting 9 pieces of 2 x 2, 4′ long to serve as the top. Next cut 4 pieces of 2 x 2, 15″ long for the legs. Cut 2 pieces of 2 x 2, 11³/₄″ long for the end pieces. Cut 1 piece of 2 x 2, 36³/₄″ long for the center piece, and 3 pieces of 1 x 2, 15″ long for the rails.

The legs may be assembled in one of two ways: (1) Locate and drill all holes to receive ³/₄″ dowels. Glue and dowel the center piece to the end pieces. Glue and dowel legs to end pieces. Attach rails to leg tops with long screws. (2) You may use some other method of assembly, such as nails, screws, or lag bolts. Turn the bench upside down over top pieces, space ¼″ apart, glue and nail. *SEE ALSO PROJECTS.*

Multi-Purpose Bench

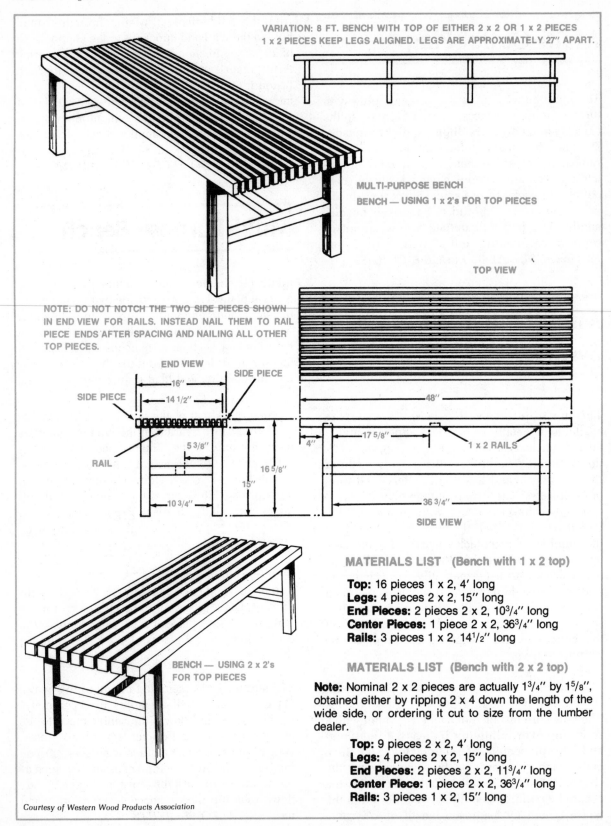

VARIATION: 8 FT. BENCH WITH TOP OF EITHER 2 x 2 OR 1 x 2 PIECES
1 x 2 PIECES KEEP LEGS ALIGNED. LEGS ARE APPROXIMATELY 27" APART.

MULTI-PURPOSE BENCH
BENCH — USING 1 x 2's FOR TOP PIECES

TOP VIEW

NOTE: DO NOT NOTCH THE TWO SIDE PIECES SHOWN IN END VIEW FOR RAILS. INSTEAD NAIL THEM TO RAIL PIECE ENDS AFTER SPACING AND NAILING ALL OTHER TOP PIECES.

END VIEW

SIDE PIECE

SIDE PIECE

16"

14 1/2"

RAIL

5 3/8"

16 5/8"

15"

10 3/4"

48"

4"

17 5/8"

1 x 2 RAILS

36 3/4"

SIDE VIEW

BENCH — USING 2 x 2's
FOR TOP PIECES

MATERIALS LIST   (Bench with 1 x 2 top)

Top: 16 pieces 1 x 2, 4' long
Legs: 4 pieces 2 x 2, 15" long
End Pieces: 2 pieces 2 x 2, $10^3/4$" long
Center Pieces: 1 piece 2 x 2, $36^3/4$" long
Rails: 3 pieces 1 x 2, $14^1/2$" long

MATERIALS LIST (Bench with 2 x 2 top)

Note: Nominal 2 x 2 pieces are actually $1^3/4$" by $1^5/8$", obtained either by ripping 2 x 4 down the length of the wide side, or ordering it cut to size from the lumber dealer.

Top: 9 pieces 2 x 2, 4' long
Legs: 4 pieces 2 x 2, 15" long
End Pieces: 2 pieces 2 x 2, $11^3/4$" long
Center Piece: 1 piece 2 x 2, $36^3/4$" long
Rails: 3 pieces 1 x 2, 15" long

Courtesy of Western Wood Products Association

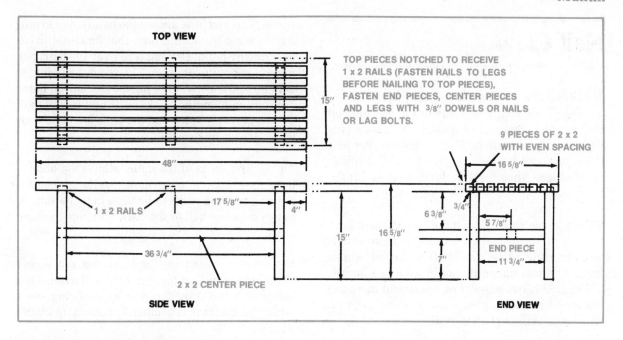

TOP VIEW

TOP PIECES NOTCHED TO RECEIVE
1 x 2 RAILS (FASTEN RAILS TO LEGS
BEFORE NAILING TO TOP PIECES),
FASTEN END PIECES, CENTER PIECES
AND LEGS WITH 3/8" DOWELS OR NAILS
OR LAG BOLTS.

9 PIECES OF 2 x 2
WITH EVEN SPACING

16 5/8"

15"

48"

1 x 2 RAILS   17 5/8"   4"   3/4"   6 3/8"

15"   16 5/8"   5 7/8"

7"   END PIECE

36 3/4"   11 3/4"

2 x 2 CENTER PIECE

SIDE VIEW   END VIEW

Multi-Zone Heating Systems

A multizone heating system is a method of controlling heat in different areas of the house with separate heating valves. Once the thermostat in a particular area is set, the valves open or close to allow a constant temperature. By using this method of heating, all rooms, even those on upper and lower levels, are kept at a comfortable temperature. *SEE ALSO HEATING SYSTEMS.*

Muntin

Muntins are vertical dividing strips between panels or vertical and horizontal bars which separate glass panes in window sashes or doors. They are made of wood or plastic and are available in different patterns, such as horizontal and diamond. When window glass could be purchased only in small sheets, muntins were applied so that small sheets could cover large openings. With the large sheets of glass available today, muntins are used mainly for decorative effects in traditional architecture. Instead of actually dividing or supporting small glass panes, muntins are overlaid on the large glass panes. Muntins can be snapped into metal grommets in the window sash and removed easily for cleaning or painting the one large pane instead of many smaller ones. *SEE ALSO MOLDING & TRIM.*

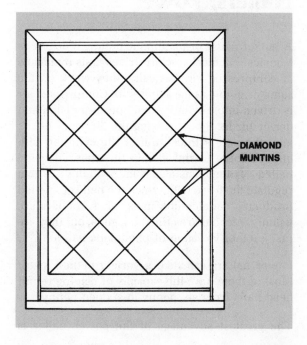

DIAMOND MUNTINS

Nail Claw

A nail claw has a sharp-edged claw at one end of a lever for driving under sunken nailheads and pulling. The claw end of these tools has varying degrees of curvature or offset which serves as a fulcrum. Use a hammer to pound the claw under the nailhead, then rock the lever back to lift the head.

Where space won't permit the use of a nail claw with an offset design, use a puller with an almost straight claw. After the nail is started, slip a block of wood under the bar to act as a fulcrum. These nail claws may be of hexagonal or round stock and have an average length of 11 to 14 inches. *SEE ALSO HAND TOOLS.*

Courtesy of The Stanley Works

Nail Claw

Nailers, Power

A power nailer or pneumatic nailing machine is a device that mechanically drives nails by means of compressed air. Basically, they work on the same principle as the staple gun. Compressed air is driven into a cylinder that houses a piston and driver blade. By depressing the "trigger" of the gun, the nail is forced out of the cylinder with enough force to sink it into the material being nailed. Nailing guns also come with devices that regulate the force with which the nail is expelled producing countersunk nails. These nailers are usually referred to as finishing guns, but they are just another variation of pneumatic nailers.

Power nailers can take a variety of nail sizes. Most of them have the capacity of driving round head nails from six penny to sixteen penny.

The greatest advantage of the power nailer is speed. The machine allows the handyman to nail five to ten nails in the time that he could drive only one by hand. Driving well over 100 nails per minute is not uncommon. The second advantage is in appearance. With a pneumatic nailer, there are seldom hammer marks surrounding the nail; the wood rarely splits and the nails are almost always driven in straight.

The compactness of the nailer allows the handyman easy access to corners, overhead beams, cramped spaces and can be used in toenailing. A handyman can nail in the dark with one of these guns.

Most nailers must be flush against the object being nailed before the nail can be driven. This safety factor keeps the gun from firing even when the machine is accidently picked up by the trigger.

The power nailer is loaded with one to three clips of nails. Most clips contain 25 to 30 nails depending on the size. One nailer holds round head 6d to 8d nails in a coil. Three hundred 6d or 250 8d nails can be loaded at one time.

These guns are rather expensive to own, but can be rented from almost any reputable rental house. Before purchasing one, it might be wise to rent a pneumatic nailer to be sure of its capabilities.

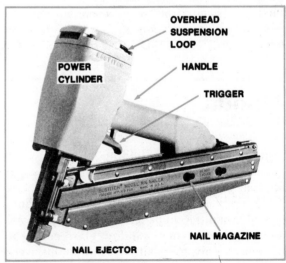

Courtesy of Bostitch, a Textron Co.

A typical power nailer.

Nail Hiding

Nail hiding, like countersinking, is a method of blind nailing. With blind nailing, no nail heads are visible on the surface of the wood. To hide nails, raise a chip of wood at the point to be nailed with a small chisel, leaving the chip attached at one end; drive a finishing, or headless, nail into the resulting hole until the nail is flush with the wood; finally, glue the chip back into place over the nail. If done properly, the nail is invisible, and the wood shows no trace of being tampered with.

A simpler method of nail hiding is called countersinking. With this method, a finishing nail is hammered almost flush with the surface. Then a nail set and hammer are used to sink the nail head flush or slightly below the wood surface. The nail heads are then covered with spackle or plastic wood to hide them, prevent rusting and to provide a smooth surface for further finishing or painting. *SEE ALSO FASTENERS.*

Nailing

Nailing is the process of driving a nail into a surface with a hammer. The hammer and nails used depend upon the job to be done; upholstery hammers and those used on construction sites differ in appearance and weight. When nailing, hold the hammer close to the end of the handle so that both the wrist and forearm actions force the nail into the wood. A nailset may be used to protect the wood from hammer scars when driving a nail flush with or slightly below a surface. When nailing close to the end of a board, predrill a hole slightly smaller than the nail shank to ease the stress on the fibers, and blunt the pointed end of the nail to avoid splitting. *SEE ALSO FASTENERS.*

Nails
[SEE FASTENERS.]

Nail Set

A nail set is a small steel punch used to start a hole for a screw or drive the head of a nail or brand below surface level. Ranging from $1/_{32}''$ to $1/_8''$, the point of the nail set should be smaller than the nail head to help eliminate surface marring. The nail should be driven close but not flush with the surface. Using the nail set, one blow should drive the nail below the surface. After the heads are sunk to a depth equal to their diameter, putty or wood filler can be used to fill the hole. *SEE ALSO HAND TOOLS.*

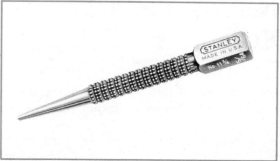

Courtesy of The Stanley Works

Nail Set

National Association of Home Builders

The National Association of Home Builders, NAHB, is primarily a lobbying organization. It acts as a liaison between the Federal Housing Administration, the Veterans Administration and the Farmers Home Administration and the home builder. The National Association of Home Builders also provides an information service dealing with laws or any other information that might effect the builder. The association publishes a weekly newsletter and one larger monthly issue, *Journal Scope,* that provides up-to-date information relevant to home builders. Benefits of belonging to this organization include educational seminars, lobbying power and updated information publications.

National Board of Fire Underwriters

The National Board of Fire Underwriters has been merged into the American Insurance Association. The phamplets and brochures produced by the board, and now by the association, provide guidelines and standards for industries, as well as insurance companies, concerning proper and adequate fire preventive measures.

National Electrical Code

The National Electrical Code, Underwriter's Laboratories, Inc. and electrical inspectors insure safe wiring methods and the use of safe equipment in the home. These safety measures are beneficial to the home craftsman whether he is engaged in wiring a house or replacing a light socket.

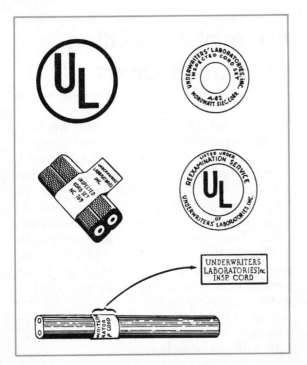

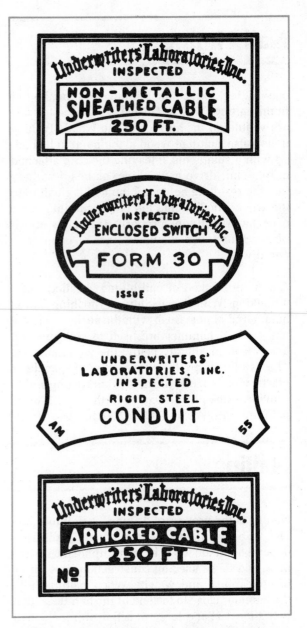

Underwriter's Laboratories Inc. places a variety of labels and tags on tested and approved products.

The National Electrical Code is a set of rules and regulations governing the acceptability of wiring devices and techniques. The code book may sometimes be called the "electrician's Bible," as no wiring job will be approved by electrical inspectors unless it follows the specifications of this Code. The standards set forth in the Code are not binding by law; i.e. they are not legislation of governments. However, most local governments provide legal enforcement of the Code through ordinances and/or state laws. Local governments often decree a supplementary Local Code to support the National Code.

Although the Code is strictly adhered to by electricians, it should not be used by the home craftsman as a manual, but as a safety guide. He should consult it to be familiar with accepted safety practices as the Code will not tell him *how* to actually perform wiring techniques.

Another assurance of safety is the label of the Underwriter's Laboratories, Inc. Supported by manufacturers, power companies and insurance companies, the Underwriter's Lab tests electrical equipment for safety and efficiency. Underwriter's approves and labels all devices that pass their qualifications and also keeps a list of all 'approved' or safe equipment. Thus, a manufacturer who would like to make his device reputable would see Underwriter's for testing and approval. One of the several different labels used by Underwriter's means that the material has met this standard according to the purpose for which it was intended. This organization does not guarantee the quality of the piece, but rather, sets a minimum standard of safety for manufacturers. For instance, two fuses might be tested, both receiving Underwriter's approval, however, one might last two weeks and the other two months. One might just barely meet the minimum standard while the other might well surpass it.

An electrical inspector is an expert who, after close examination, judges the wiring job to be safe and properly installed. Most power companies require an inspection certificate issued from a qualified inspector before they will connect any wiring job to their power source. Some local governments require that a license be bought by the person installing the wiring before work can begin. However, this is not usually necessary for the professional who is not working on his own home and who is contemplating electrical wiring as a livelihood. The home craftsman should check with Local Codes and ordinances to be sure. *SEE ALSO ELECTRICAL WIRING.*

National Fire Protection Agency

The National Fire Protection Agency was found in 1896 to advance the theory and methods of fire protection. Primarily financed by insurance companies, the remainder of the funds are derived from fees collected from members such as cities and manufacturers. The benefits of belonging to the agency include a ten volume set of preventative fire measures plus phamplets containing rules, guidelines and precautionary measures on topics such as clothing, floor and wall covering, building materials and fire extinguishers. The purpose of the National Fire Protection Agency is to provide reasonable measures to minimize loss of life and property damage due to fire.

Natural Draft

Natural draft is heated air which rises up the chimney without assistance of a blower or any mechanical device. *SEE ALSO HEATING SYSTEMS.*

Needlenose Pliers

Needlenose pliers is a thin-nosed instrument used in electrical work or delicate assembly proj-

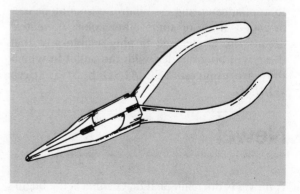

Needlenose Pliers

ects. Because of the long, thin nose, a needlenose pliers is helpful in bending and shaping wire, such as at terminals. Useful in retrieving small objects that fall into inaccessible places, some needlenose pliers have noses bent at angles to get around obstacles. This pliers is also capable of wire cutting. *SEE ALSO HAND TOOLS.*

Neutral Wire

There are two main wires to a circuit, the "hot" wire that is color-coded *black* and the "neutral" or ground wire, color-coded *white*. Regardless of the type of wiring system being installed, there will always be only two basic wire colors.

There are a few rules to remember about installing wiring that will make such installation simple and safe:

1. The wires are always connected to wires of their respective colors.

2. The terminal screws of outlet receptacles are metal-coded (i.e. brass and chrome) so that the white wire connects to the chrome screws and the black wire to the brass screws.

3. Switches do not have separate ground screws. They are grounded through the receptacle box terminal screws in which they are inserted.

4. The neutral wire must always be continuous because, should a short circuit or lightning occur, the wire will carry the electricity to the ground.

In appliance wiring the neutral wire may be color-coded green or some other color. A neutral green wire is attached to plug adapters so that these will be grounded with the outlet in which they are plugged. *SEE ALSO ELECTRICAL WIRING.*

Newel

A newel is the main post that connects the beginning of the stair railing, or balustrade, to the bot-

tom tread. It serves as a support for the bottom stairs. If there is a landing included in the stair case, a landing newel may be used. For a balustrade that ends at a wall, a half newel may be used. *SEE ALSO STAIR CONSTRUCTION.*

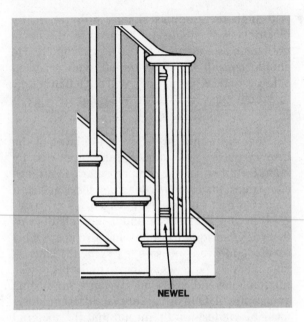

NEWEL

Night Light

A night light is a low-wattage bulb in a socket which is plugged directly into a wall outlet. It is a safety device used primarily at night to provide constant light in any room of the house. Night lights may be switch-controlled by combining them with a wall switch at the doorway or with outlets near the baseboard. These lights usually have a partial plastic covering. *SEE ALSO LIGHTS & LIGHTING.*

Nippers

Nippers are plier-shaped instruments with blunt noses. Generally used for cutting heavy wire and nails, nippers can strip insulation without damaging the wire. Nippers can also be used for twisting wire and other light-weight materials.

Special types of nippers are available, such as end-cutting nippers, which are capable of mosaic tile cutting. *SEE ALSO HAND TOOLS.*

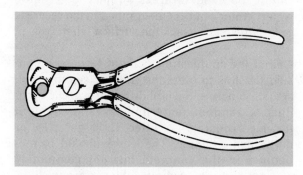

Nippers

Nipples

Nipples are short lengths of galvanized steel pipe. Available in lengths up to six feet, nipples are used to end, in a short space, a pipe system or join two galvanized steel pipes that have an opening between them. *SEE ALSO PIPE FITTINGS.*

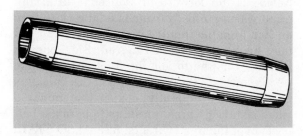

Nipples

Nominal Pipe Sizes

Nominal pipe size or stated size may be larger or smaller than the actual diameter of the pipe. Although most people size according to inside diameter, the majority of charts size pipe by the actual outside diameter. When size factor is critical, double check brands in case of variations in sizing methods. *SEE ALSO PIPE SIZES.*

Nominal Size
[SEE LUMBER.]

Nonbearing Wall

A nonbearing wall is a wall that supports only its own weight and none of the structural load. *SEE ALSO WALL & CEILING CONSTRUCTION.*

Nonglossy Varnish

A nonglossy varnish finish, rarely used anymore, is similar to semi-glossy varnish in appearance. However, nonglossy varnish has a group of solids that break up the surface disrupting the gloss giving it a cloudy finish, whereas the semi-glossy finish breaks up the surface chemically giving it a translucent film. *SEE ALSO WOOD FINISHING.*

Nonmetallic Sheathed Cable

Nonmetallic sheathed cable is a common type of cable containing two or three paper-wrapped wires encased in another layer of paper and finally enclosed in a moisture and fire resistant fabric covering. It is used in indoor permanently dry locations and known by trade names such as Romex, Cresflex, Loomwire, etc. In the National Code, nonmetallic sheathed cable is called Type NM. Another kind of nonmetallic sheathed cable is called Type NMC and is designed for wet loca-

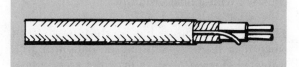

Nonmetallic Sheathed Cable, Type NM

tions and outdoors. The wire in Type NMC is imbedded in a solid sheath of plastic. *SEE ALSO WIRE SIZES & TYPES.*

Nonskid Finish

A nonskid finish is a textured concrete surface that is not slippery when wet. Sidewalks, garage floors and driveways are safer if they are *roughened* before drying. A kitchen broom will produce a more textured surface than a paint brush or push broom because of the coarser bristles. A wood float or steel trowel may be used to form swirls; light patterns are created during final troweling while heavier lines are made when the concrete is too soft for troweling.

A broom will make a simple non-skid finish.

Scoring is especially attractive on driveways and long sidewalks. This is done after smoothing the concrete with a float or darby.

The travertine finish has no definite pattern since it is made by dashing mortar on a wet, troweled surface. Smooth over the area to take down the high spots. Rock salt produces a simi-

lar effect except that after the concrete has hardened, the salt is washed away leaving a pitted surface. Neither this nor the travertine technique should be used in areas subject to freezing water. Water can become trapped in the recesses of the finish and crack the surface when frozen.

One of the simplest methods of forming a nonskid finish is to press the rim of a can into wet, smooth concrete. Several different size cans produce a random pattern. Leaves pressed in troweled concrete are effective as a border or decorative grouping. The leaves should be embedded in the concrete but not completely covered and removed after the surface is stiff.

Exposed aggregate concrete is easily produced by hosing down the surface after the concrete has begun to harden. Because the aggregate may be uneven after hosing, flat pebbles can be added to balance out the rough areas. *SEE ALSO CONCRETE.*

Nosing

Nosing is the forward or side edge of a stair tread which normally extends a little more than an inch from the tread. It is usually rounded, but may be beveled or chamfered. Side nosing, which is mitered to join the front nosing of the tread, conceals the dovetailing of the balusters and treads. Frequently, nosing is eliminated when installing carpet on stairs to permit a better fit over the tread corners. *SEE ALSO STAIR CONSTRUCTION.*

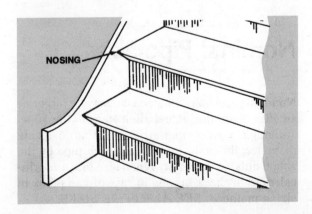

Nut Drivers

A nut driver is used in loosening and tightening nuts, in the same way that a screwdriver is used with screws. Instead of a blade, the nut driver has a socket which covers the head of the screw or nut that is being adjusted. Nut drivers are designed for woodworking, electronics and mechanics.

Because each usually fits only one size nut, nut drivers may be obtained in sets that contain seven of the most popularly used sizes from 3/16″ to 1/2″. The handles are color coded according to the head size of the nut driver. An automatically adjusting nut driver which operates by a locking mechanism of six collet chuck fingers adjusts as the user pushes down the driver. The collet fingers stay locked until the driver is pulled up after the nut has been loosened or tightened. A good automatic nut driver will have an unlimited range of adjustment, and will even lock onto bent or damaged screw and nut heads. Another adjustable type contains a nest of several hex sockets. When the driver is pushed down, the correct socket slips down to hold the nut. Another valuable extra for a nut driver is an extension handle, especially an interchangeable one that takes not only nut driver bits, but also hex and screwdriver bits. *SEE ALSO HAND TOOLS.*

Courtesy of The Stanley Works

Nut Driver

Nuts & Bolts

Next to screws and nails, nuts and bolts are the most popular forms of fasteners. Bolts are usually made of steel, are sometimes galvanized and have one of three different kinds of heads: round, hexagonal, or square. They have threads that either run the entire length of the shaft or part way leaving a smooth upper shank.

There are two types of bolts: machine and carriage. The machine bolt has to be kept from turning as the nut is tightened on the threads. A tool must be kept at both ends to prevent twisting. The ends must not be allowed to descend into the nut or the object being bolted. If the machine bolt needs to be tightened or adjusted, the end must be accessible.

A carriage bolt has a tapered shoulder that bites into the wood as the nut is being tightened. This prevents the bolt from turning as the nut is adjusted. This allows for the head to be sunk into the material being bolted.

When using a bolt, cut a circular hole slightly larger than the diameter of the bolt. Thread the bolt through and secure with the appropriate type nut.

Both machine and carriage bolts range in size 3/4 inch to 30 inches. The following chart will help you choose the size needed for any project. *SEE ALSO FASTENERS.*

BOLT SIZES AND LENGTHS

Diameter In Inches	Threads Per Inch
1 1/2	6
1 3/8	6
1 1/4	7
1 1/8	7
1	8
7/8	9
3/4	10
5/8	11
9/16	12
1/2	13
7/16	14
3/8	16
5/16	18
1/4	20

Oak

American oak is divided into two separate groups known as "white oak" and "red oak". The two groups are separated by certain technical and botanical distinctions. These are seven of the principal characteristics:

Red Oak

1. Acorns require two years to mature.
2. Bristle-tipped leaf lobes.
3. Reddish heartwood.
4. Sour, unpleasant odor of freshly cut wood.
5. Few pores in summer wood.
6. Heavily textured wood due to broad annual rings.
7. Heartwood not especially durable under conditions favoring decay.

White Oak

1. Acorns mature in one season.
2. Rounded leaf lobes.
3. Tan or brownish heartwood.
4. Distinct, but not unpleasant odor of freshly cut wood.
5. Small, numerous pores in summer wood.
6. Finely textured wood due to compact annual rings.
7. Heartwood quite durable under conditions favoring decay.

Oak is the most famous of all the hardwoods in the world, and in the United States, it is the most widely used hardwood. Because of the fine physical properties and the tasteful beauty of oak, it has made a tremendous contribution to the development of this country. It stands up well under adverse moisture conditions, planes easily, turns well and can accept most any type of finishing treatment.

Oak is widely used as a flooring material and is in much demand by the furniture industry. Under normal conditions, oak flooring will outlast the life of the building into which it is installed. Other uses include: millwork, interior finishes, boat structures, barrels and kegs. *SEE ALSO WOOD IDENTIFICATION.*

Oakum

Oakum is a loosely twisted hemp or jute fiber that is saturated with tar or a derivative of it. Easily handled because of its rope-like qualities, oakum is used to caulk seams or pack joints. *SEE ALSO PLUMBING MATERIALS.*

O. C.
[SEE ON-CENTER.]

Offset Hinges

Offset hinges are a type of fastener with one leaf wider than the other and one leaf offset. This type of hinge is generally used on cabinets with flush and lipped doors. Offset hinges are also manufactured for use on chests. They may be semiconcealed or concealed. *SEE ALSO HINGES.*

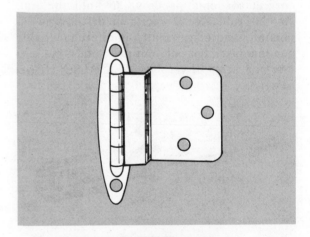

Semi-concealed Offset Hinge

Offset Screwdriver

Offset screwdrivers are designed for work in hard-to-reach areas. Its lever-type handle is usually four- to five-inches long with tips at either end running in 90° angles from the blade. The offset screwdriver may have standard tips on both ends, a standard at one end and Phillips at the other or Phillips at both ends. Though it's small in size, the offset screwdriver provides leverage for up to 10 times the turning power of a regular screwdriver. *SEE ALSO HAND TOOLS.*

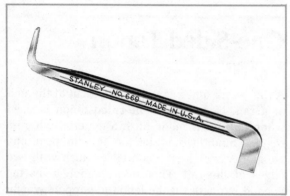

Courtesy of The Stanley Works

Offset screwdriver with standard heads.

Offset Turning

Offset turning is done on a lathe and involves working with an object that has a projection, such as a cabriole leg, which makes it off center when mounted. Offset turning is hazardous only in that clearance must be allowed for the projection and low speeds maintained to avoid excessive vibrations and possible work damage. Always mount the wood on the lathe from center-to-center, disregarding the projection. *SEE ALSO LATHE.*

Ogee Bit

The ogee bit and the Roman ogee bit are router bits which are used primarily for decorating furniture of various periods. The bit forms a type of S-shaped curve when used on the edge of a piece of stock. *SEE ALSO ROUTER.*

Oil Finish

An oil finish consists of boiled linseed oil brushed or swabbed onto the furniture surface. The oil gives wood, particularly walnut, a pleasing, natural appearance. This type of finish is applied in much the same manner as a varnish finish. The oil should be allowed time to penetrate the wood, then removed by wiping. An oil finish withstands heat rather well, although it is not very resistant to other abuses. This type of finish is easily patched by rubbing a small amount of the oil into the scratched place. *SEE ALSO WOOD FINISHING.*

Oil Paints

Oil paints have an oil base and are used in some ways like latex paints. Since latex paints have more advantages, such as being easier to apply, having a quicker drying time and a tough finish, oil paints are not as popular as the latex ones. When applied to masonry, the oil in the paint may combine with the alkali, deteriorating to make a soapy film which is not resistant to weather. This can cause flaking, peeling and chalking. There are non-chalking oil paints available to help increase resistance to alkali. Non-chalking oil paints should be applied to brick, concrete blocks, asbestos cement and stucco. Oil paints can be used for wood and metal siding, galvanized surfaces, iron surfaces, wood frame windows, steel windows, aluminum windows, shutters and other trimming and metal roofs; it can also be used for walls; a gloss enamel is best for kitchens and bathrooms. Most of these surfaces should have a primer or sealer applied before the finish coat. The durability of oil paints is about four years. *SEE ALSO PAINTS & PAINTING.*

Oils & Lubricants
[SEE LUBRICANTS.]

Oil Stain

An oil stain is one of the most frequently used stains because it is easy to apply. Usually in paste form and made from finely ground powders combined with turpentine or benzine, oil stains are applied with a rag or brush. Always wipe across and with the grain of the wood. After drying for 10 to 15 minutes, the stain is wiped off with a clean rag. A coat of shellac or varnish is applied for protection. Oil stains come in many colors and natural wood shades. *SEE ALSO WOOD FINISHING.*

Oilstone

An oilstone is a whetstone with oil rubbed on it. This stone may be used for the finish sharpening of cutting tools such as knives and axes, smoothing edges of glass and honing angles. The oil on the stone prevents small steel particles, which are ground off the tool, from stopping up the pores of the stone. Normally oilstones are artificial, but they can be made from natural stones, such as Arkansas stone or Washita stone.

To take care of a new oilstone, soak it in oil for a few days if it is not one of the oil-filled kind. The stone should be kept in a closed box covered with a plastic wrap and have a few drops of oil left on it.

Tools should be sharpened on the whole surface to keep a flat and even surface. A mixture of half machine oil and half kerosene will work well on most stones, although there is a special oil which may be purchased. Stones made from natural rock usually work better with water.

After the stone has been used, wipe the dirty oil off with a cloth. A stone that becomes glazed can have its cutting qualities restored by applying gasoline or petroleum naptha or by scrubbing it with an abrasive powder or sandpaper. *SEE ALSO TOOL SHARPENING.*

On Center

On center, abbreviated o.c., is a measure of spacing for studding, rafters and joints from the center of one member to the center of the next one.

One-Sided Tenon

A one-sided tenon is a projection cut at the end of a rail. Normally, a one-sided tenon is used when the rail is made of thin material where a regular tenon would be too thin to bear any weight. A one-sided tenon is cut flush with two edges of the rail. This side position gives the needed strength for the tenon to support weight after it is inserted into a mortise. *SEE ALSO MORTISE & TENON JOINT.*

Opaque Finishes

Opaque finishes, such as colored shellac, enamels, and colored lacquer, are used for durability and beauty in wood finishes.

The same materials found in clear finishes are also used in opaque finishes. Enamel is really varnish with added pigments. Colors are added to shellac and lacquers similarly.

Colored shellac comes in white, which can be tinted with all types of colorants, and black. It is used as a primer and sealer for wood which is to be painted or enameled. Colored shellac is best used as the first coat for large pieces of furniture.

Lacquers, used in opaque finishes, are quick-drying so that many coats may be applied to a surface within a day. Lacquers are found mostly in sprays, but are also manufactured for brushing.

The pigments in high-grade enamels provide protection as well as color. Enamels are, therefore, more durable than good varnish though their drying time is slower. These enamels are applied the same as varnish, in several coats with sanding and smoothing in between.

There are three types of enamels: glossy, semi-glossy and flat. Their durability decreases from glossy down to flat. Flat enamel is similar to regular paint and is more often used for plaster than for wood.

Open-End Wrenches

The size of an open-end wrench is determined by the size of the opening rather than by the length of the wrench. The openings on open-end wrenches are fixed rather than adjustable, and are set usually at a 15° angle so that flipping the wrench allows for the continuous turning of a nut in 30° arcs. The open end of the wrench should fit the size of the nut exactly, so that the wrench will not slip and wear away the corners of the nut. For this reason, it is a good idea to own a collection of open-end wrenches, which contain a wrench for nearly every size nut. Typical open-end wrench sets may contain six wrenches with openings from 1/4″ to 1″ or ten wrenches with openings also ranging from 1/4″ to 1″.

A flare-nut wrench is a special type of open-end wrench that is used for air conditioner, oil burner and refrigerator tubing connections. *SEE ALSO HAND TOOLS.*

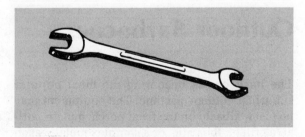

Open-End Wrench

Open Grain Wood

Open grain wood is wood with large, coarse pores close to the annual ring, such as ash, chestnut, oak or walnut. *SEE ALSO LUMBER.*

Open Riser

Open riser is a type of stair construction in which the riser members, the vertical boards between the treads, are eliminated. This type of staircase is generally constructed in basements or used for special effect purposes in a main stairway. The treads are supported by various devices such as metal brackets or dado cuts made in the stringers. *SEE ALSO STAIR CONSTRUCTION.*

Orange Shellac

Shellac is a resinous substance used as a wood filler and finisher. There are two types of shellac; orange and white. Orange shellac is the natural color of shellac; white has been bleached and appears clear.

There is much controversy among furniture makers as to the choice of shellac. Although the color of shellac does not produce great difference in the final color on the wood, most experts choose the white shellac. However, there are other experts who claim orange shellac gives wood an added glow. The best rule to follow is to apply white shellac on lighter woods such as ash, beech and maple and orange shellac on rosewood, mahogany, walnut and other dark varieties of wood.

Orange shellac thins with common alcohol and dries quickly. It is not as durable as varnish, but is pliable and does not make chalky scratches. Under normal wear, it will not flake or chip off.

Like varnish, it protects the wood and gives warmth to the grain.

Another desirable quality is the short time it takes to set up on the wood surface. After one hour the rough spots can be sanded with a fine abrasive sandpaper or no.00 steel wool. It is then ready for another coat. Finish the project with a good furniture polish and it is complete.

Orange shellac is also becoming popular in the craft of decoupage. Orange shellac, applied as the last coat to a project, gives light colored subjects an antique yellow appearance. This is particularly useful when decoupaging documents or photographs that need an antique look. *SEE ALSO WOOD FINISHES.*

Orbital Sander

Orbital sanders have a rotary motion that makes almost invisible sanding marks at an average rate of 4,600 per minute. The orbital sander is used primarily for finishing rather than removing material, and is particularly effective on miter joints and checkerboard patterns where there is more than one grain direction in the sanding area. Some orbital sanders are equipped with the additional feature of straight-line sanding. By flipping a lever, the action of the sander changes from orbital to straight or vice versa. Sandpaper is easily changed by one of several methods depending on the model. It is important that the sandpaper or abrasive cloth be secured tightly to avoid possible wood damage due to a loose fit which could knock the sander out of control. *SEE ALSO PORTABLE POWER TOOLS; STATIONARY BELT & DISC SANDER.*

Oriel Window

An oriel window is a large bay window projecting from the wall and supported on brackets or a cantilever.

Outboard Motors & Maintenance
[SEE RECREATIONAL BOATS & BOATING.]

Outboard Motor Storage

To prepare an outboard motor for postseason storage, first check to make sure that all water drain holes in the gear housing are open and that the flushing plug is removed so water will drain out. Drain the carburetor float chamber, and remove the fuel filter bowl. Clean and replace the filter element and the gasket. Disconnect the fuel line and allow the engine to run at idling speed until it stops, indicating that the carburetors are dry. Drain the fuel tank and clean it to remove any gum and varnish build-up.

Drain the gearcase and refill with the correct lubricant. Use a rust preventive around the powerhead. Disconnect and remove the spark plugs, and then place a teaspoon of light oil into the ports and crank the motor several times to lubricate the cylinders. Wipe over the entire motor with an oil-soaked cloth and store covered to keep off dust and debris. An outboard motor may be stored separately in a standing position or left attached to the boat. If the motor is left on the boat, make sure that it is tilted out of the water. *SEE ALSO RECREATIONAL BOATS & BOATING.*

Outdoor Barbecues

The barbecue is becoming the most popular suburban outdoor pastime. The equipment may be just a hibachi on the front porch, a plain portable grill on the patio, or a complex metal wagon complete with electric spit. The most desirable is the permanent structure of brick, stone or concrete block.

PLANNING THE BARBECUE

Before you install a barbecue, decide whether it should be portable or permanent. If you decide that a portable grill or hibachi is good enough for you, then location is no problem. But once you have decided to build a permanent edifice, you have to decide where you want it. If you already have a patio, the choice is usually narrowed down, as a barbecue should logically be located within close range of, preferably next to, the patio. Accessibility to the kitchen is a prime requisite for both patio and barbecue. The kitchen will remain your primary work and clean-up center, no matter how well equipped your barbecue.

Courtesy of Filon Division of Vistron

Courtesy of Superior Fireplace Company

For those who barbecue less frequently, there is a wide variety of portable units.

Courtesy of Masonite Corporation

Courtesy of Electric Char-B-Que

Even if you live in a warm area, there will be times of the year when the weather will make barbecuing, if not impossible, at least unpleasant. In northern climates, some sort of windbreak is desirable and in the south you will need protection from the sun.

Take advantage of the protections already available, like the side of the house, garage, fences or hedges. Do not consider the wind only as disadvantageous; a fresh breeze is a welcome help for fire starting. A barbecue should be faced toward gentle winds to insure a good draft. Where winds are quite strong, a side exposure may be more prudent, with some sort of windscreen provided, too. A chimney for the

The Layout of a Barbecue Unit with an Electric Spit

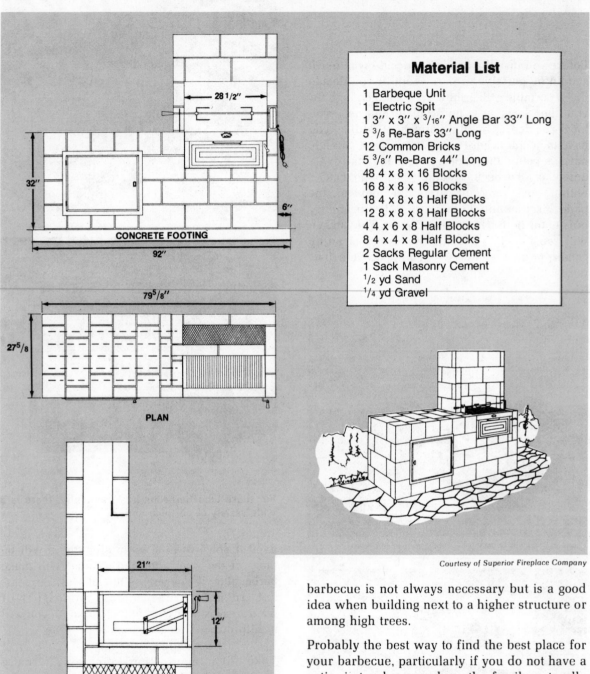

28 1/2"

32"

6"

CONCRETE FOOTING

92"

79⁵/₈"

27⁵/₈

PLAN

21"

12"

2

FILL WITH DIRT OR GRAVEL

6"

4"

40"

Material List

1 Barbeque Unit
1 Electric Spit
1 3" x 3" x ³/₁₆" Angle Bar 33" Long
5 ³/₈ Re-Bars 33" Long
12 Common Bricks
5 ³/₈" Re-Bars 44" Long
48 4 x 8 x 16 Blocks
16 8 x 8 x 16 Blocks
18 4 x 8 x 8 Half Blocks
12 8 x 8 x 8 Half Blocks
4 4 x 6 x 8 Half Blocks
8 4 x 4 x 8 Half Blocks
2 Sacks Regular Cement
1 Sack Masonry Cement
¹/₂ yd Sand
¹/₄ yd Gravel

Courtesy of Superior Fireplace Company

barbecue is not always necessary but is a good idea when building next to a higher structure or among high trees.

Probably the best way to find the best place for your barbecue, particularly if you do not have a patio, is to observe where the family naturally congregates in the backyard. Likely places for a barbecue are in close proximity to a swimming pool, a garden house, a "Florida room," gazebo or other structure. A clump of trees or shrubbery will provide shade, privacy and a natural windbreak, but beware of low-lying branches which can catch on fire.

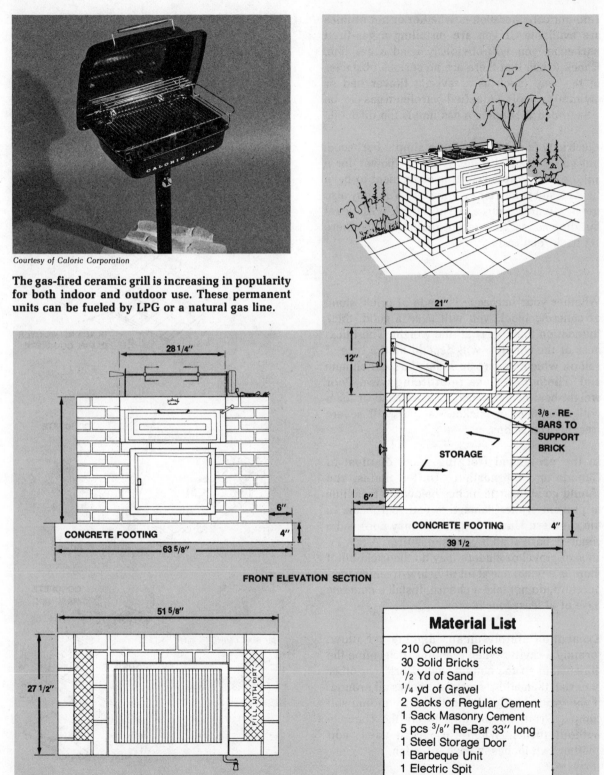

Courtesy of Caloric Corporation

The gas-fired ceramic grill is increasing in popularity for both indoor and outdoor use. These permanent units can be fueled by LPG or a natural gas line.

28 1/4"

6"

CONCRETE FOOTING   4"

63 5/8"

FRONT ELEVATION SECTION

21"

12"

3/8 - RE-BARS TO SUPPORT BRICK

STORAGE

6"

CONCRETE FOOTING   4"

39 1/2

51 5/8"

27 1/2"

FILL WITH DIRT

Material List

210 Common Bricks
30 Solid Bricks
1/2 Yd of Sand
1/4 yd of Gravel
2 Sacks of Regular Cement
1 Sack Masonry Cement
5 pcs 3/8" Re-Bar 33" long
1 Steel Storage Door
1 Barbeque Unit
1 Electric Spit

Courtesy of Superior Fireplace Company

Plans for a Gas-Fired Barbecue Unit

Another consideration is whether or not utilities are available. If you are installing a gas-fired barbecue, you will obviously need a gas line. Check to see that there are no serious obstacles in the way (such as a favorite flower bed or swimming pool). Liquefied petroleum gas can be substituted if running a gas line is too difficult.

Electricity is not a must for a simple barbecue, but you will need some source of power for a spit or other appliance. It is convenient to have light close by, too, for evening use. You may also need a water source. Also, check with local building codes. Is a permit required? Are there set-back regulations?

LAYING THE FOUNDATION

Whether your barbecue is made of brick, stone or concrete block, you will need a good, thick foundation to support all the weight. The thickness of the concrete will depend on the type of soil on which you are building, the local climate and whether you use reinforcing wire. Poor weight-bearing soils such as loose sand or loam will necessitate a thicker slab, as will severe freezing conditions.

In the prolonged freezing areas of most of Canada and the northern United States, you should go at least 16 inches below the frost line to prevent winter damage to your barbecue. In the southern United States, you may not need a concrete base at all if your soil is firm. A few inches of gravel or cinders may do the trick, but if there is any chance at all of below-freezing temperature, do not take a chance. Install a concrete base of at least four inches.

Excavation simply means digging a hollow, forming a cavity. When planning, determine the dimensions of the bottom row of brick or other material, then add at least two inches all around. If the ground is level and the surrounding soil compact, you may be able to lay the concrete without forms. When forms are used, add another two inches in each direction.

Lay out the area as described, then mark with a string. If you set the string a little above the soil line and use a line level, you can use the same

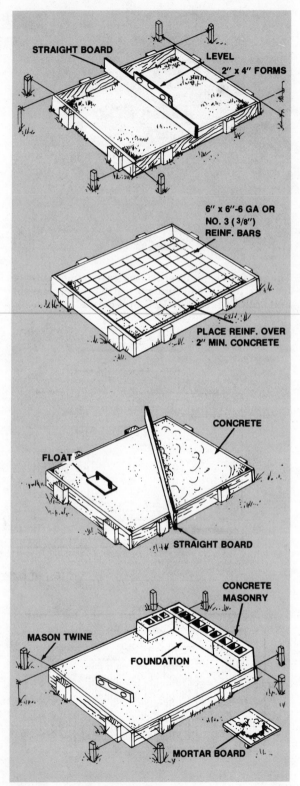

Courtesy of the Portland Cement Association

Layout for the Foundation

string to determine the correct depth of your excavation. Just add the height above the soil line to the depth of the excavation and measure down. If you want a 12-inch-deep foundation, for example, set the string two inches above the soil line and dig a 14-inch-deep hole.

When the forms are built, it helps to coat the inside with some old, heavy oil. This will facilitate removal of the wood after the foundation has cured. Check each side of the form with a level, then use a long straightedge with the level on top to check opposite walls and diagonal corners for level.

Before you pour the concrete, soak the excavation thoroughly with the garden hose and let the water stand in it for a while. When it has almost drained, start to pour the concrete. If the mix is put into a dry hole, the water from the concrete will be sucked out, causing too rapid drying and a crumbly foundation.

For smaller areas, dry ready-mixed products simplify the job greatly. (The same holds true for mortar and other cement mixes.) If you prefer to mix your own, however, the proportions are one part portland cement to three parts sand and four parts gravel.

LAYING BRICK

Use chalk to draw the outline of the barbecue two inches in from the edges of the foundation. Set dry bricks in place to check your measurements, allowing approximately 1/2 inch between each one to represent a mortar joint. If everything seems to fit, you can start bricklaying.

If you are using grates set into the mortar, be sure to put them in place while the mortar is still wet. When laying the firebed, pitch it slightly toward the front (1/4 to 3/8 inch) to allow for drainage.

When mortaring the top course of the brick, try to achieve a smooth surface without concave or beveled joints. This type of top is much easier to work on. You may want to cover the top course with a layer of concrete, ceramic tile, stone or other material, but a smooth brick finish will do

just as well. Pitch the top row slightly away from the fire so that water will drain away.

Firebrick, which is always used for indoor fireplaces, is not as necessary outdoors because there is usually plenty of air circulation out-

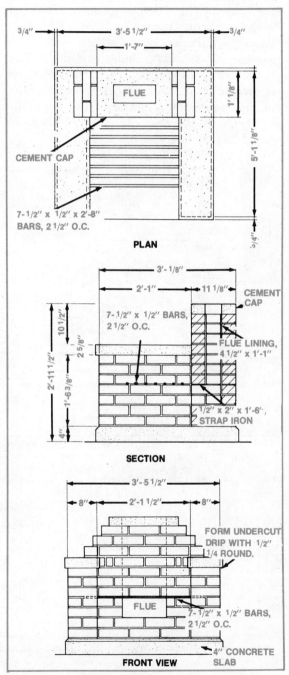

Courtesy of Superior Fireplace Company

Using a Firebrick Lining

doors, which keeps the temperature of the brick from becoming as hot as it would in an enclosed area. Furthermore, firebrick is brittle and can be damaged by cold winter weather. Hard-burned brick is a good substitute.

If you do use firebrick, lay it so that the large surface faces the fire. There is plenty of insulation using the narrow dimension. Use special fire-clay-cement mortar, or substitute fireclay for lime in your own mix. Butter firebrick lightly, allowing only $1/16$ to $1/4$ inch between bricks for better insulation. Cut firebrick more carefully, too, making shallow guide cuts on all four sides before giving the sharp final blow. Firebrick should be laid as dry as possible.

WORKING WITH STONE

Stone comes in a wide variety of sizes, shapes, colors and consistencies. Basically, there are two types of building stone: round, flinty-hard stones used in rubble masonry, and softer, stratified stones used for *ashlar* stonework. Granite, basalt and similar round stones are very difficult to work with, but they are much more resistant to erosion and extremes of temperature. Shale, sandstone and other types of wallstone are brittle and relatively easy to cut into desired shape. They cannot be used next to fire, however, because they chip, crack and sometimes explode, nor does this type of material hold up well to extreme cold.

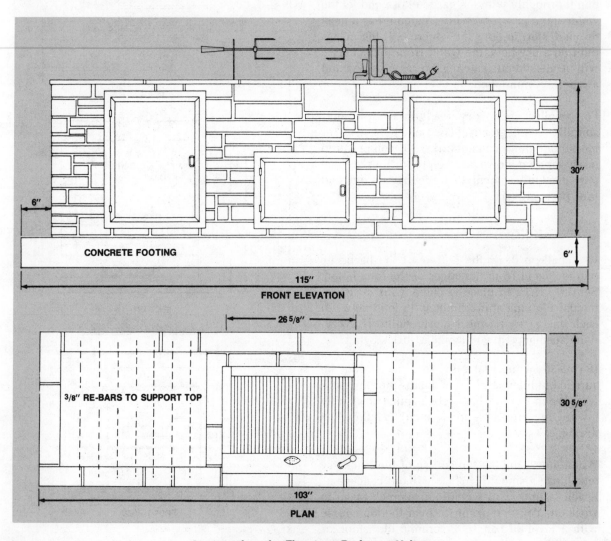

Construction of a Flagstone Barbecue Unit

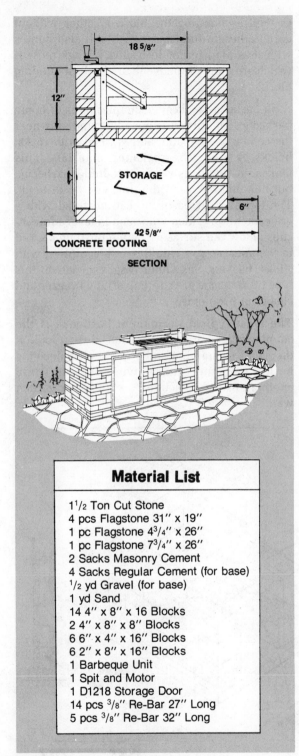

18 5/8"

12"

STORAGE

6"

42 5/8"
CONCRETE FOOTING

SECTION

Material List

1½ Ton Cut Stone
4 pcs Flagstone 31" x 19"
1 pc Flagstone 4¾" x 26"
1 pc Flagstone 7¾" x 26"
2 Sacks Masonry Cement
4 Sacks Regular Cement (for base)
½ yd Gravel (for base)
1 yd Sand
14 4" x 8" x 16 Blocks
2 4" x 8" x 8" Blocks
6 6" x 4" x 16" Blocks
6 2" x 8" x 16" Blocks
1 Barbeque Unit
1 Spit and Motor
1 D1218 Storage Door
14 pcs ⅜" Re-Bar 27" Long
5 pcs ⅜" Re-Bar 32" Long

Courtesy of Superior Fireplace Company

A round-stone fireplace can often be built with field stone found on your own property. If you have a strong back and an eye for pleasing effect,

a rubble fireplace is quicker and certainly less expensive. Working with boulders, however, is not at all simple. It is very difficult to work out an attractive pattern, and the work becomes much more difficult as you progress. One problem is that the round stones are almost impervious to water and, therefore, do not bond with mortar as well or as quickly as more porous materials. In many ways, though, a rubble barbecue is easy to build. No firebrick or other material, except for mortar, is needed. Just keep piling up the stones and mortar until you have reached the height and design that pleases you.

Using Stratified Stone

There are two basic ways to build a fireplace with stratified stone. One is to build a core of firebrick or hard-burned common brick. This is the firepit, and the stone is then laid around it. This type of barbecue can use uncut wallstone, but this method uses more stone and is therefore more expensive. Juggling the large stones into the right pattern is also a problem.

Perhaps the best way for the inexperienced stoneworker to proceed is to use much cheaper and easier-laid materials as a core, with a firebrick or hard-burned brick lining and stone veneer. A cinder or concrete block wall is laid first, with the hard-burned brick used to line the wall and floor of the firebox. Quarrycut stone is used as a veneer. This is easy to work because it is cut into pieces of uniform four inch thickness. Since you use only a thin veneer of stone, metal ties should be used to bind the stone and the block. Mortar will cover the ties.

CONCRETE BLOCK BARBECUES

Because of the hollowed-out structure, concrete block is lighter than it looks, yet it maintains most of the great strength and durability of poured concrete. Since block does not hold up well to intense heat, most block fireplaces are either lined with firebrick or hard-burned common brick or utilize a manufactured firebox. The cast-iron firebox can be used with stone or brick, too, but it is particularly well suited to block.

The principal drawback to a block barbecue is its rather unesthetic surface appearance. This

Courtesy of Westinghouse Electric Company

Rubble-stone barbecue is strong and good-looking. With outdoor lighting, it can be used at night, too.

as well as bonding the block together without using conventional mortar. Block also comes with several different decorative facings, most of which are more attractive than standard building block.

A pit barbecue makes the simplest type of home barbecue. The firepit is usually round, dug near the center of the patio, and is lined with rocks, bricks or other fire-resistant materials. This makes an inexpensive, easy-to-build barbecue, but bending down all the time can be difficult. The top of a pit barbecue can be fitted with a grate, or simply filled with sand to level a few inches below the surface. The food is then cooked in the open as you would over a campfire, with sticks, baskets, etc. Other disadvantages to this type of barbecue are shutting off the breezes and clean-out problems.

The most typical permanent barbecue is the counter-height type. But do not always look at them as free-standing individual units, since the barbecue is more attractive when built into another structure such as a retaining or garden wall.

can be minimized, however, by a *sand coat* of cement (thin, mortar-like mix), stucco or by using one of the new mortars which can be applied to the face of the block after it is set in place. This type of material acts as a finish coat

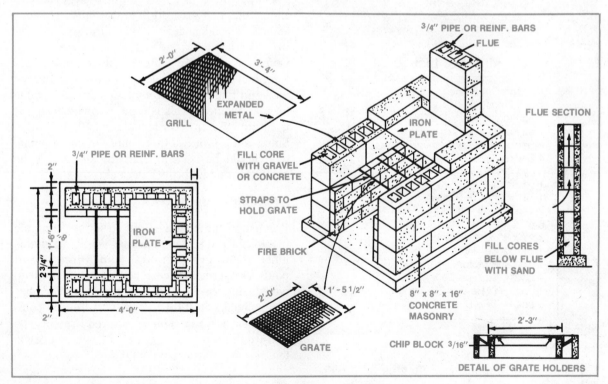

Courtesy of the Portland Cement Association

A Concrete Block Barbecue Unit

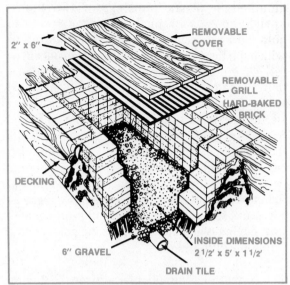

2" x 6"

REMOVABLE COVER

REMOVABLE GRILL

HARD-BAKED BRICK

DECKING

6" GRAVEL

INSIDE DIMENSIONS 2 1/2' x 5' x 1 1/2'

DRAIN TILE

Courtesy of Western Wood Products Association.

The pit barbecue is simple to construct.

Courtesy of the Portland Cement Association

Shallow fire pit is used for heat or simple barbecues like hot dogs on the end of a stick.

USING YOUR BARBECUE

One of the first things a homeowner should learn is how to build a charcoal fire. A simple device, a type of chimney, can prove of enormous help. Buy one at outdoor stores or make one yourself out of an old bottomless pail or similar tapering metal object. The secret is in getting a draft to pull the flames upward. Place the chimney so that air can enter under it and escape at the top.

An electric fire starter is convenient, as is a built-in gas firer.

Other handy accessories are some good tools such as a roasting fork, spatula, turning fork, cooking tongs, basting brush and a wire "cage" for steaks or hamburgers.

CARE AND MAINTENANCE

It is a sound practice *not* to clean the grill and other metal parts after cooking. The cooking grease is actually good protection from the elements and will help inhibit rust. The grease will burn off the next time you use it and help fan the flames. Any excess grease can be eliminated with a wire brush if it does not burn off.

If you are using brick or porous stone for your barbecue, protect it during the winter with a good masonry sealer. Apply the sealer every year or two to avoid water damage. When spring arrives, break the unit in like a new one. Wait until it dries out, then cure it slowly with a small fire kept burning for a few hours.

When using any kind of metal barbecue, portable or permanent, remember that fire gradually eats iron away. Spread foil over the surface of any metal grill using charcoal, and insulate portable grills with gravel, sand or material (but take care not to cover up air holes).

Outdoor Drainage Pipe

[SEE DRAINAGE PIPE.]

Outdoor Lighting

Weatherproof, low-voltage outdoor lighting systems are safe, economical to operate and easy to install. Spotlights and area lights around patios and along walkways can make after-dark entertaining a colorful pleasure. On the practical side, outdoor lighting makes a home more livable. Moreover, a well-lighted home is a more secure home. Burglars steer clear of homes shielded by protective outdoor lights.

1103

"Snapit" by Cable Electric Products, Inc.

Modern low-voltage outdoor lighting systems operate on only 12 volts, rather than the full 120 volts a power line delivers. This makes low-voltage lighting *safe* and allows installation to be done by the handyman rather than the skilled, but costly professional electrician. (A 120 volt outdoor system falls under regulation of the local municipal electrical code, all 120 volt outdoor componenets and wiring must be in compliance with local standards, buried well below the ground surface. Municipal electrical inspection may be required.) With 12 volt lighting systems, the restrictions are greatly eased. Power to operate the lights is furnished by a step-down transformer from the lethal power line. This means that shock hazard is virtually reduced to zero.

Another advantage of low-voltage lighting systems is they generally require fewer costly watts to operate. Each 12 volt lamp in a typical system requires only 18 watts of power. This means that six 12 volt lamps can be run for about the same price *one* 120 volt spotlight.

LAMP TYPES

Low-voltage outdoor lighting systems may use automotive-type bulbs, in tough reflectorized enclosures, or sealed-beam lamps, similar to those used in car headlights. The lamps are mounted in plastic housings of two kinds: upright spots, with push-in-ground stakes to hold the light erect, and *mushroom* fixtures, in which the light shines up against a translucent or reflective dome that sheds even, area illumination on pathways or plantings. Wall and post mounting means are also available for added flexibility in setting up a lighting scheme. Systems are sold with a certain number of lights that total a power consumption within the rated capacity of the transformer. (Generally, there is enough capacity to handle one or two additional lights and many manufacturers supply these as accessories.) All lamps feature *clip-on* connectors, having two insulation-piercing points and a screw-on fitting.

The connector is simply placed over the 2 wire, 12 volt line from the system transformer, then screwed down until the two piercing points bite into the supply wires. This simple connection method makes hookup quick when the right location for a light is found or re-location fast if effect gained on the first try is not satisfactory. There is no need to patch the tiny holes left in the cable if a connection is moved.

INSTALLING AN OUTDOOR LIGHTING SYSTEM

Most low-voltage lighting systems include a secondary supply line of 100 foot length, plus cables on each lamp of 25 foot length. This combination allows considerable flexibility in laying out the lighting system for a home.

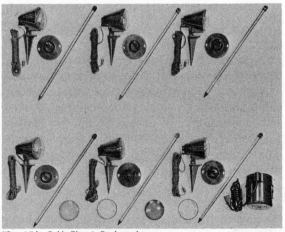

"Snapit" by Cable Electric Products, Inc.

The weatherproof transformer is usually installed in a protected location, such as a corner or behind stonework. The power cable attached to the transformer should be plugged into a nearby, weatherproof outlet. Do not use an extension cord. It can be lethal outdoors and is in violation of almost every electrical code for permanent use in an outdoor circuit. Either install, or have an electrician install, an outdoor 120 volt outlet for the low voltage lighting system.

The average household 120 volt circuit is fused at 15 amperes. This means that its capacity is 1,800 watts. To see if an existing outdoor outlet circuit will handle the lighting and other outdoor needs, add the wattages of all lights, motors, pumps, etc., which will be used *at one time,* powered by this line. If this totals more than 1,800, a separate circuit should be run from the house main panel.

Underground 120 volt wiring offers maximum safety and convenience. Wire of types USE or UF can now be used underground without enclosing in conduit or lead sheath. Either type of cable should be buried at least 12 inches deep, as protection against accidental severing by ground-breaking tools and equipment. If the electric cable cannot be buried this deep, it should be fastened with cable straps to the underside of 1″ x 4″ redwood boards. This will act as a protective covering against garden tools. Where the cable emerges from underground, it must be protected by conduit or greenfield secured to a post. In all cases, *this outlet must be grounded.* Weatherproof outlets should always

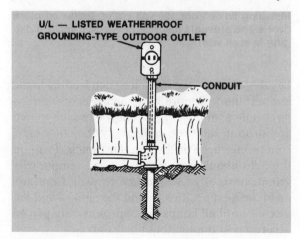

be used. They can be installed on fence posts trees or buildings. An inside switch for the system may also be desired so that power to the lighting system can be turned on from inside the home.

Alternatively, if the outlet is always *live,* a lighting system in which the transformer housing also contains a time switch (with levers that determine when the lighting system will be switched on and off) can be chosen.

PLANNING A LIGHTING SCHEME

With the system laid out so that the alternatives the available cabling affords can be seen, consider next what lighting effect you are trying to achieve. If the idea is to illuminate trees or plantings, spotlights are the logical choice. Here, the two major lighting methods, *uplighting* and *downlighting* can make your property's trees beautiful.

In an uplighting situation, one or more spots are staked in the ground below a tree and directed up into its branches. This produces an everchanging pattern of illumination and silhouetting as breezes stir the leaves, providing enjoyable viewing.

Downlighting of trees requires placement of spots in upper branches, so that the light shines down through the leaves, colorfully illuminating the ground below. Shifting patterns of color and shadows are thus projected onto the ground surface, providing an inviting, soft background for leisurely conversation or strolling.

Plantings or outside statuary can also be illuminated by colorful spots, carefully placed so that the light source is not apparent to the observer. If the color of the blooms is to be preserved and displayed, choose the color of the light cast upon the plantings with particular care. A red light will dramatically enhance the color of roses — but, the greens around it will show up a muddy brown! A green light is best for foliage, but may distort the hues of orange and red blossoms. If the objective is to enjoy the natural beauty of a garden by night choose a white or bluish-white light source to illuminate the plantings, and splash colors elsewhere.

A pool or patio can be ringed with light by using mushroom lamps providing area downlighting. The soft, diffused light shed by these lamps can be augmented by spots illuminating nearby features of interest. Try to avoid placement that subjects people within an area to the direct harsh glare of a spot. This creates a feeling of being on stage and also interferes with the comfortable conversational grouping of guests. Try to locate lighting so that reflective light falls on the area of activity.

Falling water and colorful lighting are natural partners in creating a striking exterior decor. A fountain, waterfall or reflecting pool illuminated by spots or special underwater lamps becomes a scene of beauty. Glare is a principal enemy in this case, and the placement of lights should carefully avoid lighting angles which bounce annoying reflections back at the viewer.

Lighting of a house exterior must be planned with extra care. Low key color can be added by area or walkway downlighting with mushroom lamps. Spots placed in soffits under the eaves or on nearby trees can shed soft downlight on lawn and plantings immediately forward of the house, creating a subdued reflection of color onto the house itself. Avoid spots on the lawn shining directly on the house. The harshness of this lighting treatment suggests the appearance of a model home in a new development. Try the more subtle approach of indirect illumination.

INSTALLING CABLING

The 12 volt cable leading from the transformer to the lights *can* be left on the ground surface, but it is better to bury it. This will prevent accidental trip-ups and inevitable breaks by mowers and garden tools.

A good technique for burying the cable is to use an edging tool to slice a narrow trench in the earth to a depth of three to four inches. Once the earth is incised, use the tool to lift out the divot. In a short time, a neat, inch wide trench that is easily and invisibly closed up later will result.

Lay wire into the trench, feeding toward the first light hookup position. When you are opposite the right spot, connect the lamp wire to the feeder cable. Be sure that the insulation-piercing teeth bite through each wire to assure good contact.

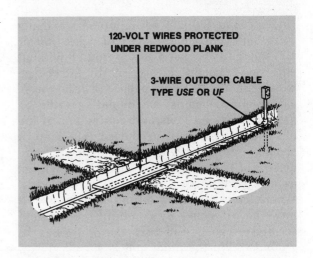

Installing an outdoor 120 volt outlet. Redwood plank over wires prevents damage or shock if you are digging in area later.

Lay the wire into the branch trench leading to the lamp. If there is more wire than is needed, dig a large hole about midway along the branch trench and drop in the excess. Feed out the other side, continuing through the branch trench. Position the light about as it should be and temporarily groundstake or secure to tree or wall. Continue on to the next position — and the next — and the next — until all lamps are approximately placed according to the lighting plan.

PLACING THE LAMPS

Spots may be affixed to short stakes if groundlevel placement is desired, or to long stakes if a light is to be located above surrounding plantings. Alternatively, the spot mounting bracket can be secured to a wall, shingle, fence or tree, using appropriate fasteners. Angle the mounted spot to create the desired lighting effect, then, tighten the wing nut to lock the light at this angle.

Mushroom lamps have attached stakes for insertion into soft earth adjoining walkways. Be sure to leave at least 18 inches clearance between the lamp dome and path edge. *SEE ALSO LIGHTS & LIGHTING.*

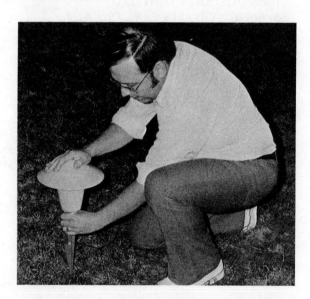

Outdoor Plumbing

Basic knowledge of outdoor plumbing may be necessary for maintaining working order in lawn fixtures or equipment used for beautification and recreation.

The outdoor faucet (or sill cock) supplies water for gardening. Also called a hose bib, this faucet is threaded for a hose attachment. It is mounted on the wooden sill of the house structure and should contain a stop-and-waste drain valve in its supply pipe connection inside. This valve shuts off water to the outside faucet and, through a vent, lets air into its crossing section of pipe for drainage. The vent's brass cap which opens it to admit air, should be attached to the outer end of the valve.

Adding an outdoor faucet can be accomplished in a few easy steps. The new pipe for it may be connected to other inside pipes by replacing their elbow fittings with T-fittings. Connections should be made available for later access without having to cut through the wall. Replacing or adding these connections sometimes requires soldering. The fittings should be of the same type as other home plumbing: copper tube or galvanized pipe.

To prevent an outdoor faucet from freezing in winter, a stop-and-waste valve must be used if the pipe leading to the faucet slants upward toward the outside wall or is level. Water will always drain out with the valve closed, the waste cap removed, and the faucet left open. If the pipe slants toward the outside, water will come out through the faucet opening while air moves in through the waste opening. If the pipe slants toward the inside, water will drain through the opened waste cap into the cellar. This cap should be replaced when draining is complete.

If the outdoor faucet has no stop-and-waste valve, a *freezeproof faucet* may be added to the outdoor plumbing fixtures next to a basement wall. This faucet, with its handle outside and the valve inside the basement, is designed to permit automatic drainage each time the faucet is shut off. This eliminates the nuisance of having to reopen an outdoor faucet on winter days.

Lawn sprinklers require an outdoor water-pipe system which should be designed for above frostline complete drainage, especially in winter-cold areas. If there is no basement into which the main pipe may lead and drain through a stop-and-waste valve, the pipe may be slanted into a small pit. At this position, the pipe may be connected to an outdoor faucet which has a stop-and-waste valve inside the house. This will allow drainage into the pit.

Lawn sprinkler systems may be installed by use of sprinkler system kits. Be sure the system is installed with a vacuum-breaker a foot or more above the highest sprinkler outlet if it is an in-the-ground type. This breaker prevents interference with the house water supply. If a permanent sprinkling system is not installed, portable sprinklers are acceptable substitutes. A lawn sprinkler can provide needed moisture in a couple of hours or less. The moving sprinkler often provides less wetness than other types. Though slow in delivery, another type, the part-circle impulse sprinkler has good results. Perforated-hose sprinklers made of plastic are good buys.

After summer, check-ups for sprinklers include the removal and cleaning of nozzle tips and inspection and replacement of worn washers. All parts should be dried; bushings and bearings oiled with water-proof grease. Cover all metal surfaces with oil also.

If a motor-driven pump is used in the sprinkling system, it should be primed for starting by pouring water into it to establish suction. Motor-driven pumps, which force water by pressure, to supply plumbing fixtures, come in different types such as the lift pump, deep-well piston pump, submersible pump and jet pump. Sometimes water is provided for sprinkling during the draining of an outdoor swimming pool by use of a centrifugal pump that may be ordered by mail.

When drawing water from a well supply, outdoor plumbing methods should not draw more water than the motor pump can supply. Drawing down the well's water level below the pump's intake system will run the pump dry, causing serious damage.

In wintertime, outdoor pump-house pumps may exert little water pressure following cold spells. This may result from a frozen copper slim tube to the pressure switch, which prevents the switch from clicking on at low pressure. Holding a small flame under this tube for a minute or so will usually thaw it and start the pump.

Pinhole leaks in plastic pump pipes or leaky valves may start a pump even when no water is being drawn. Look down into a well through its waste cap to spot leaks. New valves often take several days of usage to seal properly.

One outdoor plumbing attachment, affixed to the house, is the plumbing vent, which is a big pipe (3 inches or wider) through the roof top of the house. It prevents air-locks and blockage in the plumbing system and commonly has a collar and flange fitted around it under and above shingles. The air vent in the system may expand and contract, causing the collar to loosen. A special kind of roof-repair cement can correct this. *SEE ALSO PLUMBING SYSTEMS.*

Outdoor Wiring
[SEE OUTDOOR LIGHTING; WIRING SYSTEMS, ELECTRICAL.]

Outlet Repairs
[SEE SWITCHES & OUTLETS.]

Outlets
[SEE SWITCHES & OUTLETS.]

Outlet & Switch Boxes

Outlet and switch boxes are used in every room of the home to enclose outlets, switches, wire and cable joints and to mount light fixtures. The boxes also protect the connections between household wiring and these electrical devices and make the connections accessible inside the house.

Most switch and outlet boxes are metal, but for farm use, boxes made of bakelite or porcelain are becoming common. Outlet and switch boxes have partially loosened circles or "knockouts" in their backs and sides to admit wires and cables and built-in clamps to secure these wires and cables. Small holes in the back of the box and adjustable mounting brackets on the box permit direct fastening to house studding. Screws in-

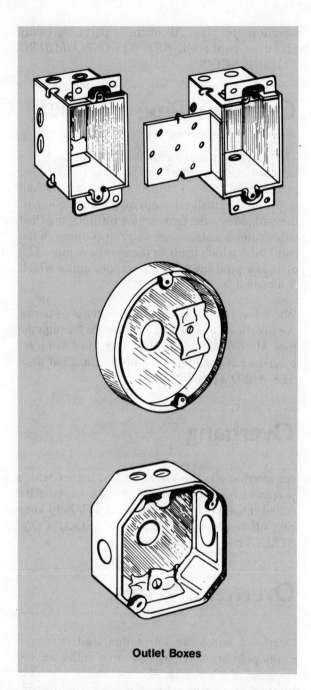

Outlet Boxes

switches and outlets are flush-mounted in a rectangular wall box. Each box holds one device, but it can be "ganged" or joined to form a larger box that can hold two or more switches or outlets. Surface-mounted rectangular wall boxes have rounded corners and covers to prevent accidents caused by sharp, exposed corners. Another type of box is square or octagonal in shape and is used to enclose wire connections, although it can be used for switches and outlets or to mount light fixtures, too. There are shallow, round boxes that fit in thin walls or act as ceiling fixture boxes. *SEE ALSO SWITCHES & OUTLETS.*

Outside Corner Molding

Outside corner molding, which is rounded in styling, provides a fully-shaped cap for the joint formed by the outside corners of a room. *SEE ALSO MOLDING & TRIM.*

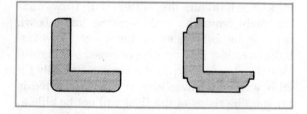

Outside Framed Walls
[SEE WALL & CEILING CONSTRUCTION.]

Outside Try Square

An outside try square is a try square or combination square used for measuring outside angles for trueness and for checking warps in boards. To test outside angles in joints for squareness with a try square place the inside edge of the square's blade perpendicular to one surface of the joint so that the same edge of the blade of the tongue is also perpendicular to the second sur-

serted in the tabs of the box hold switches, outlets, and other devices in place. Outlet and switch boxes are covered with detachable plates, since these devices and their wiring connections cannot be left exposed, and must also be within easy access.

Outlet and switch boxes can be flush- or surface-mounted in walls, ceilings and floors. Most

face, which will run at a 90° angle. When both edges of the square are perfectly even with each surface joint, the angle is square. You can use this same method in checking for warps in boards. In using the combination square for this purpose, place the long, flat end of the handle along one side of the surface, and run the blade at a 90° angle on the second surface. Any light appearing between the blade or handle and the surface will indicate where the board is warped. *SEE ALSO HAND TOOLS.*

Ovens & Stoves
[SEE RANGES & OVENS.]

Overflowing Toilet Tank

An overflowing toilet tank can be caused by one malfunction or possibly a combination of many. Normally when something goes wrong with the tank mechanism, the water will flow continuously from the tank into the toilet bowl, through the soil pipe and to the sewer. However, if the overflow pipe becomes clogged or the refill tube develops a leak, the tank will eventually fill with water and overflow. If the float valve is broken, the rising of the float will not be able to exert pressure on the valve and cut off the water. Consequently, the water will keep running and

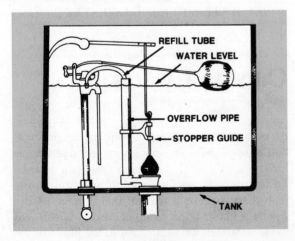

Toilet Tank

overflow the tank. All of these parts are easily fixed or replaced. *SEE ALSO PLUMBING EMERGENCIES.*

Overflow Pipe in Toilet

The overflow pipe in a toilet is located inside the tank but leads into the toilet bowl. In the flushing process, the tank is emptied and the stopper ball goes into the flush valve opening in the bottom of the tank. When the tank begins refilling, the float valve causes a stream of water to go through the refill tube which leads to the overflow pipe. The overflow pipe supports the stopper guide which is attached by a setscrew.

Water level in the toilet tank should not go above the overflow pipe. If water continues through the pipe after flushing, the float may need to be replaced or repositioned by lifting the float arm. *SEE ALSO TOILET.*

Overhang

An overhang is the lower part of a roof which projects over the exterior walls of a house. Also called the eave, a good overhang will help keep rain off house walls. *SEE ALSO ROOF CONSTRUCTION.*

Overhead Wires

Overhead wires are wires that lead from the utility pole or other power source to the service entrance of a building. This method of wiring is known as the overhead wiring technique. Although this is the quickest method of wiring, there are several disadvantages in overhead wiring.

One of the more severe disadvantages is the threat of storms. Flying debris or falling trees may knock down overhead wires causing "black-outs", or power failure, or the danger of electrocution. The wires may also be knocked down by the force of the wind which will cause the same hazards. This wiring system is also prone to cause black-outs during an "electric storm" because it provides a ground circuit for lightning.

Because of these problems with overhead wiring, modern electricians have resorted to underground wiring methods of transporting electricity from a power source to the service entrance. *SEE ALSO ELECTRICAL WIRING.*

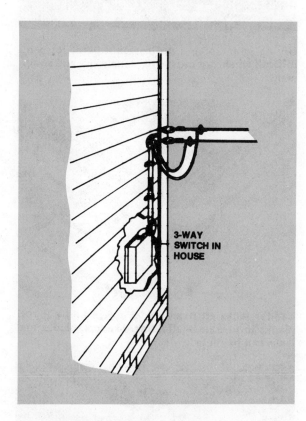

3-WAY
SWITCH IN
HOUSE

Overheating Wires

Overheating wires are often the result of an excessive amount of current flowing through a circuit, creating more friction (heat) than the wires of the circuit can tolerate. Wires are made with a specific tolerance to heat which is denoted by the wire gauge: the higher the gauge, the higher the tolerance. For instance, if a circuit and fuse are capable of carrying ten amperes of electricity but a wire of only five amperes is in the circuit, the circuit wiring will eventually overheat. Therefore, it is important to wire a circuit with the gauge of wire appropriate to the fuse protecting it. If the circuit should become overloaded by too many appliances on the same circuit, the fuse will blow, saving the wires and their insulation and preventing fires in the wall interior. *SEE ALSO ELECTRICAL WIRING.*

Overloads

Overloads in a circuit occur when the amount of electricity flowing through it exceeds the amperage capacity of the circuit. There are two types of overloads: temporary and constant. A temporary overload is caused by an electric motor, as some motors use many more amperes in starting than they do in running. A constant overload comes from the collective amperage drain of too many electrical appliances on one circuit.

To decide whether a blown fuse comes from a temporary overload, replace the fuse and turn on all but the suspected electrical appliance drawing power from the overloaded circuit. If the fuse does not blow, then a temporary overload was the problem and can be prevented by replacing the plug fuse with a time-lag fuse that has the same ampere rating. Either a time-lag fuse or a circuit breaker will allow an overload for a few seconds, allowing the motor to start without any problem.

However, if the fuse blows again, then the overload is constant. Relieve the ampere drainage by placing some of the electrical appliances that were previously on the overloaded circuit to another circuit, or by adding a new circuit to the room or workshop. To be able to decide how many appliances to remove or whether to add a circuit, compare the collective amperage of the appliances against the ampere capacity of the fuse and the gauge of the wire on the circuit. If the wire gauge will not allow replacing the blown fuse with one of higher ampere, perhaps an additional circuit is needed. *SEE ALSO ELECTRICAL WIRING.*

Padding Stain

Padding stains are those which are applied with a rag. These stains come in a powdered form and are applied by moistening the rag with diluted padding lacquer or shellac, dipping it in the stain and rubbing it over the wood. Use padding stains only for touch up work or over old finishes, and apply a coat of varnish or other material over the wood to protect it from moisture, stains and alcohol. *SEE ALSO WOOD FINISHING.*

Paint Brush Care
[SEE PAINTS & PAINTING.]

Painting Materials & Equipment
[SEE PAINTS & PAINTING.]

Painting With Rollers
[SEE PAINTS & PAINTING.]

Paints & Painting

Painting your own house is a large job, but one that is well worth the effort when you realize you can save about 75 percent of the cost of having the job done professionally. That means a $1,000 paint job will cost about $250 if you do it yourself.

To do a job of professional quality you will need to know about the right equipment and the right materials. You will also need to prepare the house properly. You can make the job easier if you have good ladders that are long enough, and if you use some type of scaffolding. Fortunately, you can rent all of this equipment, so a big investment is not necessary.

Giving your home a professional paint job isn't difficult when you use the right materials and equipment.

Ladder jacks fit over ladder rungs and support planks to make a scaffolding. Ladders, planks and jacks can be rented.

With ladders in places against the side of the house, plank is slid up the ladder to the jacks, then lifted into place.

In position on the jacks, the plank provides a convenient work platform and cuts time required to paint the house.

You can also make the work easier by dividing it into its natural segments: first preparation, then painting to prepare the house, wash it, then scrape bad areas and prime them. Caulk around windows and doors and reputty windows. Clean and paint gutter interiors.

After preparation, you are ready to paint. Begin at the top and work down. Do eaves at the top, then start on the side walls, painting the windows as you come to them. Complete one side of the house at a time.

Neatness is the mark of a good painter. Windows should be painted with no paint on the glass. There should be no paint on bushes around the house nor should there be any paint dripped on masonry adjacent to wood. A good paint job has no drips or runs because of too heavy a coat, and no thin spots because of too light a coat.

Don't attempt to hurry the job. Work at a steady, even pace. Scraping paint from places you do not want it takes a lot more time than being slower and more careful in the first place.

PAINTING WEATHER

Don't take chances with the weather when painting your house. The best days are cool, sunny ones in the spring and fall, with temperatures between 50 and 70 degrees and the next best are warm sunny ones in summer. Don't paint in the hot sun when the temperature is over 70. It is best to "follow the sun around the house," and paint those areas in the shade.

If there is a threat of rain, proceed with caution. A shower on a new coat of paint can cause problems. It is better to wait out threatening weather than to have to redo a big area. After rain, wait until the house is absolutely dry before resuming work. Oil-based paints *must* go on a dry surface. Water-based latexes can go on a damp surface, but watch for other problems such as wet grass and shrubs and wet ladder rungs which may make the job more difficult and dangerous. To be safe, paint in dry weather.

In the early spring and late fall, or whenever heavy dew is common, avoid painting late in the day. The dew may cause wrinkling of solvent-based paints and water marks on latex. Also, sudden temperature drops in the late evening may cause latex paint to fail.

HOW MANY COATS?

If you are painting new wood for the first time, three coats are recommended, because they will last longer and perform better than a two-coat job. In actual practice, however, most original paint jobs have two coats. If your new house has factory-primed siding, the factory primer can be counted as one coat.

If you are repainting your house, one coat is best. If you are painting white on white or the new color is similar to the old, one coat presents few problems. If you are painting a light color over a dark, you may need two coats to cover the old color. You may be tempted to try one heavy coat, but the result is likely to be an uneven coat and running paint. Use an even, moderate coating technique and a second coat if necessary.

Remember that you are painting to protect the wood and one good coat will do the job. If you make a thick build-up of paint through successive coatings, you may cause cracking and peeling.

HOW MUCH PAINT TO BUY?

House paints vary somewhat from brand in coverage, but on the average cover about 400 sq. ft. per gallon. *Read the label* of the brand you intend to buy and follow the coverage figures printed there.

To know how much paint to buy, find the number of square feet to be painted, and divide by the number of square feet of coverage per gallon of paint. First measure and add together the length and width of your foundation, and multiply the result by two. Find the height of the house, from the foundation to the roof, and multiply the foundation total by this height figure. The resulting number is the total square footage of the side walls of your house.

Add to this number the square footage of any other areas to be painted. If your home has considerable soffit area (eave overhang), or if you are painting the ceiling of a porch or breezeway, for example, add these square footages as well as any gable areas. To find the square footage of a gable, multiply the width by half the height. The result is approximate but useful.

Subtract from this number window and chimney areas, which you will not paint. Multiply the number of windows by the average square footage of each window. Subtract the result from the total square footage of the house. If your chimney occupies space in the side wall, multiply its width by its height, and subtract this area from the painting total.

After all this addition and subtraction, the result will be the total number of square feet to be painted. Divide this number by the coverage figure on the paint can (or by 400 if there is none on the can), and the answer is the number of gallons of paint you must buy.

HOW OFTEN TO PAINT?

Should you paint now or wait until next year? If you simply want to change colors, paint now. However, if you painted last year, it is better to live with the present color a while longer and let the existing coat weather more before putting on more paint.

The main job of paint is to protect the wood of your house, and the condition of the present coat determines when you should paint. If blistering, cracking, and peeling have exposed the wood, you should paint. If the paint is generally sound, but shows "chalking" when you rub your hand on it, reconsider before planning to paint.

Chalking is normal with most house paints. Through the action of the sun and weather, the paint slowly turns to powder on its surface. This generally is good, since rain washes off the chalk and cleans soot and other pollutants from the house. A house that is chalking normally doesn't need painting until it nearly exposes the wood. Wash the walls down with a hose and if the paint still looks good, it is not necessary to paint as yet.

Examine the house for blistering, peeling, mildew, and other problems. If you find some problem areas, but the condition is not general, repair just the affected areas. If more than a few small areas are affected, you should repaint.

PAINT PROBLEMS

If you find problem areas on your house, identify the kind of problem and take the recommended corrective action before doing the final painting.

Peeling Gutter and Downspouts

Galvanized metal is treated with an oil during manufacture. This oil must be removed or paint will not adhere. If you have new gutters, clean them thoroughly with rags soaked in mineral spirits. Change rags frequently and be sure you have cleaned all surfaces. Then paint with a rust preventive primer.

When older gutters peel, there is a good chance the fabricating oil was not properly removed in

Common gutter problem is leaking at joints, which causes rust. Stains often run onto nearby painted surfaces.

the first place. The only solution is to sand or wire brush the gutter to remove as much as possible of the old paint and paint the bare metal with rust preventive primer. Use regular house paint over the primer to finish the job.

Rusty Gutter and Downspouts

Usually the metal is rusting under its present coat of paint, and the rust is bleeding through. Most often, the problem occurs at joints. Use a wire brush to clean the area affected, getting down to bare metal if possible, and then coat with rust preventive primer.

After wire brushing of metal surface, prime all stained areas with rust-preventive paint. Leak can be treated by asphalting inside of gutter.

Blistering and peeling is most common paint problem, usually caused by moisture in the wall. Area should be scraped and sanded. Venting the wall will help prevent recurrance.

Blistering and Peeling on Walls

Moisture in the wood behind the paint is the usual cause of blistering and peeling. This moisture may come through the walls from within the house as the result of cooking, dishwashing, laundering, and steamy showers. Windows and walls near the kitchen and bathroom are most often affected, but other walls may also show signs. The moisture migrates toward the exterior and literally pushes the paint from the surface.

To correct the problem, vent the walls. You can buy small metal or plastic vents, like little louvers, at your hardware store. Buy a drill bit of the same diameter as the vents, then drill holes in the wall, and insert the vents into the holes. Usually a vent laterally every 16 inches in a problem area is sufficient. Do not vent wall areas where no peeling has taken place. If your house has lap siding, you can vent the wall by driving small venting wedges, which you can buy at the paint store, up under the siding. The wedge simply lifts the siding slightly, permitting air to circulate. Wedges are needed only where the wall shows moisture problems.

Cracks should be repaired to prevent entry of moisture. Use putty knife and vinyl spackle, which you can buy in small cans. Press spackle into crack, then scrape surface smooth. Vinyl can be painted immediately after application.

The moisture which causes the peeling may get into the wall from the outside. It can enter through uncaulked cracks, missing or deteriorated putty around window wash, deteriorated caulking around windows or doors, or a leaky roof. A trash or ice-choked gutter can force water up under roof shingles. The corrective action is to close the entry to keep the water out. Reputty your windows. Put new caulking around windows and doors. Check the wall for cracked boards, and loose nails. Look for any opening that would let water in and seal it.

One other cause of blistering could be a paint job applied too early in the spring, before all the moisture which has accumulated in the walls during the winter has thawed and evaporated. When this moisture comes through the wood as the sun warms the house, it will raise blisters in the new paint. Allow the house to "bake" in the hot sun for a month or so. Then scrape and sand the blistered areas, and repaint them. You probably won't have to repaint the entire house.

Dry Blistering

Some blistering is not caused by moisture, but by the sun. Dry blisters occur usually when you use deep colors, when you use solvent-thinned house paints or enamels, and when you paint in the hot summer sun. When the sun hits oil-based paints, especially dark colored paints, the surface of the paint dries before the solvents can escape. The vapor generated by this action raises dry blisters.

The first corrective action is to remember not to paint in the hot sun. If you do get dry blistering, scrape and sand each blister and then spot paint. As a general rule, only the blistered area itself is affected. That paint which adheres to the wood is still good.

Mildew

Especially prevalent in climates with high humidity, mildew is a fungus growth that grows on surfaces that receive little or no sunlight. Look at your north walls, and at wall areas behind shrubbery or shaded by trees. Mildew looks like smeary dirt on the wall, but actually is a growing, spreading fungus. If you paint over it, the mildew will come right through the new coat, probably stronger than before. To determine whether a black area is mildew or dirt, dab the surface lightly with household bleach. If the spot is mildew, it will quickly bleach out. If it is dirt, it will not be affected by the bleach.

Before painting, remove mildew by washing with a solution consisting of $1/3$ cup of trisodium phosphate and $1/2$ cup of household bleach in four quarts of water. Scrub the surface and let it remain wet for five minutes. Then rinse thoroughly with clean water. Use rubber gloves and goggles while applying this solution, and be sure all suspect areas are treated. If mildew isn't completely removed, the spores continue to grow. In sections of the country where mildew is a constant problem, you can hire a contractor to clean the surfaces with high pressure equipment. This is effective in killing mildew in cracks, corners and crevices, where it can hide and is difficult to remove.

If you have a mildew problem, you can buy mildew-resistant house paint to help combat it. This paint probably won't completely eliminate the problem but it can slow down the reappearance of the fungus.

Scaling or Intercoat Peeling

Look for this problem in areas not exposed to the

weather, such as under eaves or on porch ceilings. You can see the last coat peeling away from the previous coat. There are two causes for intercoat peeling. First, salt deposits form on the surface of house paints. In areas exposed to the weather, these deposits are washed away by nature. In protected areas, you must do the washing before you paint or the salts remain to interfere with bonding of the new paint.

Second, hard, glossy surfaces, such as enamel, do not allow coatings to bond thoroughly. As these surfaces expand and contract due to climatic changes, the inadequately bonded paint loosens. If you used a glossy paint on your shutters at one time and now have scaling, this is the reason.

To prevent scaling, always wash unexposed areas of the house before painting. Use a solution of trisodium phosphate (about a half a cup in a bucket of water) and scrub the area with a brush on a long handle. You can simply wash the areas with a hose, but the result is less certain. Then sand the surface to provide satisfactory bonding for the succeeding coat of paint. Latex paints have very little penetrating action. They rely on their adhesion qualities, and therefore must be applied to a sound, well-prepared surface. Sanding roughens the surface and gives them something to cling to.

Staining of Shingled Homes

If brownish stains appear on the surface of a painted home finished in cedar or redwood shingles, the problem is from moisture pushing the water soluble stain used in the wood to the surface. To correct this condition, first coat the shingles with a good oil-based primer, and allow it to dry for several days. If the staining still shows, add another coat of primer. When painting, force as much paint as possible up under the shingle courses. Be sure that the edges of all shingles, and the points where the shingles meet, are all well coated.

Checking and Cracking

Checking is a short break in the paint film. Cracking consists of long breaks. Both occur on new homes and old homes, for different reasons.

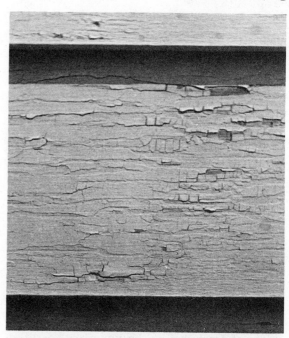

Checking, also called alligatoring, is caused by putting on second coat before first is dry, or by application of incompatible paint. This must be scraped and sanded.

On new homes, checking and cracking is often the result of raw siding being painted before it was thoroughly dry. As it dries, the fibers split with the grain, allowing water to get into the raw wood and start a peeling process. On old homes, checking and cracking are more likely to be caused by a buildup of coats of paint over the years. The thick coating loses its flexibility, and no longer expands and contracts with the wood underneath. This causes checks which then permit the entry of moisture, which in turn, lengthens the checks into cracks.

On new homes, correct the problem by scraping and sanding to remove all peeling and cracked paint and then repaint. If the wood has now dried out, there should be no repetition of the problem. On older homes, you will have to strip off all the old, brittle paint and start over. Use a chemical paint remover or an electric burner to do the job. A butane torch can be used, but must be handled with extreme care. Power sanding will do the job, too, but can be tiring if you have a large area to strip. Once you have stripped the paint, you are dealing with raw wood.

Apply a good primer coat first, and follow it with a finish coat or two.

Wrinkling of Paint

This is a problem with oil-based paints and enamels. It happens when the paint is applied in too thick a coat, and is common when a painter tries to use only one coat on an area when he really should use two. It also can occur if you paint when the temperatures are too low. The only solution is to take off the paint and start over. To prevent the problem, brush out oil-based paints thoroughly, making a good even coat that is not too thick.

Alligatoring

If you have a painted area that looks like the hide of an alligator, you have a problem caused by incompatible paints. The drying action of the top coat (usually a hard finish paint or enamel) is different from that of the undercoat (a softer, more flexible finish). The result is a separation of the top film. The solution is to sand the alligatored area until it is smooth, dust it and spot prime it. Allow the primer to completely dry before applying the finish coat.

Nail Popping and Staining

As wood dries out or flexes because of weather,

Two problems here: rust from nails bleeding through and popped nails. Prime nails with rust-preventive paint before applying final coat of house paint. Redrive popped nail and drive second nail nearby to reinforce.

the nails holding it may work their way out. These popped nails should be taken care of during the painting. One solution is to pull out the old nail and replace it with a larger one, preferably of the annular ring type, which you can buy at your hardware store. A second solution is to simply reset the old nail and drive a second one of the annular ring type next to it. Nailhead stains on paint come from non-coated steel nails which were used in construction. These rust under the paint, and the rust bleeds through. If the nail has popped, replace it with a larger one, using a zinc-coated or aluminum nail instead of non-coated steel. If it has not popped, clean the area with a wire brush, then countersink the nail $1/8$ inch below the surface. Fill the hole with caulk and spot prime the area.

WHICH PAINT TO USE?

House paints are divided into two types according to the way they are thinned: solvent-thinned paints and water-thinned paints. Solvent-thinned paints (the solvent usually is mineral spirits) are alkyd-resin base or oil-base paints. Water-thinned paints, usually called latex paints, are made of acrylic or polyvinyl acetate. You can expect good results from either solvent-thinned or water-thinned house paints when used on typical wood houses. Each has good longevity and each offers certain advantages and disadvantages.

Alkyd-based paints

These offer optimum hiding power; one-coat coverage; good adhesion to most surfaces; and a durable, glossy finish. They brush on smoothly and spread well. They are good on surfaces where there has been excessive chalking. Alkyd-based paints are good where one coat is to be used on an older home with many coats of paint. They penetrate to help bind the old paint to the surface. They require solvent for cleanup, take up to a day to dry, (depending on the weather) and must be applied to an absolutely dry surface. They may be used on a surface already painted with latex.

Latex paints

These paints are easy to apply, fast drying and they can be applied on a damp surface. They are porous, so moisture can escape from the wall, which minimizes blistering and peeling. Latex paints are easy to clean up with water and are especially good in holding color and not fading. Latex paints dry on the surface, not penetrating the wood. They do not adhere well to chalky surfaces.

You can select either type for your house. Consider these points when selecting a paint: If you have a masonry first floor, with wood siding on the second floor, ask for a chalk resistant paint for the wood surface. A chalking, self-cleaning paint will run on to the brick or stone below.

Primer or Undercoating

The primer is the first coat on new wood, so it is important. Get one from your dealer that is compatible with your finish coat, probably made by the same manufacturer. There are solvent-thinned and water-thinned primers. Solvent-thinned primers are recommended on those woods — redwood and western red cedar — that contain water soluble pigments. The primer seals the wood against moisture and protects the paint against staining.

Thickness of application is important in a primer, so follow the recommendations on the label (usually 400 sq. ft. per gallon). Solvent-based primers often are applied as basecoats for latex paints on surfaces which might not otherwise accept the latex paint. If you paint your house a deep color, the finish coat will cover better if the primer used is a gray or neutral color rather than white.

STAINS

Exterior stains are oil or synthetic color agents that contain various preservatives to beautify, penetrate and protect wood. They are available in transparent, semi-transparent and solid colors, in both the oil and latex bases. They are used on new or previously stained or painted wood surfaces, such as shingles, shakes and siding.

When using any stains, you must maintain a continuous wet edge of the work in order to avoid lap marks. When applying stain to vertical sid-

ing, start at the top of several boards, and work continuously to the bottom. On horizontal siding, start at one corner and work continuously on several boards to the opposite corner. Do not apply stain in direct sunlight nor at temperatures below 50 degrees.

Porous surfaces rapidly soak up stain, so coverage may vary from 150 to 450 square feet per gallon, depending on the product and on the condition of the surface. The surface must be clean, dry, and free of mildew, particularly when using semi-transparent stains.

As you work, pause frequently to stir the stain. When applying more than a single can, you may find a slight difference in color between cans. To minimize this problem, apply about three-quarters of the first can, then open a second can and pour half of its contents into the first. This inter-mixing "averages" the color.

Transparent coatings such as varnishes, synthetic resins and other clear films are not generally recommended for exterior use on wood products. They permit ultraviolet light to degrade the wood surface, causing loss of adhesion and cracking of the surface in less than two years. Marine or spar varnishes for exterior use can be used on doors which are adequately protected from rain or sun.

PAINTING TRIM

Trim paints are made for use on wood trim, windows, screen frames, shutters and other small areas. Solvent-thinned trim paints provide good leveling so as not to leave brush marks, dry quickly, have a good gloss and good one-coat hiding properties.

The newer latex trim enamels, available in stain-tone or gloss finishes offer these same advantages plus additional ease of cleanup when the job is finished. When painting your house, you do not have to use a trim paint unless you choose to. Regular house paint, either alkyd or latex, can be used to coat these areas.

MASONRY

Masonry, including brick, cement, stucco, cinder

block, and asbestos cement, can be painted and repainted. Masonry latex paints are made for the job, but many latex paints made for use on wood can be used, too. Check the label to make sure. Rubber-base masonry paints, solvent-thinned, are available, and are especially good for concrete floors and swimming pools because they set up a barrier against water penetration. Portland cement paints come in powder form to be mixed with water before application and become an integral part of the masonry after application.

If the surface has previously been painted, go over it carefully with a wire brush, cleaning away all chalk and loose paint. Old chalking is a serious problem in painting masonry. To eliminate the problem, you can buy special primers for use with latex when it is to be applied over old paint. You can also buy masonry paints containing fillers, which fill the rough surface and make it smooth.

PAINTING METAL

When painting any new metal item, whether it is a gutter, metal windows, or an ornamental grille or railing, remember to first remove the oil coating by wiping thoroughly with rags soaked in mineral spirits. Otherwise, any paint you apply will peel. (Be careful to dispose of rags correctly when you have finished, as they are a fire hazard).

Once you have cleaned the new metal, apply a metal primer as a first coat. You will find rust preventive and other specially formulated paints for use on metal at your paint store, in both primers and finish coats. For existing metal work which has previously been painted, use sandpaper, steel wool, and scraper to get rid of all old paint and any rust. Preparation of the surface determines how good the final job is. You can leave any paint which adheres firmly, but get rid of any cracked paint.

Aluminum objects can be painted with any house paint. Aluminum which has been exposed to the weather shows a gray discoloration, but this need not be removed before painting. It actually serves as a good base for the paint. Wipe

the surface clean with mineral spirits and then paint. New aluminum, which hasn't developed this gray surface should be treated with a metal conditioner available at paint stores. For a sound paint job on aluminum, it is best to apply a prime coat first. Any wood or metal primer compatible with your finish coat is satisfactory.

Copper, gutters and flashing, for example, doesn't need paint for protection, but is sometimes painted to protect adjoining areas from staining. If you want your copper to show its natural color, clean it with a metal polish, wipe with a solvent, and then coat with a clear exterior lacquer. This will prevent later discoloration, and also protect adjoining woodwork from staining.

FLOORS, DECKS, AND STEPS

You will find floor and deck enamel at your paint store made to take the heavy beating that comes from heavy foot traffic. The most common mistake made in applying floor paints is putting down too heavy a coat. The object, usually, is to provide a heavy surface to take wear. An excessively heavy first coat takes a long time to dry, and sometimes can remain tacky for a long period after the job is finished. The best method is to apply two or three moderate coats, allowing each coat to dry thoroughly before applying the next.

If there are worn spots in the old paint from heavy traffic, clean and prime the bare area before applying the finish coats.

PAINTING EQUIPMENT

You can make house painting much easier by using the right equipment. This includes everything from ladders and brushes to scrapers. You can buy some equipment, such as good brushes, but for big items such as extension ladders, rental is often best because they represent too big an investment for occasional use.

Ladders. For interior work, a five foot step ladder is adequate, but a six foot ladder gives you a little more reach for outside work. If yours is a single story house, you will find a straight ladder 12 or 14 feet in length is satisfactory. For two story homes, you will need an extension ladder, which should be long enough to extend from the ground to a foot or more above the edge of the roof when set in position for climbing.

You can get extension ladders with two sections which come in lengths up to 40 feet. Longer ladders are more difficult to handle on the ground, but a properly-sized ladder makes for safer, speedier work when it is in place. Most rental companies offer extension ladders in 32, 36 and 40 feet lengths.

Planks and Scaffolds. Using just one ladder when painting a large house means a lot of climbing and shifting of the ladder. You can avoid this and get the work done a lot faster by using some type of scaffolding which permits you to work over a large area before changing the setup.

Don't build your own scaffolding out of 2 x 4s unless you thoroughly understand engineering and design. Homemade scaffolds too often collapse and cause injury. You may be able to rent pipe scaffolding near your home instead.

One of the least expensive and most effective methods is the use of the ladder stage, which is made by suspending a plank between two ladders to make a work stage. The ladders are put into position, and ladder jacks are attached at the desired height by hanging each over two consecutive rungs of the ladders. Two men then take the plank up the ladder, slide it on the side rails until it reaches the jacks, and then lift it into place. If the ladders are set safely and properly (the distance from the bottom of the ladder to the wall should equal one-quarter of the ladder's height), ladder stages are safe and convenient.

Planks for ladder stages can be rented. Some are metal, or prefixed length, and others are made to telescope so the length can be adjusted. If you want to make your own plank, 12 feet is a good length.

The board should be two inches thick and (according to the safety code) 20 inches wide. To achieve this width, you can use two 2 x 10s held together with battens.

Drop Cloths. To do a neat professional job, cover the area under your work with drop cloths. Professionals use duck dropcloths, but these are heavy and expensive. You can buy lightweight, inexpensive plastic drop cloths in sizes up to 9 x 12 ft. Use these to cover shrubs, ground plantings, roof and masonry areas, sidewalks and driveways. You will have to anchor them with weights to prevent their blowing away. You can attach them to the building to cover masonry walls, window sills and so on by using masking tape.

BRUSHES AND ROLLERS

A top quality paint brush is a good investment, since it lasts a long time with care, and enables you to do superior work in less time. Brushes come with either natural (hog) or synthetic (nylon) bristles. Natural bristles are recommended for thin-bodied coatings such as varnish and shellac, but they should not be used with water-thinned paints because the bristles absorb water and become soggy. Nylon brushes should be used with water-thinned latex paints.

When buying a brush, look for quality. The bristles should feel full and somewhat spongy. A full-bristle brush holds more paint. The bristle ends should show a number of fine, branch-like splits. These split ends help the brush hold more paint and to cover the surface with fewer passes. A good brush contains bristles of four or more different lengths for good flexibility and a tapered effect.

For a neat job, use a paint shield at points where masonry joins wood.

Hold the brush up to the light and try to look through it. There should be no gaps at the tip. If what you see looks like a picket fence, then the brush probably doesn't have enough long bristles. When you press the brush gently down on a hard surface, the bristles should not fan out too much.

Types of brushes. For painting a wall, get a $3^1/_2$ or 4 inch brush. Add an angled sash brush, two inches wide, for windows, frames, and narrow surfaces. A narrow brush, 1 to $2^1/_2$ inches wide, with a chiseled edge is good for varnish or enamel applications. Finally, complete your collection with an inexpensive calcimine brush. These come in four to eight inch widths and are useful for dusting surfaces after scraping and sanding.

Brush is traditional house painting tool, but roller can speed up the job. Roller ramp suspended in 5-gal. can is convenient to use on ladder or scaffolding.

Type of Paint	Smooth Surface Plaster Wallboard Panelling	Semi-Rough Surface Sand Finish Textured Panels Cement Block	Rough Surface Cinder Block Stucco Brick Chain Fence
ROLLER SELECTION CHART			
Water-based paint	Short Nap synthetic $^1/_8''$ to $^3/_8''$	Medium nap synthetic $^3/_8''$ to $^3/_4''$	Long nap synthetic $^3/_4''$ to $1^1/_4''$
Solvent or oil base paint	Short nap synthetic or mohair $^1/_8''$ to $^3/_8''$	Medium nap synthetic $^3/_8''$ to $^3/_4''$	Long nap synthetic $^3/_4''$ to $1^1/_4''$
Lacquers	Pure mohair	Medium nap lambskin	Long nap Lambskin

Notes:
Lambwool covers not recommended for water base paints. Short nap covers recommended for glossy paints. Generally, the rougher the surface, the longer the nap.

Selecting the right roller is a matter of matching the roller fabric cover and nap length to the type of paint you use and the surface you coat. As a general rule: the rougher the surface, the longer the nap.

Trays. To use a roller, pour paint into a roller tray which forms a pool at one end. After creating the roller in this pool, you work it out lightly on the corrugated end of the tray before carrying it to the wall. New trays are now available with reservoir cans attached to the bottom. These can hold half a gallon of paint, and the roller tray can be filled by simply tilting the unit.

Pad Applicators. Pad applicators were originally designed for applying stains to striated shingles and shakes, but now a variety have been made for use with latex paints. A pad applies paint as smoothly as a brush, but does it faster. In addition, pads are made with small wheels mounted in their sides, which permit you to paint on it. These pads are useful when painting the top of the wall, where the ceiling is a different color.

Pad applicators have mohair pads, often backed

Rollers. Paint rollers make quick work of coating large, flat areas, and can be used for both inside and outside work. One effective method of painting a house is to use a roller to apply paint to a section of wall, and then follow up by brushing the section with long, sweeping strokes. This insures solid coverage.

by foam rubber. The pad is coated in the roller tray in the same manner as the roller, and should be used with a backward and forward or up and down motion, followed by strokes across the area painted.

Care and Cleaning

Brushes, rollers and other painting equipment represent a moderate investment and it should be protected. Most such equipment is intended for long use, but some homeowners tend to think of it as only for the job at hand. You can save money by buying good equipment at the outset and then caring for it properly. A major part of this care consists of proper cleaning after use.

Cleaning a brush. You clean a brush used in a solvent-thinned paint in the same way you clean a brush used in water-thinned paint — by wash-

Turn brush upward and work all paint out of the heel. Neglect of this part of washing is common mistake.

ing it. The difference is that one is washed in solvent and the other is washed in water.

First, soak the brush in water or solvent for a few minutes. The best cleaner for a solvent-thinned paint is mineral spirits. Next work the bristles against the side of the container, or pick the brush up in your hands and work the paint out. Turn the brush upright and work to get out all paint lodged in the upper bristles near the heel. Failure to do this will ruin a good brush. Use a wire brush to scrape any hardened paint from the heel and the handle.

When all paint has been squeezed out, spin the brush between the palms of your hands to remove the excess moisture. If the brush was cleaned in mineral spirits, wash it in detergent and water before spinning. Now shape the brush with your fingers, putting it back into its original tapered shape.

Shape the brush with your fingers, tapering it and flattening it. Brush should end up "chisel" shaped.

Finally, wrap the brush for storage. Many brushes come in shaped cardboard protectors. Save this for storage purposes. Otherwise, make a wrapper from heavy paper, folding it so the brush is both tapered and flat. If the brush is to be stored for a number of months, saturate with linseed oil.

Cleaning a roller. Begin roller cleaning by scraping all excess paint from the roller with a roller cleaning tool. Then remove the cover from the roller and wash it in the proper solvent, water or mineral spirits, depending on the paint that was used.

When all the paint has been removed, wash the cover in warm soap and water. Put the cover back on the roller for a few minutes to spin out any excess moisture, and then stand it on one end to dry. This prevents the formation of flat spots on the nap. Finally, wrap the cover in aluminum foil for storage.

If a cover hasn't been thoroughly cleaned, the fabric will become still after drying. It is better to use covers in this condition, as they may not give good even coverage.

To clean a roller, first use roller painting tool to squeeze excess paint out. Tool can be bought in any paint store.

Using inexpensive dish mop, spread asphalt along bottom and sides of gutter. Be sure gutter joints are well covered. Throw mop away when job is done.

Slip roller cover off of roller and wash in bucket of water. Work roller nap thoroughly with your fingers to get all paint out.

Painting Gutters

The exterior of gutters should be checked for rust or peeling paint. Wire brush rusted areas and loose paint, then prime the scraped area with rust preventive paint. Use regular house paint as a finish coat. It is a good idea to paint the inside of the gutters as well, using either a rust preventive paint or asphalt varnish. Clean the inside completely and allow it to dry before painting. Apply asphalt varnish by pouring puddles of it every few feet the length of the gutter. Then spread it to the bottom and sides with a dish mop making sure that the joints are well coated as you work. Discard the dish mop when you have finished.

EXTERIOR PAINTING

Exterior painting begins by preparing the surface. Spend plenty of time at this, because the more thorough you are in getting the house ready for paint, the better the new paint job will serve you.

Begin by locating all problem areas, where there has been blistering, cracking, checking or rust. Try to determine the cause of each problem and take any corrective action at this time. Scrape any bad areas, sand them smooth, and give them a spot priming. If there is any paint to be removed, do it now and then prime the area.

Check your windows and reputty those that need it. Scrape out the old dried putty first. Form new putty in a ball in one hand and, with the putty knife in the other hand, work new putty onto the window along one side. Now draw the knife along this putty at an angle, forming the final triangular bead by touching the glass as you go. Carefully lift one end of the excess putty on the glass and, with your fingertip, roll it up. You can roll all of the excess putty off the glass quickly in this manner, leaving a neat straight edge.

Check your walls for popped nails, cracked boards and areas that need caulking. Scrape out any old, dried caulk that has been separated from the wood, and recaulk the area, using a caulking gun. Check the gutters for rust, and nearby wood for rust stains.

Washing the house. Every house should be washed before it is painted. On exposed side walls, wash with a hose to clean off chalking and any accumulated air pollutants. Make sure you wash areas not exposed to the weather such as soffits and porch ceilings, also. Wash these areas with a solution of trisodium phosphate (half a cup in a gallon of water), using a long-handled brush, to clean off salts which have accumulated on the paint surface. If you do not do this, you can expect peeling of the new paint later on.

If there is any evidence of mildew on the house, wash it with a mixture of water, trisodium phosphate and household bleach. This fungus must be destroyed completely or it will come through the new coat. Rinse off all areas which have been washed with cleaning solutions and permit them to dry before you begin painting.

Caulk all places where moisture may enter since moisture will cause paint failure later. Pay special attention to windows and doors.

START AT THE TOP AND WORK DOWN

Begin painting at the top of the house and work down. Start with the peak, cornice and overhang and then begin on the side wall. When you paint clapboard siding, paint the undersurface of the lap first, then the face of the board. Paint just as far as you can comfortably reach from the lad-der, if you are using a single ladder. It is dangerous to attempt to lean or reach beyond a comfortable arm's length. You may cause the ladder to slip or tilt.

Paint four or five boards in this manner, then move your ladder to a point about four feet beyond the coated area, and continue painting across the house in the same manner. Don't paint from the top to the bottom of the house, as this may leave lap marks. If you are right-handed, begin painting at the right side of the house; left-handed, left side.

If you are using a brush, use long smooth strokes. Alkyd-based and oil paints should be brushed back and forth several times for a well-spread coat. If paint gathers along the edge of the clapboard, the paint is being applied too heavily.

Do not brush latex paint out as much as alykyd or oil. Use the same long, smooth strokes, however, excessive brushing cuts the film of this fast drying paint, causing brushmarks. Apply the paint generously, then give it one or two back and forth strokes and leave it alone. If you apply latex paint with a roller and then brush it out, the same rule applies: one or two long sweeping strokes of the brush to secure a good cover, then stop.

Dip your brush about $1/_3$ the length of the bristles into the paint and tap it lightly against the inside of the can. Do not pull the bristles across the lip of the cap because this robs the brush of half of its carrying capacity.

When painting with a color, use $3/_4$ of a gallon, then open a new can. Stir, then pour half of this paint into the old bucket. This assures no perpectible change of color as you paint.

Painting windows. Paint the windows as you come to them. Paint the mullions and sash first, then the frame using an angular sash brush. If you mask the glass with masking tape, allow a slight margin between the tape and the wood of the window so that the paint can contact the glass. If you do not mask, go back later with a razor blade scraper and clean the excess paint from the glass.

Apply pressure to the head of the scraper with one hand while you push with the other. For a smooth job, sand edges of paint which remains on wall.

INTERIOR PAINTING

The advent of the roller and water-thinned-latex paints have revolutionized interior painting. Application is simple, there is no heavy paint odor, and the cleaning is easy with water. It is actually possible to paint a room during the day and entertain in it that evening.

You can divide the work of painting a room into four parts: getting the room ready; painting the ceiling; painting the walls; and painting the trim. Once the room is ready, begin by painting the ceiling, followed by the walls, and then the trim. Use inexpensive lightweight plastic drop cloths to cover the floor and any furniture you cannot move out of the room. Rollers tend to splatter slightly, especially if you roll fast, so the floor and furniture need protection.

Getting Ready to Paint

Normal house temperature, 70 to 72 degrees, is ideal for painting. Get the room ready by first removing curtains, drapes, pictures, lamps, and all furniture you can carry to another room. Heavy furniture can be placed in the middle of the

floor and covered with a drop cloth.

Next repair cracks and nail holes in the wall. Use a spackling compound, which you can buy in powder form or ready-mixed. Fill small holes and cracks in one swipe of the putty knife. Larger holes should be filled in two stages, with the first application permitted to dry before the last is put on. Let the patches dry thoroughly, and then sand smooth. Finally, spot prime the area.

If the room is dirty, wash the walls and ceilings before painting. Wash the ceiling first. Prevent hard-to-remove wall washing streaks on lower parts by washing the wall from the baseboard upward. You may have to rinse the clean wall twice, but this is better than worrying about the paint covering dirty streaked areas.

Now remove wall switch and outlet plates. Remove the collars of ceiling lights, allowing them to hang freely away from the ceiling. If you have a chandelier, be sure to cover it with plastic before painting above it.

PAINTING

Paint the *ceiling* first. If you are using a brush, dip it $1/3$ to $1/2$ the bristle length into the paint, then slap it against the inside of the can and apply to the ceiling. Unload the brush with sweeping, crescent-shaped strokes in a small square area. Finish strokes all the same direction for uniform appearance. Always finish stroke into the previously painted area, and not into the unpainted area.

If you use a roller, you will find one with an extension that permits you to work without a ladder is a good idea. As you roll, overlap each rolling stroke about 50 percent with the previous one. Make the finishing strokes all in one direction, not back and forth.

Pick the short dimension of the ceiling and paint across one end of the room first. You can begin by "cutting in" the edge of the ceiling with a brush or applicator pad, use your roller right up to the edge and cut in when you paint the wall. Paint out from the edge toward the center of the room, working down one side of the room and back the other.

The walls. Begin by cutting in at the junction of the ceiling and walls, beside doors, windows, and next to baseboard trim. Use a brush or an applicator pad for this. The cut-in strip should be two to four inches wide.

Coat the roller and carry it to the wall. Make a W pattern on the wall, then turn the roller and roll across the W to fill it in. Continue until the area is well covered, then begin in an adjacent area with another W. Work with the roller right up to the cut-in strips at the trim.

The Trim. Use a cardboard shield or one you have purchased to protect the wall surface as you paint the windows and trim. Use masking tape on windows to keep paint off the glass and speed up the painting.

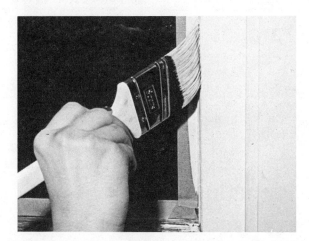

Masking tape makes window painting easy. Trim brush is tapered for this type of work.

Trim enamels are applied with an angular sash brush. The objective is to coat the trim with a glossy film that has no brush marks. Brush the paint into place, then use a final stroke to "lay" the paint smooth.

FINISHING HARDWOOD FLOORS

Hardwood floors are a valuable asset in your house, and they deserve to be kept in top shape.

These floors can be restored to their original luster through refinishing. Tools needed for the job — a floor sander, a floor edger, and a polishing machine — can be rented. When properly done, the refinishing process removes the old finish but very little of the wood. The life of the floor isn't reduced.

A word of caution: Floor sanding must be done carefully and with skill or the floor may be marred.

Before sanding, take a nail set and hammer and go over every inch of the floor. Carefully countersink each nail about $1/16$ inch. Over the years, the nails have moved toward the surface, and will tear the sandpaper if they are not set below the surface.

The floor should be given two or more sanding cuts. Begin with a No. 2 (coarse) grit to remove the old finish. This cut should be made at an angle of 45 degrees to the grain of the wood. Put successively finer paper in the machine for other cuts, making these cuts with the grain of the floor. The final cut can be made with a No. $1/2$ fine grit paper.

When operating the sander, work carefully. (Practice by sanding an old sheet of plywood laid flat.) Keep the machine moving at all times, for when you stop, the belt continues to move and will cut gouges in the floor surface. The only way to remove deep gouges is by sanding them out, which leaves a depression in the floor. The sander also may leave burn marks if permitted to stop while still on.

You have a choice of finishes which you can apply to the newly-sanded floor. These include varnish, shellac, lacquer and polyurethane. However, most flooring manufacturers today recommend a clear or colored penetrating floor sealer. Check your dealer for available brands.

After the sealer has dried thoroughly, complete the refinishing by buffing and waxing the floor. Use a rented heavy-duty floor polisher for this. Begin by buffing the floor with a fine steel wool pad. Then polish the floor, using a good quality paste wax or a liquid rubbing wax designed for use on hardwood floors. Use the buffing brush on the polisher to bring the wax to a high polish. Don't use a self-polishing wax, as these waxes contain water and could raise the grain of the wood.

Paint Spraying
[SEE AUTOMOBILE BODY REPAIRS; SPRAY GUN.]

Panel Adhesives
[SEE GLUES & GLUING.]

Paneling With Boards
[SEE WOOD PANELING.]

Paneling With Prefinished Plywood
[SEE WOOD PANELING.]

Paperhanger's Tools & Equipment
[SEE WALLCOVERINGS.]

Paperhanging
[SEE WALLCOVERINGS.]

Parallel-Jaw Pliers

Parallel-jaw pliers, due to their compound-leverage design, have unexcelled gripping power. This additional leverage also aids the wire-cutting action of the tool. Besides fitting snugly on nuts, parallel-jaw pliers are able to cut a 10-penny nail. A straight, head-on grip on the wire to be cut is possible since there is an opening between the handles through which the wire can be fed. Such an advantage is quite helpful when making splices or winding springs around a form.

These pliers can be purchased with either smooth or serrated jaw edges. The smooth-edged pliers are useful in breaking away cuts of narrow glass. SEE ALSO HAND TOOLS.

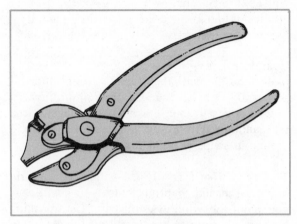

Parallel-Jaw Pliers

Parapet

A parapet is a low wall or railing which is on the edge of a roof, bridge, balcony, terrace or platform for protection. SEE ALSO ROOF CONSTRUCTION.

Pargeting

Pargeting is a thin layer of plaster or mortar which is used on brick or stone to produce a smooth or decorative surface. SEE ALSO CONCRETE.

Paring Chisel

A paring chisel is a woodworking chisel which has a thin blade. This tool is used without a hammer for light and precise shave cuts, such as in joint fitting. The new-ground cutting edge is normally beveled to 25 degrees and re-ground to 15 degrees. This makes it cut easier, but the thin edge is more likely to chip. SEE ALSO HAND TOOLS.

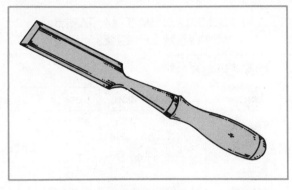

Paring Chisel

Parquet Flooring

Parquet flooring is a patterned wood floor of variegated squares or blocks. These blocks are made of wooden strips glued or wired together. The blocks are installed like other floor tiles except that the wood grains of adjoining blocks are laid perpendicular to each other to produce a decorative pattern. *SEE ALSO FINISH FLOORING.*

Parrot-Nose Plier Wrench

A parrot-nose plier wrench is a combination of a pipe wrench and pliers. Because of its nose-shape, this wrench aids the plumber in reaching objects normally unobtainable by ordinary wrenches. Useful for pipe and tubing, a parrot-nose plier wrench exerts a powerful grip. *SEE ALSO HAND TOOLS.*

Particle Board

Particle board is a hard board made from pressing particles of wood shavings or slivers into a panel. The particles are held together with a binder, such as a synthetic resin. Particle board is used in cabinet doors and counter tops because it is strong and will not warp. *SEE ALSO DRYWALL.*

Parting Strip

A parting strip or stop is a thin strip of wood used in the side and head jambs of a double-hung window. This stop separates the upper and lower sash.

Paste Wood Filler

Paste wood filler is a paste used to fill holes or crevices in wood. Since it is very thick, paste wood filler must be thinned with turpentine or benzine. Turpentine is recommended because it dries slowly; thus, the length of time to work with the paste is extended. Paste wood filler is available in a variety of colors. Light and darker hues can be made by using colors-in-oil mixed with the filler.

To apply paste wood filler, rub the substance over a two square foot area. Using a clean, stubby paint brush, rub the paste across the grain and then with the grain. About ten to fifteen minutes after the paste has been applied, it will turn gray or dull. With a rough towel or piece of burlap, wipe across the grain until most of the paste has been removed from the surface.

If the handyman begins wiping too soon, the majority of the paste will be wiped away. If wiping is delayed too long, the excess paste will dry and will not be able to be wiped away.

After the excess paste has been wiped away, wait overnight before lightly sanding and applying a finishing coat. Although the paste may look dry within a few hours, it is not and sanding will ruin the surface.

Patio Construction

[SEE BRICK & STONE WORK; PATIOS.]

Patio Fences

[SEE FENCES & GATES.]

Patio Furniture

OUTDOOR WOODWORKING

If you have never built anything for outdoor use, you should be aware that most woods, with the exception of redwood and cedar, hold up very poorly to the elements if left unprotected. A coat of wood preservative, followed by a primer, then a finish coat, is recommended for spruce, pine, fir and other common construction woods. Sealer-stains (exterior) are also very popular. Red cedar and redwood weather to attractive silvery-gray shades without rotting and are best for outdoor uses.

Plywood and hardboard contain glue, and come in interior and exterior grades. Always use the outdoor grades, which contain glues that are impervious to weather.

Courtesy of Western Wood Products Association.

Attractive, comfortable furniture makes this poolside patio a most pleasurable spot. Clustered around the barbecue pit are benches of Douglas fir 2 x 4s set on edge, with 4 x 4 legs, finished with a handsome dark sealer stain.

ROUND UMBRELLA TABLE WITH BENCHES

MATERIALS LIST

Number	Description	Use
TABLE		
1 piece	8′ 2 x 6	Top
2 pieces	10′ 2 x 6	Top
1 piece	12′ 2 x 6	Top
3 pieces	8′ 2 x 6	Legs and rail pieces
1 piece	4′ 2 x 6	Center piece and braces
BENCHES		
3 pieces	8′ 2 x 6	Tops
1 piece	6′ 2 x 6	Rail pieces
1 piece	10′ 2 x 6	Legs
1 piece	3′ 2 x 6	Braces

HARDWARE (all galvanized or zinc plated)

10	³/₈″ x 8″ machine bolts
10	³/₈″ x 6″ machine bolts
6	³/₈″ x 4″ machine bolts
68	³/₈″ washers
4	⁵/₁₆″ x 6″ lag bolts
16	¼″ x 2″ lag bolts
3 lbs.	8d box nails
glue (for exterior use)	

Courtesy of Western Wood Products Association.

This attractive round table can be used with or without an umbrella. You can leave out the holes for the shaft and drill them later on should you decide to add the umbrella. The table with its three curved benches will seat six adults or nine youngsters.

Courtesy of Western Wood Products Association.

Although hand tools can be used to make this project, it is easier to cut the curves through 2 inch lumber with a band or long-bladed saber saw. A rented saber saw is suggested if you do not own one. All parts are cut from 2 x 6 lumber. The more weather-resistant west coast types are preferred.

The Table Top

First cut out rail pieces and notch as shown in "rail piece" and top view. Drill all holes ($7/16$

inch diameter for $3/8$ inch machine bolts) before nailing to top pieces.

If using a saber saw to cut out the top pieces, cut 2 x 6s to length with square ends. Use five pieces 5 feet long, two 3 feet long and two pieces 2 feet long. Mark the centers of each board and lay best side down with centers lined up and space $1/4$ inch apart. Position rail pieces $8^1/_2$ inches from center line, attach with glue and 8d galvanized nails.

Now turn the top over and drive a small finishing nail into the very center of the middle board. Make a string compass 2 feet 2 inches long, using the nail as the center and mark off the circular outside edge. Cut on the line with your hole for the umbrella shaft. (For a band saw, cut each piece to shape before attaching. Plane or sand any imperfections.)

Legs and Center Piece

To make the table legs, cut 42 degree angles on the ends of each leg, with $36^3/_4$ inches from the long point to the short point (along each side).

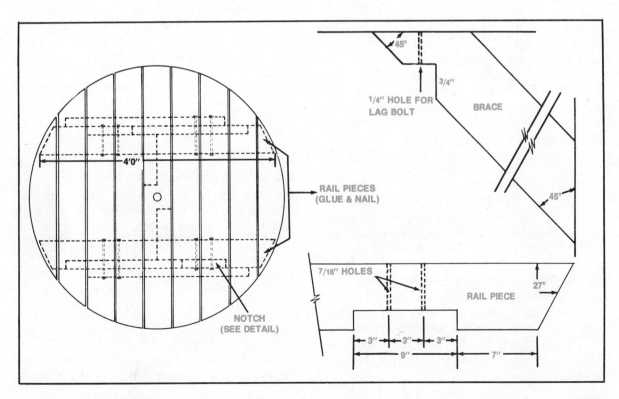

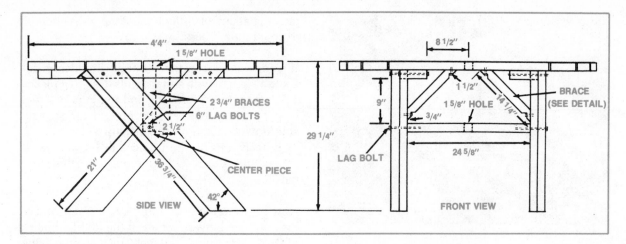

Clamp or nail the legs temporarily to the rail pieces. Make sure that the bottoms of the legs are parallel to the tops and that they are properly crossed. Mark the position of the holes and drill. Attach the legs to the rail pieces with appropriate bolts and washers.

Next drill two $1/4$ inch holes through the legs on each side on line with where they cross. Each hole should be $2^1/2$ inches from the outside intersection and will be used for attaching the center piece.

Cut out a $24^5/8$ inch long centerpiece from a piece of 2 x 6 and mark $1/4$ inch holes in the ends $1^1/2$ inches from each edge. Hold up the centerpiece to the holes in the legs to see if the marks line up properly. Adjust the marks if necessary and drill the holes into the wood about 2 inches. Also make another $1^5/8$ inch hole for the umbrella shaft. Attach the center piece with six-inch lag screws and washers.

To keep the lumber order simple, the leg braces are ripped from a 16 inch piece of 2 x 6, but you can simply buy 2 x 3s if you do not have a good ripsaw. (Be sure to double the amounts on the materials list). The braces have 45 degree angles at both ends and measure $14^1/4$ inches from long point to long point (along the longer side). Cut right-angle notches at each end, with the top notch starting $1^1/2$ inches from the end and the bottom $3/4$ inch. Notches are $3/4$ inch on each side. Drill $3/16$ inch holes through the notches into the top and each leg. Attach with 2 inch lag bolts and washers.

Making the Benches

For each bench, lay out two pieces of 4 foot long 2 x 6 spaced $1/4$ inch apart. Using another string and pencil compass, mark an arc with a four-foot radius starting $1^1/2$ inches from the outside edge of the first 2 x 6. Cut on this line and use the scrap piece from the outside 2 x 6 for the other side of the bench.

Next cut rail pieces that are 10 inches long as shown (long point to short point), with a 77 degree angle at each end. Notch per detail drawing and drill a $7/16$ inch hole with a center $2^1/8$ inches from the outside edge of the notch. Glue and nail 10 inches from the center of the bench.

Legs are cut from ripped 2 x 6 or two 2 x 3s as described under table braces. Saw ends to 56 degree angles on top and bottom, with 18 inches along each side (long angle to short angle). Set in position on rail pieces and mark holes. Drill $7/16$ inch holes at each mark. Using washers and $3/8$ inch machine bolts, attach legs to rail pieces. Clamp legs together in correct position and drill $7/16$ holes all the way through. Bolt as before.

Braces are made from 2 x 6 ripped in quarters (or 2 x 3 ripped in half). The braces are 17 inches long along the longer side, with 55-degree angles on the bottom and a 35-degree angle on top. Since there are no notches, the two-inch lag bolts must be inserted into holes predrilled ($3/16$ inch diameter) at an angle.

To save extra measuring, make one bench, put it

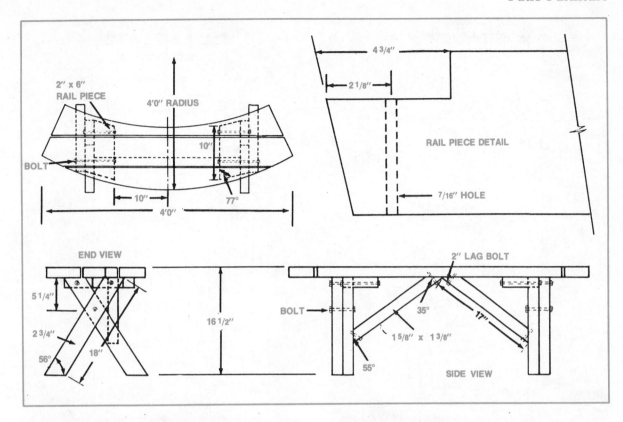

together to see if everything fits, then take it apart and use the pieces as patterns for the other two.

MODERN PLYWOOD AND CANVAS STOWAWAYS

MATERIALS LIST

Number	Description	Use
WOOD		
4 panels	³/₄" x 4' x 8 A-A EXT-DFPA (or MDO plywood)	Basic parts
16 pieces	1³/₈" x 28 ¹/₂" round stock	Chaise, chairs
2 pieces	¹/₂" x 48" dowels	Chaise, chairs
4 pieces	³/₈" x 48" dowels	Chaise, chairs
HARDWARE		
8 sets	Glides	All furniture
12	1" metal clips with 24 screws	Tables

MISCELLANEOUS

Canvas for chaise and chairs, surfacing putty for filling exposed plywood edges, and No. 120 grit

Courtesy of American Plywood Association

These plywood and canvas units look great in the surf, but they will be more at home on your patio.

sandpaper, as needed. Nonlead base undercoat and finish coat of high grade exterior type enamel for plywood, as needed. (Optional: clear sealer for plywood edges, round stock and dowels.)

Patio Furniture

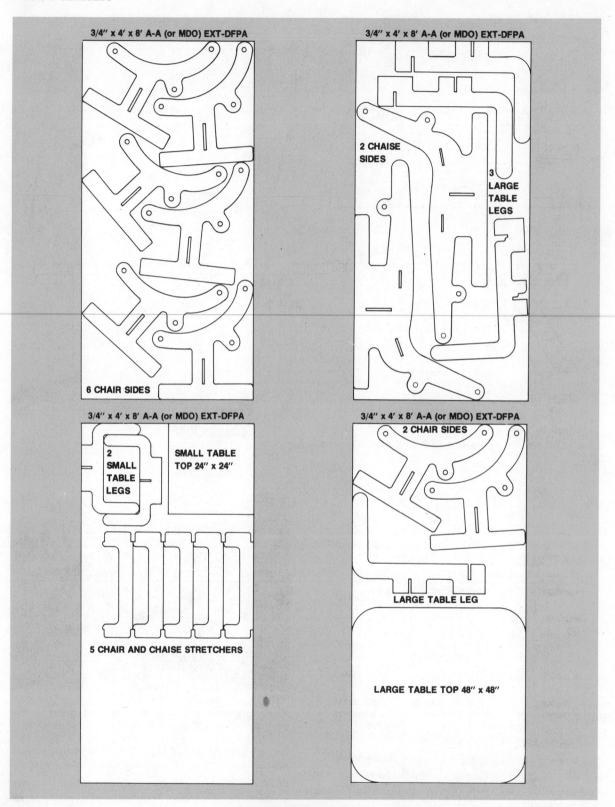

3/4″ x 4′ x 8′ A-A (or MDO) EXT-DFPA

6 CHAIR SIDES

3/4″ x 4′ x 8′ A-A (or MDO) EXT-DFPA

2 CHAISE SIDES

3 LARGE TABLE LEGS

3/4″ x 4′ x 8′ A-A (or MDO) EXT-DFPA

2 SMALL TABLE LEGS

SMALL TABLE TOP 24″ x 24″

5 CHAIR AND CHAISE STRETCHERS

3/4″ x 4′ x 8′ A-A (or MDO) EXT-DFPA

2 CHAIR SIDES

LARGE TABLE LEG

LARGE TABLE TOP 48″ x 48″

Plywood panel layout

The photo shows these modern plywood and canvas units in the surf for effect, but they are really designed for the patio. There are seven pieces in all, including four chairs, each one designed for comfort, durability and easy storage. Dowels and a few screws hold all parts together, which are easily removed for quick winter knock-down.

Grid drawings of chaise and chair sides are pro-

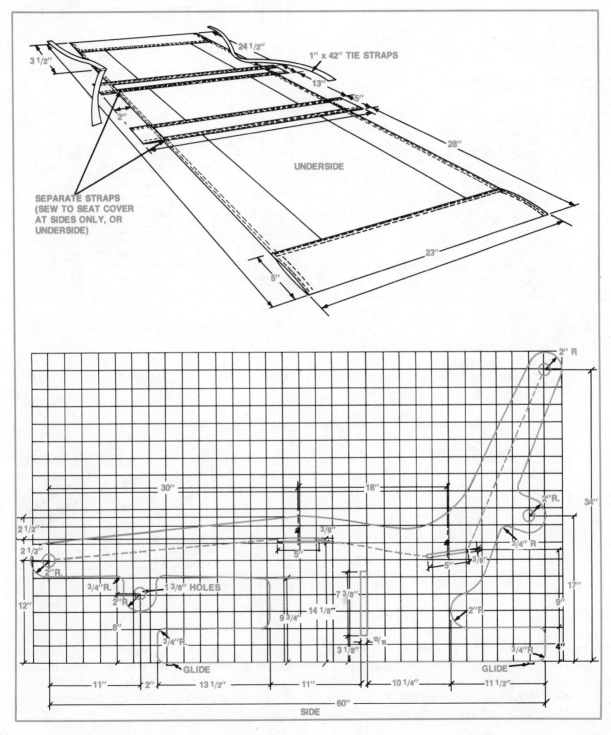

vided to aid in cutting the proper curves. When making matching parts, make a cardboard template and trace it where needed. Regular tools can be used, but a saber or jigsaw will greatly speed the work.

Materials consist mainly of A-A exterior plywood or MDO (medium density overlay) plywood, which has a pressurized hard resin coating. A few dowels, some round stock, canvas and hardware complete the material list.

The panel layouts show four plywood sheets laid out for most economical use. (You can use the leftover half sheet to make an extra coffee table.) If you are not building all the units, cut out the templates and make your own layout before cutting. Be sure to allow for saw kerfs while laying out.

Chaise and Chairs

You will need at least two chaise sides, so use a cardboard template. To lay out, use 2 inch square graph paper for those on the grid in the drawing. Check your template with the dimensions given. When accurate, transfer the template to the plywood. You will also need one stretcher for the chaise. The same stretchers are used for the chairs, so make a cardboard template if you intend to make chairs, too.

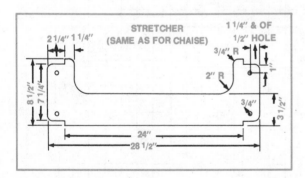

Cut the round stock and dowels to the lengths shown, and drill $\frac{3}{8}$ inch diameter holes through the round stock for the dowels. If you do not have a sewing machine or are inexperienced at sewing, you may need to have a tent or upholstery firm make the canvas covers. Before you paint the chaise, assemble it to make sure all

parts fit properly. If it all fits, disassemble, wipe clean and paint.

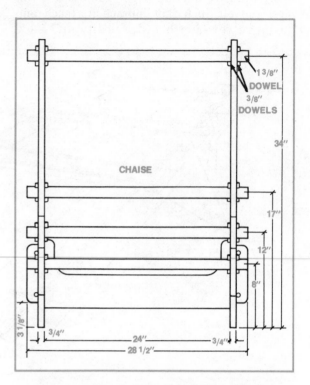

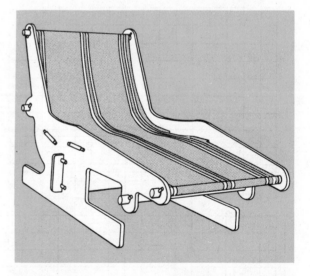

The chairs are made in much the same way as the chaise. Use the chair grid pattern to make a template for the sides. The stretcher pattern is the same as that used for the chaise, and the same template can be used.

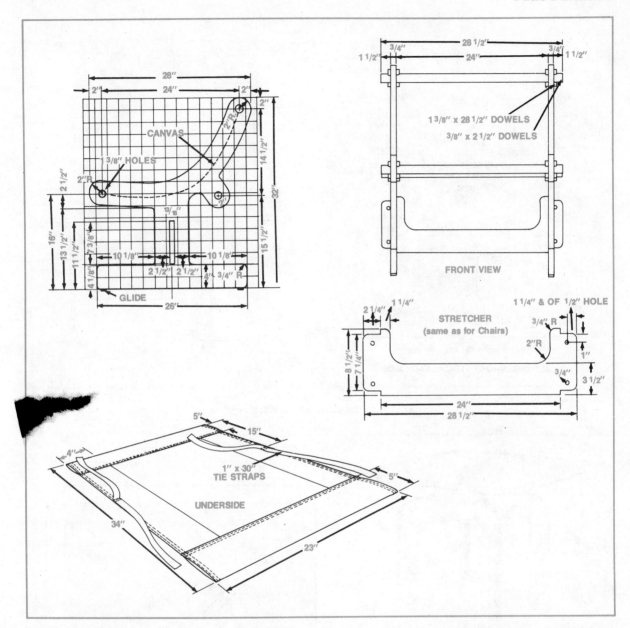

Making the Tables

The large patio table is a 4 foot square and the top is made from a half sheet of plywood as shown. Corners are cut to a 7 inch radius. The legs are four pieces of plywood cut as shown. They are attached to the top with eight one inch metal corner clips and 16 screws.

Draw a cardboard template for the legs, cut out three of them the same, then add wider notches to the fourth as shown. (The legs will not fit together without them.) Draw lines 16 inches in from each edge as shown, then drill and screw in metal clips inside each line as shown. Set the legs against the clips and make sure that they all fit together properly. If they do, mark the holes, predrill them, and screw the legs in, saving the one with the wider notch for last. Disassemble and paint.

The small coffee table has a top two feet square, and is supported by two interlocking plywood pieces. Make a cardboard template and use it to

Patio Furniture

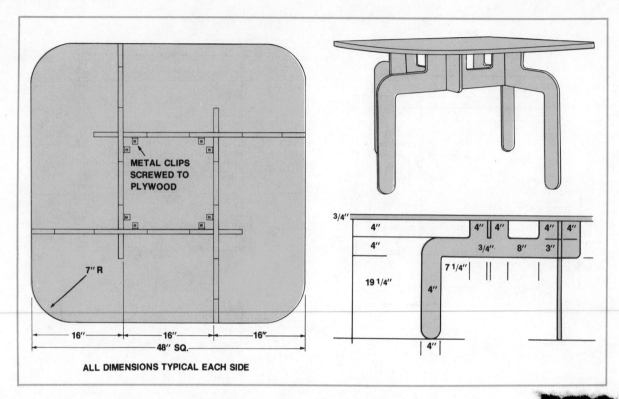

METAL CLIPS
SCREWED TO
PLYWOOD

7" R

16" | 16" | 16"

48" SQ.

ALL DIMENSIONS TYPICAL EACH SIDE

3/4"
4"
4"
19 1/4"
4"
4"

4" | 4" | 4" | 4"
3/4" | 8" | 3"
7 1/4"

(Large table plans and rendering)

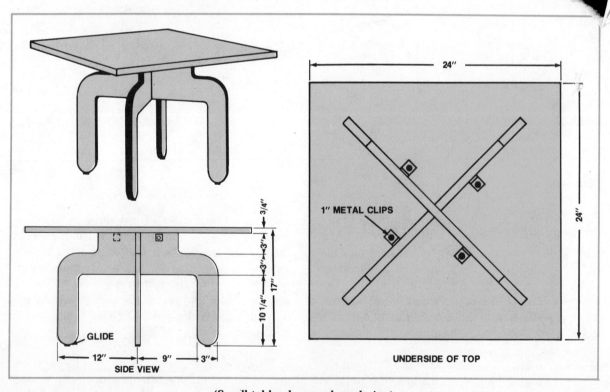

24"

1" METAL CLIPS

24"

UNDERSIDE OF TOP

3/4"
3"
3"
17"
10 1/4"

GLIDE

12" | 9" | 3"

SIDE VIEW

(Small table plans and rendering)

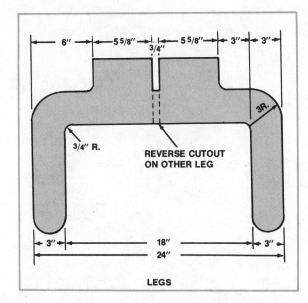

6″ 5 5/8″ 3/4″ 5 5/8″ 3″ 3″

3R.

3/4″ R.

REVERSE CUTOUT
ON OTHER LEG

3″ 18″ 3″
24″

LEGS

The seat should be about 16 inches wide, and can be any length desired up to eight feet. Relatively smooth brick should be used, with the top of the seat coated with silicone and waxed for a comfortable surface.

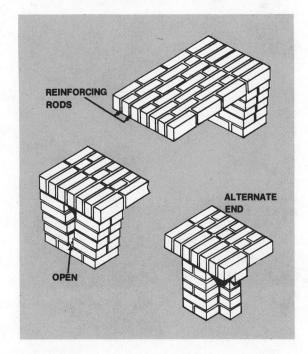

REINFORCING
RODS

OPEN

ALTERNATE
END

draw the two leg pieces. Note that one leg has a reverse cutout so that the two parts can interlock.

After all parts are cut out, draw diagonal lines across the underside of the top. Interlock the table legs and set them along the lines. Mark screw holes for the four metal corner clips. Predrill holes and put together. If all parts fit, disassemble and paint.

Finishing

Sand any rough edges (the plywood surfaces should need little or no sanding). Fill edges and any gouges with surfacing putty, then give the edges a coat of clear sealer.

For exterior use, water-based latex house paints are recommended. Trim paints can be used if bright colors are desired. All surfaces should be primed with compatible paint, preferably by the same manufacturer, as the final coat. Install metal glides to bottoms of legs.

BRICK SEAT

To make a brick bench, lay the brick for the seat first, using $1/4$ inch reinforcing rods along each longitudinal mortar joint. While the mortar hardens (three or four days), build two piers about five courses high as shown.

Other Ideas

If you are handy and have some imagination, there is no limit to what you can create in outdoor furniture. The illustrations show some wood furniture you can make out of redwood, red cedar or other weather-resistant woods.

Patios

Today, the patio or terrace is thought of as another room of the house, a much-used second living room. It can simply be a grassy area for lounging, but it is usually more clearly defined by concrete, brick, flagstone or some other material. The patio can be adjacent to the house or it can be in a separate location on the lot. It can be open, fenced, roofed or enclosed on one or more sides. It may surround a swimming pool or a cooking pit.

Courtesy of Western Wood Products Association.

The outdoor living area has become as important as any other room of the house.

PLANNING THE PATIO

Perhaps the ideal location for your outdoor living room is directly outside of, and connected by sliding glass doors to, the family room, kitchen or living room. This convenience will pay off especially if you entertain frequently.

Your home's design may not accommodate an attached patio, or you may prefer to locate it in a far corner of your lot, for privacy or to take advantage of a view. Depending on where you live, you will want to orient the patio to take advantage of, or to block out, the sun. A patio that faces the south will almost surely need a roof and some sort of sun screen. An eastward-facing patio gets the morning sun while a westward-facing patio will be exposed to the hotter midday sun. An attached patio that faces north will be shaded by the house during most of the day. Prevailing breezes are still another consideration in your planning.

As an extension of the home, although not necessarily a physical part of it, the patio should be planned to complement the home's architectural features. Shape and size must be considered in relation to the house and to the shape and size of the lot. In most cases, a patio should be larger than the rooms inside the house, with plenty of room for oversized lounging furniture. In some instances, however, a small, intimate, private patio is preferred outside a master bedroom or even a bath.

When selecting materials for your patio, consider the setting as well as the architecture of the

Courtesy of Western Wood Products Association.

If a swimming pool is part of your plans, the patio can be built around it to accommodate poolside loungers.

house. For example, patterns can be created with flagstone or brick or modular concrete units to harmonize with the terrain and textures of the natural surroundings and at the same time complement the lines and features of the house. Other key factors in the choice of outdoor building materials include durability, ease of maintenance, quick drying and non-skid properties.

Concrete is a long-time favorite for patios, and can be employed in a number of ways such as small modules, easy for the home handyman to manage, a slab, alternate squares of plain and pebbled concrete, tinted concrete to offset glare and concrete patio blocks. Other popular materials are brick, flagstone and tile. Often, a combination of two or more of these is employed.

Concrete Patio

Carefree concrete makes a fine patio surface, and a slab construction is the most popular type. A gridwork of redwood lumber embedded in a concrete patio can give it a pleasing appearance. It also makes it easy for the weekend worker to do the job in stages. First excavate the area of the patio as necessary, and prepare the subgrade with gravel or cinder fill. Construct a gridwork of 2 x 4 lumber, face-nailing it together with 8d common galvanized nails. The grid can be of whatever dimensions seem to work best with the patio and its surroundings: 4 foot squares, 2 x 4 rectangles, a random design or whatever gives the best accent and pattern to the area. For forming wide radius curves, use 1 x 4 lumber. Form short radius, curved corners with hardboard or ¹/₄ inch plywood. Hold the gridwork in place

Courtesy of Western Wood Products Association.

Redwood lumber set at random angles into the concrete patio provides a casual counterpoint to the formal Western cedar pergola. Dividing the patio in this manner also makes it easier to build; work can be done in stages.

Courtesy of the Portland Cement Association

Exposed aggregate, brushed and textured concrete finishes. Techniques for these decorative effects are described in the section on CONCRETE

with 1 x 3 stakes driven into the ground around the perimeter. Stake forms closely at curves. Set all stakes well below the top edges of the lumber forms before nailing.

Once the gridwork is in place, you can do the concrete work in easy stages, just a few squares or rectangles at a time. Either mix the concrete and pour it by hand or rent a small mixer. If you plan to make the entire patio in one operation, it

is best to order ready-mixed concrete brought to the site by truck.

Strike off the poured concrete flush with the top edges of the redwood boards. Then apply the desired finish, as described in the CONCRETE entry, and allow to cure thoroughly. Exposed-aggregate, brushed and decorative finishes are especially desirable for patio surfaces, adding textural interest. A checkerboard effect, alternating squares of brushed concrete with exposed-aggregate for example, is another possibility.

Another way to build a concrete patio is to cast individual modules in manageable sizes, then lay them on a base of sand or well-compacted soil. The modules can be square, rectangular, circular or any shape you wish. Details for estimating concrete needs, mixing, pouring and curing are included in the section on CONCRETE. You can cast the modules in your basement or garage during the off-season, then lay them when the warm weather arrives.

To make a form for square or rectangular blocks, use 2 x 2 lumber (up to 12 inches square) or 2 x 3 lumber (for larger modules). Cut the form pieces 6 inches longer than the intended concrete module size. Cut notches halfway through each form piece, 1 1/2 inches wide and 1 1/2 inches in

Courtesy of Westinghouse Electric Corporation

Dramatically lighted patio is of rectangular blocks with grass planted between for a natural appearance.

Area in foreground is laid with 12-inch square patio blocks; larger blocks are used outside the house at right.

from each end. Then simply fit the pieces together; they come apart easily for reuse. For circular blocks, cut strips of 1/8 inch hardboard, 2 inches wide for blocks up to 12 inches in diameter and 3 inches wide for larger blocks, slightly more than three times longer than the intended diameter (remember the formula: circumference = pi (3.1416) x diameter. Bend the strips into a circle, with smooth sides turned inward. Where the ends meet, wrap securely with heavy duty tape. Then wrap the outside of each circle with tape to make a sturdy form. Circular forms can be reused as can the lumber forms. You need make only one form, but it is recommended that you make several so that you can cast a number of blocks at a time. Grease the insides of the forms before use, then place them on tarpaper on a flat surface, such as a concrete basement or garage floor. After pouring and smoothing the concrete, leave the forms in place for a few days. They can then be removed for reuse, while the cast blocks are allowed to cure for at least a week. When the concrete modules have been set in place on an excavated base, the joints between them can be filled with sand. Or you may wish to plant grass or some other greenery between the units for a natural effect. In the case of round patio blocks, you can fill in with

gravel or tanbark. Very striking effects can be achieved with colors, such as deep blue or black-colored circular blocks with white pebble fill.

You can also buy ready-made patio blocks at building supply stores and garden centers. These are usually 2 inches thick and typically measure either 12 inches square or 8 inches by 16 inches (many other sizes are also available). These are laid similarly to the method described previously.

Courtesy of Ponderosa Pine Woodwork

An eastward-facing patio gets the morning sun. One that faces the west will be exposed to the heat of mid-afternoon.

Courtesy of the California Redwood Association

Rugged brick set in a bed of sand makes a delightful garden patio. Redwood A-frame shelter offers protection from sun and wind.

BRICK PATIO

Color, pattern, high abrasion resistance and relative ease of working make brick a desirable material for a patio. Available in a variety of sizes and colors, brick can be set in a bed of mortar over a concrete slab, with mortar applied between joints, or it can simply be laid in sand over well-tamped, compacted earth. Either way, you can make any number of pleasing designs.

Drainage is an important factor in construction of a brick patio. When subjected to excessive moisture, brick may be susceptible to efflorescence (a whitish crust caused by mineral salts in the brick rising to the surface), stains, growth of fungi or molds or disintegration caused by freezing and thawing in the absence of moisture. Slope patios at least 1/8 inch per foot away from buildings, retaining walls or other

structures that will cause water to collect on the surface. Provide gutter drainage, if necessary, locating gutters at the edges of the patio to prevent water from adjacent areas draining onto the patio.

Unless you live in an area where there are extremely sharp temperature changes or very severe winters, no special foundation need be used with a brick patio. Bricks can simply be laid in a bed of sand. In colder areas, winter freeze-thaw cycles might create a swell or roll in the patio, displacing some bricks. This is a simple matter to correct come springtime; just take up and reset the bricks in the affected areas.

To make such a simple brick patio, excavate the area to a depth of approximately 4 1/4 inches. The brick paving will tend to spread or shift unless restrained, so provide an edging at the perimeter. The easiest way to do this is by building a frame of redwood 2 x 4s, nailing them together with galvanized nails and fastening the frame securely in place with stakes driven into the ground outside the 2 x 4s. (Make sure there are stakes at all 2 x 4 joints.) You can also make an edging of bricks set in a soldier course (on end), but these too may tend to shift unless they are set in mortar or restrained by a lumber or concrete frame.

Spread a bed of sand 2 inches thick in the excavation, and tamp it down firmly. Tie strings across the excavation from opposite edgings and use a level to check the evenness of the sand base; fill or cut down where necessary, remembering to maintain the drainage pitch. When the sand bed is completed, set bricks in place, allowing a ¹/₂ inch joint between all units (or use the modular-size paving bricks and lay them tightly together).

There are several methods of finishing off the brick patio. You can sweep sand over the surface, filling all the joints, then spray it with water to settle the sand and repeat the process until the joints are flush with the brick. A second method is to sweep a dry mixture of three parts of very fine sand to one part portland cement over the surface. Make sure all the cement is swept from the face of the brick, then spray with a fine mist of water until the paving becomes damp. Spray intermittently to keep damp for several days. Still another method is to mix 2 ¹/₂ parts sand to one part portland cement to make a pourable grout. Fill the joints with this, carefully cleaning spilled grout from the brick faces with a piece of burlap as you go along.

If you live in an area with a very high water table or where the soil is heavy clay, lay the brick on a cushion of gravel to provide below-surface drainage and to prevent any large upward capillary flow of moisture. In this case, omit the sandbed, which would sift down into the larger material and cause uneven settlement, block drainage and provide a capillary path for subsurface moisture. Set the brick directly on the gravel bed, and finish off the joints the same as on sand.

If you live in an area where winters are particularly severe, you will probably want to build your brick patio on a concrete slab, which involves considerably more work but will produce a highly weather-resistant result. Dig footings for the slab well below the frost line (check with local building authorities to get this information).

When the slab has cured thoroughly, mix mortar as described in the entry on BRICK. Start laying brick in one corner of the patio, spreading enough mortar ¹/₂ inch thick on the slab for two or three bricks. Butter brick side and end with mortar and set in place. Tool the joints before mortar has a chance to set. The joints can be made flush with the surface or they can be made concave by running a ³/₄ inch pipe along them. Use a damp piece of burlap to wipe excess mortar from the brick surface as you go along. When the patio is completed, keep the brickwork damp for about a week to allow the mortar to cure.

FLAGSTONE PATIO

As a natural material, flagstone is uniquely suited to use in your outdoor living room. It is available in rectangular pieces or irregular cuts or you can have it cut, matched and keyed. It provides a handsome and rugged patio floor that, if properly laid, will stand up to the most severe weather. Unfortunately, it is also quite expensive. Slate is somewhat cheaper, and is often used in place of flagstone.

Courtesy of the Bilto Corporation

Terrace in the corner formed by two walls of the house is sheltered from prevailing winds. Basement entry makes it convenient for storage of outdoor furniture.

Courtesy of Western Wood Products Association.

Combination of flagstone, concrete circles, river rock and a wood deck blend this patio beautifully into its surroundings.

Like brick, flagstone or slate can be laid in a bed of sand or gravel, but the larger pieces are more susceptible to heaving than are the smaller brick units. Therefore, it is preferable to build your flagstone patio on a concrete slab base.

When the slab has cured, lay the stones "dry" to check pattern and color match. When you are satisfied with the appearance, pick up the stones individually, spread a layer of mortar on the slab and set the flagstones in place. Keep spaces between the stones as uniform as possible. Fill these spaces with mortar, flush with the surface of the stones.

Baked clay tiles also make a durable patio surface, somewhat more formal in appearance than the other materials. The tiles are set similarly to flagstone. While they can be laid in a sand bed, it is best to put down a slab foundation and set the tiles in a mortar at least 3/4 inch thick.

THE PATIO ROOF

The advantages of having at least a portion of your outdoor living room covered are many and obvious. Properly planned, the patio roof can be a major architectural asset to your house. A continuous roof line, for example, may make a small, disproportionately high dwelling appear longer, lower and much better balanced. You may be able to combine the patio area with a carport or a hidden storage area for lawn and garden equipment, which could also serve as a wall for the patio to shut out unwelcome winds or an unsightly view.

The important consideration is that the structure relate in some way to the house itself, even though it may be unattached and some distance from the house. Similar roof lines may establish this relationship, or the use of similar materials. A common trim color for both house and patio covering is another good tie-in feature.

Courtesy of Western Wood Products Association.

Free-standing pergola of Douglas fir provides patio privacy and filters out harsh sunlight.

Post and beam construction is generally preferred for patio coverings. This type of structure allows you to build while leaving the sides open to the outdoors. The posts can be metal columns, either sunk into concrete foundations or with base flanges that are lag-bolted to the concrete piers, or the posts may be lumber, usually 4 x 4s or 4 x 6s. These similarly can be set into concrete foundations or bolted to metal U-brackets set into concrete piers. Unless the lumber is strongly rot-resistant, such as redwood, it should be thoroughly impregnated with a preservative such as pentachlorophenol before being put into position.

Basic construction involves erecting the posts and bracing them temporarily in place. Then the beams (doubled 2 inch dimension lumber or 4 inch lumber in most cases) are fastened to the posts. Next, rafters are set in place, similar to ordinary roof framing, but spacing will depend on the finish material to be used on the roof.

The roof can be covered in a variety of ways. If a sun break, rather than a complete shelter, is desired, you can fasten 1 x 2s or 2 x 3s on end across the rafters, allowing a gap between each board.

To filter the sunlight while shutting out the precipitation, install a fiberglass roof. Available in a variety of colors and patterns, this tough material is designed for do-it-yourself installation. It comes in corrugated panels, and is installed directly to the rafters with nails or screws.

You can, of course, install a conventional roof, with plywood or tongue-and-groove sheathing finished off with asphalt shingles or other material to match the rest of the house. But, unless you live in the deep South, this alternative tends to defeat the whole purpose of the patio.

One final note of caution: before you advance too far in planning your patio shelter, check your local building codes. While the patio itself may not necessitate any permits, there may be requirements or limitations concerning the type of covering structure you can erect, or how close you can build to your property line.

Paving

Paving is the act of covering an area, such as a sidewalk, driveway or road, with concrete, brick, stone or asphalt. *SEE ALSO BRICK & STONE WORK: CONCRETE.*

Paving Blocks

Home made or purchased paving blocks may be used as stepping stones for a path or sidewalk or to pave a driveway. To construct paving blocks, build square or rectangular wooden forms from 2 x 4 stock. Install hinges on three of the four corner joints for easy removal of the block. Place a hasp on the fourth corner and use a wooden peg to keep it closed. To keep the concrete from sticking to the forms, oil all the surfaces or cover them with waxed paper.

Before pouring the concrete, the closed form must be resting on a level surface. When working on a garage floor, driveway or sidewalk, cover the area under and around the form with building paper to prevent adhesion between the two concrete surfaces. If the form is on a wooden board, cover the board with a sheet of polyurethane.

Using a trowel, fill the form halfway and gently shake it to release any air bubbles and pockets in the concrete. Insert any reinforcement desired and finish filling the form to slightly over the top. Pack down the concrete, shake the form again and, using a board, scrape the excess off the top. A float or trowel may be used to finish the surface. After the concrete is dry, release the hasp and remove the block. *SEE ALSO CONCRETE.*

Pebble Concrete

Pebble concrete, which contains stones embedded in the surface of the slab, adds a distinct decorative quality to sidewalks, patios and porches, driveways, entryways of homes and even fireplace hearths. The use of pebble concrete eliminates the need for time-consuming fine troweling, and the textured surface is nonskid. The pebbles are sold by building and patio supply dealers and transit-mixed concrete manufacturers in 100 lb. sacks, in a variety of shapes, sizes and colors. The use of the darker pebbles lessens glare and obscures staining.

The pebbles are distributed over the concrete immediately after it has been poured and leveled off. The stones may be placed close together or spaced far apart, and combinations of different colors and sizes may be used, depending on the desired effect. The pebbles are packed into the concrete with a darby or a 2 x 4 plank. Pounding may be required to press the stones into concrete that has stiffened slightly. The surface of the slab is then smoothed over with a wood float so that no holes or stones can be seen. After the concrete has begun to harden, the slab is lightly hosed and brushed with a broom. If this treatment dislodges the pebbles, the concrete should be allowed more time to harden. This hosing and brushing process should expose the pebbles as full as possible, and also maintain a relatively smooth surface on the slab. *SEE ALSO CONCRETE.*

Pebble Paving, Mosaic
[SEE MOSAIC PEBBLE PAVING.]